The Politics of Dissent

The Politics
of Dissent

*Pacifism in France
1919–1939*

NORMAN INGRAM

CLARENDON PRESS · OXFORD
1991

Oxford University Press, Walton Street, Oxford OX2 6DP
Oxford New York Toronto
Delhi Bombay Calcutta Madras Karachi
Petaling Jaya Singapore Hong Kong Tokyo
Nairobi Dar es Salaam Cape Town
Melbourne Auckland
and associated companies in
Berlin Ibadan

Oxford is a trade mark of Oxford University Press

Published in the United States
by Oxford University Press, New York

British Library Cataloguing in Publication Data
Ingram, Norman
The politics of dissent: pacifism in France 1919–1939.
1. France. Pacifism, history
I. Title
327.1720944

ISBN 0-19-822295-5

Library of Congress Cataloging in Publication Data
Ingram, Norman
The politics of dissent: pacifism in France 1919–1939/Norman
Ingram.
Includes bibliographical references and index.
1. Peace movements—France—History.   2. Pacificists—France—
History.   I. Title
JX1961.F8I54   1991
327.1'7'0944—dc20
90-36856

ISBN 0-19-822295-5

75780

Typeset by Rowland Phototypesetting Ltd
Bury St Edmunds, Suffolk
Printed and bound in
Great Britain by Bookcraft (Bath) Ltd
Midsomer Norton, Somerset

To my parents

Acknowledgements

Many people and organizations have helped me enormously during my six years of postgraduate study. First and foremost, I must thank the Commonwealth Scholarship Commission in the United Kingdom for the provision of the scholarship which enabled me to undertake doctoral studies at the University of Edinburgh in the first place. I am grateful to the Social Sciences and Humanities Research Council of Canada for providing me with the doctoral fellowship which allowed me to spend two delightful years in Paris doing research. I spent the 1984–5 academic year as a student at the Institut d'études politiques de Paris where I attended the doctoral research seminars of Pierre Milza, Serge Berstein, Michel Winock, Jean-Pierre Azéma, and Jean-Marie Mayeur, to all of whom I am grateful for this entrée into the world of the French historian. I am thankful to the Killam Trust for honouring me with the post-doctoral fellowship at the University of Alberta which has allowed me to prepare the manuscript for publication relatively untroubled by other concerns. Finally, I should like to record my thanks to Professor John C. Cairns, Dr Martin Alexander, Dr Martin Ceadel, Dr Patricia Prestwich, Dr Jo Vellacott, Professor Robert Wilcocks, Mr Michel Dreyfus, and to my examiners, Dr Robert Anderson and Dr Peter van den Dungen, all of whom have given most generously of their time and thoughts at various stages. I am particularly indebted to my supervisor, Professor Maurice Larkin, first for his congenial and scholarly supervision of my Ph.D., and secondly for recommending its publication to the Clarendon Press.

I have made use of many libraries and archives during the past five years. My thanks go to the staffs of the following institutions: the Service historique de l'armée de terre (Château de Vincennes), the Archives nationales (Paris), the Bibliothèque du Protestantisme français (Paris), the Library of Congress (Washington), the National Archives of the United States of America (Washington), the Swarthmore College Peace Collection (Swarthmore, Pennsylvania), the Bibliothèque nationale (Paris), Edinburgh University Library, and the National Library of Scotland (Edinburgh). Specifically, I should like to thank Mlle Odile Patrois and Mme Thérèse Muller of the Bibliothèque de documentation internationale contemporaine at Nanterre, and the late Myrtle Solomon who kindly gave me access to the un-sorted and un-catalogued archives of the War Resisters' International which were at that point stored in her Chelsea garage before finally being transferred to the International Institute for Social History in Amsterdam.

I should also like to thank my editors, Mr Robert Faber and Dr Anthony Morris, as well as their staff at Oxford University Press, for their efficient and professional handling of my manuscript. What for them might seem commonplace has been anything but routine for this neophyte author, and I am grateful to them for guiding me gently through the successive stages of publication.

Many friends in Edinburgh and Paris have helped me in innumerable ways, large and small, and I thank them all. Last, but by no means least, I am profoundly grateful to my family for the support they have given me through six years of postgraduate study. Above all, though, I should like to thank my parents, to whom this book is dedicated, for providing me with the loving home, stimulating environment, and so very much more that I shall probably never know.

N.I.

University of Alberta
October 1989

Contents

ACKNOWLEDGEMENTS   vii

ABBREVIATIONS   xi

Introduction   1

PART I. *PACIFISME ANCIEN STYLE*, OR THE PACIFISM OF THE PEDAGOGUES

1. Peace through Justice, or the Old Pacifism Defined   19

2. A Decade of Optimism (1919–1929)   40

3. Cracks in the Foundations (1928–1933)   56

4. The Rise of Pessimism (1933–1938)   93

5. Peace through Justice Reaffirmed (1938–1940)   110

PART II. *PACIFISME NOUVEAU STYLE*, OR THE POLITICS OF DISSENT

6. The Origins of the New Pacifism   121

7. Years of Growth (1930–1934)   134

8. Challenges to *Intégralité* (1934–1938)   179

9. Munich and all that (1938–1939)   223

PART III.   *THÈMES ET VARIATIONS*, OR FEMINIST
PACIFISM IN INTERWAR FRANCE

10. Feminist Pacifism and the LIFPL   249

11. France meets the International   286

    Conclusions   311

BIBLIOGRAPHY   322

INDEX   349

Abbreviations

AGM	Annual general meeting
AN	Archives nationales, Paris
APD	Association de la paix par le droit
BDIC	Bibliothèque de documentation internationale contemporaine, Nanterre
BIP	Bureau international de la paix
BN	Bibliothèque nationale, Paris
DD	Dossiers Duchene
DFG	Deutsche Friedensgesellschaft
IEC/CEI	International Executive Committee/Comité exécutif international
LICA	Ligue internationale contre l'antisémitisme
LICP	Ligue internationale des combattants de la paix
LIFPL	Ligue internationale des femmes pour la paix et la liberté
L.o.N.	League of Nations
LROC	Ligue pour la reconnaissance de l'objection de conscience
MIR	Mouvement international de la réconciliation
PCF	Parti communiste français
PD	*La Paix par le droit*
PH	*La Patrie humaine*
RR	Romain Rolland
RUP	Rassemblement universel pour la paix
SCPC	Swarthmore College Peace Collection
SFIO	Section française de l'internationale ouvrière
SHA	Service historique de l'armée de terre, Château de Vincennes
V.d.P.	La Volonté de paix (when italicized this is the newspaper of the same group)
WILPF	Women's International League for Peace and Freedom (the English name of the LIFPL)
WRI	War Resisters' International

I should greatly encourage young people looking for a thesis topic in history to study the origins and development of conscientious objectors. (Romain Rolland to Pierre Ceresole, Oct. 1923, *Rolland and Gandhi Correspondence* (New Delhi: Ministry of Information and Broadcasting, 1966), p. 381.)

Nous roulons, en apparence, l'éternel rocher de Sisyphe. Constatation amère, et qui découragerait d'aucuns. Mais nous sommes de ceux qui ne désespèrent jamais. Aussi bien trouvons-nous, jusque dans l'aveu de notre déception, des raisons positives d'envisager l'avenir avec une confiance réfléchie. ('Appel-programme', *PD* 30/1–2 (Jan.–Feb. 1920).)

Introduction

In response to a 1934 survey on the 'crisis of pacifism', Marcel Déat wrote that 'it has often been said that nations do not have the same sociological age, that the same institutions do not have the same meaning everywhere'.[1] His comment is particularly apposite with regard to the history of pacifism and peace movements in France. While there is a large body of historical writing on pacifism in America, Britain, and Germany, the dearth of historical writing on the French peace movement of this century is almost complete.

What are the reasons for this strange neglect? Was France immune to the political phenomena which affected the rest of the interwar world? In fact, quite the opposite was true. The France of the twenties and thirties was alive with a plethora of pacifist groups of various inspirations and orientations. A large compendium of information about Franco-German peace groups published in 1932 under the patronage of André Tardieu listed fifty 'pacifist organizations' in France and a further seventeen groups which 'sympathized' with pacifism.[2] Four years later, the Centre international de documentation antiguerrière in Paris published a peace yearbook for France which contained over 200 organizations described as 'pacifist'.[3] On the surface, then, it would seem that the French peace movement was a hale and hearty creature enjoying large support within the French body politic. To some extent, this was true. Certainly until about 1933, large sections of French political society

[1] Marcel Déat, 'Réponse à l'Enquête sur la crise du pacifisme', PD 44/2 (Feb. 1934), 78. Unless otherwise indicated, all translations from French or German into English are mine.
[2] See 'Les Organisations pacifistes françaises' and 'Les Groupements sympathisants français' in Nous voulons la paix (Paris: SRIP, 1932), 27–110.
[3] Annuaire de la paix (Paris: Centre international de documentation antiguerrière, 1936).

sought to portray themselves as 'pacifist'. There was tremendous support for Briand,[4] and, as will become clear in Part I, important figures of the French intellectual and political élite had close connections with what is described here as *pacifisme ancien style*.

But it is important to underline that, in contradistinction to the British or the German experience, there was no large, all-encompassing pacifist organization in France. There is no French equivalent—in numbers at least—either of the Peace Pledge Union or of the German Peace Cartel. The French peace movement of the interwar period was a lively and probably numerically significant force, but it was also a balkanized, splintered movement. Indeed, one of the theses of this study is that the predominantly political (as opposed to ethical) nature of French pacifism is a feature which differentiates it from Anglo-Saxon pacifism. This emphasis on the political produced a shotgun effect in terms of its practical impact on the world of French politics. As the editors of the 1936 *Annuaire* commented

May we be permitted to draw one conclusion from the work here presented: it is the *number* of Organizations, even those genuinely pacifist, and the *extraordinary dispersion of efforts* for peace, among people who have the best will in the world. And we can add without fear of contradiction that these Organizations are often almost totally ignorant of one another's work.[5]

The editors noted the warm reception they had received from all groups in compiling the *Annuaire* but remarked that in such a time of international tension, one had to wonder whether these dispersed efforts for peace would be effective.[6]

The first point, then, to bear in mind in approaching a study

---

[4] The old-style pacifists supported Briand most energetically. His conception of peace was closely allied to their 'ideological' or 'collaborative' stance. The support for Briand within the new pacifism was more nuanced and tended to recall the Socialist Briand of the turn of the century. The LICP refused to be represented officially at Briand's funeral, underlining its sectarian attitude to French political society, even in the case of a man whom in other respects it admired. See for example Robert Tourly, 'Sur une tombe', *PH* 106 (9 Mar. 1934), 1; see also the announcement that, unlike some pacifist groups, the LICP would not participate in the state funeral, in *PH* 15 (12–18 Mar. 1932), 1; see also Victor Méric, 'Le Véritable Briand', *PH* 17 (26 Mar.–2 Apr. 1932), 1.

[5] *Annuaire*, 11–12.

[6] Ibid. 12.

of French interwar pacifism is the tremendous diversity of men, women, and organizations struggling, often in almost complete isolation, for peace. There were many groups which appear to have consisted of chiefs, but few Indians; it is equally the case that many of the groups listed in the two works cited above would not in the normal scheme of things be considered as 'pacifist'. For example, both works list the Trait d'union, a naturist group, as one of the pacifist associations in France. There are also many instances in both compendia of Masonic groups and positivist associations as well as the more mainstream groups supporting the League of Nations. The Carnegie Endowment for International Peace and the Interparliamentary Union are also mentioned. Groups promoting cultural or student exchanges with Germany figure prominently, as indeed do the veterans' organizations and the political parties most likely to be friendly to peace ideas. The impression, therefore, is one of some semantic confusion about what was understood by the word 'pacifist', in addition to organizational effervescence. No doubt many of the groups listed in these prospectuses would be more at home classified merely as 'internationalist', or as something else entirely. For many, it is clear that peace was not their primary reason for being.

Having said that, it seems obvious that great portions of the French public in the interwar years considered themselves to be 'pacifists', whatever that word may mean. While there are indications that the word had begun to take on pejorative tinges during the Great War, it was nevertheless a fairly common thing to hear a politician proclaim himself a pacifist. One has only to think of Briand, and the great urge to peace which he incarnated, to see the truth of that. There are other examples, too. Édouard Herriot, for example, in a speech on 1 February 1925 at the Trocadéro to raise money for a monument to peace, seemed to divide French society into the pacifist and nationalist camps when he cried, 'It is we pacifists who are the most true to the teachings of the war'.[7] The year previously, Charles Richet (1850–1935) had written that the French soul was 'profoundly pacifist' and in 1932 he stated that France was the 'most pacific of all peoples'; he went so far as to argue that even the extreme right in France held 'no idea more dearly than that of

---

[7] Cited in Jules Prudhommeaux, 'La Propagande: Le Monument de la réconciliation: Une manifestation émouvante au Trocadéro', *PD* 35/2 (Feb. 1925), 83.

peace'.[8] Even as late as 1937, in the face of a clearly worsening international situation, Théodore Ruyssen (1868–1967), the president of the Association de la paix par le droit, could state quite confidently that since the formation of the APD pacifism had made 'tremendous conquests'. 'It is not an exaggeration to say that today pacifism is everywhere'.[9] But in fact, this very success—or apparent success—for the pacifist idea had become one of its weaknesses. Ruyssen underlined that there were now so many types of pacifism that the movement had become 'frankly strangely incoherent'. If the end desired remained the same, the methods for reaching it, and the social and political analyses which underpinned them, had become almost irreconcilably different.[10]

This leads quite naturally to the problem of definition when discussing French pacifism. If pacifism is often equated with Communism by the man in the street in France, the reality was certainly

[8] See Charles Richet, 'Soyons tous les enfants de la paix!', *PD* 34/3 (Mar. 1924), 105–7; Charles Richet, 'La Vraie Figure de la France', *PD* 42/7–8 (July–Aug. 1932), 321–3; and Charles Richet, 'La Vraie Figure de la France', *PD* 43/3 (Mar. 1933), 97. Charles Richet was one of the grand old men of French pacifism. He was professor of medicine at the University of Paris and also held a chair at the Collège de France. In 1913 he won the Nobel Prize in Medicine for his work on anaphylaxis. He was a long-time member of several of the most important pre-World War I French peace societies, including the Société française pour l'arbitrage entre nations, founded by Frédéric Passy, of which he eventually became president. See Sandi E. Cooper, 'Charles Richet', in Harold Josephson (ed.), *Biographical Dictionary of Modern Peace Leaders* (London and Westport, Conn.: Greenwood Press, 1985), 807–9.

[9] See Théodore Ruyssen, 'Le Cinquantenaire de la Paix par le droit', *PD* 47/2 (Feb. 1937), 49–51. Ruyssen was a member of the French intellectual establishment. He took his *agrégation* in philosophy in 1892 as a *normalien* in the same class as Élie Halévy and Émile Chartier (Alain). He also held a doctorate, and studied for some time in Germany at the Universities of Berlin and Leipzig. As a philosopher he was a specialist on Kant. He taught at several *lycées* before being appointed to the Universities of Aix-Marseille (1904–6), Dijon (1906–8), Bordeaux (1908–21), and Grenoble (1939–45). For most of the interwar period (1921–39), Ruyssen was secretary-general of the Union internationale des associations pour la Société des nations and was based first in Brussels and then in Geneva. A man of prodigious literary output, Ruyssen published widely as a philosopher and was well past his ninetieth birthday when he finished the third volume of his *Les Sources doctrinales de l'internationalisme*, 3 vols. (Paris: Presses universitaires de France, 1954–61). See Jean-François Sirinelli, *Génération intellectuelle: Khâgneux et normaliens dans l'entre-deux-guerres* (Paris: Fayard, 1988), 90; and Sandi E. Cooper and Bernard C. Weber, 'Théodore Eugène César Ruyssen', in Warren F. Kuehl (ed.), *Biographical Dictionary of Internationalists* (London and Westport, Conn.: Greenwood Press, 1983), 647–8.

[10] Ruyssen, 'Cinquantenaire'.

different in the interwar years. As a quick glance at the tergiver-
sations of the PCF during the twenties and thirties on the question of
peace will show, French Communism in the interwar period was
intermittently and opportunistically antimilitarist and internationalist, but hardly pacifist. Indeed, it is one of the basic premisses of this
study that none of the political parties in interwar France can
justifiably be considered 'pacifist'. Being multi-interest political
groupings, the parties all had other concerns which, with the pressure of political events on a multitude of fronts, caused peace and
pacifism to wax and wane in importance as the political seasons
changed. Because the line has to be drawn somewhere, this study will
therefore not be about the position of the French political parties on
the question of peace. Other writers have examined this aspect of
interwar history—indeed, it is probably true to say that what little
has been written about peace *in any connection* in French history has
been done from this angle.[11] Others, such as Antoine Prost, have
dealt with 'pacifism' as a function of a larger whole, as *one* aspect
of the experience of another group.[12] The few works which do
attempt to treat the question of French pacifism proper usually
do so less than dispassionately and are often derisory in their

---

[11] See for example Michel Bilis, *Socialistes et pacifistes, 1933–1939: Ou l'intenable dilemme des socialistes français* (Paris: Syros, 1979); Philippe Robrieux, *Histoire
intérieure du parti communiste 1920–1945* (Paris: Fayard, 1980). See also Richard
Gombin, 'Socialisme et pacifisme', in René Rémond and Janine Bourdin (eds.), *La
France et les Français en 1938–1939* (Paris: Presses de la FNSP, 1978), 245–60.

[12] See Antoine Prost, *Les Anciens Combattants et la société française*, 3 vols.
(Paris: Presses de la FNSP, 1977), esp. iii: *Mentalités et idéologies*, 77–119. A work
which goes beyond the confines of this study and is also an example of one which
discusses pacifism as a function of other concerns (in this case admittedly closely allied
to many of the concerns of interwar French pacifists) is Jean-Claude Delbreil,
*Les Catholiques français et les tentatives de rapprochement franco-allemand (1920–
1933)* (Metz: Centre de recherches relations internationales, 1972). See also Barnett
Singer, 'From Patriots to Pacifists: The French Primary School Teachers, 1880–1940',
Journal of Contemporary History, 12 (1977), 413–34. See also Isabel Boussard, 'Le
Pacifisme paysan', in Rémond and Bourdin, *La France et les Français en 1938–1939*,
59–75. See also Jean-François Sirinelli, 'Khâgneux et normaliens aux années vingt',
thèse de doctorat d'état, Université de Paris-X, Nanterre, 1986, 5 vols., which
contains some interesting material on the extent to which this rather specialized milieu
of French society became impregnated with pacifist ideas. Mr Yves Santamaria is
currently preparing a doctoral thesis on 'Le PCF dans la lutte pour la paix, 1932–
1936' under the direction of Annie Kriegel. For several years Jean-Marie Mayeur has
run a joint research seminar at the Sorbonne and the Institut d'études politiques on
'Les Églises chrétiennes devant la guerre et la paix', but so far nothing has emerged in
published form that I am aware of.

superficiality.[13] The end result leaves one with the impression that perhaps, after all, the French *are* different and that they were spared the agonizing debates over the problem of peace between the wars which beset the rest of the Western world.

But such a supposition is, of course, false. It ignores the fact that one of Europe's best-known pacifists in the interwar period was a Frenchman—Romain Rolland—and that in fact the very word 'pacifism' is French in origin.[14] How has this state of affairs come to pass? No doubt one reason is the legacy of the Second World War in France with all that that event conjures up in the historical imagination: Vichy, collaborationism, defeatism, the *épuration*, and so on. As one French commentator has written:

In denying the virtue of war, rendered sacrosanct by tradition, pacifism shakes established ideas. It is lumped together with defeatism, with cowardice, with treason.

Pacifism has, therefore, often taken on a pejorative connotation. It is

[13] Perhaps the most glaring example in the latter category is J. B. Barbier, *Le Pacifisme dans l'histoire de France (de l'an mille à nos jours)* (Paris: La Librairie française, 1966). See also Jean Defrasne, *Le Pacifisme*, Collection 'Que sais-je?' (Paris: Presses universitaires de France, 1983). See also Jean-Pierre Cattelain, *L'Objection de conscience*, Collection 'Que sais-je?' (Paris: Presses universitaires de France, 3rd edn. 1982). See also Marcel Merle, *Pacifisme et internationalisme XVIIe–XXe siècles* (Paris: Armand Colin, 1966), which is a useful collection of texts from a variety of authors, not all of them by any means French, with rather little in the way of analysis. Two other works which deserve mention are Nicolas Faucier, *Pacifisme et antimilitarisme dans l'entre-deux-guerres* (Paris: Spartacus, 1983) and Michel Auvray, *Objecteurs, insoumis, déserteurs: Histoire des réfractaires en France* (Paris: Stock/2, 1983). The first is a personal memoir by the companion of Louis Lecoin and is useful for details about one aspect of interwar French pacifism. Auvray's book is by a present-day militant and conscientious objector and is also useful for detail, although at times rather polemical in approach. On the earlier antecedents to French pacifism, see Elizabeth Souleyman, *The Vision of World Peace in Seventeenth and Eighteenth-Century France* (New York: G. P. Putnam's Sons, 1941); see also Peter Brock, *Pacifism in Europe to 1914* (Princeton, NJ: Princeton University Press, 1972). Finally, see J. B. Duroselle, 'Les Précédents historiques: Pacifisme des années 30 et neutralisme des années 50', in *Pacifisme et dissuasion: Travaux et recherches de l'Institut français de relations internationales sous la direction de Pierre Lelouche* (Paris: IFRI, 1983), 241–52.

[14] On the place of Romain Rolland within French and European pacifism, see my 'Romain Rolland, Interwar Pacifism and the Problem of Peace', in Charles Chatfield and Peter van den Dungen (eds.), *Peace Movements and Political Cultures* (Knoxville, Tenn.: University of Tennessee Press, 1988), 143–64. On the origins of the word 'pacifism', which was first used at the Universal Peace Congress in Glasgow in 1901, see Roger Chickering, *Imperial Germany and a World without War: The Peace Movement and German Society, 1892–1914* (Princeton, NJ: Princeton University Press, 1975), 14–15.

perversion. It is to peace what formalism is to form, simplism to simplicity, sentimentality to sentiment.[15]

He goes on to say that 'pacifism played its role in the birth of the Vichy regime'.[16] Thus, in the French mind, the notion of pacifism occasions distressing memories of a particularly difficult time in recent history.

Clearly the usage of the word 'pacifism' contained several shades of meaning in the interwar years, and the same is true today. The historian is thus faced initially with a definitional problem in beginning an examination of interwar French pacifism. One of the most important recent contributions to the historiography of the modern peace movement is Martin Ceadal's book on interwar British pacifism, which despite its Anglocentricity is an important work for two reasons. First, Ceadel attempts to define what is meant by pacifism, to delineate the boundaries between pacifism and what he calls *pacificism*, following A. J. P. Taylor's unfortunate usage. The former he defines as 'the belief that all war is *always wrong* and should never be resorted to', and the second as the 'assumption that war, though *sometimes necessary*, is always an irrational and inhumane way to solve disputes, and that its prevention should always be an over-riding political priority'.[17] The problem with this definition is that it is arguably artificial. As Ceadel himself admits, both of the above positions were described as 'pacifist' during the interwar period in Britain. The same is even more the case in France where the word *pacifisme* described the whole spectrum of pacifist activity. It was only in the late twenties that French pacifists began to feel the need to distinguish between ordinary pacifism which had a long history in France and the arrival of a new and more radical pacifism which was christened *pacifisme intégral*.

To separate the different strands of pacifism from one another like this in the case of France would leave us with only half the story of the interwar French pacifist experience. As Roger Chickering justly remarks in his study of the pre-war German peace movement, to do

[15] Defrasne, *Le Pacifisme*, 3.
[16] Ibid. 111.
[17] Martin Ceadel, *Pacifism in Britain, 1914–1945: The Defining of a Faith* (Oxford: Clarendon Press, 1980), 3. Taylor's derivation may be found in A. J. P. Taylor, *The Troublemakers: Dissent over Foreign Policy, 1792–1939* (London: Hamish Hamilton, 1957), 51 n. 5.

so would be to exclude 'from the category of pacifist the very people who invented the term as a self-designation'.[18] Instead, he defines as a pacifist anyone 'who holds war to be wrong and has made a personal commitment to pursuing the kinds of activities he believes will lead to its systematic elimination from international affairs'.[19] Chickering's definitional approach has much to commend it.[20]

The basic limitation of this study will be that of definition. We shall define as pacifist those men, women, and organizations in interwar France for whom peace was a primary, consistent, and overriding concern and goal. This may seem a rather fluid definition, but it has the advantage of limiting the field of endeavour almost immediately. This is not, therefore, a study of political parties in interwar France. Whilst undoubtedly many of the parties, especially the Socialists, Communists, and Radicals, in varying ways and at different times, did express pacifist concerns, their primary purpose was never the achievement of peace as a goal in itself. In like manner, it would be interesting, but beside the point here, to consider in great detail the contribution made by such organizations as the Ligue des droits de l'homme, or the veterans' groups, to the struggle for peace. Both of these organizations had other, and more dominant, concerns and are therefore beyond the scope of this study.

Two further types of organization or thinking which were sometimes confused with pacifism in France must also be excluded. The first is the series of groups which grew out of the Amsterdam Congress against Imperialist War in 1932 and the congress held against Fascism the following year at the Salle Pleyel in Paris. Aside from the fact that this movement, which became known as Amsterdam-Pleyel, has already attracted its own chroniclers,[21] it is clear that it, too, had limitations on its attitudes towards what types of international wars might be resisted. Having said that,

[18] Chickering, *Imperial Germany*, 16.   [19] Ibid.
[20] The American–European Consultation on Peace Research in History, held 24–9 Aug. 1986 at Stadtschlaining, Austria, tended in its majority to follow something like the Chickering definition, referring to 'peace advocacy' rather than pacifism *per se*.
[21] See for example Rosemarie Schumann, *Amsterdam 1932: Der Weltkongreß gegen den imperialistischen Krieg* (East Berlin: Dietz Verlag, 1985). See also the doctoral thesis by Yves Santamaria cited above. A group which seems to have evolved in the opposite direction to the Amsterdam-Pleyel movement was the Comité de vigilance des intellectuels antifascistes. See Nicole Racine-Furlaud, 'Le Comité de vigilance des intellectuels antifascistes (1934–1939): Antifascisme et pacifisme', *Le Mouvement social*, 101 (Oct.–Dec. 1977), 87–113.

Amsterdam-Pleyel lurks like an *éminence grise* behind large parts of this study. Although international in scope and directed in some measure by the needs of Soviet foreign policy, its leading lights and greatest organizational successes were undoubtedly French. Amsterdam-Pleyel began as a protest against one sort of war—imperialist war—and ended up largely as the cover for an antifascist movement which accepted the idea of war as a potential necessity in an ideological crusade to protect the revolution and its home in the Soviet Motherland.

Secondly, at the end of the thirties there is the thorny question of the position of the extreme right in France on the question of war and peace. There is little doubt that for many partisans of the right, the political situation in Europe had undergone a complete reversal with the Nazi seizure of power in 1933. As Joseph Folliet pointed out in a perceptive essay, the traditional poles within French political society seemed to have been reversed by the time of the Munich crisis of 1938.[22] Whereas sections of the left were now clamouring for action against Hitler, parts of the extreme right seemed to some contemporary pacifists to be supporting many of the traditional theses of pacifism. This today may seem bizarre. It is clear that the *pacifisme des munichois*, or at least of those among them who were normally on the political right, was completely opportunistic in inspiration and had nothing to do with pacifism as it is here defined or was normally understood at the time. As will become evident in Part II, the political sea-changes occurring in France in the late thirties did provide French pacifists with a tremendous dilemma—to collaborate or not with these strange political bedfellows? Most pacifists refused to have anything to do with such a marriage of convenience; some, however, succumbed to the temptations of the *hic et nunc* and in so doing compromised their cause.[23]

Moving beyond the problem of definition to that of typology, one is confronted with several recent and competing conceptual approaches to the history of pacifism. Reinhold Lütgemeier-Davin, for example, divides the peace movement up into two broad categories: what he calls 'organizational pacifism' and 'radical pacifism'. In the former are subsumed the categories of 'scientific',

[22] See Joseph Folliet, *Pacifisme de droite? Bellicisme de gauche?* (Paris: Éditions du cerf, 1938).

[23] See especially ch. 9 ('Munich and all that') for a discussion of this problem.

juridical, and democratic pacifism, as well as an idealistic ethical-humanitarian pacifism. Radical pacifism he divides into non-violent and revolutionary tendencies. Overlapping between the two are the religious pacifists and a 'pedagogical' pacifism.[24] This division has much to commend it in an analysis of the French example. Following this schema, what is here denoted as *pacifisme ancien style* would represent an example of 'organizational' pacifism, while *pacifisme nouveau style* would be a clear case of 'radical' pacifism, incorporating both non-violent and revolutionary elements.

Ceadel's definitional approach is arguably unhelpful in the French or European context, and his analytical structure, taken largely from Weber and the sociology of religion, has some limitations in its applicability to the French case. The very subtitle of his work, 'The Defining of a Faith', indicates the extent to which the religious analysis underpins his argument. Nevertheless, there is much in his study that is suggestive for a history of the French peace movement of the same era. Ceadel distinguishes between what he calls the 'inspirations' for pacifism and its 'orientations'. The former he divides up into three further subcategories: religious, political (i.e. Socialist or anarchist), and humanitarian. The humanitarian inspiration was, according to Ceadel, the one major philosophical advance made by interwar pacifism, because it attempted to derive a value-neutral, utilitarian justification for pacifism. Pacifism can moreover have three orientations according to Ceadel: sectarian, collaborative, and non-violent. Depending on the political climate of the day, pacifism therefore either retreats into a sectarian stance which condemns completely the society around it and withdraws into purity; or else, it is tempted out of its shell into collaborative arrangements. The third possible orientation he defines as non-violence which 'presupposes exceptionally favourable circumstances', is the 'most optimistic' of the three, and 'assumes that pacifism can be applied as an immediately effective policy in the world as it is.'[25] Somewhat paradoxically, Ceadel writes that 'the most confident and impressive

---

[24] Reinhold Lütgemeier-Davin, *Pazifismus zwischen Kooperation und Konfrontation: Das Deutsche Friedenskartell in der Weimarer Republik* (Cologne: Pahl-Rugenstein Verlag, 1982), 13–17.

[25] Ceadel, *Pacifism in Britain*, 15–16. It should be noted that in his latest book, Ceadel distinguishes still further between the 'utilitarian' and the 'humanitarian' inspirations for pacifism. See Martin Ceadel, *Thinking about Peace and War* (Oxford and New York: Oxford University Press, 1987), 151–4.

pacifism has resulted where pacifists have been driven, by disagreement with a society convinced of the inevitability of war, into a sectarian orientation'.[26]

The use of the term 'non-violent' presents problems for the student of French pacifism as Part II makes clear. For many French integral pacifists of the thirties, pacifism did not mean non-violence at all. They envisaged the application of violence to situations on an individual or civic level with surprising equanimity. Non-violence seems out of place as an orientation for pacifism; rather, it is nothing more than a case of extreme collaboration for pacifists. Ceadel weakens his case for a tripartite division of orientations by writing of the bipolar nature of pacifist orientation: '. . . pacifism is pulled in two opposed directions in its relationship with society: towards preserving its purity; or towards maximizing its political relevance.'[27] It is simpler and conceptually clearer to limit the discussion of orientation to the sectarian–collaborative dichotomy. Violence and non-violence are better left to a discussion of tactics. This question constitutes one of the fundamental differences between the Anglo-American, essentially religiously or ethically inspired, view of what constitutes pacifism, and on the other hand, the French and German view which incorporates both violent (usually revolutionary or anarchist) and non-violent elements.

Ceadel has recently expanded his typological analysis of pacifism in another important and thought-provoking book.[28] He distinguishes between 'war pacifism' (or 'modern-war pacifism') and 'force pacifism', a distinction which contributes greatly to an appreciation of the interwar French pacifist position on the problem of violence. As we shall see, for many French pacifists it was war that was objected to, and not the use of force as such.

Of particular interest is Ceadel's final chapter which deals with 'the determinants of the debate'. He argues that a state's political culture 'predisposes its citizens towards certain views of international relations'; and he proposes that the 'degree of liberalism in a state's political culture and the degree of security in its strategic situation' are essential to an understanding of how nations view the problem of war and peace. Ceadel describes France as a 'non-liberal'

---

[26] Ceadel, *Pacifism in Britain*, 16–17.
[27] Ibid.
[28] Ceadel, *Thinking about Peace and War*.

culture which 'though granting asylum to foreign radicals, . . . has no tradition of tolerating pacifist sects'.[29] Above all, he writes,

French anti-war campaigning has been political, being an extension initially of radical and then of socialist and communist partisanship. It has thus been severely handicapped by the left's tradition of Jacobin nationalism. Although strongly opposed to militarism, it has always felt the need to defend the achievements of the French Revolution, notably republicanism, against foreign attack as well as aristocratic reaction.[30]

Finally, Ceadel considers the question of strategic situation, and persuasively argues that for a nation like France in the late thirties 'extreme insecurity' was the order of the day, an insecurity which could produce either pessimistic pacifism or defeatism[31]—and in France it did both. The French war-and-peace debate was therefore conducted around the two poles of a basically non-liberal political culture and an exposed, extremely insecure strategic position. This explains a great deal about the French pacifist debate, particularly in its dissenting, sectarian, utopian form, discussed in Part II of this book.

It is clear that the Ceadel typology can be applied to the French example with some degree of success. The old-style pacifists would therefore represent the collaborative orientation, and the new-style pacifists a sectarian stance. The feminist pacifists present a problem, however. They were at the same time both collaborative and sectarian in their orientation, although increasingly collaborative as the thirties progressed. In the immediate post-war period, however, the Ligue internationale des femmes pour la paix et la liberté represented in France both an absolute rejection of war and the society which engendered it, and paradoxically also a collaborative position of involvement with political society in an attempt to prevent its recurrence.

Thus, despite the major contribution made by Ceadel to the typology of pacifism, there remain problems of interpretation. A further criticism one might raise is the extent to which the sociology of religion approach is applicable to the far more secular French example. Admittedly, one is speaking here merely of an analytical

---

[29] Ceadel, *Thinking about Peace and War*, 172.
[30] Ibid. 173.
[31] Ibid. 184–5.

tool, which in many ways has much to commend it, but in studying the French case, one cannot help but be struck by the essentially political and secular nature of much of French pacifism.

Roger Chickering's approach to the typology of pacifism is similar in some respects to Ceadel's, although he does not follow the strict definition of pacifism employed by the latter. Chickering's typology is based on Karl Mannheim's work on the sociology of knowledge. He distinguishes between what he calls a 'utopian' pacifism which 'conceives of war as an inseparable aspect of a social and political order that is utterly corrupt and beyond rehabilitation', and on the other hand an 'ideological' pacifism which 'rejects war because of the threat it poses to a social and political order that is basically sound and praiseworthy'.[32] Thus, in Chickering's typology, utopian pacifism is largely a 'sectarian and chiliastic phenomenon', the province of 'marginal sectors of society'. The difference between the two types of pacifism is reduced to the following: 'Whereas utopian pacifism anticipates a radical personal or collective solution to the problem, ideological pacifism calls for moderate, constructive reform within the framework of political society'.[33] Finally, Chickering stresses that neither type of pacifism necessarily precludes what he terms 'the instrumental use of violence'. For the ideological pacifist, 'both wars of national defence and the use of collective sanctions by international agencies' are quite permissible. The utopian pacifist 'fluctuates between extreme passivity and extreme, often violent activism'.[34]

It seems clear that the Chickering typology is the most easily applicable to the interwar French case. The pacifists discussed in Part I are readily assimilated into the category of ideological pacifism, as indeed those of Part II quite easily fit the category of utopian pacifism. The feminists, once again, present a special case which is discussed in Part III. They vacillate between a utopian and an ideological pacifism, gradually moving more in the direction of the latter as the interwar period progresses.

There are conceptual similarities between the Chickering and Ceadel approaches. Ceadel goes one step further than Chickering in differentiating explicitly between inspirations and orientations, but

[32] Chickering, *Imperial Germany*, 19.
[33] Ibid. 19–20.
[34] Ibid. 21.

his inclusion of non-violence as an orientation seems out of place in a description of European, or at least French, pacifism. There were many pacifists within the Ligue internationale des combattants de la paix, for example, who espoused a violent, *civil* response to the threat of war. The use of non-violence as a criterion for establishing orientation thus seems irrelevant in the French context, the imposition perhaps of an Anglocentric conception of what rightly constitutes pacifism on the European situation. In this sense, Chickering comes much closer to the mark in his acceptance of revolutionary violence as one of the potential methods of pacifism.

The problem with both the Ceadel and the Chickering typologies is the lack of any sense of evolution over time. At any given moment the orientation of a pacifist group can thus be ascertained, but there is little sense of movement or change. And yet, one of the theses of the work here presented is that there was a great deal of movement and change over time. As will become clear, French pacifism evolved remarkably over the period in question. In 1919, what is called *pacifisme ancien style* defined the essence of French pacifism from which all subsequent variations were to evolve. Over the course of the twenties, with the rise of pessimism, fears of another war, and the growing feeling that little had fundamentally changed in the European situation since 1918, a gradual realization that a more radical pacifism was needed overcame some pacifists. This is not to say that this radical response to war was entirely new; it was not. There had been 'integral' pacifists before 1930, but what is new at the end of the twenties is the fact that these isolated instances of absolute, 'integral' pacifism began to coalesce into a proper movement with its own ideas, leaders, and publications. In so doing, it emerged into the body politic and became a force in French politics.

These, then, are the two fundamental dichotomies in this study: that between old-style pacifism which was, to use Chickering's typology, largely ideological in orientation; and the new-style pacifism, which was more utopian. A variation on this theme is to be found in the feminist pacifism of the Ligue internationale des femmes pour la paix et la liberté which is discussed in Part III. Feminist pacifism followed a trajectory in opposition to the development from old- to new-style pacifism. As Part III makes clear, the feminists of the LIFPL were *pacifistes nouveau style* before the distinction even existed. But they were never entirely utopian or sectarian in their orientation; they maintained close links with political society despite their espousal of an absolute pacifism. As the interwar years progressed, this orientation became increasingly 'collaborative' or 'ideological', in opposition to the evolution occurring from old- to new-style pacifism. Even within old-style pacifism, the situation was hardly static. In the age of Briand and the optimism of the twenties, the old-style pacifism followed an ascending curve bringing it close on several issues to the emerging new-style pacifism. But the rise to power of Hitler across the Rhine rapidly brought this to an end, and old-style pacifism reverted to its former ideological prescriptions for peace.

Some final comments are in order before we proceed any further. It is important to emphasize that one is dealing here with the politics of the margins. Perhaps by its very nature the politics of dissent was always, even in its collaborative, ideological forms, somewhat beyond the pale of French political society. This marginality varied from group to group, orientation to orientation, and over time. The Association de la paix par le droit, for example, seems to have had fairly close contacts with mainstream French political life. The same cannot really be said about the new-style pacifism which because of its dissenting attitude on a variety of issues seems to have maintained a fairly strict posture of sectarianism or utopianism. The point to be made is that the historian of marginality is somewhat like the medievalist, forever digging for clues to what the pacifists of the interwar period really thought. In some cases, he is successful. But in many instances, he must content himself with published primary material because pacifist archives simply do not exist. This is certainly the case in the study of French pacifism. The Gabrielle Duchene bequest at the Bibliothèque de documentation internationale contemporaine at Nanterre is rich in otherwise untraceable tracts, pamphlets, and books, but in terms of correspondence with other pacifists it is primarily useful for the history of feminist pacifism. Part III of this study is therefore heavily based on this sort of archival material. The Romain Rolland papers in the Bibliothèque nationale were also consulted, but they are unfortunately still in the process of being sorted and catalogued, and were therefore of only limited use. The author also consulted the André Trocmé papers in the Swarthmore College Peace Collection in America; this too was only of limited use because of Trocmé's tangential connection with this study. The Archives nationales and the Service historique de l'armée de terre were used primarily for information on the government's reaction to a perceived conscientious objection problem in 1933, discussed in Chapter 7. The papers of the Ligue internationale des combattants de la paix and the Association de la paix par le droit do not seem to exist; were they to be found, they would be of central interest to future scholars of French pacifism. Additional archival collections were also consulted, but the information gathered therein forms only a small part of the material contained in this book.

A second point is that the reader will perhaps look in vain for detailed practical prescriptions for achieving lasting peace, or conversely specific tactical instructions for responding to a war situation. There are a number of reasons for this. For the pacifists of the thirties especially, all energies were directed at avoiding a recurrence of war. As Victor Méric often wrote, when the next war arrived, it would all be too late. For most pacifists, the task at hand was thus largely an educative one, informing people of the dangers of war and leaving them to draw their own conclusions. It is also extremely important to realize that there was a limit to how specific even the most committed pacifist orator could be in advising or exhorting an audience to pick up the pacifist cross. As Part II makes clear, it was only too easy to fall foul of the Third Republic's laws prohibiting propaganda against the army, for example. Pacifist orators had to be content with drawing a picture and allowing their audiences to take whatever interpretation they chose from it.

One final criticism might well be that little mention is made of the impact of pacifists on French political society. In one sense, it could be argued that it was negligible because it is clear that the pacifist voice was not heard. But in another sense, as Part II demonstrates, the government was certainly worried in 1933 about the spread of integral pacifist ideas in France. Our purpose in this study, though, has not been primarily to examine the extent to which pacifism became a governmental issue in interwar France, but rather to describe the evolution and the political development of an as yet unexamined, but important, peace movement. In so doing, we move into the nebulous and marginal realm of the politics of dissent.

PART I

PACIFISME ANCIEN STYLE, OR THE PACIFISM OF THE PEDAGOGUES

1. Peace through Justice, or the Old Pacifism Defined

Pacifism was not born in France in the aftermath of the Great War. Despite the apparent aversion of modern French historiography to the treatment of the subject, pacifism has a long and respectable history in the annals of nineteenth- and twentieth-century France. Groups which claimed the achievement of peace as their primary goal are to be found well back into the early years of the last century. The earliest French peace society on record, according to Roger Chickering, was the Société de morale chrétienne which was founded in Paris in 1821 by the Duc de la Rochefoucauld-Liancourt and included such luminaries as Guizot, Lamartine, and Benjamin Constant in its membership.[1] Later in the century, under the Second Empire, Victor Hugo was arguably the most renowned pacifist in Europe. But it is above all the period following the initial consolidation of the Third Republic which saw a notable explosion in the number of French peace societies. Between 1898 and 1902 alone, according to Chickering, twenty-seven new peace societies were formed, and the years from 1899 to 1906 represented 'the period of the peace movement's greatest influence in France'.[2]

In 1902 the French societies began holding regular national peace congresses. By 1900 the Bureau français de la paix, which had been founded in 1896 by Gaston Moch (1859–1935), a former artillery captain, and which was to become the Délégation permanente des sociétés françaises de la paix in 1902, already claimed some 400 member organizations, most of them admittedly not societies whose

---

[1] Roger Chickering, *Imperial Germany and a World Without War: The Peace Movement and German Society, 1892–1914* (Princeton, NJ: Princeton University Press, 1975), 331.
[2] Ibid. 339.

primary concern was the achievement of peace.[3] However, by the time of the outbreak of the First World War, 'the French peace movement was, organizationally at least, an impressive phenomenon. It included in 1913 twenty-eight different societies devoted to popularising arms limitation and arbitration'.[4] In Chickering's view, the rise of the peace societies in late nineteenth-century France is directly attributable to the crisis of the Dreyfus affair and the growing influence of Radical republicanism. This process brought the peace movement in from the cold, as it were. The politics of the margins moved much closer to the centre of French political life. As Chickering puts it, 'Radicalism and pacifism were closely related phenomena. Like the peace movement, Radicals advocated the rigorous application of democratic principles, distrusted soldiers, renounced all but defensive wars and called for arms limitation and arbitration of international disputes'.[5]

Of the many pre-war French peace societies, probably the most important and influential[6] was the Association de la paix par le droit, which was formed in 1887 by six *lycéens* in Nîmes, and which had an unbroken existence spanning more than half a century until it finally dissolved in the aftermath of the Second World War.[7] The Association de la paix par le droit represents better than any other competing organization the *pacifisme ancien style* which was the point of departure for all subsequent developments within French pacifism. The APD typified the bourgeois, liberal, internationalist tradition within French pacifism which believed in the inexorable march of humanity towards a better future in which war would be banished under the aegis of arbitration and conciliation between mutually enlightened powers who would voluntarily disarm and

---

[3] Chickering, *Imperial Germany*, 339; see also obituary on Gaston Moch in *PD* 45/9 (Sept. 1935), 377–8; see also Sandi Cooper, 'Gaston Moch', in Harold Josephson (ed.), *Biographical Dictionary of Modern Peace Leaders* (Westport, London: Greenwood Press, 1985), 645–7.

[4] Chickering, *Imperial Germany*, 339–40.   [5] Ibid. 338.

[6] This view is shared by Chickering, *Imperial Germany*, 337.

[7] On the origins of the Association de la paix par le droit see ibid. 337–8; see also J. Prudhommeaux, 'L'Origine, le développement et le fonctionnement de l'Association de la paix par le droit', *PD* 38/12 (Dec. 1928), 513–18; Henry Babut, 'Les Origines de la Paix par le droit', *PD* 38/4–5 (Apr.–May 1928), 169–75; Ernest Roussel, 'Les Origines de la Paix par le droit', *PD* 38/1 (Jan. 1928), 10–15; Jacques Dumas, 'Les Origines de la Paix par le droit', *PD* 38/3 (Mar. 1928), 105–12; see also: Henry Babut, 'Notes brèves sur nos origines', *PD* 48/6–7–8 (May–June–July 1938), 254–6; J. Prudhommeaux, 'Un demi-siècle d'activité de la revue "La Paix par le droit"', *PD* 48/6–7–8 (May–June–July 1938), 269–77.

pool their coercive forces into a single army under international command. The APD exemplified all that was best in the French 'scientific' approach to peace, in its continuing search for what it termed a 'positive' peace which had to be constructed slowly and patiently over time.

Part I will therefore largely be about the evolution of the Association de la paix par le droit over the course of the interwar period. Other organizations could have been chosen to represent traditional French pacifism, but none so clearly epitomizes its spirit and methods as the APD. There are other reasons, too, for concentrating our attentions on the APD. As an organization, it swallowed up several of the more important pre-war groups and thus established a sort of hegemony over French pacifism in the immediate post-war period. For example, one of the oldest French peace societies, the Ligue internationale et permanente de la paix, which had been founded in 1867 by Frédéric Passy (1822–1912)[8] and others, became the Société française des amis de la paix and finally in 1888, under the influence of the Englishman Hodgson Pratt (1824–1907),[9] the Société française pour l'arbitrage entre nations.[10] When the young *lycéens* of Nîmes formed their association in 1887, it was to Passy that they looked for an honorary president. However, by the immediate post-war years, the Association de la paix par le droit had overtaken the Société française in importance and in 1922 the two associations merged, retaining the name of the APD and its organ.[11]

So much for the organizational legacy of the pre-war years. But what about the post-war era? Did the APD retain its position of pre-eminence in the interwar period? The answer is almost certainly affirmative within the parameters of the old-style pacifism with which we are concerned in this section. The victory of the Allied powers in 1918, Wilson's fourteen points, and more especially the founding of the League of Nations created an explosion of societies in France whose *raison d'être* was to support the work of the League. In many ways, these societies, of which there were many, were logical

---

[8] See Sandi E. Cooper, 'Frédéric Passy', in Josephson, *Dictionary*, 730–2.

[9] See John V. Crangle, 'Hodgson Pratt', in Josephson, *Dictionary*, 767–9.

[10] Chickering, *Imperial Germany*, 334–7.

[11] On the fusion of the two societies, see Charles Richet and Théodore Ruyssen, 'Fusion de la Société française pour l'arbitrage et de l'Association de la paix par le droit', *PD* 32/2 (Feb. 1922), 57–8. For a short account of the links between the two organizations see Jacques Dumas, 'La Société française pour l'arbitrage entre nations', *PD* 32/2 (Feb. 1922), 59–65.

off-shoots of the pre-war work of the APD. They represented the culmination of all that the Association wished to achieve in international life. And they were not surprisingly closely connected with the APD in terms of shared membership, shared ideals, and, in the case of some, shared organs. For example, Théodore Ruyssen, the long-serving president of the APD, was also the secretary-general of the Union internationale des associations pour la Société des nations.[12] Jules Prudhommeaux, one of the founding six from Nîmes, was the secretary-general not only of the APD, but also of the Association française pour la Société des nations. Jules-L. Puech was the editorial secretary of the Association's review, also entitled *La Paix par le droit*; and his wife was the president of the Union féminine pour la société des nations and also vice-president of the APD. In 1931 the APD announced that, in light of a recent friendly agreement, its review would be open to news and announcements from the Association française pour la Société des nations, the Comité français de coopération européenne, the Union féminine pour la Société des nations, and the Fédération française des associations pour la SDN.[13] The APD was thus the nexus between the pre-war societies which had worked for the creation of something like the League of Nations, and the plethora of post-war groups which sprang up to nurture and defend the fledgeling Geneva institution. In terms of membership, leadership, intellectual content, and the pooling of printed resources the Association de la paix par le droit thus stands out as the most important and influential of the French peace societies which collectively make up what we have denoted here as *pacifisme ancien style*. The theme of interpenetration of the French peace societies is one to which we shall return later in this section, together with its antithesis, the balkanization of French pacifist efforts.

For the moment, though, it would be useful to take a brief look at the thorny question of membership and circulation figures in order to gain some sort of appreciation of the size of the APD. Thorny, because in the history of marginality, even in the case of relatively mainstream groups such as the APD, the historian feels very much like the medievalist dealing with the imponderables of quantifica-

---

[12] Mention is made of Ruyssen's election to this position in Edmond Duméril and J. Prudhommeaux, 'L'Assemblée générale de l'Association de la paix par le droit' (Poitiers, 31 Oct.–1 Nov. 1921), in *PD* 31/12 (Dec. 1921), 404.

[13] See the 'Avis' printed on the inside cover of *PD* 41/2 (Feb. 1931).

tion. Nevertheless, it seems clear that after the quite natural slump in membership figures occasioned by the Great War, the APD quickly began to climb out of the trough towards a membership which varied between roughly 5,000 and 7,000 members for most of the interwar period. Two non-dated reports from the interwar period, written in English, apparently for the Society of Friends, and contained in the Swarthmore College Peace Collection, put the membership of the APD variously at 8,000 and 20,000.[14] The latter figure is certainly too high and the former might be slightly inflated as well. Combing through the various reports presented over twenty years of annual general meetings the following figures for membership can be gleaned: 6,000 members in 1929, rising to around 7,000 in 1935 and falling to 6,000 again in 1938.[15] This compares with pre-war figures of 1,200 in 1902 and about 4,000 in 1912.[16] The pre-eminence of the APD within old-style French pacifism is further illustrated by a list of the membership charges exacted on the French members of the Bureau international de la paix which had its headquarters in Geneva. *Le Mouvement pacifiste* reported that in 1926 the total contribution of French peace societies to the work of the Bureau, by reason of 5 centimes per member, was just over 151 Swiss francs. Of this sum, 98 francs came from the APD, and a further 5.65 francs from its Paris section directly. Following this line of reasoning, the APD claimed (or at least paid for!) only some 2,000 members in 1926. Whatever the accuracy of the global figures, the APD's contribution to the BIP was four times higher than the next largest French contributor. That said, the French total pales into insignificance beside the 956 Swiss francs paid by the German peace societies and the 808 francs paid by the various British groups.[17]

There seems to have been a fairly high turnover in the Association's membership, too. Auguste Laune, the Association's indefatigable treasurer (and a founding member) complained at the 1938

---

[14] 'Pacifist Organizations in France' (1928?) and 'France', both in SCPC, CDG-B (France), Box 2.

[15] An obituary on Séverine mentions 6,000 members; see *PD* 39/6 (June 1929), 251. See also J. Prudhommeaux, 'L'Assemblée générale de la Paix par le droit' (Marseille, 27 Dec. 1935), *PD* 46/2 (Feb. 1936), 68; J. Prudhommeaux and J. Lahargue, 'L'Assemblée générale et le Congrès du cinquantenaire Nîmes, 19–21 avril 1938', *PD* 48/6–7–8 (May–June–July 1938), 249.

[16] Chickering, *Imperial Germany*, 337 and 344.

[17] 'Tableau des cotisations versées en 1926 au Bureau international de la paix,' *Le Mouvement pacifiste* (Oct. 1927), 146–7.

annual general meeting of 2,500 memberships or subscriptions to the review which had not been renewed over the preceding five years. Clearly the worsening international situation, coupled with the effects of the financial crisis which had finally reached France (in 1932), was much to blame for this state of affairs, but nevertheless it seems that it represented a continuing problem for the APD. In this same financial report, Laune noted that over the course of its fifty-year existence the Association had lost a total of 30,000 members or subscribers.[18]

Turning to circulation figures for the APD's organs, the situation is broadly similar. Not all subscribers to the review *La Paix par le droit* or to the more popular broadsheet *Les Peuples unis* created following the 1924 annual general meeting, were necessarily members of the Association. That said, the subscription rate for *La Paix par le droit* was a close mirror of membership figures in the Association. In 1920 the review had a print run of about 5,000 copies. This compared with 8,000 copies printed in the first seven months of 1914 and 6,000 in the last five.[19] By 1924 the circulation figures had risen to 8,000 again, falling to 5,500 in 1927, and only 5,300 in 1935, despite a rise to 7,000 in 1931.[20]

The above figures give a rough quantitative idea of the nature of the APD, but they say very little about the sort of person who was likely to be found in the ranks of this Association. Unfortunately little information is available which would provide a precise and objective analysis of the sort of 'pacifist' likely to join the APD. Still, it is possible to paint an impressionistic picture of the APD which will give us at least an approximation of the sort of membership it had.

The first point to be made is that one could almost call the old-style pacifism under discussion in this section the *pacifisme des professeurs*, such is the level of activity of teachers of all grades within the APD. Barnett Singer has written of the extent to which the *instituteurs* of the late Third Republic became imbued with pacifist ideas, and Jean-François Sirinelli in his recent massive *doctorat-*

[18] Laune in Prudhommeaux and Lahargue, 'L'Assemblée générale', 249.

[19] Jules-L. Puech, 'Notre revue', PD 30/11–12 (Nov.–Dec. 1920), 367.

[20] See: J. Prudhommeaux and Georges Cadier, 'L'Assemblée générale de la Paix par le droit', PD 34/7–8 (July–Aug. 1924), 273; J. Prudhommeaux and J.-L. Puech, 'L'Assemblée générale et les fêtes du XLème anniversaire', PD 37/12 (Dec. 1927), 443; J. Prudhommeaux, 'Notre Assemblée générale', PD 41/12 (Dec. 1931), 577; J. Prudhommeaux, 'L'Assemblée générale de la Paix par le droit', PD 46/2 (Feb. 1936), 62.

d'état paints a picture of *khâgneux* and *normaliens* in the twenties affected by much the same system of ideas.[21] The APD was the creation and preserve of academics. A 1932 list of almost sixty local groups of the APD provides the following breakdown by occupation of the group presidents or secretaries: thirteen professors, directors of schools and faculties, or inspectors of education, one *instituteur*, two pastors, six medical doctors, one industrialist, three present or sometime mayors, one *premier adjoint* (to the mayor of Nîmes), one *conseiller-général*, one *conseiller-municipal*, one retired military officer, one newspaper director, and one court clerk, for a total of thirty-two local group presidents for whom the occupation is given or can be deduced. Another twenty-seven groups provide no information as to the occupation of their presidents.[22] If one examines the APD's executive committee and Conseil de direction the predominance of the professorial element is even more noticeable. Taking 1932 once again as the point of reference, in that year the executive committee was composed of people who represented the cream of the French intellectual élite. The president, Théodore Ruyssen, was a professor at the University of Brussels, having previously taught at the University of Bordeaux. As vice-presidents in 1932 were Jacques Dumas (1868–1945),[23] a doctor of laws and a justice at the Cour de cassation in Paris, and Marie-Louise Puech who was president of the Union féminine pour la Société des nations. The secretary-general was Professor Jules Prudhommeaux,[24] the

[21] See Barnett Singer, 'From Patriots to Pacifists: The French Primary School Teachers, 1880–1940', *Journal of Contemporary History*, 12 (1977), 413–34; J.-F. Sirinelli, 'Khâgneux et normaliens aux années vingt', thèse de doctorat d'état, University of Paris-X, Nanterre, 1986, 5 vols.; see also J.-F. Sirinelli, *Génération intellectuelle: Khâgneux et normaliens dans l'entre-deux-guerres* (Paris: Fayard, 1988).

[22] See 'Association de la paix par le droit' in *Nous voulons la paix* (Paris: SRIP, 1932), 28–31.

[23] Dumas was educated at the Universities of Montpellier and Paris, from which latter institution he took his Doctor of Laws degree in 1893. He was a founding member in 1887 of the Association des jeunes amis de la paix in Nîmes. After working briefly in a government ministry, Dumas entered the judiciary in 1897 and stepped down as president of the APD. He finished his career as a justice of the Supreme Court of Appeal in Paris. See Théodore Ruyssen, 'Jacques Dumas', *PD* 51/2 (Nov.–Dec. 1947), 51–3; and Jules-L. Puech, 'La Paix par le droit (1887–1947)', *PD* 51/2 (Nov.–Dec. 1947), 33–41; and Sandi E. Cooper, 'Jacques Dumas', in Josephson, *Dictionary*, 231–3.

[24] Jules Jean Prudhommeaux was born in 1869 and died sometime after 1948 in France. He was one of the founding members of the Association des jeunes amis de la paix, and for many years the European director of the Carnegie Endowment for

footnote continued overleaf

secretary in charge of propaganda was Edmond Duméril who was a *professeur agrégé* at the *lycée* in Nantes, and who was to receive his doctorate in German literature in 1934, and finally the secretary in charge of the reviews was Jules-L. Puech who held doctorates in law and letters, and in 1934 was to be honoured with the ribbon of the Legion of Honour. The treasurer of the Association was Auguste Laune, a businessman. Of the three members at large in the executive committee one finds Georges Scelle,[25] professor of international law at the University of Geneva, Célestin Bouglé, at that time assistant director of the École normale supérieure but who was to finish his career as director in the rue d'Ulm, and Georges Cadier, director of a newspaper in Nantes. This rather long list goes some way to showing the extent to which the APD was very much the creation and preserve of part of the French liberal, educated élite. The honorary president of the Association was Charles Richet, professor at the Faculty of Medicine of the University of Paris and Member of the Institute. Other names of some renown are to be found in the list of members of the Conseil de direction; one example is that of Justin Godart, senator for the Rhône. And the list could go on.[26]

In terms of the type of pacifist attracted to the APD in the interwar period, more could be said about the links between the Association and Ligue des droits de l'homme, Freemasonry, the Radical Party, and the extent to which the APD reflected Protestant ideals within a Roman Catholic tradition. In ending this introduction to *pacifisme ancien style*, however, one should point out the intimate relations between it and the official world of French politics, in short its central place in an important part of French political culture, especially during the twenties. With men like Painlevé, Paul-Boncour, Godart, and Pierre Cot—to name but four—interested in the work of the APD, it is perhaps not surprising to find that in 1929 the Association was given the official accolade of being *reconnue d'utilité publique*.

---

footnote continued

International Peace. See Albert S. Hill, 'Jules Jean Prudhommeaux', in Josephson, *Dictionary*, 770–1.

[25] Georges Scelle was born at Avranches in 1878. He took first place in the *agrégation* in public law in 1912, and taught 1912–19 at the University of Dijon. During the Great War he distinguished himself by winning the Croix de guerre. See Jean-François Sirinelli, *Génération intellectuelle*, 230.

[26] For a list of the members of the Conseil de direction and the Comité exécutif of the APD, see the inside cover of *PD* 42/6 (June 1932). Additional information on Puech and Duméril can be found in *PD* 44/7–8 (July–Aug. 1934), 304–5.

ORIGINS

It is interesting to note that despite its later 'scientific' or juridical pacifism, the Association de la paix par le droit began its existence very much as the result of an ethical and moral rejection of war. The writers of the monthly news column in the *PD* referred in 1926 to the department of the Gard as the 'cradle of our association'.[27] As has been mentioned above, the APD was formed in the spring of 1887 by six *lycéens* in Nîmes, the capital of the Gard, and like the ripples caused by a pebble dropped into a still pond the ideas of the APD spread out from Nîmes across France, following in many cases the careers of the original six and their converts to the cause. It is probably no accident that this association was formed in one of the areas of France most imbued with Protestant ideas.[28] The connection between the APD and Protestantism was to remain strong over the course of its entire life. Several members of the APD's committee were clergymen in the Reformed Church of France. In fact, one of the founding six, Henri Babut, was the son of a pastor and went on to study Protestant theology in Montauban before being ordained himself. The influence of Protestant ideas from England was also important in the formation of the APD. These ideas seem to have been transmitted to the young *lycéens* of Nîmes as a result of a voyage undertaken by the oldest of the founding six, L.-A. Barnier, who became the first president of the fledgeling association, then called simply the Jeunes Amis de la paix. As Jules Prudhommeaux wrote in 1928, Barnier 'had brought back from a trip to England, which had placed him in contact with several members of the Society of Friends (Quakers) who were committed to ideas of peace and arbitration, the new faith which he hastened to share with his comrades'.[29] Ernest Roussel, writing of the origins of the APD, said that it grew out of an adolescent discussion group called 'La Gerbe'. For him the pervasive influence of Protestant ideas was self-evident:

The Gerbe was Protestant in spirit, for we were mostly of Huguenot origin, which was only natural in Nîmes. We represented different nuances of religious belief. To tell the truth, I think that only one of us had a real faith;

---

[27] Charles Rousseau and Jules Prudhommeaux, 'Dans le Gard: A Caveirac', *PD* 36/5 (May 1926), 234.

[28] See Brian Fitzpatrick, *Catholic Royalism in the Department of the Gard, 1814–1852* (Cambridge: Cambridge University Press, 1983), 15–17.

[29] Prudhommeaux, 'L'Origine', 513.

he has become a pastor and an admirable one. But we were all sons of the Reformation, through our critical spirit and faith in the value of the things of the mind and of the conscience.[30]

The initial programme of the Jeunes Amis de la paix was comprised of two points: (1) 'Suppression of permanent armies—creation of national militias to guarantee the internal police'; and (2) 'Creation of a tribunal of international arbitration endowed with a special code'.[31] Following the suggestion of Frédéric Passy, the order of the two points in the programme was inverted, the suppression of armies being a result of the creation of international tribunals according to him.[32] The name La Paix par le droit was suggested by Pastor Charles Babut who gave the young Association 'in three words, a principle, a programme, and a hope in a better Future'.[33] Despite the early influence of Quaker individualism on the nascent Association, it quickly affirmed a measure of conformity with Third Republic military demands. After one of its early members became a conscientious objector, the APD included an article in its statutes which read that 'Active and ordinary members [membres actifs et membres adhérents] undertake to submit to the military laws of their country, if they have not yet satisfied them'.[34] Thus, without labouring the point, it is clear that what began in an élan of individualistic moral or religious conviction was quickly transmuted into an essentially political and juridical programme no less fervently espoused for all that. This very early change is important and is one to which we shall return, especially in the debates on conscientious objection within the APD in the late twenties and early thirties, but it is important to note that almost from the outset pacifisme ancien style in France had a social and juridical epicentre rather than a religious or primarily ethical one. The insistence on justice or 'right' in the Association's rather epigrammatic title is one which was to provide both strengths and weaknesses in its approach to the problem of peace in interwar Europe; strength no doubt in its perspicacious analysis of the dangers posed by Hitlerian Germany, but weakness also in its blurred vision of the world of the twenties created at Versailles.

[30] Roussel, 'Les Origines', 12.
[31] See 'Facsimilé' of the original programme in PD 37/12 (Dec. 1927), 428.
[32] Prudhommeaux, 'L'Origine', 513–14.
[33] Roussel, 'Les Origines', 13.
[34] Prudhommeaux, 'L'Origine', 515.

One further point needs to be made in this introduction to the pre-war nature of the APD's pacifism, that is to say, its relations with the organized working class. As early as 1904–5 the Association had become aware of the need to develop some sort of position on the pacifism or antimilitarism of large swaths of French syndicalism. Within the pre-war French working class the fight against war had overtly mechanistic dimensions with little in the way of ethical nuance. The argument was quite simple: rid society of the capitalist class and wars would disappear forever. The violence of the syndicalist analysis of war and how to prevent it seemed to be peculiarly French. As Prudhommeaux said in a speech on the relations between pacifism and the working class delivered at the fourteenth International Peace Congress in Lucerne in September 1905, 'For very diverse political and social reasons (absence of obligatory military service, etc.), American federationism and English trade unionism have not adopted the violent attitude of French syndicalism with regard to militarism and capitalism.'[35] German trade unions, he noted, contained substantial conservative and Catholic elements. It was precisely the existence of more conservative elements within the trade union movement which dictated the course of action pacifists must follow. It was necessary 'to go to these moderates and speak a language which is appropriate to their needs and preoccupations'; this would 'stop them on the slope which is leading them to extreme positions'.[36]

For Prudhommeaux, what was important was to search out a common ground. The end was the same for both groups—the bourgeois and working-class pacifists alike—what differed was the method or means to achieve that end. For the pacifists of the APD and the international congresses it was international arbitration and conciliation, in short the growth of a positive international order. For the working class, it was the overthrow of capitalism. The answer lay in what Prudhommeaux called 'a voyage of reciprocal exploration'.[37] Thus, from almost its earliest days, the APD and its leading thinkers were aware of the existence and ideas of the other main protagonist of peace in the pre-war and later in the interwar period.

---

[35] J. Prudhommeaux, 'Les Rapports du pacifisme et du mouvement ouvrier', *PD* 15/11 (Nov. 1905), 430.   [36] Ibid.   [37] Ibid. 433.

THE APD AND THE GREAT WAR

With twenty-seven years of pacifist activity behind it in 1914, the APD was already an association of middle-aged men by the time of the Great War. What was its position during the cataclysm? And perhaps more importantly, did the experience of the Great War produce a dramatic change in the Association's pacifist thinking?

The answer to the above questions is that in fact very little changed in the APD's approach to peace as a result of the Great War. Despite the attacks of the censor's scissors, the review continued to appear regularly, albeit in somewhat truncated format. Meetings continued to be held, and the men and women of the APD simply waited out the war while continuing to publish their prescriptions for a better world. This is not to say that the old-style pacifists did not feel the tragedy of the situation. They most certainly did and were greatly moved by it. But, like so many other thinking men and women in those bloody years, they believed that the war was being fought for a higher ideal and that the world which would emerge from the mud of northern France would be a better one. As Charles Richet and Théodore Ruyssen put it in an appeal for 'Peace through Justice' published in January 1918:

Our readers know what our propaganda has been. But it is useful in these troubled and passionate times to recall it one more time. It can be summed up in one word: from the very first day of the war we have tirelessly advocated the policy which has finally brought North America and two-thirds of South America to the side of the Allies. Let us dare to say without boasting, because it is the simple truth, that we were Wilsonians, not before Mr Wilson, but before the President of the United States had proclaimed to the universe the doctrine which was to lead to the intervention of the New World in the European war. We have thought, written and repeated untiringly since the tragic days—doubly tragic for pacifists—of July 1914, that the aggression of force against justice must be opposed by force without flinching, even at the price of the worst sacrifices—but that this force must spring from a desire for peace, a just peace, organized, durable, as tenacious, as irreducible as the desire for war itself.

In judging moreover this war of defence and liberation necessary, we have abandoned none of our convictions of old. We continue to think, for reasons which we have developed a hundred times, that between civilized men war is a monstrous anachronism and an avoidable evil. Just because it is imposed, we do not believe it holy, nor beautiful, nor salutary; we fulfil with firmness, but with sadness, a cruel duty, and we preserve intact our desire to struggle against the international anarchy from which this war was born.[38]

This long citation defines clearly the APD's position during the Great War. With the benefit of hindsight there was certainly nothing subversive about it, although to the bellicists of the day (a species with which we are no longer familiar) there was no doubt much about it that caused concern. The APD was thus thoroughly patriotic during the war. Its members did their duty. Ruyssen, though too old for active service, worked for a time as a sort of volunteer nurse, looking after the wounded in a hospital in Nantes. Félicien Challaye (1875–1967),[39] who was a committee member in the twenties, and of whom much more will be heard, served as a simple sergeant in the territorial army, and so on.[40]

If the trauma of the Great War did little to change the APD's basic *Weltanschauung*, it did, however, force it to define its position with regard to other pacifists who drew different lessons from the wartime experience, and also with regard to the erroneous, but tenacious and damaging, conclusions reached by public opinion about the nature of pacifism. Taking the latter point first, several writers in the *PD* were at pains to distinguish between pacifism and defeatism, and to emphasize that the APD's programme of positive prescriptions for peace in no way affected its view of what it considered to be a just war. In a short article published before the war had ended, Gustave Belot protested at the insinuation by the judge in the Hélène Brion trial that there was something subversive about pacifism:

Whether it pleases him or not, Pacifism in the proper sense of the word is exactly the same thing in time of war as in time of peace. What do we have to do in order to make people understand that the true idea of Pacifism is that of a *regime of international law*—an idea which the state of war cannot annul?

[38] Charles Richet and Théodore Ruyssen, 'Pour "La Paix par le droit"', *PD* 28/1–2 (Jan. 1918), 2.

[39] Challaye is one of the key figures who made the transition from the old-style pacifism to integral pacifism in the thirties. His political evolution finally brought him close to collaboration during the Second World War, but he was acquitted of the charge after 1945. Challaye was educated first at the University of Lyon, and then at the École normale supérieure where he took his *agrégation de philosophie* in 1894. He also studied at the University of Berlin 1898–9 and won a travel grant which enabled him to travel around the world in 1899–1901. This journey exposed him to the Far East and he became an important opponent of colonialism and imperialism in France. See James Friguglietti, 'Félicien Challaye', in Josephson, *Dictionary*, 152–3.

[40] Félicien Challaye, 'Pour la paix sans aucune réserve', *PD* 42/4 (Apr. 1932), 149; J.-L. Puech, 'A propos des articles Challaye–Ruyssen', *PD* 42/4 (Apr. 1932), 153–4.

Pacifism is decidedly not Bolshevism. It has never consisted in compromising or obstructing the defence of the nation . . . This perpetual caricature that is made of pacifism is an intolerable calumny . . .[41]

The war experience and public opinion seem to have taken their toll on some readers of the *PD* however. F. Lepine, an *inspecteur de l'enseignement primaire* in Reims, wrote a long open letter to Ruyssen published in the review in which he raised the question of pacifism and defeatism. Lepine distinguished between the pacifism of a Passy which had 'nothing in common with anarchism or antimilitarism', and a certain 'equivocal pacifism' which 'cohabits happily with the class war, with doctrines of hatred and civil war' and ends up 'lowering itself to antinational and antisocial heresies'. As a prime example of this he cited Barbusse who in his view preached violence and did not distinguish between anarchism, antimilitarism, and pacifism. This attitude could only lead to a situation like that in Russia under the Soviets. Ruyssen's response was clearly in favour of pacifism as opposed to defeatism. He defended Barbusse by arguing that his characters in *Le Feu* 'curse war, *but they fight it*', and he said that he was still looking for the European pacifists of whom Lepine wrote 'who fail to recognize the necessity of resisting savage violence by force'. Such pacifists were not to be found in the ranks of the APD in any case.[42]

In October 1918 when the German demand for an armistice became known, Ruyssen wrote a public letter to Clemenceau asking that the war be ended as soon as possible within the bounds of what was just. But he underlined the dangers for France contained in what he called the 'phobia of peace' which certain public personages seemed to be experiencing—a phobia which saw anyone envisaging peace as either pusillanimous or a traitor. It is perhaps indicative of the extent to which the APD was itself sensitive to these charges that he underlined to Clemenceau that 'we are pacifists, we are not defeatists', reminding the Tiger that in 1916 he had written to Ruyssen that he 'liked' the APD's 'pacifism'.[43]

[41] Gustave Belot, 'Encore le mot "pacifisme"', *PD* 28/7–8 (Apr. 1918), 109.

[42] F. Lepine, 'Pacifisme ou défaitisme?' (letter of 1 Jan. 1918 with response by Ruyssen), *PD* 28/3–4–5–6 (Feb.–Mar. 1918), 49–55. For favourable comment on Barbusse, see *PD* 28/1–2 (Jan. 1918), 41–3.

[43] 'A M. Georges Clemenceau (lettre adressée à M. Clemenceau au lendemain de la demande d'armistice formulée par les Empires centraux par le Comité directeur de "l'Association de la paix par le droit", Bordeaux, 8 octobre 1918)', *PD* 28/21–2 (Nov. 1918), 332–3.

Richet and Ruyssen saluted the end of a war which they believed ought never to have occurred, but for which they believed there were some direct and crushing responsibilities as well as other more imponderable, indirect ones. They celebrated the return of Alsace-Lorraine, but even more perhaps the remaking of the map of Europe on revolutionary principles which the end of the war seemed to promise. Let there be no doubt: Richet and Ruyssen did not have a social experiment on Marxist lines in mind. They were referring to the revolutionary principles of the early French Revolution, the spirit of '92, when they wrote, 'Yes, this war is revolutionary. It achieves the work of our ancestors of '92, compromised by Napoleon. In all of central Europe crowns are falling in cascades: stunned, the sovereigns are fleeing the popular wrath . . .'[44] *La guerre du droit* thus assumed at its climax almost mythical proportions for the republicans of the APD. It represented the culmination of a revolutionary struggle begun and then derailed almost 130 years previously.

The euphoria brought on by the end of the war died away rather quickly however as it became apparent that the peace which was emerging from the ashes was not a perfect one. The APD's pronouncements on the state of international affairs, the Versailles Treaty, and the tasks facing post-war pacifism are a mixture of optimism and despair. On the one hand the men of the APD saw tremendous hope for progress in the post-Versailles world, but equally they could not help but be disturbed by the incompleteness of the post-war system. In an *Appel-programme* published at the beginning of 1920, for example, the APD spoke of the horrors of the war which was finally over, but registered disappointment that what had been fought as the war to end all wars already seemed to have given birth to a bastard peace. The League of Nations was a 'pale and imperfect' creation which did not 'even dare to pronounce, in the name of organized humanity, a definitive and absolute interdiction of war'. The Paris Peace Conference was a failure because it had succeeded neither in constituting an international police force nor in enforcing an obligatory solution of all disputes by means of law. In the words of the APD's tract, 'Tomorrow, almost as much as yesterday, war remains possible in an anarchistic world'.[45]

[44] Charles Richet and Théodore Ruyssen, 'La Fin de la guerre', *PD* 28/21–2 (Nov. 1918), 330.
[45] 'Pour la paix par le droit: Appel programme', *PD* 30/1–2 (Jan.–Feb. 1920), 2.

But however imperfect the post-war world might be, it had to be lived in and the APD saw the League of Nations as the indirect creation of pacifist hands. Never before had they felt so much that they were moving in the same direction as the march of History; their 'lifeboat was lifted up by the rising tide'.[46] Whereas before the war the APD's task had been the promotion of international arbitration and warning against the coming catastrophe, during the war it had been the fulfilment of its patriotic duty, and after the war its horizons had to be broadened to go beyond its old formulas to demanding the creation of a League of Nations endowed with real powers of international organization including that of an international police force. As Ruyssen reiterated later in the year following the APD's first post-war annual general meeting, public opinion was in complete disarray because it seemed that the promises made during the war were not to be fulfilled, and that two years after the armistice the most the French government could offer was a reduction of the length of military service from two years to eighteen months. Added to this was the defection of the Americans from the Geneva experiment and the sniping attacks of some Socialists who persisted in seeing the League as nothing but the tool of imperialist oppressors. The pre-war challenge thus remained the same for the APD, although amplified and extended by the creation of the League, which was 'too young, too infirm, too contested not to have need of being defended'.[47]

Thus, despite the admitted problems inherent in the new order born of Versailles, the APD saw its mission clearly as the support and extension of an international system based upon a desire for peace achieved through respect for law. Within the APD however there continued to be some dissension as to the nature the Association's post-war pacifism ought to have. Some members thought the Association was going too far in its reconciliation with the former enemy; others thought quite the contrary and saw in the APD's reticences an unwillingness to move forward in the fight for peace and reconciliation. In 1920, for example, the review had carried an article about relief to famine-struck areas of Europe, especially with regard to saving the lives of young children. Some readers took great exception to the fact that the appeal was directed at saving the lives of *German*

---

[46] *PD* 30/1–2 (Jan.–Feb. 1920), 3.
[47] T. Ruyssen, 'Au travail', *PD* 30/11–12 (Nov.–Dec. 1920), 354–5.

children too! Ruyssen replied by saying that he pleaded guilty: 'We admit our pity for the starving child, even if his father is guilty, because it is a double misery to be hungry and also the son of an assassin or thief.'[48] A year later, however, R. Périé, an *inspecteur d'Académie honoraire*, took fundamental issue with the review over its attitude with regard to Germany. Périé argued for more mutual tolerance and forgiveness. The problem with the Versailles Treaty was that it was the judgement of men who were prosecutors and judges in their own court. The argument over whether or not reparations constituted a war indemnity was pedantic. Périé accepted the principle of restitution, but argued that in order for it to be valid, and deemed to be valid by the offending party, it had to be the result of a judgement handed down by a competent tribunal —'that of a universal, ecumenical League of Nations'. The fundamental issue though was one of attitude towards Germany and the reconciliation necessary for the rebuilding of Europe; echoing an Englishman who was in no way a Germanophile, Périé wrote that the Germans 'were not born with a double dose of original sin'.[49]

The mild dissent of a Périé was certainly not matched by many readers of the *PD*. Jules Puech, the review's secretary, complained in a 1924 article that 'many readers think that the only truth worth repeating is the governmental truth which is disseminated by certain more or less official newspapers'.[50] This was fine during the war, although even then the *PD* was not prepared to become a *bourreur de crânes*. But Puech argued that the time for such mindless and uncritical conformity had long since passed. The APD and its members had to regain their critical faculties and to praise and condemn public policy where necessary. The apparent lack of the dissenting spirit amongst the rank and file of the APD, if Puech's comments are to be given any credence, reflects the views of wider French society on pacifism. One contributor writing in the review in 1922 said that pacifism frightened people. During the war it somehow became synonymous with 'defeatism', and since the victory, although everyone was in favour of peace, no one wanted to be called a pacifist. But a pacifist was merely someone who was a 'partisan of peace', and thus all men who earnestly desired peace must be pacifist.

[48] T. Ruyssen, 'Réponse à quelques objections', *PD* 30/5 (May 1920), 134.
[49] R. Périé, 'Scrupules pacifistes' (letter to Ruyssen), *PD* 31/7 (July 1921), 237–40.
[50] Jules-L. Puech, 'Notre "sainte cause"', *PD* 34/4–5 (Apr.–May 1924), 165.

On this basis, France and Germany could both be divided politically into parties of war and parties of peace.[51] Seven years later the problem remained much the same as Ruyssen exasperatedly attacked the misconceptions of the popular press about the nature of pacifism. His ire had been raised by Louis Lafon—'this pastor, doctor without charity of a religion of love'—who had defined pacifism as a utopian belief held basically by fools.[52] And yet again Ruyssen defined to his uncomprehending detractors the *pacifisme ancien style* of the APD:

Is it necessary to emphasize yet again that pacifism is anything but a march to the stars?—that on the contrary it is an attempt to organize peace through the real, secular experience of civilian life, and not according to some chimerical plan? . . . What is fanciful in that? . . . In 1914, it was not pacifist idealism which was listened to, but the desperate pessimism of the believers in force, for the greatest benefit of the canon founders of all countries.[53]

Ruyssen's pacifism, this pacifism of the APD, showed little sign of self-doubt about the rectitude of its position in the twenties. It was a pacifism based on justice, and Ruyssen and his fellow pacifists believed they knew what that entailed. It meant condemning those who deserted justice and Right for opportunistic reasons.[54] It meant condemning the veterans' organizations for their equivocal stand on national defence which made the whole question one of individual conscience.[55] It meant a rapid end to the honeymoon with Barbusse once the latter's conception of peace became evident. Louis Bosse described Barbusse's prescriptions for peace as a 'project for a mechanical paradise'.[56] The problem with Barbusse's thinking was that it reduced peace to an 'all or nothing' concept. Bosse argued instead for the necessity and value of partial steps; Barbusse's method was the panacea of a lazy mind. What made such an argument even stranger in Bosse's view was that the teleology was the same; Ruyssen and Barbusse differed only on means. Barbusse

---

[51] René Lauret, 'Pourquoi le pacifisme est décrié', *PD* 32/2 (Feb. 1922), 72–3.

[52] T. Ruyssen, 'Polémiques', *PD* 39/10 (Oct. 1929), 357. Lafon was director of *La Vie nouvelle* and also contributed to *Le Temps*.   [53] Ibid. 358.

[54] 'Une idée . . . turque: Lénine, lauréat du Prix Nobel', *PD* 28/1–2 (Jan. 1918), 43. Criticism of Lenin's nomination by the University of Constantinople for the Peace Prize on the grounds cited.

[55] T. Ruyssen, 'L'Internationale des anciens combattants', *PD* 30/6–7 (June–July 1920), 204. Ruyssen's comments are actually just an introduction to a report on the Geneva Conference by F. Gouttenoire de Toury which follows.

[56] Louis Bosse, 'Quelques réflexions sur un projet du paradis mécanique', *PD* 31/1 (Jan. 1921), 3–6.

was proposing a 'messianic mysticism' in which 'in the final analysis [he] wants to create peace out of peace. There will be no more war when we have done away with all causes for war . . .'[57] With regard to the question of the class struggle and civil war, Ruyssen wrote that all members of the APD's committee detested the latter but that at the social level there was no defined doctrine held by members of the APD.[58]

Notwithstanding these divergences with some of the representatives of the as yet unselfconscious and undefined *pacifisme nouveau style*, Ruyssen in 1925 was still affirming that the old-style pacifism was capable of working with the disparate elements within the pacifism of the twenties because the end for all was still the same.[59] As will become clear, it was only in the early thirties that the incompatibilities of new- and old-style pacifism became so marked as finally to force a rupture. But that is to jump ahead somewhat. Pacifism was beginning to change but the men and women of the APD could not at this point begin to guess to what degree. Edmond Vermeil[60] saw the beginnings of this divergence at the 1924 International Peace Congress in Berlin where the pacifist camp seemed to be divided between 'moderates' and 'intransigents'. The differences became particularly obvious in the debates on disarmament, which led Vermeil to conclude that in the pacifism of the mid-twenties there was a tendency towards 'absolutism' and 'ideology', towards 'peremptory and definitive declarations which arrange everything in the abstract, but solve nothing within the order of present reality'. In Vermeil's words, peace needed 'not only to be decreed, but to be "organized"'.[61]

---

[57] Ibid. 5.   [58] Ruyssen, 'Réponse à quelques objections', 135.

[59] T. Ruyssen, 'Le XXIV Congrès international de la paix', *PD* 35/10 (Oct. 1925), 362–3. On the growing sense of divergence felt by representatives of the 'other side' in the pacifist movement see the letter of 30 July 1925 by Henry van Etten of the Society of Friends on behalf of himself and Marianne Rauze (a left-wing pacifist) to G. Duchene asking for her co-operation in an attempt to prevent the bourgeois pacifists from taking over the XXIVth Peace Congress in Paris as they apparently had done the year before in Berlin (BDIC/DD/FΔRés 273/19/129).

[60] Vermeil was born in Switzerland in 1878. He was educated at the Universities of Montpellier, Fribourg, and Munich, and also at the Sorbonne. He was a *Docteur ès lettres* and an *agrégé d'allemand*. He taught at a number of universities, most notably at the University of Strasburg 1919–34, and at the Sorbonne 1934–51. He was also a visiting professor at Harvard University in 1931. See the entry on Vermeil in the third edition of *Who's Who in France* (Paris: Éditions Jacques Lafitte, 1957).

[61] Edmond Vermeil, 'Le XXIIIème Congrès international de la paix de Berlin', *PD* 34/12 (Dec. 1924), 453–4.

Kurt Hiller (1885–1972), one of the German 'intransigents', said in a private conversation with Vermeil at the Congress that the two strands of pacifism must continue to coexist within the bosom of the same movement, but this was to become an increasingly unattainable, and indeed undesirable, ideal by the end of the decade.[62]

Pierre Cot summed up the differences between what he called the 'French' conception of peace and the 'Anglo-Saxon' idea of peace in an important article published in the spring of 1929. The Kellogg–Briand Pact attempted to dispense with war simply by condemning it; what shocked the French mind in his view was that this simple condemnation of war did nothing actively to organize peace:

For France the heart of the problem is less to pronounce a solemn and platonic anathema against war than to work towards the organization of peace. The land of Descartes and of Voltaire prefers techniques to canticles . . . The Anglo-Saxon, it has been said, tours the world with his Bible and the Frenchman with his Code. Let us not be embarrassed by this natural and national penchant. We have a conception of peace which is more juridical than mystical. But justice, too, supposes an ideal.[63]

The end of the war had seen these two conceptions of peace confront one another in the creation of the League of Nations. The French had held to a belief in a system of positive international law in which recourse to international violence would be *forbidden* and nations *obliged* through a system of sanctions, including that of an armed international force, to conform to the new international order. Cot believed that for the Anglo-Saxon nations, on the other hand, the question of sanctions assumed an entirely secondary importance behind a merely moral condemnation of unjust wars by international public opinion, which would express itself through two agencies: a moratorium on wars and a public debate on the causes of the conflict. In his view, the Anglo-Saxon conception carried the day.

---

[62] PD 34/12 (Dec. 1924), 454. See also Karl Holl, 'Kurt Hiller', in Helmut Donat and Karl Holl (eds.), *Die Friedensbewegung* (Hermes Handlexikon) (Dusseldorf: ECON Taschenbuch Verlag, 1983), 186–8; see also Karl Holl, 'Kurt Hiller', in Josephson, *Dictionary*, 408–10; see also Lewis D. Wurgart, *The Activists: Kurt Hiller and the Politics of Action on the German Left, 1917–1933* (Philadelphia: Transactions of the American Philosophical Society, 1977). The same observations on the Berlin Congress were also made by another observer from the APD—see L. Léontin, 'Après le Congrès de la paix de Berlin', PD 34/12 (Dec. 1924), 457–8.

[63] Pierre Cot, 'La Conception française de la lutte contre la guerre', PD 39/4–5 (Apr.–May 1929), 164.

There was thus according to Cot a fundamental dichotomy of views within the former Allied camp as to the method of achieving peace.[64]

This conception of pacifism was clearly inimical to that increasingly espoused in the Anglo-Saxon world and by the more avant-garde German pacifists. But it was also increasingly at variance with the movement of ideas within French pacifism itself. As will become clear later in Part I, the challenges of the new pacifism caused momentary cracks to appear in the APD's *pacifisme ancien style*, but by the end of the thirties the international crisis had caused the wagons to be pulled into a circle and the fundamental ideas of the old pacifism to be reaffirmed. What is apparent however is that though the decade of the twenties represents a period of relative hegemony for the APD and its ideas within French pacifism, there were already signs that the pot was beginning to boil. Not for much longer would the struggle for the same goal suffice; the question of means and the definition of what sort of peace was being fought for gradually assumed paramount importance.

[64] Ibid. 164–70. There was, of course, dissent over the nature of French pacifism even within the pages of the *PD*. See for example A. Vulliod, 'La Valeur du Pacte Kellogg–Briand', *PD* 39/6 (June 1929), 214–21, in which the author (a professor at the University of Nancy) argued for the moral versus the juridical approach to peace: 'A mon sens, cette constatation nous amène à reconnaître que l'œuvre de la paix constructive est essentiellement une œuvre pédagogique et morale. Il existe sans doute (suivant une façon de dire qui est en faveur) une technique de la paix; mais les organes de cette technique sont commandés par l'énergique volonté de paix qui se trouve actuellement vivante dans un grand nombre d'âmes, sur tous les points du globe . . .' (220).

2. A Decade of Optimism (1919–1929)

The decade from 1919 to 1929 was largely one of guarded optimism for the old-style pacifism. There was no ignoring the tremendous upheaval European society had to face, but the overall picture was one of an international order which was slowly, however imperfectly, rising above anarchy to a state inspired by reason and law. There continued to be wars, but the rule of law was increasingly to be seen in action at Geneva and elsewhere. This chapter will examine the nature of the APD's optimism, its reaction to the international developments of the twenties, and its position on the question of Franco-German *rapprochement* in the light of the debate over war guilt.

Underlying the events of the whole decade was the fundamental question of Franco-German reconciliation and all of the tangential issues which this topic conjured up. The APD was clearly in favour, in theory at least, of a fundamental reconciliation between the two former enemy nations, but it will be argued here that precious opportunities for such a reconciliation were lost because of the Association's fixation with what it in all good faith considered to be the question of justice and 'Right' in France's relations with Germany. Blinded by this conception of Right and convinced of the entire rectitude of France's cause, the APD was guilty of not providing all the support it could have done to the feeble liberal, democratic, and pacifist elements within the struggling Weimar experiment.

As has already been noted, the APD believed implicitly in the rightness of France's role in the Great War, a war which had been forced upon it. The question of war origins and responsibilities is one which the review continued to comment on during the twenties. For example, in a 1920 number Ruyssen debated the question of responsibilities with Louis Guétant of the Clarté group. While recognizing that the Central Powers did not bear exclusive responsibility for the conflict, Ruyssen nevertheless argued that they bore primary responsibility.[1] He continued to hold to this line the following year in a review of *Les Origines de la guerre* published by the Société d'études documentaires et critiques sur la guerre, in which while accepting that the brochure of Morhardt, Demartial, *et al.* was in places 'troubling', he argued none the less that the Russian mobilization was not war, and that one could not logically construe war guilt from a simple mobilization order.[2] Commenting in 1922 on a polemic which had broken out in the German press between representatives of different strands of German pacifism on the question of war guilt, Ruyssen came round to admitting that Article 231 of the Versailles Treaty bothered him, not because it was an inaccurate representation of what he believed to be the case, but simply because Germany had been forced to 'recognize' its war guilt. 'The moral error, which is serious, is of having forced Germany to declare that it recognized that which in fact, aside from a clear-sighted minority, it had in no way recognized. In short, a lie was extracted from it.'[3] When Victor Margueritte (1866–1942)[4] published his *Appel aux consciences* in 1925, Ruyssen exasperatedly attacked it for its vanity and naïveté. He did not believe that the treaties could or would be revised. He did not deny that Article 231 was wrong, but argued that in that case Germany ought never to have signed the treaty. What appeared to shock him greatly was that the *Appel* was signed not

[1] Louis Guétant and Théodore Ruyssen, 'Les Responsabilités de la guerre I et II', *PD* 30/10 (Oct. 1920), 328–33.

[2] Théodore Ruyssen, review of *Les Origines de la guerre* published by the Société d'études documentaires et critiques sur la guerre, in *PD* 31/7 (July 1921), 267.

[3] Théodore Ruyssen, 'De quelques polémiques allemandes sur les responsabilités de la guerre', *PD* 32/3–4 (Mar.–Apr. 1922), 113.

[4] Margueritte achieved infamy in interwar France with the publication of his novel *La Garçonne* (1922) which shocked readers with its open discussion of sexuality. He was the son of a famous French officer in the Franco-Prussian War. He served for a time himself as a cavalry officer, but resigned in order to devote himself to a career as a writer. His novel *La Patrie humaine* provided the title for the newspaper of the Ligue internationale des combattants de la paix when it was formed in 1930. Margueritte was closely involved in the new pacifist movement which arose in the early thirties. See James Friguglietti, 'Victor Margueritte', in Harold Josephson (ed.), *Biographical Dictionary of Modern Peace Leaders* (Westport, London: Greenwood Press, 1985), 604–6.

only by the usual names of the Société d'études—Georges Demartial (1861–1945),[5] Charles Gide (1847–1936),[6] Gouttenoire de Toury (1876–1965),[7] and Mathias Morhardt (1863–1939)[8]—but also by more mainstream pacifists such as Victor Basch (1863–1944),[9] Gaston Moch, and Marc Sangnier (1873–1950).[10] In his view the continued talk of treaty revision was an unnecessary troubling of the waters:

> In my opinion, it is too late, or too early, to stir up these memories. Too late if one wants to return to texts legally signed and for which no procedure for revision which is at once practical and peaceful is conceivable; too early if one claims to be able to deliver a definitive judgement on Articles 227 to 231 . . . It is surprising that the pacifists or ultra-pacifists who composed or signed the *Appel aux consciences* do not realize the danger that their

[5] See James Frigulietti, 'Georges Demartial' in Josephson, *Dictionary*, 203–5. Demartial was a senior civil servant with the Ministry of Colonies and a government commissioner with the Bank of Indochina. World War I shocked him out of his comfortable middle-class complacency and he began to enquire into the origins of the conflict. Together with other intellectuals he founded the Société d'études documentaires et critiques sur les origines de la guerre in 1916. He became an active supporter of the new-style pacifism discussed in Part II. His visceral anti-government position survived into the Second World War during which he published his final major work, *1939: La Guerre de l'imposture* (Paris: Éditions Jean Flory, 1941).

[6] See Linda L. Clark, 'Charles Gide', in Josephson, *Dictionary*, 321–2. Gide was a renowned economist who held a chair at the Collège de France. He challenged *laissez-faire* doctrines and was a supporter of feminism, pacifism, anti-alcoholism, and consumers' co-operatives.

[7] Fernand Gouttenoire de Toury was the son of an aristocratic family. He was educated at the Saint Cyr military academy. He left the army in 1901 in disgust at the treatment of Captain Alfred Dreyfus. He returned, however, in 1914 and lost a leg in an attack on German positions, for which he received the Legion of Honour. The war experience so embittered him, however, that he turned his attention to politics and was active for many years in the Ligue des droits de l'homme. He joined the Communist Party in 1920, but left it in 1922 in disagreement with its authoritarian tendencies. See James Frigulietti, 'Fernand Gouttenoire de Toury', in Josephson, *Dictionary*, 351–3.

[8] See Albert S. Hill, 'Mathias Morhardt', in Josephson, *Dictionary*, 660–1.

[9] Victor Basch was born in Hungary and died in 1944 at the hands of the Gestapo and Milice in Lyon. He was a professor at the Universities of Nancy, Rennes, and at the Sorbonne. He served first as vice-president, and then as president of the Ligue des droits de l'homme (1909–40). See Françoise Basch, 'Victor Basch', in Josephson, *Dictionary*, 55–6.

[10] See Albert S. Hill, 'Charles François Marc Marie Sangnier', in Josephson, *Dictionary*, 833–5. Sangnier was the founder of one of the precursors of the Christian Democratic movement in France, Le Sillon, which sought to reconcile the Church and the Republic. He was also active in the pre-war and post-war Catholic peace movement, and is famous as the founder of the French youth hostel movement. He was elected to the Chamber of Deputies in 1919, but could not gain re-election.

campaign is causing to the present peace; imperfect peace no doubt, unjust peace even on more than one point, but real peace, and just peace on many points of primary importance . . .[11]

As an address to German pacifists voted at the APD's annual general meeting in Poitiers in 1921 put it, the APD 'registered with great satisfaction the assurance it had received that numerous were the democrats in Germany and Austria who were resolved to execute the treaties in so far as was possible'.[12]

The equation of liberal, democratic, and pacifist Germany with the worst of Wilhelmine Germany was an unfortunate and short-sighted position taken by the APD and other French and international pacifist bodies immediately after the War. It is a difficult historical judgement to make, but it seems clear in retrospect that for the future good of Europe the French pacifists ought to have 'gone the extra mile' in their first post-war contacts with the Germans. In an article in January 1919, however, Ruyssen replied negatively to the sugges-tion of Benjamin de Jong van Beek en Donk, secretary of a group called the Organisation pour une paix durable, that a conference of pacifists, including the Germans, should be held as soon as possible. He was not willing to forgive and forget. He wrote that 'an attempt at an *entente* which postulated forgetting [the German aggression] or abstaining [from condemning it] would be vitiated in its very principle'.[13] There were certain facts which could not simply be forgotten: the invasion of Belgium, the official theory of the 'scrap of paper', submarine warfare, inhumane warfare, the destruction of civilian property, and so forth. 'My first act,' he wrote, 'in an assembly in which I might meet German or Austrian pacifists would be to ask them if they totally repudiate all of these acts.'[14] *Rap-prochement* and reconciliation should be left for a time to allow passions to cool; the time had not yet come for it. The German pacifists, liberals, and democrats had enough to contend with

[11] Théodore Ruyssen, 'Encore l'Article 231!', *PD* 35/5 (May 1925), 203.
[12] Edmond Duméril and Jules Prudhommeaux, 'L'Assemblée générale de la Paix par le droit' (Poitiers, 31 Oct.–1 Nov. 1921), *PD* 31/12 (Dec. 1921), 408.
[13] Théodore Ruyssen, 'Le Mouvement pacifiste: Pour et contre la reprise des relations pacifistes internationales', *PD* 29/1 (Jan. 1919), 48. On the Organisation pour une paix durable and de Jong van Beek en Donk, see Peter van den Dungen, 'Benjamin de Jong van Beek en Donk', in Josephson, *Dictionary*, 477–8.
[14] Ruyssen, 'Le Mouvement pacifiste', 48.

internally, he thought, and so did the French trying to ensure that the domestic chauvinists did not get out of hand.[15]

A manifesto of the Deutsche Friedensgesellschaft which came to the APD by means of an English translation, thus escaping the censor, was treated to the same rejection. The German manifesto asked that the new Germany not be treated like the old and insisted that something new was happening in the country. The APD, while claiming not to want to see unjust measures applied against the former enemy, noted that, first, the German pacifists had never, to their knowledge, protested against the declaration of war against France, or against the invasion of Belgium; secondly, that they had never protested against the 'excesses' of the German armies, or more specifically against submarine warfare; thirdly, that they had only protested against certain clauses of the Treaty of Brest-Litovsk; and finally, that they had never, either before or during the war, recognized that the Alsace-Lorraine question was a valid one.[16] The French attacks centred largely on Ludwig Quidde and Alfred Hermann Fried (1864–1921)[17] whose attitudes during and since the war were deemed by the French pacifists to have been equivocal if not duplicitous.[18]

In these early months of 1919 it seemed that for the French pacifists no good thing could come out of Germany. Edmond Duméril acerbically attacked Mathias Erzberger as a convert of *la dernière heure* when the latter proposed a '*German* project for the League of Nations' (the emphasis is Duméril's), and commented caustically that 'it took four years of atrocious war in order for the first project for a League of Nations to be formed in German political circles. How can one believe in the sincerity of a conversion the stages

---

[15] Ruyssen, 'Le Mouvement pacifiste', 49.

[16] 'Un manifeste de la Société allemande de la paix', *PD* 29/1 (Jan. 1919), 54–6.

[17] See Roger Chickering, 'Alfred Hermann Fried', in Josephson, *Dictionary*, 303–5.

[18] For attacks on Quidde see 'Les Responsabilités de la guerre et le professeur Quidde' in *PD* 29/1 (Jan. 1919), 56; for the Fried controversy, see Gaston Moch, 'Un réquistoire nécessaire: Alfred Hermann Fried', *PD* 29/4 (Apr. 1919), 155–68; see also 'Le Journal de guerre d'Alfred H. Fried' (comprising two letters, one from Fried to Ruyssen and a response by Gaston Moch) in *PD* 29/7–8 (July–Aug. 1919), 312–25; a final response by Fried may be seen in Alfred H. Fried, 'Un dernier mot', *PD* 29/9–10 (Sept.–Oct. 1919), 401–2. See also Puech's negative comments on the 8th German Peace Congress in J.-L. Puech, 'Le 8ème Congrès allemand de la paix', *PD* 29/7–8 (July–Aug. 1919), 362–4.

of which have been the same as those of the defeat?'[19] The Erzberger project also provided Duméril with another occasion to wax cynical over the motives behind Erzberger's July 1917 resolution in the Reichstag calling for a peace without annexations.[20]

Sooner or later, however, French and German pacifists had to meet one another. The executive committee of the Bureau international de la paix, which was largely controlled by Frenchmen or Belgians, emphasized to the German pacifists in late April 1919 that before any meaningful reconciliation could occur the German pacifists would have to recognize Germany's preponderant responsibility for the outbreak of the war, and also its present responsibility to ensure that full reparation was made for the ensuing damages.[21] When French and German pacifists finally did meet in Berne under the auspices of the BIP for the first time in four and a half years in late August 1919, the meeting occasioned some sharp and frank exchanges of views. A resolution proposed by Ruyssen concerning Germany's primary responsibility for the outbreak of war was however passed by the Council of the BIP.[22]

The German pacifist camp was divided on the question of war guilt and reparations. There were those like Dr Fritz Röttcher (1879–1946),[23] a principal contributor to the *Völkerfriede* (the organ of the DFG), who argued for acceptance of the Versailles Treaty. Others, such as Fried, who directed the *Friedenswarte*, attacked the treaty. Fried wrote that 'I regret that the victory of democracy has not resulted in a democratic peace ... the treaty is radically antipacifist ...'[24] In February 1921 the DFG, over the signatures of

---

[19] Edmond Duméril, 'L'Allemagne et la Société des nations: Le Projet de Mathias Erzberger', PD 29/2–3 (Feb.–Mar. 1919), 65.   [20] Ibid.

[21] Correspondence between the BIP and the Deutsche Friedensgesellschaft about the reopening of relations between international pacifism and German pacifism can be found in 'Le Bureau international de la paix', PD 29/7–8 (July–Aug. 1919), 357–9.

[22] See Ruyssen's account of this meeting in Théodore Ruyssen, 'Le Renouveau du pacifisme et le Bureau international de la paix', PD 29/9–10 (Sept.–Oct. 1919), 403–16. This meeting also discussed in broad terms the problems created for old-style pacifism by the continued disaffection of the working class, the suspicion of pacifism held since the war by the middle classes, and the difficulties posed by the new doctrines of non-resistance which were especially to be felt in England.

[23] See Karl Holl, 'Fritz Röttcher', in Josephson, *Dictionary*, 819–21.

[24] Cited in 'Chronique: La Révision du traité de Versailles: La Paix par le droit et la guerre: La Paix avec la Russie' (letters from A. H. Fried, A. A. Warden, and Louis Guétant, with comments by Ruyssen), PD 30/3–4 (Mar.–Apr. 1920), 90; see also Théodore Ruyssen, 'Les Pacifistes allemands et le Traité de Versailles', PD 30/1–2 (Jan.–Feb. 1920), 32–8.

Hellmut von Gerlach (1866–1935),[25] Dr Ludwig Quidde (1858–1941),[26] and Dr Helene Stöcker (1869–1943),[27] appealed to the BIP about the dangers for future peace posed by Versailles and especially by the reparations question. They claimed that Germany was unable to pay the reparations and that the treaties did not constitute a genuine and lasting peace: '. . . the decisions of the Paris conference do not guarantee peace, they compromise it. They will be the source of struggles without end.'[28] In the DFG's view, the treaty would have as its only result a rise in the activity of Bolshevism and extreme right-wing circles in Germany.[29] Even the warnings of a German pacifist such as Hermann Fernau (b. 1884),[30] respected by the APD, seem to have fallen on deaf ears. In a 1921 article published in the review, Fernau argued essentially the same case as the other German pacifists, making the point that without a peace of reconciliation founded on much mutual indulgence, the only winners would be the political reactionaries and the German Communists. He accused France of resorting to the same methods and ideas as Imperial Germany in its attempts to have the treaties respected at all costs: 'Speaking too often as a conqueror to the conquered, . . . French policy not only is in contradiction with the noble promises of the French Revolution, but what is worse, is playing the game of those in Germany who are the sworn enemies of France.'[31] Fernau saw Germany being pushed into the arms of Bolshevism because it was being cut off from its occidental heritage. French policy was having as its only effect the discrediting of the Versailles Treaty along with nascent German democracy. He called for the creation of a dike to stop the rising tide of folly which threatened to overthrow democratic civilization in Germany and he proclaimed that 'Franco-German *rapprochement* is this dike'.[32]

The view taken of the German revolution was also less than warm.

[25]   See Karl Holl, 'Hellmut von Gerlach', in Josephson, *Dictionary*, 319–21.

[26]   See Karl Holl, 'Ludwig Quidde', in Josephson, *Dictionary*, 774–7.

[27]   See Amy Hackett, 'Helene Stöcker', in Josephson, *Dictionary*, 904–6.

[28]   'Message adressé au Bureau international de la paix par la Société allemande de la paix au sujet des décisions de la Conférence de Paris' (with response by Ruyssen), in *PD* 31/3–4 (Mar.–Apr. 1921), 119.   [29]   Ibid.

[30]   See Lothar Wieland, 'Hermann Fernau', in Josephson, *Dictionary*, 277–8. Fernau was the pseudonym of Hermann Latt. It is not known when Fernau died. Although he was active in the Deutsche Friedensgesellschaft in the 1920s, he seems to have disappeared from the scene thereafter.

[31]   Hermann Fernau, 'De la nécessité d'un rapprochement franco-allemand', *PD* 31/2 (Feb. 1921), 55.   [32]   Ibid. 57.

Marie-Louise Puech writing in 1924 said that 'There has not been a German Revolution; it has still to be accomplished. Worse still, a large part of the [German] nation does not even hate its republic, it is ashamed of it.'[33] This, she said, was in contrast to the French Revolution which 'glorified the victory of the French people over a regime and a caste'.[34]

Thus, to recapitulate the argument so far, the first few years of the interwar period were ones of intransigence for the men and women of the APD *vis-à-vis* Germany. This intransigence expressed itself not only with regard to the political nation, but also unfortunately in equal measure with regard to those very elements in Germany which were trying to create something new out of the defeat. The APD, at least until 1922, failed to take note of these attempts and of the danger to be incurred in not supporting them wholeheartedly. The APD's short-sightedness can perhaps be forgiven; the hatred engendered by a disaster of the magnitude of the Great War must surely take years to die down. Jules Puech, writing in 1920, said that three options were open to French pacifists: one was to have nothing whatsoever to do with the former enemy; the second was to rush at the Germans with arms open in reconciliation; and the third was to have as little as possible to do with them, while letting time take its healing course. It was the latter he recommended. 'That is all; I shall not suddenly, on command, love *en bloc* a people whom I regret not having better killed when I was a soldier . . .'[35]

1922 seemed to be a watershed year in terms of the APD's, or at least Ruyssen's, views on *rapprochement* with Germany. It also marked the return of a healthy scepticism about French government policy towards the former enemy. Ruyssen participated in 1922 in the first post-war visit to Germany by an official delegation of the Ligue des droits de l'homme. The group visited Berlin, Essen, Dortmund, and Bochum, speaking before bourgeois and working-class audiences. Generally they were very well received and Ruyssen came back with some favourable impressions. Frenchmen living in Germany believed that Germany had disarmed almost to the zero point, and Ruyssen seemed convinced that German youth was searching for new paths and was in no way reactionary. For all that, the economic difficulties spelled trouble for the Weimar Republic,

---

[33] M.-L. Puech, 'De l'Allemagne', *PD* 34/9 (Sept. 1924), 333.   [34] Ibid.
[35] Jules-L. Puech, 'Chronique: La Paix avec l'Allemagne', *PD* 30/1–2 (Jan.–Feb. 1920), 27.

and he reckoned that 90 per cent of Germans did not accept the war-guilt clause, and even amongst those that did there was great doubt about Germany's ability to pay its reparations. All of this led to a net impression of pessimism for Ruyssen. Perhaps as a result of this pessimism, the voyage to Germany seemed to produce a sort of 'road to Damascus' experience in him. He continued to affirm Germany's guilt, but blamed France for not being more indulgent and far-sighted in its treatment of its neighbour, a position in sharp contrast to the polemics in which he had previously engaged with German pacifists over the question of reparations, for example:

... our country, hated but secretly admired, could conduct a magnificent campaign of clarity and conciliation (in Germany), if we finally practised with regard to our vanquished neighbour a policy different from the detestable methods which we have abused for four years ... while England tries clearly to deal gently with Germany, we continue to talk of 'sanctions' which could very well mean a new occupation should Germany fail to fulfil its latest promises. That these measures are justified by Germany's failure to keep a good number of promises, one can easily agree. But what is certain is that they have ulcerated the German people to the core without it having any idea of the sacrifices we have consented to on our side ... What does it profit us to be right in the essence of our demands, if we succeed neither in forcing Germany to pay, nor in reconciling her to us?[36]

By 1923 and the Ruhr crisis, the APD was thus far less dogmatic in its support of French policy and condemnation of Germany. The Ruhr occupation and the larger question of reparations payments which it represented became the focus of criticism on the part of the APD. At the Association's annual general meeting in Nantes in February 1923, the Ruhr question was debated. Ruyssen both condemned the occupation and upheld the principle of reparations at one and the same time, arguing that 'we must bring German opinion round to the belief that the present situation is all the same motivated by its attitude'; he recognized that the task was a difficult one and doubted that the French would succeed with the means currently being used.[37]

---

[36] Théodore Ruyssen, 'La Ligue française des droits de l'homme en Allemagne', *PD* 32/7–8 (July–Aug. 1922), 286 and 291; Théodore Ruyssen, 'Pour le rapprochement franco-allemand: La Ligue des droits de l'homme et le Bund neues Vaterland', *PD* 32/2 (Feb. 1922), 90–1, describes the visit of a delegation from the Bund neues Vaterland comprised of von Gerlach, Nicolai, and Lehmann-Russbüldt to Paris.

[37] Ruyssen cited in Jules-L. Puech, 'Assemblée générale de la Paix par le droit, Nantes, 10 et 11 février 1923', *PD* 33/4 (Apr. 1923), 142; the executive committee of

The Assembly adopted a resolution which, while noting that the French interpretation of the treaty was correct, conceded that the French view was not shared by many former allies, nor by the Germans. Consequently, it asked that this interpretation be submitted to the International Court of Justice for arbitration. On the heart of the matter—reparations—the Assembly agreed that the methods used up until 1923 had been largely sterile in their success in getting the Germans to pay up, and that the Ruhr occupation was costing more than it was bringing in. The Assembly demanded that the Allies give up these ineffective methods which were only leading to the danger of renewed war, and that the problem be submitted to the League of Nations for resolution along the lines of its work in Austria and Upper Silesia.[38]

Jules Prudhommeaux, writing in March 1923, was even more pessimistic about the effects of the Ruhr occupation. He attacked the popular press for brazenly misrepresenting the state of French public opinion; there was no unity behind the government's action in the Ruhr. 'The labouring masses in their rough common sense', he wrote, 'have understood since the first day of the military intervention . . . that it would not fail to be economically useless, politically dangerous, and morally discredited.'[39] Far from being a popular move, Prudhommeaux saw nothing but negative results flowing out of the Ruhr decision: reinstitution of censorship on news coming out of the Ruhr basin, France divided against itself to the point where civil war was spoken of, and international opinion turned completely against it. He called for pacifists of all nations to join together in a united front and to avoid sterile polemics with one another over the French action.[40]

The two events of the 1920s which mark the apogee of the APD's burgeoning optimistic faith in the new order created at Versailles were undoubtedly the Locarno Pact of 1925 and the Kellogg–Briand

the APD had already condemned methods of coercion and military occupation in anticipation of the Ruhr occupation at its meeting on 18 December 1922, as inefficacious, upsetting to French allies, and damaging to the work of German democrats. The committee continued to affirm nevertheless the rectitude of France's claims to reparations, and asked the French government to seek redress through the League of Nations, and a restructuring of the world economic situation. See: 'La Politique internationale: Deux ordres du jour sur les réparations: La Paix par le droit et la Ligue de la République', *PD* 33/1 (Jan. 1923), 29–31.

[38] Puech, 'Assemblée générale', 143–4.
[39] J. Prudhommeaux, 'Le Problème des réparations et le pacifisme international', *PD* 33/3 (Mar. 1923), 119.
[40] Ibid. 122.

Pact of 1928. Prudhommeaux, writing in October 1925, declared that the Locarno accords opened the way towards the realization of the dream of a United States of Europe held by Mazzini and Victor Hugo. Locarno also restored France to its proper, generous place in the European constellation: 'France becomes herself again, and Germany, which will be forever honoured in the annals of history for having taken the initiative in its memorandum of 9 February 1925, enters at last into this society of nations where, as Vandervelde said, "there are no more enemies, where there are no more conquerors, nor conquered, but only peoples united under the sign of equality".'[41] The APD congratulated Briand on a pact which 'opened a new era in the relations between France and Germany'.[42] Indeed, Prudhommeaux went so far in his article as to suggest that in return for the generous gesture of the Germans in agreeing to guarantee the Franco-German frontier, the French might consider doing something about the 'unfortunate' Article 231 of the Versailles Treaty.[43] Another commentator, writing the following month in the PD, stressed the 'capital fact' that the Locarno agreement had transformed 'into a state of law, juridically established and modifiable only by legal procedure, the pure state of fact (état de fait) which the European statute of 1919 constituted with regard to Germany'.[44] Locarno was a victory of 'common sense, of international order, of peace founded on the organized forces of justice; a victory, consequently, of Republican France'.[45]

The Kellogg–Briand Pact produced another élan of optimism in 1928, despite the reserves which Pierre Cot was to express about the conception of peace embodied in it, as we have seen above. Prudhommeaux noted with satisfaction that the Pact had as its consequence the creation of a solidarity between old world and new for the maintenance of universal peace and that it brought the United States in from the cold.[46] Georges Scelle wrote that the Pact had a juridical importance, and perhaps even more a political and psychological value. But its potential impact lay in the ability of public opinion to support it:

[41] Jules Prudhommeaux, 'Le Pacte rhénan et la Conférence de Locarno', PD 35/10 (Oct. 1925), 387.   [42] Telegram cited ibid.   [43] Ibid. 386.
[44] Edmond Laskine, 'La Victoire de Locarno', PD 35/11 (Nov. 1925), 431.
[45] Ibid. 433.
[46] J. Prudhommeaux, 'La Politique internationale et la SDN: La Mise hors la loi de la guerre: L'Accord est fait', PD 38/7–8 (July–Aug. 1928), 317.

The Kellogg Pact is a new step on the path of war against war. It is certainly not the last. It depends on public opinion and on the development of democratic institutions that the stages which remain to be achieved be crossed more or less rapidly. Or better said, it depends individually on the will of each one of us to hasten the advent of peace. It is entirely a question of civic and moral education.[47]

The APD was not immune to the highly individualistic conclusions drawn by many pacifists as a consequence of the Kellogg–Briand Pact. Francis Delaisi, for example, suggested that pacifists ought not to count upon a 'domesticated and deluded' parliament to ensure that war remained a crime. Instead he recommended that people pin all their hopes on the Kellogg Pact in order to oblige governments to take it seriously. And taking this argument to its logical conclusion, Delaisi proclaimed that if forced to choose between his mobilization papers and the Kellogg Pact which made war a crime, he would choose the Pact. Furthermore, he declared his faith in the higher power of the League of Nations which alone had the authority to condemn an aggressor. If France should be in violation of the Pact, then Delaisi announced that he would refuse to fight. Governments thought they were merely signing a scrap of paper, but Delaisi declared that 'we take them at their word, and we hide behind their signature. We, too, are for conscientious objection, but we transport it from the religious sphere to the juridical.'[48] The Kellogg–Briand Pact, by creating what appeared to be a supra-national juridical court of last resort in the case against war, sparked off the *pacifisme nouveau style* which will be dealt with in Part II.

A reaction more in keeping with the APD's usual rather conservative approach to peace was that of Georges Scelle in a report and resolution on how to bring the French constitution into line with the Kellogg Pact and the prescriptions of the League, which he presented to the 1928 annual general meeting. Scelle's motion, adopted unanimously by the Assembly, envisaged the amendment of Articles 8 and 9 of the 1875 constitution such that all future treaties would have to be ratified by the Chamber and the texts deposited with the League, and that any declaration of war would have to be in conformity with

---

[47] Georges Scelle, 'Le Pacte Kellogg (fin)', *PD* 38/10 (Oct. 1928), 441. For the first part of this article see *PD* 38/9 (Sept. 1928), 356–65.

[48] From Francis Delaisi's report, 'Les Garanties intérieures de la paix, conséquence du Pacte Kellogg', in J. Prudhommeaux, 'L'Assemblée générale de la Paix par le droit, Bordeaux, 2 et 3 novembre 1929', *PD* 39/12 (Dec. 1929), 458.

the prescriptions of the Kellogg Pact and the Covenant of the League of Nations.[49]

The Kellogg–Briand Pact marked in many ways the high-point of the interwar period for French pacifists. In 1928 it seemed as if the international order created at Versailles was finally beginning to function properly. Locarno had shown a new Germany prepared to live in peace with a new France. The legacy of Briand and Stresemann, together with the new-found interest of the United States in the affairs of Europe, augured well for the future. Another five years would pass before it became impossible to ignore the hair-line cracks growing and lengthening in the plaster of European peace. In the intervening time the elusive goal of a comprehensive disarmament agreement would dance tantalizingly, but forever out of reach, before French pacifist eyes. But that is to leap ahead somewhat.

Before concluding this examination of the first decade of the interwar period, however, it would be useful to look briefly at the practical measures for peace employed by the APD. In its official publications, the APD listed its means of action as (1) the organization of public or private lectures; (2) the creation of local or regional groups for propaganda and discussion; (3) the publication of brochures, tracts, and other works destined for propaganda; (4) the publication of the review *La Paix par le droit* and the more popular bulletin *Les Peuples unis* alone or in conjunction with other societies; (5) encouraging the composition of works, through competition or otherwise, in connection with its programme; (6) maintaining relations with other groups in France or abroad which were interested in the same goals.[50] This rather general list of the Association's activities makes clear the largely educative and platonic nature of much of the APD's work. This is not to deny its usefulness, merely to point out the obvious, namely that propaganda of this type is very difficult to assess in terms of its efficacy. One is dealing here yet again with the unquantifiable imponderables of recent history. There is no doubt that such activity was of some use in that it contributed towards the creation of a climate of ideas, which by their nature were often very slow in coming to fruition. But bear fruit they did. Many of the ideas

[49] See the report and resolution of Georges Scelle, 'Pourquoi doit-on et comment peut-on mettre la constitution française en accord avec le Pacte Briand–Kellogg et les prescriptions de la Société des nations?', in Jules Prudhommeaux, 'L'Assemblée générale de Nancy (suite)', *PD* 39/1 (Jan. 1929), 7–11.

[50] See 'Association de la paix par le droit' in *Nous voulons la paix* (Paris: SRIP, 1932), 28.

and principles of the APD took shape in the interwar years in Geneva; indeed the very idea of Geneva and the League could be said to epitomize the goals of the Association. In the dark hours of 1938, Ruyssen was to look back to an autumn day in 1922 when he and Prudhommeaux stood on the steps of the Salle de la réformation in Geneva which served as the provisional seat of the League of Nations Assembly. The Comte Clauzel, then secretary-general of the Ministère des Affaires étrangères, emerging from the hall, noticed Ruyssen and Prudhommeaux and cried, 'There are the forefathers of the League of Nations!'.[51]

The APD's primary method of propaganda after the publication of its two organs was probably the public lecture. These varied in topic and number from year to year but they were a constant of the Association's activity during the interwar period. In 1928 for example some fifty public lectures were given by members of the APD.[52]

Another important aspect of the Association's work was its attempt to reach French and European youth with the pacifist message. One of the ways this was done was the publication each year of a brochure entitled *La Jeunesse et la paix du monde* which was given away to targeted groups around the world. In 1933 the brochure had a French print run of 108,000 copies and a further print run of about 250,000 copies in Dutch, Polish, English, Welsh, Esperanto, Chinese, and Malaysian.[53]

With many of the members of the APD belonging to the teaching profession at all levels, it is not surprising to find a strong interest in the pedagogy of peace within the Association. Throughout the interwar period members of the APD participated in commissions and international conferences on the problems of peace education. There was also much interest in the task of monitoring both French and German school history texts in an attempt to have the bellicist examples removed from school curricula.[54]

During the 1928 election campaign members of the APD were

[51] Cited in Théodore Ruyssen, 'La Paix par le droit: Rapport: Documents de l'Assemblée générale et du Congrès du cinquantenaire', *PD* 48/6–7–8 (May–June–July 1938), 268.

[52] J. Prudhommeaux, 'L'Assemblée générale de Nancy', *PD* 39/1 (Jan. 1929), 4.

[53] Cited in Jules Prudhommeaux, 'Notre Assemblée générale, Paris, 30 et 31 décembre 1933', *PD* 44/2 (Feb. 1934), 54.

[54] For more detailed examinations of this aspect of the Association's propaganda

footnote continued overleaf

encouraged to present motions to election rallies for approval. The 1927 annual general meeting of the Association proposed three types of motion: one in favour of the League of Nations in which electoral candidates pledged to work towards an increase in the League's authority, the provision of means whereby the League could effectively fulfil its peace-making role, and the engagement to submit, without exception, all conflicts in which France might find herself to the arbitration of the League. A second motion asked candidates and electoral meetings to vote in favour of continued efforts for 'gradual disarmament'. Finally, a third resolution called for the establishment of 'economic peace' through the lowering of tariff barriers and the creation of a European customs union.[55] Electoral candidates were also to be sent a questionnaire asking them if they accepted the APD's programme of support for the League and whether they were a

which we unfortunately do not have the space to deal with here, please see: Roger Lévy, 'Société des nations et coopération intellectuelle depuis dix ans', *PD* 40/6 (June 1930), 218–25; Dr Siegfried Kawerau, 'Les Livres d'histoire en Allemagne, notamment depuis 1923', *PD* 37/3 (Mar. 1926), 104–11; Dr Siegfried Kawerau, 'Où en est l'Allemagne dans l'amélioration de ses livres d'histoire?', *PD* 41/10 (Oct. 1931), 449–52. Siegfried Kawerau (1886–1936) was a school reformer and pacifist who came repeatedly into conflict with the nationalist leagues and the Nazis in Weimar Germany. He died in 1936 after three years in a Nazi prison. For a biographical sketch of Kawerau, see Reinhold Lütgemeier-Davin, 'Georg Siegfried Kawerau', in Josephson, *Dictionary*, 495–6. See also J. Hadamard, 'Un nouveau pas à faire dans la voie de la paix: Les Manuels scolaires', *PD* 40/1 (Jan. 1930), 1–4; Jules Prudhommeaux, 'La Paix par l'éducation, l'histoire à l'école', *PD* 35/2 (Feb. 1925), 61–8 and 35/3 (Mar. 1925), 99–107; Jules Prudhommeaux, 'Pour la paix par l'école', *PD* 38/7–8 (July–Aug. 1928), 293–306; *PD* 38/9 (Sept. 1928), 366–75; and *PD* 38/10 (Oct. 1928), 419–31. On the work of the Comité d'entente des associations françaises pour la paix par l'éducation of which C. Bouglé was the president, see the reports on its five national conferences in which Ruyssen and Prudhommeaux participated: *PD* 41/3 (Mar. 1931), 129–61; *PD* 42/5 (May 1932), 201–36; *PD* 43/4–5 (Apr.–May 1933), 125–52; *PD* 44/4–5 (Apr.–May 1934), 145–76; *PD* 45/3 (Mar. 1935), 116–34 and *PD* 45/4 (Apr. 1935), 172–92. On the two international conferences on the teaching of history, see Georges Lapierre, 'La Conférence internationale pour l'enseignement de l'histoire', *PD* 42/7–8 (July–Aug. 1932), 346–9 and Charles Rousseau and J. Prudhommeaux, 'La IIème Conférence internationale pour l'enseignement de l'histoire', *PD* 44/10 (Oct. 1934), 399–400. Finally, for a very thorough set of observations on French and German school history texts which covers the period from the French Revolution onwards and is a rare example of collaboration with Nazi scholars, see 'Les Manuels d'histoire allemands et français: Résolutions adoptées par la commission d'historiens allemands et français, réunis du 25 novembre au 1er décembre 1935, pour examen des rectifications qu'il y aurait lieu d'apporter aux manuels scolaires des deux pays', *PD* 47/6 (June 1937), 209–17 and 47/7 (July 1937), 257–71.

[55] See Jules Prudhommeaux and J.-L. Puech, 'L'Assemblée générale et les fêtes du XLème anniversaire' (Nîmes, 30–1 Oct. and 1 Nov. 1927), *PD* 37/12 (Dec. 1927), 448–9 and 464–5.

convinced supporter of it. The questionnaire had already been used with some success in the election campaign of 1924.[56]

The final and perhaps most important aspect of the APD's external propaganda during the interwar period was its commitment to the idea of summer schools in different parts of France and indeed elsewhere in Europe. Taking 1932 as an example, the Association ran Colonies internationales de vacances at Saint-Claude, Boulogne-sur-Mer, and for the fifth time at Thonon in the Jura. Sixty-two young girls took part in the summer school at Thonon, down from about 130 in 1930. Additionally, the Association's president, Ruyssen, for many years led a course in Geneva sponsored by the Union internationale des associations pour la Société des nations. This course—which became known as the *cours Ruyssen*—involved 272 students in 1930, of whom 80, including 17 *boursiers*, came from France through the good offices of the APD. Numbers began to fall later in the thirties, but the figures given provide some indication of the size and range of these summer schools to which several members of the APD were active contributors.[57]

Thus, the APD's position towards the end of the 1920s can be qualified as one of growing optimism in a new international order which the Association believed was partially inspired by its own ideas. The distrust of Germany, and especially of German pacifists, began to wane by about the time of the Ruhr crisis and diminished further with the signing of the Locarno accords. The Kellogg–Briand Pact capped a decade of achievement for pacifists and internationalists and the future began to look brighter than it had for some time. During this first decade under discussion there was little to challenge the APD's vision of the world and the pacifist's place in it. Germany was clearly wrong, French bellicists were clearly not helping the situation, and after 1925 it was equally clear that international anarchy was gradually being set aside. The fragile edifice was not to stand for long, however. Cracks soon began to appear in the APD's own vision of what constituted pacifism, as well as in the nature of international relations upon which this view was based.

---

[56] Ibid. 448.
[57] See Jules Prudhommeaux, 'Notre Assemblée générale', 55; see also J. Prudhommeaux, 'L'Assemblée générale de Boulogne-sur-Mer', *PD* 41/1 (Jan. 1931), 25. The numbers of students attending the international summer school in Geneva had fallen by 1933 to 129 students, albeit from 18 different countries. Madame Prudhommeaux organized the Thonon school and in Geneva M. Angles, Mme Thibert, Jacques Dumas, André D. Tolédano, Ruyssen, and Prudhommeaux took part.

3. Cracks in the Foundations (1928–1933)

Modris Eksteins has commented on the approximate ten-year time lag between the end of the Great War and the explosion of war literature describing the event.[1] The same slow process of internalization and subsequent expression can be seen in the development of pacifist ideas in France in the interwar period. Preceding chapters have shown how, despite the impression of some representatives of the old-style pacifism that it had changed, the principles espoused by the APD remained relatively constant during the first decade of the interwar years. The APD and its ideas retained the vestiges of their pre-war hegemony in French pacifism at least until 1928 when the approach to the question of peace began noticeably to change as more radical, integral methods of tackling the problem arose. It is not the purpose of this chapter to examine in a systematic way the content of the *pacifisme nouveau style* which began to appear in significant form from about 1928 onwards—that will be left to Part II—but what will be discussed here is the extent to which these questions of methods, principles, and goals were discussed within the confines of old-style pacifism. Finally, in addition to examining the changing nature of pacifism within the APD, the changes in the international situation will be examined in so far as they impinged upon the world of growing optimism inhabited by the liberal, bourgeois pacifists.

[1] Modris Eksteins, '*All Quiet on the Western Front* and the Fate of a War', *Journal of Contemporary History*, 15/2 (1980), 345.

CONSCIENTIOUS OBJECTION, OR THE INDIVIDUALIZATION OF FRENCH PACIFISM

Probably the most important development in the five-year period under discussion here was the 'individualization' of pacifism. We have noted in preceding chapters of Part I that from almost its earliest days the APD was much concerned to avoid 'negative' approaches to peace such as conscientious objection, and instead to concentrate on the development of 'positive' measures for peace, primarily through juridical and educational means. The essential point was that the conquest of peace was a social goal, pursued collectively and not individually. The first crack therefore in the view of peace held by the APD and the old-style pacifists was the increasing attempt after 1928 to make peace a question requiring a response purely on the individual level. In most cases this meant conscientious objection.

Of all the pacifist doctrines developed in the interwar period, conscientious objection was probably the 'least French'. As a concept it originated in the Anglo-Saxon world and although it did have its adherents in France, it never became a widely recognized method of resistance to war. The French pacifist preference was always for the creation of large movements (which paradoxically were rarely achieved) with an emphasis on the collective conquest of peace. Nevertheless, it is true to say that conscientious objection did occupy the French mind (and certainly its government) for much of the interwar period. As Ruyssen noted in 1926, the French had been impressed to see that even with the Great War in full swing, the British authorities had not hesitated to admit cases of conscientious objection, and so from a position of intransigent refusal, French opinion was gradually evolving to the point where people were asking, 'Why not?'.[2] Ruyssen argued for acceptance of objection if it could reasonably be proved that the person in question was sincere in his beliefs and willing to accept a longer, harder, and perhaps personally more dangerous service in place of his military duties. The bottom line for the APD seems to have been to ensure that social duties were performed. Discussing the differences between the Anglo-Saxon and the French, essentially Latin, approach to

---

[2] Théodore Ruyssen, 'L'Objection de conscience', *PD* 36/9–10 (Sept.–Oct. 1926), 331. See also Ruyssen, 'L'Idolâtrie patriotique', *PD* 35/1 (Jan. 1925), 1–4, in which he likened the plight of COs to that of the Huguenots who went into voluntary exile under Louis XIV.

conscientious objection, Ruyssen wrote that the former sprang 'from a moral and religious individualism' and that its greatest obstacle in France was quite simply that 'the average Frenchman is not tolerant'.[3] This together with the nation's long tradition of Catholicism and authoritarian centralism combined to make the acceptance of objection very difficult. Interestingly, Ruyssen recognized that the root of the problem might well be the idea of the 'nation in arms' which constituted a strong and established revolutionary tradition in France. As an indication of Ruyssen's essential conservatism and cautious conformism, he did not however see conscientious objection as a legitimate means of lessening this militaristic hold over the nation's soul.[4]

The APD considered the question of conscientious objection for the first time in the post-war period at its annual general meeting in Paris in late December 1925. Paul Allégret, the director of the École de droit de Limoges, presented the main report on the subject to the Assembly along with some ideas about how to resolve the issue to the contentment of all concerned. He gave a historical overview of the question, going back to the 1904 Congrès national de Nîmes, at which he had also been charged with presenting a report and motion on the same subject. His main concern then, as now, had been to ensure that there was no 'attack on patriotic sentiment, nor on the dignity of the law, but only the manifestation of sympathy for those who are guilty only of interpreting to the letter the maxim "Thou shalt not kill"'.[5] The question of conscientious objection had also been on the agenda of the Congrès universel pour la paix held in Paris in September 1925. The Ligue pour la reconnaissance légale de l'objection de conscience had presented a motion in favour of it, and in the commission charged with preparing a resolution on disarmament Georges Pioch (1873–1953)[6] had managed to have a motion

---

[3] Ruyssen, 'Objection de conscience', 332.

[4] Ibid. 333–7.

[5] Paul Allégret, 'Le Devoir militaire, et le scrupule de conscience: Avant et après la Grande Guerre: Une solution: Rapport présenté à l'Assemblée générale de la "Paix par le droit"', PD 36/4 (Apr. 1926), 145–6.

[6] See James Friguglietti, 'Georges Pioch', in Harold Josephson (ed.), Biographical Dictionary of Modern Peace Leaders (Westport, London: Greenwood Press, 1985), 752–3. Pioch came from a modest family background. He nevertheless received a lycée education in Paris. He worked as a proof reader for several newspapers and wrote poetry and short stories in his spare time. He eventually joined the staffs of musical and literary reviews such as Musica, Comœdia, and Gil Blas. He joined the newly formed French Communist Party in 1920, but despite becoming a prominent

adopted in favour of the abolition of obligatory military service, and the acceptance as an interim measure of the right of objection. When it came time for the full Congress to vote on the resolution, however, it was defeated by a vote of 193 to 144 in favour of a substitute resolution proposed by Ferdinand Buisson (1841–1932)[7] which underlined that the only means of achieving universal disarmament, and hence an end to military service, was by adopting the Geneva Protocol which imposed on nations obligatory arbitration and the renunciation of the use of brute force; as long as international law remained incapable of guaranteeing the peace, the Congress recognized the right of nations to impose military service on their citizens.[8]

With this as a backdrop, Allégret argued in favour of accepting conscientious objection but with severe conditions attached: he could not support a motion such as Pioch's which he thought anarchic. Even the proposal that COs should serve a period of duty one-third longer than ordinary conscripts appeared too easy to him, too much a temptation for cowards. Instead, he proposed that conscientious objection be recognized on condition that the objectors perform their duties in times of peace either abroad in the colonies, or else in very dangerous work such as the care of people in infectious disease wards of hospitals. In time of war, the objectors would be used as stretcher-bearers in the most dangerous part of the line, in the forward trenches and between the barbed wire in no man's land. Only thus could the state ensure that objection did not become the easy way out for cowards.[9] Anticipating the conclusion which many pacifists would draw from the Kellogg–Briand Pact by some three years, Allégret proceeded to add a further distinction to his argument. He believed that there were many young men who were prepared to fight if the cause were just, but who categorically refused to shed their blood in a war of colonial conquest or continental aggression. The concept of a just war was thus of paramount importance. But how to define such a war? The Geneva Protocol of

---

figure in the party, left it in 1922 over questions of discipline. By 1924 he had returned to the socialist fold. Pioch was also an important member of the Ligue des droits de l'homme, although he (along with several others) broke with that organization in 1937 over the issue of its support for French intervention in the Spanish Civil War and its refusal to denounce the Moscow Purge Trials.

[7] See Albert S. Hill, 'Ferdinand Édouard Buisson', in Josephson, *Dictionary*, 123–4.

[8] Allégret, 'Devoir militaire', 149–53.

[9] Ibid. 155–6.

1924 had declared that all wars of aggression were crimes. Allégret saw this as the first manifestation of the new international republic which the members of the APD had been striving for. It was therefore up to the League of Nations in all future conflicts to pronounce on the rightness of any war. This put the convinced pacifist in the position of having potentially to choose between his Minister of War and the League. There was only one choice possible, the League: 'It is the lesser evil which must be chosen, and the lesser evil is that of not allowing oneself to become an accomplice of an aggressor, it is opposing injustice.' To those who would condemn this attitude as defeatist and antipatriotic teaching, Allégret responded rhetorically by asking, 'is it not in reality defending one's country? Do we conceive it, do we wish it to be anything but an instrument and a force for justice?'[10]

At this 1925 AGM Pierre Ceresole, the Swiss engineer behind the creation of the International Civilian Service which sought to send young men to disaster-stricken areas of Europe in a non-military form of active service to society, spoke to the Allégret report. He optimistically foresaw the day when by their sheer number the example of conscientious objectors would have a pacifying effect on the world. The question of objection thus assumed not merely an individual importance, but also a social, collective value in the fight against war. This idea, already present in French pacifism in the mid-twenties, was to find fuller expression in the debates over the efficacy of conscientious objection in the thirties.[11]

The traditional French argument against a special regime for those whose conscience forbade them to take arms was argued 'vehemently' by Célestin Bouglé, who said that it was totally inadmissible for an association which had 'law' at its base to demand recognition for those who flouted it. In Bouglé's view, the proposals in favour of objection were 'pure anarchy'. The League of Nations had to be founded upon respect for the law, and this respect could only be guaranteed through force. Bouglé declared that 'nothing could be more dangerous than to ask it to intervene in support of those who deny the law in favouring, despite their good faith, cowards and deserters . . .'.[12]

---

[10] Allégret, 'Devoir militaire', 156.
[11] See J.-L. Puech, 'L'Assemblée générale de la Paix par le droit', PD 36/1 (Jan. 1926), 17.
[12] Ibid. 18.

The discussion became so agitated that the Nancy group proposed to adjourn it to the following year. It was finally decided however to accept a compromise resolution from Allégret which emphasized the necessity of adopting the principles enshrined in the Geneva Protocol thus permitting general disarmament and in the long run an end to obligatory military service. In the meantime, it asked the League of Nations and the International Court of Justice to define specifically the limited number of cases in which a country could legitimately defend itself so that there could be no equivocation on the subject.[13]

There to all intents and purposes the subject lay for another five years until the full debate on the theory and practice of conscientious objection at the 1930 annual general meeting. In the meantime there was some discussion of the subject in the review. One reader wrote to ask whether, given his stand as an objector in 1904 and again in 1913, he might legitimately remain a member of the Association. Ruyssen replied that he could because although he had refused to carry arms, he had always remained at the disposal of the military authorities and in fact served as a nurse and stretcher-bearer during the Great War.[14]

In the autumn of 1926 the review also ran an *enquête* on conscientious objection which elicited far fewer responses than the enquiry earlier in the year on the alleged dangers of toy soldiers to children's growth and development.[15] Four out of the seven responses were in favour of the legal recognition of objection, one was rather confused, and two were completely against the idea. L. Léontin, a regular contributor to the journal, wrote strongly against conscientious objection for the usual French republican reasons, primary amongst them being the fear of a 'praetorian' army which he seemed to think Britain suffered from.[16] The review continued to publish short notices from other pacifist groups about conscientious objection, too. A manifesto sent out by Runham Brown of the War Resisters' International merited simply the comment that the APD did not believe the WRI's approach actually solved the 'grave' problems

---

[13] Ibid. 18–19.

[14] E. Guiton and Théodore Ruyssen, 'A propos de l'objection de conscience' (2 letters), *PD* 36/2 (Feb. 1926), 68–9.

[15] 'Enquête sur l'objection de conscience', *PD* 36/9–10 (Sept.–Oct. 1926), 337–41 (5 responses); 'PS à l'Enquête sur l'objection de conscience' (2 responses), *PD* 36/12 (Dec. 1926), 439–40; for the *enquête* on toy soldiers see 'Les Jeux de soldats', *PD* 36/5 (May 1926), 193–213; and *PD* 36/6 (June 1926), 253–5.

[16] 'Enquête', 439–40.

posed by conscientious objection.[17] Jules Prudhommeaux and his wife also attended the Bierville Congress organized by Marc Sangnier at which two resolutions in favour of sharply delimited conscientious objection were passed.[18]

The first of the trials of conscience to receive public attention, that of Georges Chevé in 1927, caused the APD to pause and reflect however. Prudhommeaux, writing in early 1928 after Chevé's sentencing in Rouen, saw clearly the potential conscientious objection had if it should ever develop into a 'movement'. He pointed out that the verdict solved nothing for the authorities because the question would re-pose itself in six months' time when Chevé left prison. He foresaw the chaos which would result if 'only fifty thousand Chevés in France stood up one after the other, and as many in the other militarized countries'; it was plain that should this ever occur, governments, moving slowly from 'disquiet to terror, would suddenly realize that international disarmament had something good about it'.[19] But the APD contented itself with calling for Chevé to be given the benefit of the 'political' regime in prison, instead of being classed as a common criminal.

Two years later when Eugène Guillot was sentenced along with another CO to a one-year prison sentence the APD's reaction was much the same. Prudhommeaux criticized the Conseil de guerre which condemned them as being composed of career officers and a magistrate who by reason of their 'déformation professionnelle' were incapable of seeing beyond the letter of the law. It is interesting to note that once again an intelligent man like Prudhommeaux pointed out the logical inconsistency of such a policy on the part of a government which was one of the originators of the Kellogg–Briand Pact.[20] This demand on the French government to be consistent with its own proclamations was thus not one used only by other pacifist groups less intellectual than the APD.

A discussion on European political union at the 1929 AGM of the Association showed to what extent some French pacifists were

[17] 'Un manifeste pour l'abolition du service militaire obligatoire', PD 36/12 (Dec. 1926), 472.
[18] 'Le Congrès de Bierville', PD 36/9–10 (Sept.–Oct. 1926), 369–72.
[19] J. Prudhommeaux, 'L'Objection de conscience: Georges Chevé', PD 38/3 (Mar. 1928), 142.
[20] J. Prudhommeaux, 'Guillot et Perrin, objecteurs de conscience', PD 40/4 (Apr. 1930), 137–8.

confused about the motives behind conscientious objection. Régis de Vibraye suggested that a federated Europe would provide a way out of the moral dilemmas posed by objection because it would allow for the creation of an international police force to take the place of national armies. Each nation would furnish a contingent of its own which would be filled entirely through voluntary subscription. But as a Mr Lowery from the Society of Friends pointed out in the ensuing discussion, it was not the *character* of the army—be it international or national—that was called into question by objectors but rather the simple fact of being obliged to kill one's fellow man. With either sort of army, the problem remained.[21]

The 1930 AGM of the APD saw the question of conscientious objection debated most thoroughly, however. The two rival tendencies in the debate were represented by Pastor Henri Roser,[22] the secretary of the Mouvement international de la réconciliation (the French branch of the International Fellowship of Reconciliation based in London), and by the president of the Association, Théodore Ruyssen. Roser made an eloquent case for both the 'humanitarian' objectors and those, like him, of the radical Christian persuasion. Ruyssen countered by inviting the audience to 'come back down to earthly reality' and opposed Roser's arguments by saying that one must render to Caesar the things that are Caesar's. However noble the motives of the conscientious objectors might be they constituted a 'disastrous romanticism'. Violence still ruled the world, and against it the rule of law had to prevail. Ruyssen invited his listeners to meditate on Pascal's dictum: 'Justice is impotent without Force and Force is tyrannical without Justice. Since we cannot make Force just, let us at least make sure that Justice is strong.'[23]

Ruyssen maintained that the problem of peace was insoluble from the purely individual point of view and that only a juridical statute regulating the relations of nations would establish peace in the world, thus rendering the question of conscientious objection

---

[21] See J. Prudhommeaux, 'L'Assemblée générale de la Paix par le droit, Bordeaux, 2 et 3 novembre 1929', *PD* 39/12 (Dec. 1929), 451–3.

[22] Henri Roser was born in 1898 or 1899 and died on 6 Jan. 1981. During the twenties and subsequently he was the leading light of the MIR. He was a convinced conscientious objector and spent several years in prison for his beliefs. See *Le Monde* of 21 Jan. 1981, 14, for an obituary. See also *Cahiers de la réconciliation*, 48/2 (Feb. 1981) for a series of articles commemorating Roser.

[23] Cited in J. Prudhommeaux, 'L'Assemblée générale de Boulogne-sur-Mer (suite)', *PD* 41/2 (Feb. 1931), 75.

irrelevant. Three resolutions were presented to the assembly: one by Roser, another by Ruyssen, and a third by René Valfort and Félicien Challaye, which was similar to Roser's. A composite resolution was drawn up which was passed unanimously. Despite Ruyssen's apparent objections to conscientious objection in his speech to the assembly, the final resolution called for an end to universal and obligatory military service which was called 'a heritage of the Napoleonic regime' which could not 'be considered an essentially democratic institution'. The resolution demanded instead the creation as soon as possible of a statute regulating the situation of the conscientious objectors, and as a temporary measure in this direction proposed the creation of a civilian form of service in France.[24]

The assault on obligatory military service continued the following year with another report by Henri Roser, this time on 'The Equivalents of Obligatory Military Service: International Civilian Service and the Voluntary Rescue Service'. Roser argued that the motion before the AGM was the logical outcome of the previous year's resolution at Boulogne. Using Pierre Ceresole's International Civilian Service as his example, Roser demonstrated the successes this idea had enjoyed since the war, having helped enormously at the scene of several major natural and human disasters in Europe.[25] This type of civilian service had its opponents in France, however:

. . . the anarchists reject it energetically, because for them, a civilian service is still the State domesticating the individual . . . military service that is ashamed of itself, hidden, camouflaged by the State which in time of war would quickly transform it without a care for the agreements undertaken. There are others who argue that with modern warfare, the distinction between the two services is an illusion since everything—the road that one rebuilds, the wool one weaves, the tree one cuts down in the forest

[24] Prudhommeaux, 'L'Assemblée générale', PD 41/2 (Feb. 1931), 77. For Roser's resolution see Edmond Duméril, 'Pour notre Assemblée générale', PD 40/10 (Oct. 1930), 373–5.
[25] See Roser's report and the ensuing discussion in Jules Prudhommeaux's 'Notre Assemblée générale', PD 41/12 (Dec. 1931), 598–602. Roser listed the areas in which the Service Civil International had provided assistance since the war: 'à Esnes, près de Verdun; aux Ormonts, dans le canton du Vaud, en 1924; à Someo, dans le Tessin, la même année; dans les Grisons, en 1926; dans le Liechtenstein, en 1928, et enfin, pour la plus grande gloire du service civil et le plus grand profit de notre pays, en 1930, à Albefeuille-Lagarde, près de Montauban, au lendemain des terribles inondations dont vous n'avez pas perdu le souvenir. Cette année même, Ceresole et ses vaillants sont allés à Bryn-Mawr, au secours du Pays de Galles ravagé par le chômage, pour essayer, par la mise en train d'industries nouvelles, de rendre à des malheureux la volonté de vivre. Un autre groupe travaille en Argovie.'

—immediately finds its wartime use once violence is let loose. Finally, one last objection: civilian service, affirms M. Alexis Danan, has the unfortunate effect of diverting integral pacifists from the only attitude which is logical, that recommended by the great Einstein: total resistance, the categorical refusal to play any role in the drama.[26]

Roser saw, however, two advantages to the institution of a civilian service. First, it would give legal sanction to the refusal of military service, thus reconciling it to the law and social order. Personally, he was not entirely convinced by this argument, because in good primitive Christian manner, he believed that a little martyrdom now and again did not hurt the cause. Secondly, though, he argued that if a civilian service were instituted in the manner of Ceresole's project, it would become a beneficial 'school of solidarity', something the obligatory military service was not. In order for it to have this virtue, however, it would have to be voluntarily consented.[27] He objected to the APD's motion because it proposed that COs should serve a longer term of civilian service than military service. If COs themselves had the right to demand this extension, it seemed to him that an external association such as the APD did not. Moreover, the extended service idea was not logical. If one accepted that a civilian service was superior to military service, in terms of dignity and educative value, then logically the Association ought to have the courage of its convictions in demanding its institution pure and simple.[28]

The discussion on the resolution exposed the equivocal nature of some pacifists' attitudes to conscientious objection. René Valfort argued that incorporating objectors into the nursing and stretcher-bearing corps of the army still made them supporters of war. 'What they demand', he declared, 'is to make war impossible, and not to occupy a place which shelters them from the obligation of killing their fellow man.'[29] This is one of the strands of the CO argument which highlights the contradictions within pacifist theory on it. The point to be made about the APD's discussions of conscientious objection is how disparate the thinking was and how unconscious

[26] Ibid. 599.

[27] Ibid. 599–600. For a personal view of the degradations of military life in the twenties, and a critique of the social utility of this experience and its effects on young men, see André Trocmé, *Autobiographie*, 140 ff. in SCPC DG-107 Acc. No. 79A-52. See also Albert S. Hill, 'André Trocmé', in Josephson, *Dictionary*, 959–61.

[28] Roser's report in Prudhommeaux, 'Notre Assemblée générale', 600–1.

[29] Ibid. 601.

the APD seemed to be of its internal contradictions. On the one hand there were those who believed that military service was a social obligation but could not see beyond this to a civilian service which would fulfil the same role. There were those who advocated a civilian service on humanitarian or religious grounds, and wavered between a belief in the necessity of a substitute service for social reasons, and those who took the 'esoteric quasi-pacifist'[30] position, close to anarchism, that no demands could be made of certain objectors. There were also those within the APD who argued simply in favour of obligatory military service on grounds of equality before the law, the needs of national security, and the imperative in Republican France of avoiding the creation of a 'praetorian' army. Still others, like Ruyssen, seemed prepared to vote in favour of the legal acceptance of conscientious objection out of scruples more at home in the Ligue des droits de l'homme. For these pacifists there was no question of objection being a method of fighting war: what they were concerned to do was purely and simply to protect the wounded individual conscience. Finally, there were those like Prudhommeaux who began to see the potential effects an organized campaign of conscientious objection would have on the military system in France and elsewhere, but who lacked the courage or conviction to draw the necessary logical conclusions. Others in this camp, such as René Valfort, did grasp the nettle of collective objection but in so doing objection became a mere method (amongst many presumably) of resisting war, and no longer a matter of individual conscience alone.

The connections were never established in the APD between conscientious objection, moral disarmament, and the nascent integral pacifism. The former was accepted to the limited extent that it was perceived to be a question of human conscience and dignity with no direct connection to pacifist theory. When this connection was established by some pacifists, objection was rejected as a method of fighting war. The same can be said of moral disarmament, which was preached throughout the interwar period. The connection between the individual or people who are morally disarmed and a conscientious objection to killing other people in similar circumstances was never fully developed. Finally, in the period up until at least 1933, there seemed to be no inkling on the part of the APD's leadership that

---

[30] The typology is Ceadel's: see *Pacifism in Britain, 1914–1945* (Oxford: Clarendon Press, 1980), 10.

both of these positions, taken to their logical conclusions, essentially spelled integral pacifism. Thus, in the same year in which the APD passed resolutions in support of a special statute for conscientious objectors and recognized that objection was 'respectable' and a method of resisting war, it also categorically rejected the idea of integral pacifism.[31] Conscientious objection was always viewed as an essentially negative approach to peace and therefore of little value. To the extent to which COs were defended, it was for purely humanitarian reasons.

The failure to draw logical conclusions, to force the issue, to go beyond what might be called a rather anodyne *pacifisme des pantouflards* can be seen in Prudhommeaux's comments about the recidivism of Eugène Guillot at the end of his first prison sentence for objection. Prudhommeaux wrote that the Kellogg–Briand Pact seemed to have created a new and essential fact in law and in logic with regard to the COs. By making war a crime, it also made the preparation of war a crime. Having taken this step, Prudhommeaux could go no further, however, than to say that the Pact had thus created a *civic* conscientious objection. In his considered opinion, the individual refusal of military service 'in France at least and given the present state of things, would not resolve the enormous problem of War and of Peace: this Guillot will never be the shepherd of a flock large enough for one to hope for that'.[32]

At the 1932 AGM the topic reappeared under different guise, this time as a debate on the relative merits of obligatory military service versus a permanent regular army. André Lecomte of the Jeune République presented a report in favour of the permanent army, but in the end the Assembly pronounced itself incapable of taking an enlightened decision.[33]

In 1933 Henri Roser tried to distinguish between conscientious objection strictly as a function of conscience, and objection based upon the desire to find a way of combating war. He was responding to allegations printed in the *PD* that Pastor Nick in the Côtes-du-Nord was running a sort of 'school for COs' in which young men were being encouraged and organized to refuse their military service.

[31] This subject is dealt with fully later in this chapter.

[32] J. Prudhommeaux, 'Un récidiviste de l'objection de conscience: Eugène Guillot', *PD* 41/2 (Feb. 1931), 108.

[33] See 'Notre Assemblée générale, Pau, 29 octobre–1er novembre 1932', *PD* 42/12 (Dec. 1932), 535–6 and 541.

This allegation was completely untrue according to Roser, who saw in it an occult attempt to make conscientious objection seem a threat to the security of the state. Roser also responded to the stories in the press about the mutilation of a statue of Déroulède in Paris by Gérard Leretour, a sometime objector, and his (and others') use of the hunger strike as a weapon. Roser wrote that though he understood the motives of desperation behind these acts he could not condone them. Most importantly, however, Roser distinguished between what he considered genuine *conscientious* objection and an ersatz objection which saw itself as merely one tactic among others in the fight against war—an attitude epitomized by the hunger strike. The argument was that objection on whatever grounds was good because it drew attention to the 'extremely grave peril of war and of conscription'. But in that case, according to Roser, one could no longer speak of conscientious objection as such—'a tactic, a technique of opposition to war, perhaps, but no longer the unconditional submission of the conscience to an ineluctable truth'. The distinction had to be made, in his view.[34]

Whatever the specific motives of most objectors, conscientious objection continued to receive support, not as a method of resisting war so much as a question of pure conscience, until late in the 1930s. In 1936, for example, the review published a petition written by André Philip, then professor in the Faculty of Law at the University of Lyon, demanding the reform of the law regulating the penalties meted out to convicted COs. Under existing legislation, it was theoretically possible for a convinced objector to spend his entire life from the age of 20 to 48 in prison for his beliefs if the law were applied rigorously. Ruyssen signed the petition, and readers of the *PD* were invited to do the same. The appeal was for signatures from

---

[34] Henri Roser, 'L'Objection de conscience et la légalité: Lettre ouverte à M. le rédacteur de "La Paix par le droit"', *PD* 44/1 (Jan. 1934), 22–3. The article containing the erroneous allegations is J. Prudhommeaux, 'La Condamnation de "l'objecteur" Philippe Vernier', *PD* 43/10 (Oct. 1933), 402–3. Roser developed this distinction even further in his response to the 'Enquête sur la crise du pacifisme' in *PD* 44/2 (Feb. 1934), 71–3 in which he argued that the logical conclusion of pacifism was conscientious objection. He differentiated, however, between 'genuine' CO with its emphasis on the imperatives of the individual conscience, and CO used merely as a tactic by other pacifists. He underlined forcefully the religious conception he had of pacifism and argued that the spiritual side of the question must be predominant. For Roser no progress ever occurred without a spiritual origin. In this sense Roser comes very close to making pacifism an example of Weber's 'ethic of ultimate ends'—an idea developed further in the case of British pacifism by Martin Ceadel.

people irrespective of their attitude towards objection, and the list of luminaries who signed the petition is impressive.[35]

Thus, it can be seen that the APD hardly presented a unanimous face to the world on the question of conscientious objection. Within the association there were several strands of thinking on the subject, all of them at least initially under the delusion that they were talking about the same thing. But it is clear that the conception of objection held by these different strands varied enormously. These differences gradually became more and more apparent. Officially, the APD was in favour of legislation which would attenuate the harsh penalties inflicted upon genuine objectors, but equally it could never bring itself to pronounce in favour of conscientious objection as an efficacious method of war resistance. Having said all that, it is clear that Ruyssen (and perhaps, by extension, the APD as a whole) had progressed markedly since his speech in the early twenties to the Congrès belge pour le progrès des idées morales, in which he had exalted the moral value of war and attacked those who had shirked their duty in the hecatomb.[36]

THE CHALLENGE OF INTEGRAL PACIFISM

The second and more important challenge to the APD's view of pacifism in the early thirties was that of integral pacifism. If conscientious objection constituted a crack in the façade, then integral pacifism represented a veritable fissure. The discovery of such irreducible differences of outlook and doctrine within pacifism was even more shocking in that the debate burst upon the APD from

[35] For the text of the petition, see 'Pour la réforme d'une loi inhumaine', *PD* 46/2 (Feb. 1936), 97–8. Amongst early signatories of the petition were *inter alia*: Régis de Vibraye, Paul Langevin, Jacques Maritain, Michel Alexandre, André Gide, Jean Guéhenno, Georges Guy-Grand, E. Mounier, Élie Gounelle, Théodore Ruyssen, André Philip, Wilfred Monod, Paul Rivet, Alain, André Chamson, Joliot-Curie, J.-R. Bloch, Albert Bayet, Jules Isaac, Georges LaPierre, Jean Giono, René Maublanc.

[36] See Théodore Ruyssen, 'La Guerre et la morale (extrait d'un discours prononcé à l'ouverture du Congrès belge pour le progrès des idées morales)', *PD* 33/2 (Feb. 1923), 49–52, in which Ruyssen said: 'Nous n'aurons garde, quant à nous, de méconnaître la grandeur morale de certaines heures du temps de guerre. C'est l'honneur du caractère humain de s'élever, sous l'aiguillon de l'épreuve, au-dessus du médiocre niveau de l'humanité moyenne.' Speaking of the duty which all men felt to fight in the Great War, he said, '. . . hélas! il n'est pas vrai que tout le monde ait fait son devoir. Il y a eu, en petit nombre, il est vrai, mais il y a eu quand même en tous les pays des réfractaires, des déserteurs, des lâches et des traîtres: il y a eu les mauvais prophètes du défaitisme . . .'

within in the form of the Trojan horse Félicien Challaye, who until
1932 was a member of the Comité directeur.

The debate on integral pacifism within the APD originated in a
discussion between Jacques Hadamard, professor at the Collège de
France, and Challaye in the pages of the *Cahiers des droits de
l'homme* in 1928 and 1929.[37] The discussion centred on the question
of what the Serbian reaction ought to have been to the Austro-
Hungarian ultimatum of 23 July 1914. Hadamard argued that the
Austro-Hungarian action constituted a refusal of all arbitration and
an attack on Serbian independence which had necessarily led to war.
Challaye on the other hand argued that while he in no way condoned
the Austrian action, the rest of Europe ought to have had the sense to
abstain from getting involved in what was to become so catastrophic
a generalized war.[38] This quite naturally evolved into a more theoretical discussion of what Hadamard referred to as the Tolstoyan
doctrine of non-resistance to evil. The humanitarian development of
this argument in the thirties was that anything was better than a new
blood-letting on the scale of the Great War.[39]

Hadamard reduced the 'Tolstoyan' proposition to two arguments: first, that anything was preferable to another war, and
secondly, that faced with a nation which refused to defend itself, the
aggressor would not dare to execute his crime. It was particularly this
latter argument which Hadamard sought to combat. He demonstrated that international, juridical progress founded upon universal
and obligatory arbitration of conflicts was fundamentally incompatible with the idea of non-resistance. In a Tolstoyan universe,
he argued, arbitration would become a nonsense as the aggressors
would simply refuse arbitration in favour of immediate gains.
Taking the argument from another angle, he maintained that non-
resistance would spell the end of all progress. The adversaries of the
French Revolution and of liberty still existed, and non-resistance in
the civil and international domains meant in the final analysis a
return to despotism. But despotism contained within it the seeds of
war. Non-resistant pacifists might avoid war in refusing to fight the
despot, but they would 'then have the pleasure of fighting for the

[37] See J. Hadamard, 'Pacifisme intégral?', *PD* 41/2 (Feb. 1931), 57 nn. 1 and 3.
[38] Ibid. 57.
[39] Ibid. 60. Martin Ceadel calls this the 'humanitarian' inspiration for pacifism
—in his view the most important intellectual development of interwar pacifism. See
Ceadel, *Pacifism in Britain*, 13.

despot'. History abounded with examples of this.[40] The progress realized by the Geneva Protocol in determining the aggressor in any conflict would be rendered null and void by the doctrine of non-resistance:

... this so-called avant-garde doctrine would mark a step backwards. This is perhaps our principal reason, sufficient of itself, for repudiating it.

International peace cannot be founded at the same time on the definition of the aggressor and on the theory of non-resistance of the attacked. Between one and the other, one must choose, and our choice is made. One cannot avoid the question of whether one should renounce liberty and justice deliberately in favour of peace, or whether, as we believe, peace, justice, and liberty are inseparable things, one not being able to exist without the others.[41]

Challaye responded in the November 1931 issue of the *PD* with an article in favour of 'peace with no reservations'.[42] He underlined that he was only concerned with war between peoples, that is to say, nations: civil conflicts were beyond the parameters of his argument and his pacifism. Challaye defined three attitudes possible in the face of international war. The first was the *belliciste* position, embodied by those who proclaim war to be morally beneficial and socially productive. Secondly, there were those who believed peace to be superior to war, but considered war to be necessary in some cases, and therefore legitimate. These he called the *belli-pacifistes*. Finally, there were those who condemned war in an absolute sense, whatever the circumstances. These demanded peace by any means, these were the pacifists, the representatives of *integral pacifism*.[43]

Challaye also defined the sources of pacifism. These were two. On the one hand, pacifism could arise from egotism pure and simple, 'an egotism which is in itself legitimate: it is reasonable to safeguard one's own existence, and to sacrifice it only to a cause which is worth it'.[44] But clearly this egotism could also lead to bellicism or belli-pacifism as well. Thus, pacifism arose more from moral ideas than from egotism. Challaye argued that it represented the application to relations between peoples of the commonplace commandments: 'Thou shalt not kill' and 'Love thy neighbour as thyself'.[45]

---

[40] Hadamard, 'Pacifisme intégral?', 59–61.   [41] Ibid. 67.
[42] F. Challaye, 'Pour la paix sans aucune réserve', *PD* 41/11 (Nov. 1931), 489–97.
[43] Ibid. 489.   [44] Ibid.   [45] Ibid.

While it was true that integral pacifism sprang from the application of this *morale courante*, it was absolutely false that it was logically tied to the Tolstoyan conception of non-resistance to evil according to Challaye.

Certainly the Tolstoyan must be an integral pacifist, but the integral pacifist is not necessarily a Tolstoyan. The integral pacifist, he who demands peace at any price between the peoples, can very well accept legitimate familial and individual defence. Legitimate individual or familial defence has nothing but its name in common with national defence, so-called national defence. Legitimate individual or familial defence has as its goal, and often with success, the *saving of several precious lives*; so-called national defence always has as its consequence the *destruction of innumerable precious existences.*[46]

Thus, for Challaye, the integral pacifist would not hesitate in using force to defend his mother, his wife, or his child. He would run to the aid of someone attacked in the streets. He would defend to the best of his ability Jews attacked in pogroms, and he would be free to participate in a revolt against an oppressor. 'Civil war or social war is essentially different from foreign war ... It is war between peoples, only, which is forbidden by integral pacifism as it is here defined.'[47]

There were three primary reasons for Challaye's belief in integral pacifism. The first, what he called the decisive reason, was essentially that of Bertrand Russell, namely that the 'evils of war are infinitely greater than any other solution applied to conflicts between peoples'. He claimed that viewed from this angle, integral pacifism was not a 'tissue of abstractions', or a utopia, but rather a living doctrine taken from 'contact with reality, and nourished by experience'. And the experience was that of the last war. Secondly, there was the aspect of suffering which a modern war brought about—an infinity of suffering. Warfare in the twentieth century no longer could limit its effects, horrible that they were, to the combatants. All members of society were now affected by war, and therefore by its terrible sufferings. And finally, the new means of warfare made war the worst of evils, in fact absolute evil. To this absolute evil an absolute remedy needed to be applied and that remedy was integral pacifism, 'peace without the slightest reservation'.[48]

Challaye foresaw the arguments which the belli-pacifists would

---

[46] *PD* 41/11 (Nov. 1931), 490. Challaye expressed his debt for this idea to his friend, the pacifist René Valfort.   [47] Ibid. 490–1.   [48] Ibid. 491–3.

marshal against his conception of integral pacifism. The best would be that war can safeguard national independence. To this Challaye replied that armed defence and wars are not necessary or even sufficient for the maintenance of national sovereignty. Examples of this were Andorra, Luxembourg, Switzerland, Denmark, and so forth. Perhaps more important, war in no way guaranteed national independence. Wars could be lost and with them national sovereignty. But even if war could be proved to be 100 per cent effective in preserving national independence, one had to ask at what price. This led Challaye to his major conclusion that 'a foreign occupation is preferable to a war—the acceptance of this formula could be the criterion separating the real pacifists from the belli-pacifists . . .'.[49] Challaye believed that modern warfare made the defence of the nation in reality its death. That did not imply however a total abdication in the face of aggression. If national defence were impossible by means of arms, there were other ways of resisting aggression: passive resistance and non-co-operation such as Gandhi was using in India; the appeal to the conscience of the invading people; the appeal to the conscience of other nations who could then organize an economic and financial boycott against the aggressor, and so on. The integral pacifist was thus called to resist, but not by force of arms. Integral pacifism called therefore for pacifist action on the individual level first—a personal renunciation of war as in the Einstein declaration; and secondly, a social renunciation of war through total and if necessary unilateral disarmament.[50]

The counter-attack was not long in coming. The editors of the *PD* wrote in the next number of the review that Challaye's article had caused them no small amount of grief, not only from a very hostile press, but also from many members of the Association 'who were far from sharing his views'.[51] Ruyssen challenged the philosophical and moral bases of Challaye's pacifism head on. The differences between the two men were irreducible. Ruyssen clearly believed that certain things—justice and law, incarnated in the right of peoples to dispose of their own destinies—were most definitely worth fighting for. To Challaye's claim to be speaking from the cold experience of reality, Ruyssen threw back the undeniable facts of recent history: Belgium resisting the Kaiser's army in 1914, the Danes heroically fighting the

---

[49] Ibid. 494.   [50] Ibid. 494–7.
[51] 'La Paix sans réserve?', *PD* 41/12 (Dec. 1931), 561.

Prussians in Schleswig in 1864, imposing the plebiscite on Bismarck which he was trying to avoid; and he recalled to mind the visceral importance of national identity and self-determination, reminding Challaye of 'the little peasants of Poznań who, around 1910, were whipped because they could not recite the catechism in German', to say nothing of the old men he had seen sobbing in Colmar, Strasburg, and Mulhouse in 1913, such was the depth of their feeling at being separated from France.[52] Ruyssen charged that Challaye was being illogical in limiting his concept of legitimate defence to the individual or family level; just as at these levels, so the sense of national solidarity led men to defend the social collectivity called the nation. Ruyssen's attack finished on a decidedly *ad hominem* note. He accused Challaye of reducing the whole problem of war to one of fear, of producing a 'dry theorem', of being a 'prudent bourgeois' who was teaching cowardice, of putting a long and comfortable life above all other values. To Challaye's 'swaggering' affirmation of an unconditional pacifism, even if it resulted in an unjust or dishonourable peace, Ruyssen opposed his ideal of 'peace in justice and dignity'. It was the APD's desire to see to it that force, 'which up until now has been bound up with the law of men only by accident, should be so by rule and without exception, as it is already in a large measure within human communities'.[53]

Challaye's response to Ruyssen's attack heightened the personal nature of the debate. He accused Ruyssen of cowardice himself for having spent the war as a non-combatant, while he, Challaye, despite his age, served as a sergeant in the territorial infantry and was wounded slightly. This is the classic distinction made during and after the war by those who fought at the front *vis-à-vis* those who remained behind the lines as non-combatants, or perhaps shirkers.[54] Challaye affirmed that he was profoundly attached to the idea of national independence, but he still maintained that to fight for this independence given the state of modern warfare would mean the

---

[52] Théodore Ruyssen, 'La Paix sans réserves? Non!', *PD* 42/1 (Jan. 1932), 10–12.

[53] Ibid. 14–15. The attack on Challaye continued the following month with Charles Richet, 'La Paix sans réserve est un rêve!', *PD* 42/2–3 (Feb.–Mar. 1932), 70–1.

[54] F. Challaye, 'Pour la paix sans aucune réserve (réponse à l'article de M. Ruyssen)', *PD* 42/4 (Apr. 1932), 149. On the distinctions drawn by the war veterans between *ceux du front* and *ceux de l'arrière*, see Antoine Prost, *Les Anciens Combattants et la société française, iii: Mentalités et idéologies* (Paris: Presses de la FNSP, 1977), 78–81.

annihilation of the state in any case. There was nothing 'utilitarian' about his argument at all, said Challaye; he made the case for integral pacifism from the moral point of view. True courage was being prepared to sacrifice one's life for a cause that merited it, not in causing the deaths of innocent men and women in a war. He summed up his conception of courage in Bossuet's dictum that one must 'reserve *for real service* the action of an extraordinary bravery'.[55]

The editorial secretary of the review, Jules Puech, intervened at this point in the debate and tried to smooth over the differences between the two men, by arguing that in fact Challaye's conception of pacifism was not that different from Ruyssen's. He did this by quoting from several of Challaye's books on moral philosophy which certainly seemed to point to similarities. He also cited a patriotic lecture which 'Sergeant' Challaye had given to the 109th territorial infantry regiment during the war, expressing in perfect form the patriotic pacifist sentiments of the APD. There is thus little doubt that Challaye's pacifism had changed remarkably since the war, evolving rapidly in the late twenties from one quite similar to that held by the APD to one of intransigent integral pacifism.[56]

---

[55] Challaye, 'Pour la paix (réponse)', 152. Challaye had written, 'Mais Bossuet me paraît avoir raison de soutenir qu'il faut "réserver *pour le vrai service* les actions d'une hardiesse extraordinaire".'

[56] Jules-L. Puech, 'A propos des articles Challaye–Ruyssen', *PD* 42/4 (Apr. 1932), 153–6; see also Challaye's wartime lecture in Félicien Challaye, *La Signification morale de la guerre actuelle (conférence faite au cours d'instruction complémentaire pour les sous-officiers du 109e régiment territorial d'infanterie le 29 mars 1916 par le Sergent Félicien Challaye)* (Paris: Comité de propagande socialiste pour la défense nationale, 1916). Similar sentiments were expressed in a letter to Romain Rolland written in Apr. 1915. Challaye told Rolland that he shared the sentiments expressed by the latter in articles in the *Journal de Genève*, but went on to say: 'Je suis en ce moment sur le front, depuis le début d'octobre, et même, maintenant sur la ligne de feu. Ma compagnie territoriale y a tour à tour creusé des tranchées, occupé des tranchées, entretenu une route stratégique; maintenant elle travaille à "l'assainissement du champs de bataille". Je crois avoir fait, et je suis décidé à faire, jusqu'au bout, tout mon devoir militaire; ce n'est point un lâche qui vous écrit.—Mais c'est un soldat que la guerre n'a pas fait renoncer à son idéal de bonté boudhique, chrétien et socialiste. Si je me bats, si je meurs, ce sera sans aucune haine.

Je crois que nous devons vaincre, à tout prix, pour sauver notre indépendance nationale; pour permettre aux Alsaciens-Lorrains authentiques soit de revenir à la patrie à laquelle ils sont si longtemps fidèles, soit d'obtenir une entière autonomie; pour réaliser une Europe où les peuples auront enfin le droit de disposer d'eux-mêmes librement. Mais après la victoire je souhaite et je réclame une paix définitive basée sur la justice internationale, sur le respect des droits de tous, sur une mutuelle fraternité. Je désire ardemment que ce régime de paix soit réalisé à la fois dans les esprits et les cœurs et dans les institutions internationales que n'écrasent ni n'humilient aucun peuple. Je

footnote continued overleaf

The sense that a divorce was in the offing remained strong throughout 1932 and 1933. It is hard to escape the impression that French pacifism was indeed traversing a crisis, a fundamental parting of the ways between pacifist forces which until then had been content to rely on the assumption that all pacifists were struggling towards the same peace. But as L. Emery charged in a 1933 article published in the *PD*, there were equivocations within pacifism which needed to be rectified. He wrote that in reading the recent articles of Ruyssen, and especially of Richet, he felt that he no longer understood. 'What they call "pacifism" hardly coincides any longer with what we define by this word.'[57] He defined his conception of pacifism on two levels. First, it was necessary to see that the Europe created by the treaties of 1919 was 'agonizing' and that justice had not been done. France had to be prepared to accept a reduction in her political hegemony and prestige. A pacifism which clung to the treaties was one based upon conservatism and French national advantage, not upon justice:

Thus, we arrive at the first line of division: we refuse categorically to recognize as a pacifist anyone who poses, as a prerequisite condition, respect of the existing international order and the refusal by France of new concessions. We believe on the contrary that the integration of France into a pacified Europe cannot be achieved without the abandonment of its present privileges. A definitive equilibrium is at this price.[58]

The second point of division was over the nature of modern warfare and what this implied for the pacifist case. This had nothing—or at least not necessarily—to do with religious ideas or 'quakerism'. But it had everything to do with the fact that the game had changed:

---

footnote continued

considère qu'un devoir urgent s'imposera tout de suite après la paix: rétablir le contact entre les peuples divisés par la guerre; entre les savants, entre les chrétiens, entre les socialistes, entre les ouvriers, entre les gens du monde des pays actuellement en lutte. Puis, chez nous, sauver des étroitesses chauvines le droit à une culture vraiment générale, à laquelle ne manquera point l'importante contribution de l'Allemagne; sauver le droit à Goethe et à Heine, le droit à Kant et à Nietsche, le droit à Beethoven et à Wagner.—Nous aurons de belles luttes à soutenir.

Je me réjouis à l'idée d'y participer, si j'échappe aux petites balles sifflantes et aux éclats des bruyants obus. Nous aurons, pour ce combat aussi, besoin d'un chef: vous serez le nôtre, n'est-ce pas?' And the letter was signed Félicien Challaye, Sergent au 109e territoriale, 1ère compagnie, Secteur portal 140. Letter is in BN MSS Fonds RR, F. Challaye to RR, 26 Apr. 1915.

[57] L. Emery, 'Les Équivoques du pacifisme', *PD* 43/7 (July 1933), 239.
[58] Ibid. 240.

The idea of placing force at the service of justice, and if need be, of accepting a war of national defence as the *ultima ratio* was reasonably compatible with a sincere pacifism as long as there existed an acceptable relationship between the ruins caused by war and the values which it could save. Defending a nation was then shedding a tenth of its blood with a view to a superior interest.[59]

1914 had changed all this. War was now totally out of proportion to the values which it claimed to be saving. The military defence of a nation had become a verbal relic: 'the expression no longer coincides with the reality'.[60] This in no way implied the abandonment of the nation, the acceptance of all injustices. What it did imply however was the need to rethink the way in which a nation would defend itself. No doubt many of the substitute methods of national 'defence' were insufficient, but there was no other alternative, argued Emery. The Geneva Disarmament Conference was a chicanery because it spoke of disarmament and security in the same breath. Pacifism had lost its way according to Emery and in order for it to regain its credit and its strength, it needed to redevelop a programme, and become again an ideal and a moral imperative.[61]

Responding to Emery's article, Richet admitted and defended the idea that he represented a *vieux pacifisme* in contradistinction to what he called Emery's 'neo-pacifism' which he likened to that of the Nazis in terms of its content. He defended the Versailles Treaty as having finally created a Europe in which minority and national aspirations were realized. With regard to disarmament, he believed that Germany was far from disarmed, although he did agree with Emery that any future war would be a disaster for victor and vanquished alike. Richet concluded that there were therefore no equivocations in pacifism. Old pacifists and neo-pacifists alike, he believed, were struggling towards the goal of peace. But he insisted that it was through obligatory arbitration that this peace would be achieved.[62]

Ruyssen, too, responded to Emery's article. He declared that the APD's doctrine had not changed in its essential aspects. He was not fanatically attached to the boundaries of Europe as laid down by the treaties, either, but he did believe that the European situation in 1932

[59] Ibid. 241. [60] Ibid.
[61] Ibid. 242–4.
[62] Charles Richet, 'Y-a-t-il des équivoques du pacifisme?', *PD* 43/8–9 (Aug.–Sept. 1933), 285–8.

was much more equitable in terms of national identity than certainly had been the case in 1914. To revise the treaties would lead straight to war. This did not mean though that the map of Europe created by the treaties was perfect in all respects. But the main point of Emery's essay was the same as that argued by Challaye the year before, namely that any future war would be so ruinous, so costly, so dangerous for civilization that it ought simply not to be fought under any circumstances. Submission rather than destruction was how he summarized Emery's argument. Ruyssen argued that since Emery was prepared to accept the justice of some wars up until 1914, his neo-pacifism therefore reduced itself in the final analysis simply to a calculation of risks involved in a modern war. The answer Emery arrived at was that these risks were too high and spelled doom. The notion of justice was totally absent from the calculation. Ruyssen invited Emery therefore to spell out in precise terms at what level of destruction a war became immoral, and what measure of 'justice could be sacrificed without remorse'.[63] Thus, Ruyssen, despite the definite fact that a future war would be ghastly beyond belief, did not believe that one could confidently extrapolate from it the end of civilization. Pacifist thinking in this area fell into the realm of hypothesis and conjecture, and not of fact. But beyond this argument on the magnitude of destruction, Ruyssen argued that to declare in advance that one would not defend oneself, far from preventing a war, actually encouraged aggression. The only sensible path lay in building up the notion of international law and arbitration whilst at the same time seeking to arrive at the highest level of general disarmament possible.[64]

A HOUSE DIVIDED: FRENCH PACIFISM

A third crack in the optimistic, positive pacifism espoused by the men and women of the APD was undoubtedly the amazing dispersion of efforts for peace in interwar France, and the apparent immunity of the French peace movement as a whole to any attempt to bring order out of the organizational (and doctrinal) chaos. The problem had existed for many years, but the Challaye–Emery controversy helped to bring it into focus for the APD. Right from the outset of the interwar period the APD felt crowded by the advent of new groups

---

[63] Théodore Ruyssen, 'Y-a-t-il des équivoques du pacifisme?', PD 43/8–9 (Aug.–Sept. 1933), 288–9.   [64] Ibid. 289–90.

with the League of Nations as their object. The Association felt that many of its members or potential members were being poached away in the early twenties either by the League of Nations associations or sometimes by the Ligue des droits de l'homme.[65] The APD was nevertheless able to establish itself in the early twenties as a kind of bridge between the world of pacifism and the new groups formed in support of the League. Even within the APD the two tendencies existed; Ruyssen described them in 1922 as the tendency in favour of peace and that in favour of the League of Nations.[66] The problem of balkanization remained, however. Prudhommeaux spoke at the 1924 annual general meeting of a 'crisis of pacifism' engendered by the dangerous and wasteful multiplication of efforts amongst French pacifists. An example of this existed within the APD itself. At the 1922 AGM Lucien Le Foyer (1872–1952)[67] and the Paris group he headed were attacked for lethargy; the real reason behind the attempt to unseat Le Foyer from the president's chair in Paris seems to have been the latter's creation of a rival pacifist organization called the Union populaire pour la paix universelle.[68] No love was lost either between the APD and the Délégation permanente des sociétés

[65] See for example Edmond Duméril, J. Prudhommeaux, and Théodore Ruyssen, 'L'Assemblée générale de la Paix par le droit', *PD* 30/11–12 (Nov.–Dec. 1920), 371. Ruyssen spoke of the problem of competition from the League of Nations associations: '. . . il s'agit avant tout de savoir comment nous pourrons vivre et développer notre Association sans nous heurter à la propagande des groupements nés depuis la guerre et qui poursuivent un but semblable au nôtre sous le pavillon de la Société des Nations.' Georges Cadier for the Poitou group said that '. . . la concurrence de l'Association française pour la Société des Nations nuit à notre propagande, car notre public ne comprend pas cette dualité. De plus, la Ligue des Droits de l'Homme recueille dans beaucoup de localités les adhésions de personnes favorables à nos idées' (370–1).

[66] Ruyssen cited in Jules Prudhommeaux, 'Conseil directeur de l'Association de la paix par le droit', *PD* 32/10 (Oct. 1922), 426–7.

[67] See Albert S. Hill, 'Lucien Le Foyer', in Josephson, *Dictionary*, 552–4.

[68] In his *rapport moral* for the 1924 AGM, Prudhommeaux said that 'Notre mouvement traverse une dangereuse crise de croissance. Aimez-vous le pacifisme? On en a mis partout, et c'est partout la confusion et le désordre. Entre les anciennes sociétés de la Paix et celles qui ont pour objet la Société des Nations, les divergences persistent. Il y a trop d'œuvres, trop de sociétés, trop de journaux, et la belle émulation qui enchantait d'abord les optimistes, risque d'aboutir à l'incohérence et à l'impuissance.'—cited in J. Prudhommeaux and Georges Cadier, 'L'Assemblée générale de la Paix par le droit', *PD* 34/7–8 (July–Aug. 1924), 270–6. For the attack on Le Foyer see Théodore Ruyssen, 'L'Assemblée générale de l'Association de la paix par le droit', *PD* 32/6 (June 1922), 237–46. A short description of the Union populaire pour la paix universelle can be found in Lucien Le Foyer, 'L'Union populaire pour la paix', in *Nous voulons la paix* (Paris: SRIP, 1932), 55–6.

françaises de la paix which was described by Ruyssen as a chief without any Indians.[69]

These fissures and disagreements could only worsen as the twenties flowed into the thirties. The number of groups continued to grow and the doctrines espoused by them moved increasingly in the direction of 'intégralité' whether for sentimental or for humanitarian or religious reasons. It is not our purpose here to examine in detail the nature of the pacifism of some of these groups in that they define the *pacifisme nouveau style* which will be discussed fully in the next section. However, in so far as they represented the beginnings of a break with the old-style pacifism typified by the APD, the Ligue internationale des combattants de la paix was condemned for its integral pacifism, the Ligue internationale des femmes pour la paix et la liberté was criticized for its naïve approach to international affairs, and the Volonté de paix likewise was attacked for its sentimental approach to the problem of peace.[70]

The APD's reaction to the Amsterdam Congress against Imperialist War was both positive and negative. Initially Prudhommeaux had taken a very negative line because of the increasingly evident attempts of the Communists to take over the Congress for their own

[69] On the Délégation permanente, see Théodore Ruyssen, 'A propos du 9me Congrès national de la paix', PD 31/5–6 (May–June 1921), 219–20. Ruyssen wrote '. . . qu'est-ce donc la DP? . . . Peu de choses; une façade à laquelle sont accrochés quelques noms biens connus, mais derrière laquelle il n'y a à peu près rien, ni effectifs, ni activité, ni ressources . . .'

[70] On the LICP see Ruyssen's comments to René Valfort in the debate on the crisis of pacifism at the 1933 AGM in J. Prudhommeaux, 'Notre Assemblée générale, suite et fin', PD 44/3 (Mar. 1934), 101. See also Prudhommeaux's comments in J. Prudhommeaux, 'La Ligue des combattants de la paix: Le Congrès de Montargis: Les Dissidents', PD 44/6 (June 1934), 244–5, in which Prudhommeaux called the LICP's propaganda 'ardent and courageous', but reminded readers that the APD had some fundamental reserves about the LICP programme. On the LIFPL, the APD had both positive and negative views. In 1922 Ruyssen condemned the 'empty rhetoric' of the LIFPL International Congress at the Hague which sought what he called the 'ardent, at times fanatical, demolition' of the treaties of 1919 but seemed to offer little to put in their place. See Théodore Ruyssen, 'Un Congrès féminin pour la paix à La Haye', PD 33/1 (Jan. 1923), 34–5. Later in the twenties however the APD applauded the work of the LIFPL in its investigation of the effects of chemical warfare. See Jules Prudhommeaux, 'La Guerre chimique et l'opinion: Un article de M. de Kérillis', PD 40/11 (Nov. 1930), 451–2. With regard to Madeleine Vernet and the Volonté de paix, as far back as 1921, Ruyssen had attacked Vernet's 'Appel aux femmes' as 'pathetic' and an appeal only to sentiment. See Théodore Ruyssen, 'Les Femmes contre la guerre', PD 31/3–4 (Mar.–Apr. 1921), 140–1. In 1928, after the founding of the Volonté de paix, Prudhommeaux put the readers of the PD on their guard against the 'extremists of peace' to be found in the V.d.P.'s ranks. See J. Prudhommeaux, 'Pacifisme d'avantgarde', PD 38/3 (Mar. 1928), 137–8.

ends.[71] Right up until the eve of the Congress his apprehensions about the reception likely to be reserved for 'bourgeois pacifists' grew, but after attending it, he wrote that 'this congress will remain . . . an important event of the post-war era'.[72] The credit for this success was largely due to Henri Barbusse who had managed to see that the pact of mutual toleration between the multifarious strands of world pacifism was respected.[73] That said, the organization of the Congress was chaotic and in no way designed for constructive work. The unity of tone achieved at Amsterdam was the result of an abdication on the part of many pacifist groups which allowed the Moscow obedience to impose its conceptions on the Assembly and its resolutions.[74] Later on in 1932, when local Amsterdam committees began to be formed in France and elsewhere, it became apparent to Prudhommeaux that the movement had been taken over by the Third International.[75] Despite all this, it is surprising to note how measured and friendly Prudhommeaux's reaction to his experiences at the Congress itself actually was.

The APD participated in efforts in the early thirties to remedy this balkanization of French peace efforts. Jules Prudhommeaux was most actively involved in this work and propagandized tirelessly for the creation of *cartels de la paix* which, while not limiting the independence of their constituent members, would provide a force for unity in French pacifism. We have already noted his concerns as early as 1924 at the dispersion and waste of French peace efforts.[76] By the mid-twenties some cartels had been formed and the movement towards some form of loose unity seemed to gather momentum by

[71] J. Prudhommeaux, 'Un congrès de la paix qui s'annonce mal: Genève ou Moscou?', *PD* 42/7–8 (July–Aug. 1932), 350–1.
[72] J. Prudhommeaux, 'Le Congrès mondial contre la guerre impérialiste', *PD* 42/9 (Sept. 1932), 405.   [73] Ibid. 406.   [74] Ibid. 408–9.
[75] J. Prudhommeaux, 'Les Lendemains du Congrès d'Amsterdam', *PD* 42/11 (Nov. 1932), 494–5. Prudhommeaux formulated many of the same criticisms with regard to the Rassemblement mondial des femmes contre la guerre et le fascisme which was held in Paris in Aug. 1934. It was an impressive congress—some 1,500 delegates were present—but it was overrun by the Communist and Muscovite element and was totally chaotic in terms of organization with decisions and, more importantly, the final manifesto imposed from above. In a strange speech for a 'pacifist' to make, Barbusse attacked the religious, non-violent pacifists and called women to the fight, to the revolution, to violence, if need be. See J. Prudhommeaux, 'Le Rassemblement mondial des femmes contre la guerre et le fascisme', *PD* 44/9 (Sept. 1934), 343–7.
[76] Prudhommeaux cited in Prudhommeaux and Cadier, 'Assemblée générale', 270–6.

the late twenties.[77] The formation of local peace cartels seemed to take off however in 1931, largely under the influence of a tour of France made by a mobile museum on war and peace organized by the Jeune République. Prudhommeaux estimated that during its two-week stay in Bordeaux alone, some 110,000 to 120,000 people saw the museum's display.[78] The purpose of the mobile museum was to raise the population's consciousness about the problems of war and peace until the time of the Geneva Disarmament Conference in February 1932 and the French general elections in May of that year. In provincial France it seems to have had some major successes. In Bordeaux a Cartel girondin de la paix was formed which numbered almost 200,000 members within its constituent organizations. The Cartel rouennais de la paix contained thirty-three member organizations on 1 November 1931. Unfortunately, Paris seemed to remain immune to this flurry of cartel formation and Prudhommeaux wrote that the 'dispersion of efforts [in the capital] is a scandal'.[79] Paradoxically, the new-found or at least growing unity of 1932 was to be difficult to maintain in the face of the Amsterdam movement which, too, had claims on being a unifying force in French pacifism.[80] The inspiration for the creation of peace cartels in France undoubtedly came from across the Channel where the example of the 'powerful' League of Nations Union served to highlight the insufficiencies of the French movement. Despite the very real progress made towards some form of unity in 1931–2, however, French pacifism remained divided unto itself. In 1935, for example, Prudhommeaux engaged in a discussion with Fabien France[81] in which he argued that aside from

[77] On the formation of the Lyon cartel in 1925 see J. Prudhommeaux, 'Le Cartel lyonnais pour la paix et la SDN', *PD* 36/1 (Jan. 1926), 39–40. See also J. Prudhommeaux, 'Vers l'union des forces pacifistes: Cartels et semaines de la paix', *PD* 39/11 (Nov. 1929), 425–30.

[78] J. Prudhommeaux, 'Le Tour de France du Musée "guerre ou paix"', *PD* 41/7 (July 1931), 320.

[79] Ibid. 318. See also 'Les Cartels de la paix' in *Nous voulons la paix*, 88–90. See also J. Prudhommeaux, 'Petite histoire des cartels de la paix', *PD* 42/4 (Apr. 1932), 179–82. For a more general analysis of the need in France for a unification of peace efforts, see Ernest Archdeacon, 'Pour l'unification des sociétés pacifistes', *PD* 41/7 (July 1931), 313–14.

[80] See Part III for comments on the trouble caused to local cartels by the machinations of local Amsterdam committees.

[81] 'Fabien France' was the pseudonym, according to Prudhommeaux, of a 'pacifiste très averti du mouvement d'idées contemporaines, collaborateur apprécié de la *Jeune République*'. See J. Prudhommeaux, 'La Grande Pitié du pacifisme français: Pour l'unité et la coordination des efforts', *PD* 45/10 (Oct. 1935), 391.

problems in the French national temperament which produced a splinter effect within the peace movement, there was also another difficulty. This was without doubt the politicization of the question of peace:

> . . . there exists an extreme right, a right, a centre, a left and an extreme left in pacifism. M. Herriot is a pacifist just as much as comrade André Marty, the anarchist Sébastien Faure, and the objector René Gerin. *Le Temps* (yes, indeed!) has the pretension of serving peace just as much as *Le Barrage*, but of serving it better. Hence the rivalries, the incompatibilities, the antagonisms of doctrines, or groups, or persons that make it most difficult to achieve the desired unity within the movement.[82]

Fabien France responded to Prudhommeaux's invitation to show the way forward to unity, by arguing that unity across the entire spectrum of French pacifism was impossible. Moreover, he believed, the diversity of tendencies need not be an obstacle. It was clearly impossible to group together in one society nationalists who were not genuinely interested in peace for its own sake, and on the other hand, the army of 'extremist pacifists, Tolstoyans, conscientious objectors, and anarchists of all sorts'.[83] He thought that French pacifism could do without people who wanted to preserve peace while preparing for war, and people who thought that individual or collective refusals to fight *any* war were sufficient. In France's view, there came a time when the divergence on methods signified, practically speaking, a divergence on principles.[84]

But that is to jump ahead a couple of years. The point, which ought to be clear, is that French pacifism by the onset of the thirties was experiencing a crisis of growth coupled with a crisis of confidence in the values it proclaimed. In the face of a worsening international situation, French pacifists began to arrive at increasingly radical answers to the problem of peace. Or at least, *some* did. For the old-style pacifists of the APD, the doctrine and methods remained the same, despite the temptations and hesitations of the years under discussion.

THE APD AND A DETERIORATING INTERNATIONAL SITUATION

The final assault on the world view of *pacifisme ancien style* was therefore the deteriorating international situation in the early

---

[82] Ibid. 393.   [83] Fabien France, ibid. 394.   [84] Ibid.

thirties. This situation can be reduced to three main events: the Sino-Japanese conflict in Manchuria and the apparent impotence of the League of Nations to resolve it; the general disappointment caused by the increasing failure of the Geneva Disarmament Conference to reach any substantial agreement on arms reductions; and finally, the rise of Nazism in Germany which riveted French eyes once again on events *outre-Rhin*.

Disarmament had always been an important plank in the APD's pacifist platform. Ruyssen saw success in disarmament as absolutely necessary if public opinion was to be convinced of the efficacy of the League of Nations. This disarmament would take three forms: moral, economic, and military. He believed that moral disarmament was making great progress. Economic disarmament was a slower process, but it would be realized soon that it was necessary because in it lay Europe's future. Military disarmament was the most difficult to achieve, because it was dependent on success in the other two areas, but Ruyssen believed that it, too, would see its hour come.[85] Paul Painlevé's new policy of rearmament in 1927 prompted the Comité directeur of the APD to ask bluntly in a public statement, 'Why these armaments?'[86]—especially at a time when Germany was finally beginning to accept the post-war world and had signed the Locarno accords. The Geneva Disarmament Conference disappointed pacifists because it was never able to reach beyond the concept of limitation to that of reduction of armaments. In April 1934 Ruyssen rather bitterly attacked its failure. He registered the sense of disappointment pacifists felt at the German walk-out in October 1933, but sharply criticized the French approach to the whole question of disarmament as well. Ruyssen wrote that France ought to be confident of its military superiority and that it could easily consent to sacrifices without putting its security at risk; the day that France brought to Geneva 'something other than a juridical dialectic and theoretical plans', it would restore the international confidence which was so lacking, and gain more through collective security than it might have lost in 'betting on the cause of peace'.[87]

---

[85] Théodore Ruyssen, 'Désarmement? Ou désarmements?', *PD* 39/12 (Dec. 1929), 441–2.

[86] Le Comité directeur de la Paix par le droit, 'Pourquoi ces armements?', *PD* 37/6 (June 1927), 185–7.

[87] Théodore Ruyssen, 'La Nouvelle Crise du désarmement', *PD* 44/4–5 (Apr.–May 1934), 186.

The APD cannot be accused of short-sightedness with regard to its analysis of the situation in Germany preceding the Nazi *Machter-greifung*. From at least 1930 onwards, the writers of the review were very much aware that something perhaps catastrophic was occurring in Germany, and after the Nazi seizure of power, they lost no time in denouncing the regime to their readers. Our interest is not here in a detailed analysis of the stages of the APD's *prise de conscience* with regard to Nazism, but merely to indicate that the association could not be accused of political naïveté with regard to Hitler.[88]

It is hardly surprising, given the length and breadth of some of the cracks in the edifice of old-style pacifism, that the APD should feel it necessary to institute an *enquête* on the crisis of pacifism. The review printed responses from a selected group of French pacifists whose views were thought to be fairly representative of the strands within the movement.[89]

Fascinating and varied as these responses are, our interest here must be limited to the development of this debate within the Association itself, and the decisions it came to with regard to its brand of pacifism. The issue of a crisis in pacifism was thoroughly debated at the APD's 1933 annual general meeting in Paris. This AGM was really a stock-taking on the part of the Association of its activities since the war in the face of a deteriorating national and international situation which caused everyone to ask whether pacifism had failed

---

[88] See Henri Simondet, 'Les Élections allemandes', *PD* 40/10 (Oct. 1930), 376–82; Henri Simondet, 'L'Allemagne dans le gâchis', *PD* 43/2 (Feb. 1933), 62–7; Wilfred Monod, 'L'Antisémitisme et la notion de race', *PD* 43/6 (June 1933), 198–200; Jules Prudhommeaux, 'Les Paroles et les actes', *PD* 43/6 (June 1933), 218–19 (about the divergence between Hitler's words of peace and the treatment being meted out to pacifists within Germany); Jules Prudhommeaux, 'Et si l'Allemagne résiste?—Les Sanctions économiques', *PD* 43/11 (Nov. 1933), 458–60 (in which Prudhommeaux envisaged the use of economic sanctions if Germany should refuse to rejoin the international community). Ruyssen can be forgiven for taking a view shared by many other people in late 1932, namely that the Nazi menace had reached the high tide mark in Germany and would now subside. See the account of Ruyssen's speech at the public meeting held during the Association's AGM in Pau at the beginning of Nov. 1932, in 'Notre Assemblée générale, Pau', 518–20.

[89] The responses to the *enquête* were published in *PD* 43/10–44/3 (Oct. 1933 –Mar. 1934). The following people submitted responses to the question of what was the definition, the mission, and the very programme of pacifism: C. Bouglé, Léon Brunschvicg, Max Hébert, Georges Michon, Ch. Braibant, Mgr. E. Beaupin, Thomas Barclay, Paul Passy, Georges Guy-Grand, Gaston Richard, Henri La Fontaine, Maxime Leroy, C.-G. Picavet, Charles Rousseau, M. Angles, Georges Hoog, André D. Tolédano, M. le pasteur Roser, Jacques Bois, Marcel Déat, M. le pasteur Jézequel, Roger Picard, and Charles Rist.

in its quest. Prudhommeaux's description of the meeting reads like a litany of woes delivered in what he called an 'atmosphere singularly charged with bad electricity'.[90] Wherever one looked the international situation offered nothing but irritation and disquiet. He enumerated the problems as follows: an inability on the part of nations, after the failure of the London Conference, to move beyond the most 'sterile and deceiving of dogmas, that of economic autarchy'; the 'visible decline of the League of Nations attacked not only in its prestige but in its very existence, through treasons and repeated desertions'; the impending failure of the Disarmament Conference which after two years of discussions 'goes from one prorogation to another in order to hide its impotence'; and finally, the repeated failures and defeats of democracy in a Europe which seemed to be 'three-quarters submerged by the rising tide of Fascism'.[91] The concept of 'peace through justice' seemed at once an old and a still very young slogan to Prudhommeaux. The worst of it all was that the international situation was reflected in extraordinary divisions in the pacifist camp at a time when unity was of paramount importance. Pacifists in France and around the world needed to form a common front against the enemy if they were to prevail. But, unfortunately, never had the 'dispersion of efforts been larger in the domain of practical action, and never more profound the divisions in that of doctrine'.[92]

Ruyssen presented the main report on the Crisis in Pacifism. He began by outlining the psychological reasons for pacifist confusion. Before the Great War, pacifist goals were modest and timid. The League had not yet been created. Pacifists fought war, according to Ruyssen, with a purely sentimental ideology and they had only one remedy to propose: voluntary arbitration laid down in purely bilateral pacts. Two experiences completely overturned the world of primordial pacifism: the first was the Great War and the second, flowing out of it, was the creation of the League of Nations. These two events lay at the heart of the present pacifist confusion according to Ruyssen:

From there the opposition which divides pacifists according to whether their thinking is dominated by the one or by the other of these two experiences.

---

[90] Jules Prudhommeaux, 'Rapport moral', in Jules Prudhommeaux, 'Notre Assemblée générale, Paris 30 et 31 décembre 1933', PD 44/2 (Feb. 1934), 53–8, also 49.   [91] Ibid. 49.   [92] Ibid.

For the first, it is the fact of the monstrous war which obsesses them, with its slaughter, its ruins, its abominations which renew every day for us the inexhaustible, ineluctable consequences. And thus, they feel rise in them a horror, a revolt, which obliges them to shout: 'Never again! Peace at any price!' The others, on the contrary, are attached to the League of Nations, to its promises and its acts. And thence yet another new division in peoples' minds: certain of our members, shocked by the impotence and the failures of the Geneva institution, denounce it as a dupery and look elsewhere—in a return to the state of things before the war or in the 'dictatorship of the proletariat'—for the solution to the problem. Others, the 'juridically' minded, seek to perfect, to complete, to reinforce the L.o.N., to draw out of it the super-state which will create Humanity.[93]

Ruyssen thought that there were three possible objections which could be made to the Association's device 'la paix par le droit'. The first was that there was an equivocation in the very definition of what *droit* stood for. This argument had been developed in Gaston Richard's response to the *enquête* and was one made by Alain (1868–1951).[94]

If you only admit of peace within justice or law, they say to us, you are throwing yourself outside reality, into a complete chimera. Because life is made of injustices . . . To correct these abuses, you will take the *beati possidentes* to task—and it will be war, generator of new injustices. When will this eternal flight from justice end? One speaks of the *right to love*, of the *right to happiness*. These are but aspirations, as chimerical as the absolute right of peoples to dispose of themselves. Understood thus, the right to peace is a ferment of revolt, of anarchy, and of war . . .[95]

Thus, for Ruyssen, one had to content oneself with a peace founded upon positive law, always changing, always imperfect, always referring back to rules, to codes, to a sort of unwritten law. There was nothing absolute or metaphysical about this law; it was in constant evolution. And it was necessary in this system of law to have more

[93] Théodore Ruyssen, 'La Crise du pacifisme', ibid. 62–3.
[94] Alain was the pseudonym of the philosopher Émile-Auguste Chartier. Alain was of the same generation as Théodore Ruyssen and Élie Halévy—the three shared the top honours in their class at the École normale supérieure. Alain was in many respects the philosopher of many of the strands of interwar French pacifism. On his role in the shaping of much of the interwar generation see especially Jean-François Sirinelli, 'Khâgneux et normaliens aux années vingt', thèse de doctorat d'état, Université de Paris-X, Nanterre, 1986, 5 vols. See also Sirinelli, *Génération intellectuelle: Khâgneux et normaliens dans l'entre-deux-guerres* (Paris: Fayard, 1988). See also David James Fisher, 'Alain', in Josephson, *Dictionary*, 8–10.
[95] Ruyssen, 'La Crise du pacifisme', 63.

than a judge. Sanctions were needed, in the first instance moral or economic sanctions, but in the final resort, force had to be there as a deterrent. 'This is', said Ruyssen, 'my totally realistic conception, in a still barbarous world, of peace through law.'[96]

There were two other approaches which could be taken. The first was conscientious objection which he said had been debated thoroughly enough at the Boulogne AGM. The APD's position was essentially that of the Ligue des droits de l'homme, namely that the conscience of the objector must be respected, but that conscientious objection as an organized movement was wrong and inefficacious in the struggle against war.[97]

The final approach was the generalized version of a politicized conscientious objection, namely collective non-resistance in the face of aggression, or essentially the Challaye–Emery case discussed above. Ruyssen's argument against this option was simply that the case for it was based purely on opportunistic calculations of the potential risks entailed by a modern war. Challaye and Emery had both fought in the last war apparently without any qualms. Ruyssen asked, therefore, whether one was not permitted to wonder if the risks of a modern war were not being exaggerated, and if so, at what level of destruction a war became unfightable. The advocates of non-resistance also made much of the difficulty of knowing who the aggressor was in a modern war, but Ruyssen responded that the League of Nations ought to be able to develop some competence in this area, and that nations ought to agree not to pursue any war beyond their own frontiers. But the clinching argument, in his mind, was that by disarming totally and announcing in advance that one would not fight, far from lessening aggression, one was actually encouraging it in a very fallen world.[98]

The debate was lively, to say the least. There seemed to be a general tendency at this AGM to blame the treaties of 1919 for all of the problems faced by Europe. Jeanne Mélin came right out and said that Hitler was the result of Versailles.[99] A.-M. Bloch, a *professeur agrégé de philosophie* at the Lycée Henri Poincaré in Nancy, argued that Ruyssen was too willing to accept the insufficiencies of 'positive law', and that what the Association must continue to do was proclaim the ideal or 'pure' state of law to which international relations might

[96] Ruyssen, 'La Crise du pacifisme', 64.   [97] Ibid.   [98] Ibid. 64–5.
[99] Cited in Jules Prudhommeaux, 'Notre Assemblée générale (suite)', 99.

attain. The hardline minority group was led by Jacques Bois, another *professeur agrégé de philosophie*, and René Valfort, who argued that it was a nonsense to try to achieve peace through law. Either peace was one's dominant concern, or else the law and justice were the primary values. One could not have it both ways. If justice were predominant in the mind of the APD, then logically one had to admit that the Association's device could easily become, in times of international tension, *la paix par la guerre* or *le droit par la guerre*. Bois argued in his brilliant, if a little sophistical, response to the *enquête* on the crisis of pacifism, that the only strictly logical approach for a pacifist was to believe in the achievement of *peace through peace*.[100]

In addition to the polarity which existed between Ruyssen and the holders of the old-style pacifism on the one hand, and the proponents of a more integral pacifism on the other, there was an intermediate position typified by Jules Prudhommeaux who argued that pacifists should lead the way towards the acceptance of the rule of the League of Nations in cases of international aggression. He proposed that the L.o.N. should constitute a sort of 'mutual assistance society' which by its international authority would pronounce on the rights and wrongs of international conflicts and organize an 'immediate chastisement' against any nation attacking another. He believed that this chastisement could very well consist of economic sanctions which if effectively and unanimously applied would bring any nation quickly to its knees.[101]

But as one member pointed out, Prudhommeaux's proposal did nothing to resolve the problem of how to respond to aggression in the *hic et nunc*. The organization he envisaged did not yet exist, or at least only in embryonic form. Georges Cadier remarked that Ruyssen's analysis was completely realistic, but that Prudhommeaux had his eyes turned towards the future and the ideal. And Ruyssen intervened to say that if he and Prudhommeaux appeared to be in opposition, they were in fact in agreement on essentials. It was only in their respective approaches to the present reality that they differed:

On fundamentals we are in agreement. But we approach the problem from different levels of reality. If the great problem of the organization of peace

---

[100] Ibid. 97–9; see also Jacques Bois, 'Enquête sur la crise du pacifisme, réponse de M. Jacques Bois', *PD* 44/2 (Feb. 1934), 74–7.

[101] Prudhommeaux, 'Notre Assemblée générale (suite)', 98–9.

were resolved, if there existed a universal League of Nations, controlling, in a completely disarmed world, a force which could impose itself on everybody, then, fine, the national defence would be useless. But M. Bloch has said it: the repugnance of the great nations for undertaking agreements of mutual assistance is the sad fact which must be taken into account. There are still—Japan is an example—governments of prey. Aggression is still possible, that is the present; the league of nations, super-state, obeyed by all, that is the future . . .[102]

A composite resolution was hammered out which took into account A.-M. Bloch's arguments about the need to bring existing 'positive' law more into line with the Association's vision of an 'ideal' law. The resolution was divided into three sections. The first proclaimed that the Association remained true to its device and its traditional programme. By 'Droit', it understood the 'ensemble of positive international institutions, analogous to those which assure a relative order within states', comprising (1) 'precise rules governing the relations between states', (2) 'appropriate procedures for the handling without exception of international differences', and (3) 'an international system of sanctions capable of quelling any attempt made by a state to pursue its national policies by force'.[103]

The second section underlined the Association's view of the world and the style of pacifism appropriate to it. Far from considering the present system of international law as the definitive expression of the 'needs of human society', the Association recognized that above the present positive law, there existed an ideal state of international law which had yet to be achieved. More particularly, it recognized that the treaties of 1919 were not intangible and that a revision of certain articles thereof was necessary. It believed furthermore that the League of Nations was a partial realization of the state of ideal law, and it remained resolved to seek its further development and improvement. It noted that the League had been greatly weakened by the failure to resolve the crisis in the Far East, by the indefinite adjournment of the disarmament idea, by the withdrawal of Japan and Germany, and that as a result it found itself in 1933 in a weakened position incapable of guaranteeing respect for law in the world. As a consequence of this it was only natural that the peoples would continue to seek their salvation elsewhere. The continuing inequality in national armaments nevertheless created a system in

[102] Prudhommeaux, 'Notre Assemblée générale (suite)', 99–101.
[103] Ibid. 107.

which no state could be sure of its security. This led states to seek security in offensive alliances and in an arms race which could lead directly to war. The Association saw no possible solution for law or for peace outside a revivified and widened League of Nations, a League which would be capable of constituting a genuine 'mutual Protection Society against War' for its members. For this to be possible, not only moral and economic sanctions, but also an international police force would have to be instituted.[104]

Finally, in a third section, the Association declared that while it was the duty of all pacifists to hasten the glad day when the international regime described above would become reality, in the interim it was necessary to support the idea of the national defence, despite the insufficiences and perils it enshrined, because it 'constituted in a world still subjected to the evil forces of the past, a vital necessity, carrying with it for all citizens the exercise of their duty of national solidarity'.[105]

The first section of the resolution was passed unanimously minus one vote. The second and third sections were passed by eighty-four votes to eight, although as Prudhommeaux took pains to remark in his account of the Assembly, the vote was taken purely as an indication of feeling within the Association and was without binding value.[106]

Thus ended the pivotal period of 1928 to 1933 for the APD. It had faced and dealt with the challenges posed to its conception of the world and the pacifist's place in it by reaffirming in its essentials the doctrine it had nearly always held. There was dissent—of varying degrees—within the Association but in terms of its outward programme little had changed. It had encountered, examined, and rejected conscientious objection as an acceptable method for pacifism, while at the same time demanding the recognition of the rights of conscience of individual objectors. In this it followed the same course as the Ligue des droits de l'homme. Closely allied to the problem of objection, but quite distinct in the APD's mind, was the question of integral pacifism. This was rejected outright as a position likely to lead to war rather than prevent it. In the face of an increasingly splintered, balkanized French peace movement, the APD continued to believe strongly in the necessity of union, but it came to see in the period under discussion that differences in method

<hr/>

[104] Ibid. 107–8.   [105] Ibid. 108.   [106] Ibid. 106.

between the various strands of French pacifism necessarily precluded such an arrangement. As will become clear in the next chapter, even within the confines of old-style pacifism, of the pacifism which saw as its reason for existence the support of the League of Nations, there was hesitancy and finally refusal on the part of the APD to consider outright union with other like-minded groups. But more importantly, the period 1928–33 marked the parting of the ways between the old approach to the problem of peace and the integral pacifism which was creating for itself both a doctrine and a programme in those years. Finally, the period under discussion in this chapter clearly shows the impact the worsening international situation had upon the pacifist optimism of the twenties. The post-Versailles world was breathing its last, French hegemony in Europe had passed, and the spectre of Nazi-inspired *revanchisme* across the Rhine was beginning to produce a certain degree of *Angst* in France. We turn now to an examination of the impact of the rise of pessimism on the pacifism of the APD in the period from 1933 to 1938.

4. The Rise of Pessimism (1933–1938)

The changing perceptions and values within the peace movement in the interwar period were in the final analysis more than anything else a reaction to the Nazi seizure of power which represented a sea-change of such proportions that after 1933 it was no longer possible to discuss European politics in the same manner as before. The arrival of Hitler in the German *Reichskanzlei* is thus an event of conspicuous importance to a study of French pacifism. It changed the nature of the Franco-German political debate and in so doing it fundamentally altered the content and boundaries of the pacifist response to that debate. The representatives of the old-style pacifism were much quicker to realize the importance of the Nazi seizure of power and to adjust to it accordingly than were the proponents of new-style pacifism, as we shall see in Part II. This is not to say that they immediately understood the Nazi menace. They did not. But their political *prise de conscience* in the post-1933 world of international politics was much quicker than that of some other pacifists. This was undoubtedly a function of the APD's fervent attachment to the cause of justice. The Association, much like the Ligue internationale des femmes pour la paix et la liberté, was a bicephalous entity. If, during the twenties, this attachment to justice produced a narrowness of spirit and a certain rigidity of approach to the problem of peace, it became in the thirties a source of strength and insight when faced with the dubious proclamations of peace proffered by the Nazis. Running parallel to this clear-sightedness, however, was a tendency for some members of the APD wittingly or unwittingly to allow Fascist Italy and Nazi Germany to set the tone of the political agenda in Europe for the latter half of the interwar period.

It would be useful to begin this chapter by examining briefly the reaction of the APD to the Nazi seizure of power and the changing evaluation of what Nazism meant for the peace of Europe up until about 1938. It is clear that Ruyssen especially recognized the dangers posed by Hitler very early on, although equally there seemed to be surprise that he had been successful in his bid for power. In his first comment on the *Machtergreifung*, Ruyssen set the tone for much of his future commentary by arguing for a cautious, careful, but far from pessimistic approach to the new Germany. He believed war to be possible, but not probable given the general economic distress then reigning and the still-fresh memories of the last war on both sides of the Rhine. But equally, it was clear that the peace was in danger. The rise of Nazism was largely a function of what Ruyssen now recognized to be the negative aspects of the treaties of 1919 'which have imposed on the vanquished bad borders', together with the economic crisis and the weakness of the democracies.[1] He remained convinced of the need for Franco-German reconciliation as 'the essential condition of the pacification of Europe'.[2] It had to be frankly admitted, however, that conciliatory gestures from across the Rhine were few and far between. One could not be a pacifist alone. Peace was a communal effort, and if the desire for peace were not reciprocated across the Rhine then that left the peace-loving countries two alternatives: a war of defence or else peace in servitude. 'Choose who dares!', he said.[3] What was needed was a pacifist sang-froid in the face of the challenges of Fascism and Nazism. He believed that general and simultaneous disarmament should continue to figure on the pacifist platform but it could never be a question of unilateral disarmament. Above all, the League of Nations needed to be supported and strengthened.[4]

A couple of months later, Ruyssen addressed the issue of whether Hitler could be taken at his word. In his speech to the Reichstag on 17 May 1933 Hitler had made the usual attacks on the Versailles Treaty but had also made some conciliatory statements designed for public consumption outside Germany—assurances that war was unthinkable. Ruyssen thought there were the best reasons in the world to doubt Hitler's sincerity given that, but four days previously, von Papen had revealed to the world that the word 'pacifism' had been

---

[1] Thédore Ruyssen, 'Veillons!', *PD* 43/3 (Mar. 1933), 94.
[2] Ibid. 95.   [3] Ibid. 95–6.   [4] Ibid. 94–5.

struck from the German vocabulary. German pacifists were either in prison or else in exile abroad. Thus, for Ruyssen, the olive branch extended by Hitler had to be treated with the utmost caution. It was no longer good enough to maintain that there were two Germanies —one peaceful and the other bellicose. The most that could be said was that within the newly united National Socialist version of Germany, there were two competing tendencies. He thought he saw the tempering hand of the Wilhelmstraße behind Hitler's speech and that was a good omen. In answer to his question, 'where are we going then?', he replied that 'that all depends on the solidity of the moral front which Germany, to its great surprise, has just re-established against herself',[5] and he put his faith in the Disarmament Conference.

The APD certainly did not lack for warnings about the situation in Germany from German pacifists. Hellmut von Gerlach, writing in the June 1933 number of the *PD*, discussed the idea of a preventive war against Hitler which some 'pacifists' apparently were advocating. Von Gerlach rejected such a notion categorically as against the pacifist ideal. He underlined that Hitlerism was a danger to peace, 'but it is not a guaranteed war; this must be the line taken by all pacifists'.[6] That said, he warned French pacifists about the dangers posed by weak thinking in opposing Hitler. 'He who preaches the doctrine of Tolstoy today in a country like France would assume a terrible responsibility; to apply it to a Hitler would be an invitation to the use of force.'[7]

There was a fine line separating calls for Franco-German *rapprochement* with the eyes wide open, and the calls of some pacifists for a *rapprochement* with Nazi Germany *malgré tout*. Ruyssen exemplified the former position with his early insight into the nature of Nazism and his continued hope in a peaceful future for Europe, contained within the parameters of a cautious *modus vivendi* with the Third Reich. The latter position, however, was typified by Régis de Vibraye at the Association's 1933 AGM. De Vibraye presented a report entitled 'Is an *entente* with Germany impossible?',[8] which by virtue of its political myopia seemed to open

[5] Théodore Ruyssen, 'Où allons-nous?', *PD* 43/6 (June 1933), 194.

[6] Hellmut von Gerlach, 'Guerre préventive?', *PD* 43/6 (June 1933), 197.

[7] Ibid.

[8] Report and discussion in Jules Prudhommeaux, 'Notre Assemblée générale (suite)', *PD* 44/3 (Mar. 1934), 110–17.

the way to the collaborationism of Vichy. De Vibraye was too willing by far to exculpate Hitler, to the point of claiming that *Mein Kampf* was an aberration of youth, written in the heat of the Ruhr crisis.[9] He warned against accepting the 'unintelligent' and 'nefarious' policies proposed by German *émigrés*. He qualified Blum's desire to put Germany in quarantine as 'dangerous', and viewed the threat of German expansionism in Eastern Europe with equanimity. France, and not Germany, according to de Vibraye, had become the anomaly in Europe with its rotten parliamentary institutions. As far as a potential Anschluss with Austria was concerned, de Vibraye declared that if 'the Anschluss occurred with our participation, it would consolidate the peace. Let us be arbitrators and not adversaries.'[10] Small comfort for democratic Austrians.

Von Gerlach attacked de Vibraye's naïveté and declared that he could not share his views on Hitler's sincerity. In his view, it was clear that Hitler spoke two messages: one for internal German consumption, and the other for the listening world outside Germany's borders. Between Nazi Germany and democratic France there existed a 'redoubtable moral antagonism'.[11] Wolfgang Hallgarten, another German present at the AGM, took a much softer view, arguing that Hitler should be given time to evolve in the more anodyne direction of a Mussolini. All dictators want to retain power, and in his view this meant that Hitler would gradually become more amenable.[12] De Vibraye finished the debate by calling for France to put 'her reason, her logic, her experience of revolutions' to the service of Hitlerian Germany, and thus work, 'without dangerous illusion but also without a discouraged pessimism, towards a Franco-German *rapprochement*'.[13]

There are other examples of this multiplicity of attitudes towards the conditions of Franco-German *rapprochement* within the APD. They make clear that for some pacifists the betterment of relations between France and Germany had become an end in itself, devoid of moral and political content. Hélène Lhoumeau, the daughter of Pastor Lhoumeau, the president of the Poitou federation of the Association, wrote in a letter published in the review that after a prolonged period spent abroad working as an official of the League of Nations, she had the impression on her return to France that the

---

[9] Prudhommeaux, 'Notre Assemblée générale (suite)', 117.   [10] Ibid. 111, 113–14.
[11] Ibid. 116.   [12] Ibid. 117.   [13] Ibid.

pacifist movement had been 'chloroformed' and 'emptied . . . of all dynamic force'.[14] The bottom line was Franco-German *rapprochement* and she believed that it was founded upon a misunderstanding. Instead of trying to understand Germany as it was, France was trying to impose upon it a democratic face which conformed to its own conceptions. She believed, on the contrary, that if a *rapprochement* with Germany was desired (and she certainly desired it), then it would have to be with Hitlerian Germany, and not with an exiled minority.[15]

But German voices continued to be raised against the idea that a *rapprochement* on Germany's terms was possible or desirable. Friedrich Wilhelm Foerster (1869–1966),[16] the veteran German pacifist, pleaded in a 1935 article published by the review for a 'pacifism without illusions'.[17] Foerster warned the French of the dangers they faced in Nazi Germany, predicting with amazing prescience the return of the Polish territories to Germany, the Anschluss, the dismemberment of Czechoslovakia, the colonization and penetration of Russia, and finally the consolidation of an Eastern Bloc which would turn against the West.[18] If some of the points of this prophecy were never fulfilled it was surely only providential. Foerster's prescriptions for pacifist action were threefold; first, stop any thought of treaty revision; secondly, it had to be demonstrated that the Corridor and the other limitations placed upon the German borders by Versailles were just and necessary and designed to repair historical damage from earlier wars; and thirdly, with regard to disarmament, Foerster said that it was an outright lie to say that Germany was

[14] Hélène Lhoumeau, 'Lettre à M. Ch. Rousseau à propos de "l'Allemagne contre le droit"', *PD* 44/1 (Jan. 1934), 18.

[15] Ibid. 19.

[16] Friedrich Wilhelm Foerster was one of the most important figures in German pacifism. He was variously professor of philosophy, sociology, ethics, and moral pedagogy at the Universities of Zurich, Vienna, and Munich, and the author of many books. During the Great War he was a strong supporter of Wilsonian internationalism. After 1922 he lived permanently in Switzerland, never setting foot in Germany again after being warned by friends that the same fate as that of Walther Rathenau awaited him. Foerster collaborated in the publication of *Das andere Deutschland* and in 1926 published a pamphlet denouncing Germany's secret rearmament programme. See Hans Kühner-Wolfskehl, 'Friedrich Wilhelm Foerster', in Harold Josephson (ed.), *Biographical Dictionary of Modern Peace Leaders* (Westport, London: Greenwood Press, 1985), 284–7.

[17] F. W. Foerster, 'Avertissements d'un pacifiste allemand: Pour un pacifisme sans illusions', *PD* 45/1 (Jan. 1935), 4–14.

[18] Ibid. 6.

disarmed—the Allied powers needed to seek some clarifications from Germany and pursue an energetic policy.[19]

There was thus much debate within the APD about the proper course to take in dealing with Nazi Germany. On the one hand was the Ruyssen camp which seemed to exhibit remarkably clear-sighted opinions on the nature of Nazism, and on the other hand were the occasional writers, perhaps representing a minority view within the Association, who continued to press for a more indulgent approach to the new Germany. It is instructive to consider just how much the entire commentary of the APD in these years—from both tendencies within it—was in fact determined by the pronouncements of Nazi Germany, or, to a lesser extent, Fascist Italy.[20] One has very much the impression that the pacifist camp, and other elements of French political society as well, had been reduced to the underdog role of reacting to events across the Rhine rather than determining them.

A further example of this is the way in which Fascist claims of the need for more living space, more markets, more primary materials, and so on became part and parcel of the pacifist debate within the APD at the time of the build-up to the Ethiopian War. For example, at the 1935 AGM, two well-meaning reports were presented, one on the division of primary materials in the world, and the second on the problem of overpopulation in certain countries. In both cases Italy was cited as a prime example of a country which was relatively overpopulated and had access to very limited supplies of primary

---

[19] Foerster, 'Avertissements d'un pacifiste allemand', 9–13. Foerster's thesis and conclusions were attacked by Louis François in 'Une entente franco-allemande est-elle donc impossible?', PD 45/3 (Mar. 1935), 139–43 and 'Suite', in PD 45/4 (Apr. 1935), 195–204. François's argument was basically that Foerster's thesis led straight to war, and that if a *rapprochement* with Fascist Italy was possible then why not with Nazi Germany? Moreover, many of the 'revisions' which Foerster said that the Nazis wanted to see in the Europe created at Versailles had been on the cards anyway under the Weimar democrats. He noted the strange conjunction of thought which brought together a German pacifist and the French nationalists. The tone of the article was distinctly lowered by the reversion to the old conspiracy theory: François saw occult links between Blum, the Socialists, Jewish finance, and the arms manufacturers. He concluded that there was no reason in the world why France should not negotiate with Germany.

[20] Maurice Vaïsse has commented recently on the extent to which Nazi propaganda was able to set the tone of the pacifist debate in France: 'Prenant appui sur le pacifisme ambiant, la propagande nazie a réussi à s'insinuer dans de nombreux secteurs de la société française et a développé avec éfficacité une action de neutralisation psychologique, endormant la vigilance des Français et affaiblissant leur volonté de réagir.' Maurice Vaïsse, 'Le Pacifisme français dans les années trente', Relations internationales, 53 (spring 1988), 37–52.

materials.[21] None of the statements made, nor for that matter the conclusions reached, can be reproached in the slightest for illiberality or obvious Fascist content, but it is surely not coincidental that in a year in which Germany was beginning to flex its muscle, and, more importantly, Italy was beginning to embroil itself in Ethiopia for *precisely* the issues raised in these two reports, the Association should have chosen to discuss them at its annual Congress. In a completely unconscious way, the Association's political agenda was being subtly set by forces well outside, and antithetical to, the pacifist camp.

Even someone as astute as Ruyssen, however, could be misled by the Nazi propaganda machine. Certainly up until 1935 or 1936, the APD's analysis of Nazism tended to oscillate from rejection of what Hitler said, to scepticism, through to acceptance. No doubt the desire for peace was so strong that it conditioned to some extent the response old-style pacifism made to German peace overtures. In late November 1933, Prudhommeaux could write rather contemptuously of Hitler's *pacifisme oratoire*, taking a sceptical attitude towards his sincerity but arguing at the same time that France should take Hitler at his word and see how far meaningful discussions could actually proceed.[22] In 1935, to give some measure of the oscillation which beset the APD in these first years of the Third Reich, Ruyssen responded quite warmly to Hitler's speech to the Reichstag of 21 May, declaring that it was a 'categorical affirmation of peace'.[23] He took a similar line at the time of the Saar plebiscite. He was disappointed that the vote went in favour of Germany, but declared that it had to be respected. Other problems remained to be sorted out with the Hitler government—the disarmament problem, Austria, Poland, and so on—but Ruyssen saw in Hitler's speech after the plebiscite results became known a 'precious element of appeasement': 'There is no longer, the Führer affirms, any territorial dispute

---

[21] See the report by M. Maurette, Directeur-adjoint du Bureau international du travail, on 'La Répartition des matières premières', and that by Francis Delaisi on 'Le Problème des populations en surnombre', in J. Lahargue, 'Le Congrès de Marseille de la Paix par le droit (suite et fin), 28–29 décembre 1935', *PD* 46/4 (Apr. 1936), 170–5.

[22] Jules Prudhommeaux, 'Le Pacifisme oratoire d'Hitler et Cie', *PD* 43/11 (Nov. 1933), 455–8.

[23] Théodore Ruyssen, 'Le Discours du Fuehrer', *PD* 45/5–6 (May–June 1935), 244–9. Cf. Lida Gustava Heymann's letter to Félicien Challaye criticizing his attitude to this speech in BDIC/DD/FΔ Rés. 208/16, LGH to Félicien Challaye, Zurich, 11 June 1935.

between France and Germany; let us take note of that and let us not reject the hand of friendship.'[24]

A. Bloch, the vice-president of the Lorraine group of the APD, wrote an article in 1934 in which he argued that in the world as it was, pacifists would be obliged to work with men who despised and hated the very ideas they stood for. The interwar years had been ones of mistakes: Versailles, the failure to disarm when the opportunity was there in the twenties, and the failure to negotiate more agreements with Weimar Germany, all of which now left France in the position of having to treat with Hitler. It was mortal folly to think that this could be done with one's eyes closed, using the ideas of Tolstoyan pacifism. He expressed the desire that

> our friends in the minority, our brothers in the ideal, might leave their dream world and rally around us on the basis of our resolution of last December: that of a vigorously non-conformist and revisionist pacifism, energetically set against the injustices, the hypocrisies of the treaties, but no less resolved to resist all attempts at violence, that is to say of injustice, for violence is unjust in its very principle.[25]

This seems to embody the central point in the APD's response to early Nazism: the necessity of negotiating and working with the Nazi regime in good faith, but without any illusions or false ideas about the sincerity of its statements.

The desire to believe Hitler's words was gradually shattered by his actions. The events of the thirties, far more than the pacific platitudes of Hitler, caused the scales to fall from pacifist eyes. The three crucial events up until 1938 were undoubtedly the remilitarization of the Rhineland which spelled the end of post-Versailles Locarno Europe, the Abyssinian War which brought international Fascism aggressively out of the closet, and finally, the trauma of the Spanish Civil War which became a trial of conscience for many pacifists everywhere.

The growing sense of an impending conflict in Ethiopia preoccupied the APD in mid-1935. The review published a number of articles and appeals in connection with what was occurring in Africa. Charles Rousseau, in an article examining the juridical side of the conflict, concluded that Italy had no business whatsoever in Ethiopia on the basis of the tripartite agreement of 13 December 1906, the

[24] Théodore Ruyssen, 'La Sarre a voté', *PD* 45/1 (Jan. 1935), 1–2.
[25] A. Bloch, 'Le Pacifisme a-t-il fait faillite?', *PD* 44/3 (Mar. 1934), 134.

bilateral Italo-Abyssinian friendship treaty of 2 August 1928, and more to the point on the basis of the League Covenant and the Kellogg–Briand Pact of which both nations were signatories.[26] The executive committee of the Association, in a meeting on 21 July, transmitted to Émile Borel, the president of the Fédération française des associations pour la Société des nations, a resolution on the nascent conflict in which it recommended financial, economic, and, if need be, military sanctions against Italy.[27] Likewise, at the end of August, Ruyssen in his capacity as president of the Association sent a message to the Conference for the Defence of the Ethiopian People held in Paris on 3 September. He underlined that the APD gladly associated itself with the efforts of other groups to defend Ethiopian independence against Italian aggression. The Association 'categorically condemned the attack against the system of collective security and the League of Nations' by the actions of a member state against another member state before any peaceful means had been sought to resolve the conflict.[28] But as another indication of how Fascist demands cloaked under the guise of imperialist equity were being allowed to set the agenda for the APD, Ruyssen then went on to weaken his argument by stating that the juridical aspect of the problem was only one side of it. The other aspect which had to be considered was Italy's need for more living room and access to more raw materials and markets for its industry. Thus, while 'categorically' condemning the Italian position, Ruyssen had in a sense justified it. He recommended that the League explore ways of extending the mandate system 'to all territories in which the population is not yet in a state to administer itself according to the principles of civilization'.[29] Similar sentiments were contained in a letter addressed to Pierre Laval on behalf of the Association by Ruyssen and Prudhommeaux on 3 September.[30]

In October 1935 the APD published the text of an appeal to the

---

[26] Ch. Rousseau, 'Les Données juridiques du conflit italo-éthiopien', *PD* 45/9 (Sept. 1935), 349–57. Cf. Ch. Rousseau and Jules Prudhommeaux, 'Le Conflit italo-éthiopien', *PD* 45/7–8 (July–Aug. 1935), 307–13.

[27] 'Projet de résolution soumis par le comité exécutif de "La Paix par le droit" à la "Fédération française des associations pour la SDN"', *PD* 45/9 (Sept. 1935), 338–9.

[28] 'Message à la Conférence tenue à Paris le 3 septembre 1935 pour la défense du peuple éthiopien', *PD* 45/9 (Sept. 1935), 339–40.

[29] Ibid. 340.

[30] 'Lettre à M. Pierre Laval, président du Conseil, ministre des Affaires étrangères', *PD* 45/9 (Sept. 1935), 340–1.

French people by the British League of Nations Union in favour of a common front and collective action against Italian aggression in Ethiopia. A French umbrella group, the Comité d'action pour la SDN, responded with a similar text underlining that it was happy to see the British finally won over to the collective security argument which France had been propounding for years.[31] The APD welcomed the British initiative whole-heartedly, but emphasized the dangers for France if it should refuse to go along with the British proposals. France was 'at the crossroads'; if it failed 'at this truly crucial hour' to take its part in the task of 'communal salvation' being proposed by the British, then it was probable that in the more or less immediate future it would be witness to a 'withdrawal of English policy which would have the most serious consequences'.[32]

When war finally did break out, the APD was pleased to see that the sanctions mechanism of the League appeared, at least initially, to work rather well. What was of most concern, however, was the effect the crisis had had on the *Entente Cordiale*. The British government had seen its position in Africa supported at best only lukewarmly by the French, whom Rousseau reproached for having done what Stresemann had been accused of doing in the past: '*on a finassé*'.[33] The British had asked for naval support in the Mediterranean, and the French had replied by demanding assurances of support in a future potential conflict with Germany over Austria or Czechoslovakia. This only displaced the problem and irritated the British without resolving it. Rousseau warned that the two essential planks of French foreign policy, the *Entente Cordiale* and the League of Nations, were in danger of being lost in the Ethiopian affair.[34] In a retrospective look at the crisis Georges Scelle concurred with this analysis and condemned the Laval government for reneging on the policies of collective security pursued by France for fifteen years at the very moment when Britain seemed to have come round to a

---

[31] Both texts are contained in La Paix par le droit, 'Un appel à l'opinion française: Que fera la France?', *PD* 45/10 (Oct. 1935), 386–90. The French were happy to see the British finally accepting the collective security argument. It will be remembered that Pierre Cot had underlined this as one of the fundamental differences between the French and the British conceptions of the organization of peace. See Pierre Cot, 'La Conception française de la lutte contre la guerre', *PD* 39/4–5 (Apr.–May 1929), 164–70.   [32] 'Un appel', 389.
[33] Ch. Rousseau, 'L'Agression italienne et les sanctions', *PD* 45/11–12 (Nov.–Dec. 1935), 451.
[34] Ibid. 452.

French view of this issue.[35] France's moral position as one of 'fidelity to the defence of Justice' had been lost: 'Henceforth, it is understood in Geneva that France, in defending for fifteen years the thesis of collective security, has been thinking only of saving herself against the renascent and dreaded power of Germany.'[36]

What is interesting in all of these analyses of the Ethiopian conflict is precisely the straightforward response to Italian aggression by the writers of the APD. In an earlier time, this insistence on 'justice' and the necessity of defending it, if necessary by arms, would have been the province of the right, and hardly of a 'pacifist' journal of largely Radical inspiration. But times had changed and with them the norms of political behaviour. Rousseau noted the confusion the Ethiopian conflict had caused in the French nationalist camp, where it had been expected that the aggressor to be faced in the thirties would be Germany. *Candide* had asked, 'Do you want to die for the Negus?' But as Rousseau pointed out, Frenchmen had not been asked in 1914 if they wanted to die for Sarajevo, and it was now becoming questionable what the attitude of the right would be if asked to die (potentially) for Memel or Austrian independence tomorrow.[37]

The Ethiopian conflict was the subject of a report and resolution presented by Georges Scelle to the Association's Marseille Congress in late December 1935. Scelle argued for the rigorous application of the Covenant and the defence of justice, which coincided exactly with France's interests in his view.[38] He declared that the situation far surpassed the confines of a purely Italo-Ethiopian conflict; the complete 'organization of peace was in danger'.[39] The 200-odd persons present at the Congress agreed with his analysis. A resolution, 'voted by acclamations', expressed the Congress's alarm at the confusion in French public opinion on the Ethiopian War, and went on to demand the firm application of the League Covenant in order that other nations considering aggression might be deterred therefrom.[40]

The remilitarization of the Rhineland, and the abrogation of the Locarno accords which it spelled, brought the growing threat of expansionist international Fascism closer to home for most

---

[35] Georges Scelle, 'Retrospective', *PD* 46/1 (Jan. 1936), 23–31.   [36] Ibid. 25.
[37] Rousseau, 'L'Agression italienne', 452.
[38] Scelle cited in J. Lahargue, 'Le Congrès de Marseille de la Paix par le droit, 28–29 décembre 1935', *PD* 46/3 (Mar. 1936), 114–16.
[39] Ibid. 115.   [40] Ibid. 116.

Frenchmen. It came at a time of deepening ambiguity in the attitude of the French right to Hitler, which provided, in Ruyssen's view, a strange counterpoise to the 'reservations and scepticism' of the 'so-called left-wing papers which for so long regarded Franco-German *rapprochement* as the surest means of guaranteeing the security of France against the perilous uncertainties of the present'.[41] Ruyssen noted this growing right-wing equivocation in the interview accorded by Hitler to Bertrand de Jouvenel and published in *Paris-midi* on 27 February. The de Jouvenel interview was remarkable not for what Hitler said, but for the questions which de Jouvenel left unasked and hence unanswered.[42] Ruyssen presciently predicted that on one issue, the future status of the west bank of the Rhine, the Nazis would soon move. They did, even as Ruyssen was writing his article.

Ruyssen condemned the remilitarization of the Rhineland as completely against international law and as the first step leading to war, in the East if not in the West. He saw clearly that Hitler was trying to neutralize the help France could give to the USSR and its other allies in Eastern Europe, 'in a word, take as many guarantees as possible for the success of the next war, to which the Reich is here and now resolved'.[43] It would, of course, also facilitate greatly the Anschluss of Austria. What to do? Simply take Germany at its word and demand that as a proof of its oft-trumpeted desire for peace, it withdraw its troops from the Rhine and then negotiate in good faith a solution to all of the outstanding treaty problems. And if Germany should refuse this proposal, Ruyssen advocated not instituting a system of sanctions against it which would almost surely lead to war, but rather watching Germany's every gesture and refusing to have the slightest meaningful diplomatic contact with it. The problem was, as Ruyssen now realized, that Hitlerian Germany no longer had the same concept of international law as the rest of the world. For it the only valid law was now national law, and that emanated not from evolving juridical concepts, but rather from the person of the Führer himself. He realized that on this basis it had become impossible to have meaningful conversations with the German government

---

[41] Théodore Ruyssen, 'Le Double Visage de la politique allemande', *PD* 46/3 (Mar. 1936), 135.
[42] Cf. Zeev Sternhell's comments about the importance of this interview in Zeev Sternhell, *Ni droite, ni gauche: L'Idéologie fasciste en France* (Paris: Éditions du seuil, 1983), 11.   [43] Ruyssen, 'Le Double Visage', 140.

because the two systems of legal thought now represented completely distinct and non-interlocking sets.[44] Ruyssen's conclusions about what to do in response to the Rhineland crisis were simply the following:

Neither repression, nor concessions; let us avoid war, but let us not offer to a partner from whom everything separates us the guarantees of a negotiated peace; no economic blockade, which would only cause the innocent to suffer, but a sort of moral quarantine, that it would be most profitable to organize within the framework of the League of Nations—the reaction of nations resolved to maintain the peace against any positive aggression by Hitlerian Germany.[45]

Prudhommeaux once again took a much softer line than Ruyssen. He 'begged' the French government not to take an irreparable step, and he called on Britain to make its voice of moderation heard. Clearly for Prudhommeaux, the time to stop negotiating with Hitler had not yet come. He admitted that there was much in the Nazi system that was repulsive but he urged an examination of the German position to see what constructive policies for general European peace might emerge from it.[46]

Charles Rousseau, too, rejected the arguments of some parts of public opinion and of some pacifists that Hitler was after all merely demanding equality for Germany in the international sphere. This was a very simplistic and therefore very dangerous view of the situation. He asked rhetorically whether 'the existence of a demilitarized zone has therefore become a dishonour'.[47] Like Ruyssen, Rousseau centred the problem on the completely different conception of international law held by the Nazis. Locarno had been a glimmer of hope in the regulation of European affairs, but now he foresaw Nazi aggression in the East as a result of its abrogation. The blame for the Rhineland disaster had to be laid at the feet of the French nationalists who were complaining now about the lukewarm British reaction, while only six months previously they had been unwilling to support British action in Ethiopia. The man in the street was incapable of an

---

[44] Ibid. 141–2.
[45] Ibid. 142.
[46] Jules Prudhommeaux, 'France et Allemagne: Le Péril', *PD* 46/3 (Mar. 1936), 143–5.
[47] Charles Rousseau, 'La Dénonciation des Traités de Locarno devant le droit international', *PD* 46/4 (Apr. 1936), 196.

objective view of the situation and completely uninterested in collective security, and the government did not have the courage or the intelligence to seek to convince him otherwise.[48] He underlined, too, the differences between the Hitlerian and Genevan conceptions of peace. The former put the 'vital rights' of the German people above everything, and Rousseau found it difficult to see how these could be reconciled with the ideas of the League of Nations. He concluded by reiterating his belief that peace and justice must be linked: '. . . despite the fact that one French journalist has gone so far as to write that peace takes precedence over justice,[49] we believe that to refuse today to base peace upon the force of law is to resign oneself tomorrow to suffering a peace imposed by the law of force'.[50]

The rise of pessimism was capped in 1936 by the outbreak of the Spanish Civil War. The first comment in the review came from the pen of Charles Rousseau who argued in the early autumn of 1936 for strict non-intervention and neutrality in the Spanish conflict. 'In this powder-keg which is the Europe of 1936', he wrote, 'the hour has not come for proselytism but for prudence.'[51] The desire of some extreme left-wing circles and indeed of some 'pacifists' for intervention in Spain had created an 'intervention mystique'.[52] In his view the overriding concern had to be that the general European situation was highly inflammable, no matter what one's feelings were for the Popular Front or the fears one might have at the thought of a third Fascist state on France's borders. The only sane policy was strict non-intervention and he reminded Frenchmen that the war of 1870 had also begun in Spain.[53]

There is no doubting where the APD's sympathies lay in the Spanish Civil War. For the good republicans of the Association the Spanish dilemma was nothing short of tragic, but the general consensus seemed to be that Spain was not worth fighting for, that the ostensibly civil nature of the conflict had to be respected, and that, above all else, Spain's trauma must be prevented from becoming a generalized European conflict. The latter point especially was the essential concern. Very early on, however, the writers of the review

---

[48] Rousseau, 'La Dénonciation', 197.
[49] Henri Jeanson, 'La Paix prime le droit', *La Flèche*, 21 Mar. 1936, cited ibid. 198.
[50] Rousseau, 'La Dénonciation', 198.
[51] Charles Rousseau, 'Les Événements d'Espagne', *PD* 46/8–9 (Aug.–Sept. 1936), 355.   [52] Ibid. 357.   [53] Ibid. 358.

knew full well that the democracies' attempts at non-intervention were being made a mockery of by the Axis powers. Even in Rousseau's early article cited above, fears were voiced at the 'one-way abstention' in the provision of arms to the combatants.[54] There was thus no illusion about the possibility of isolating the Spanish conflict from the rest of European society. The decision that had to be taken was whether or not to support the Spanish government knowing that it might lead to an escalation of the conflict. This the APD decided it could not do.

The Association debated the Spanish question at its Congress held in Clermont-Ferrand in late December 1936. Henri Guernut, honorary secretary-general of the Ligue des droits de l'homme presented a report and resolution on Spain, which was supplemented by two further resolutions from Ruyssen and J. Lahargue. Guernut said that France had bravely led the way in non-intervention, but it had not been followed. In the face of Italian and German duplicity, the question of intervention raised itself once again. It was heartily supported by the CGT and the Communists, but Guernut argued against it because for France to go back on her word would only serve to alienate her ally Britain. The British, he reminded his listeners, had sympathy for neither one side nor the other in the Spanish Civil War.[55] Guernut's resolution, which was passed unanimously by the Congress, did not have the courage of its convictions however. It admitted that the French government had subordinated 'its concern for the law, international usages, political friendship and military advantage' to the higher goal of Peace.[56] It had asked other nations to do the same, but had not been followed by the Fascist powers. Rather than draw the obvious conclusions from this sorry state of events, however, Guernut went on to recommend that Italy and Germany be given one more chance to come round to the French view. The policy of non-intervention, organized internationally, was to be attempted yet again, and then, and only then, if Germany and Italy refused to play according to the rules, sanctions might be applied. But that was some way down the road, and in the meantime, the APD (along with many other Frenchmen) hoped against hope that the Axis would see the light and co-operate.[57]

[54] Ibid. 356.
[55] Guernut in J. Lahargue and Jules Prudhommeaux, 'Le Congrès de la Paix par le droit, Clermont-Ferrand (suite et fin)', *PD* 47/4–5 (Apr.–May 1937), 150.
[56] Ibid. 152.
[57] Ibid.

Ruyssen's resolution called for an armistice to be arranged under the aegis of the League, and followed by a popular consultation in Spain.[58] The third resolution, that by J. Lahargue, reflected again the concerns for the economic arguments justifying Fascist aggression which have already been noted in connection with the Ethiopian conflict. It spoke of taking the legitimate economic needs of these powers into consideration and reaching an economic arrangement which would 'relieve the economic distress of the less well-favoured peoples'.[59] This sort of attitude on the part of the APD implied an unfortunate and unconscious acceptance of the attempts at rationalization employed by the Nazi and Fascist regimes in order to justify their expansionist and aggressive policies. Ruyssen had already pressed this idea in a letter to Yvon Delbos, the Minister of Foreign Affairs, together with the idea of creating areas of sanctuary in Spain for the disarmed and innocent population.[60]

1936 had not been a good year for the pacifists of the APD. The international situation seemed to be cracking apart at the seams and no one was quite sure what to do about it. As Ruyssen lamented at the end of the year, 'We have not changed, despite the treason of men and of events'.[61] In early 1937 he issued an invitation to the Association's members to join in celebrations of the APD's fiftieth anniversary. This provided him with the opportunity to reflect on the changes pacifism had undergone in the last half-century. First, it had grown enormously. There were far more pacifists in 1937 than there had been in 1887. But in growing, it had also suffered from increasing diversity, not to say increasingly strange 'incoherences'.[62] The end remained the same for all pacifists, but the inspirations behind pacifism and the methods envisaged for achieving peace were so different that the various tendencies were often mutually antagonistic. At one extreme was 'a pacifism which is primarily sentimental in its motives and negative in its conclusions'; opposing this was a pacifism 'above all rational in its principles and active and constructive in its methods'.[63] This latter pacifism, which he called the 'most constant tradition' of the APD, was one which

[58] In Lahargue and Prudhommeaux, op. cit. 153.   [59] Ibid.
[60] Mentioned in Jules Prudhommeaux, 'Notre Assemblée générale', PD 47/2 (Feb. 1937), 64.
[61] Ruyssen cited in Jules Prudhommeaux, 'Le Congrès de la Paix par le droit, Clermont-Ferrand, 26–27 décembre 1936', PD 47/3 (Mar. 1937), 105.
[62] Théodore Ruyssen, 'Le Cinquantenaire de la Paix par le droit', PD 47/2 (Feb. 1937), 50.   [63] Ibid. 51.

recognized in war a historical reality which one could not stamp out simply by means of imprecations, meetings, and verbal resolutions, and which could only be overcome if one integrated the life of nations into a general system of law, of *complete* law, implying an international law, institutions and judicial procedures, and, if necessary, sanctions—because peace has its price which must be paid.[64]

That was the pacifism of the APD, but Ruyssen recognized that there were many people within the Association who held views better typified as sentimental pacifism. It is clear from this that although the lid had been kept on the theoretical debates of the early thirties, the issues were still very much alive for the APD. If the pacifism of the Association had been discussed and 'defined' like so many articles of faith at the 1933 AGM, the faith had not really been completely internalized by all of its members. As Ruyssen said, the treason (if treason there had been) was most certainly that of men and events. The ideological attacks on the APD's conception of pacifism came at a time when the international situation and France's place in it were both worsening by leaps and bounds. As will become clear in Part II, the new-style pacifism was providing a strident alternative which became more and more attractive to some pacifists as the *ultima ratio* of the old-style juridical pacifism increasingly appeared hide-bound, dusty, and incapable of resolving the problem of peace without resort to force. As in the case of the LIFPL, whose commitment to freedom gradually took pre-eminence over the fight for peace, so for the APD the attachment to the cause of justice gradually assumed overriding importance over the question of peace. The final divorce between justice and peace occurred in the period from 1938 to the outbreak of war in September 1939, and it is to that final period that we turn now.

[64] Ibid.

5. Peace through Justice Reaffirmed (1938–1940)

The age of the Association's leadership, if not of its membership, combined with the disappointments of the thirties seem to have produced a period of sharp introspection for the APD in 1937 as it considered its future within French pacifism. In 1934 the executive committee of the Association had examined and rejected a proposal for union of most of the groups belonging to the Fédération française pour la SDN. It was felt that the APD represented an old, established, and central position within French pacifism which surpassed the johnny-come-lately groups whose sole purpose was support of the League of Nations. The Nantes group defined the Association's role in French pacifism as a 'central position ... between the extreme left, which is pacifist at any price, and a Right too ready to see in the League of Nations as it is, the ultimate stage of pacifism'.[1] By contrast the APD had been only too willing to participate extensively in the Rassemblement universel pour la paix organized by Lord Cecil (1864–1958)[2] and Pierre Cot; indeed Prudhommeaux served as a committee member of this

---

[1] Jules Prudhommeaux, 'L'Association de la paix par le droit: Séance du conseil de direction', PD 44/6 (June 1934), 250–1.

[2] Cecil was one of the founders of the League of Nations, as well as one of the founders and leaders of the League of Nations Union in Britain. As a British representative at the Paris Peace Conference in 1919, he had a hand in drafting the Covenant of the League of Nations. He won the Nobel Peace Prize in 1937. See J. A. Thompson, 'Edgar Algernon Robert Gascoyne Cecil', in Warren F. Kuehl (ed.), Biographical Dictionary of Internationalists (Westport, Conn. and London: Greenwood Press, 1983), 147–9.

organization.[3] The mid-thirties were marked, then, by continuing concern at the dispersion of pacifist efforts, and a willingness to participate as fully as possible in combined efforts for peace which did not infringe on what the Association considered to be its independence, and its central place in French pacifism.

But to return to 1937, the APD seems to have undertaken in this year a quiet stock-taking and actually briefly considered merger with another association or else the cessation of its activities. There are subtle indications that something serious was happening at the top. For the first time since 1920, the Association did not hold an AGM or congress in 1937. To be sure, many of its members were active in the French Congress of the RUP and other activities, and the review continued to be published, but the announcement in the review that the Fiftieth Anniversary Celebrations in Nîmes, no less, were being postponed has a faint air of implausibility about it.[4] This impression is reinforced by the 'pressing appeal' addressed by Ruyssen to the members of the Association and the readers of the review in late 1937. He described the executive committee meeting in Paris on 24 November at which the first question discussed was precisely whether or not the Association should disappear or perhaps merge with another pacifist body. The violent reaction against this idea of those members consulted by the committee convinced it to go ahead with the Fiftieth Anniversary Congress in the conviction that the Association de la paix par le droit would continue.[5] Secondly, it was very apparent that the APD was suffering a 'crisis of age', as Ruyssen

---

[3] For the APD's comments on, and participation in, the RUP see Ch. Rousseau and Jules Prudhommeaux, 'La Grande Pitié du pacifisme international: Le "Rassemblement universel pour la paix"', *PD* 46/1 (Jan. 1936), 43–6; Jules Prudhommeaux, 'Le Rassemblement universel pour la paix: La Conférence de Londres', *PD* 46/4 (Apr. 1936), 206–8; Théodore Ruyssen, 'Les Voies de la paix: A propos du Rassemblement mondial', *PD* 46/8–9 (Aug.–Sept. 1936), 329–32; Odette Laguerre, 'Le Congrès du Rassemblement universel pour la paix à Bruxelles', *PD* 46/10 (Oct. 1936), 397–400; Ch. Rousseau and Jules Prudhommeaux, 'Le Conseil général du RUP à Genève: Le Discours de Lord Robert Cecil: Les Résolutions', *PD* 47/4–5 (Apr.–Mar. 1937), 184–7; Odette Laguerre and Jules Prudhommeaux, 'Le Congrès français du Rassemblement universel pour la paix, Paris, 25–27 septembre 1937', *PD* 47/11–12 (Nov.–Dec. 1937), 393–9; Ch. Rousseau and Jules Prudhommeaux, 'Lord Robert Cecil, Prix Nobel de la paix pour 1937', *PD* 47/11–12 (Nov.–Dec. 1937), 417. Prudhommeaux and Ruyssen were members of the international committee of the RUP.

[4] See 'Le Cinquantenaire de l'Association: A nos amis', *PD* 47/8–9 (Aug.–Sept. 1937), 297–8.

[5] Théodore Ruyssen, 'Pressant appel aux membres de l'Association et aux lecteurs de la revue', *PD* 47/11–12 (Nov.–Dec. 1937), 385–6.

called it. Several of its most prominent militants had either been present at its birth in Nîmes in 1887, or else were of the same generation. It was time for young men and women to step forward and take the torch from the old and increasingly tired hands which had held it for so long. Many local groups also seemed to be faltering and Ruyssen appealed to the young to take over.[6]

1937 was thus a pivotal year. It marked the gradually hardening realization of most of the leadership of the APD that no more could be conceded to the Fascist powers. The two crucial events of 1938 were undoubtedly the Anschluss and the Munich crisis. Sandwiched between them was the Association's Fiftieth Anniversary Congress in Nîmes. But as we have argued above, the realization that war might not be avoidable began to penetrate the pages of the review as early as January 1938. In the first number of that year, Georges Scelle published an article in which he separated the two ideals contained in the Association's device, and spoke of peace and of justice as two distinct entities. It seemed clear to Scelle that the democracies had searched for peace outside of justice and had not found it because the dictators had cynically violated every legal precept and had prepared and waged war. The abdication of the democracies could be clearly seen in successive stages: the Japanese incursion into Manchuria in 1932 began the dismantling of collective security; the problem of unanimity demanded by Article XI of the Covenant of the League created the hole through which demands for collective action went unfulfilled; the third stage was the continuance of Japanese aggression in China which went essentially unchecked; the fourth was the failure of sanctions against Japan; and the fifth was the Italo-Abyssinian conflict. All of these, he wrote, were 'the result of the *a-juridical* policies of M. Laval and several of his successors'.[7] He

---

[6] Ruyssen, 'Pressant appel', 386–7. Mme Prudhommeaux in her *rapport moral*, given in the absence of her husband, at the AGM held in Paris on 23 Jan. 1938, described the *active* groups within the APD as: Marseille, Saint-Étienne, Montpellier, Nantes, Chatellerault, Nîmes, Bordeaux, Saint-Foy-la-Grande. Those which were *lethargic* were: Nancy, Boulogne-sur-Mer, Paris, the federations of the Languedoc, the Vienne, the Pyrénées, and Versailles. Those groups which seemed to have *disappeared* completely were: Rouen, Lyon, La Rochelle, Limoges, Saintes, Ivry-sur-Seine, the Landes, Montpezat-du-Quercy, and the federations of the Cevennes, the Charente, and Poitou. See 'Rapport moral' in M.-L. Puech, 'Notre Assemblée générale, Paris, 23 janvier 1938', *PD* 48/3 (Feb. 1938), 66.
[7] Georges Scelle, 'La Paix . . . et le droit', *PD* 48/1 (15 Jan. 1938), 4–7. Earlier in 1937 he had already commented on the end of collective security in Georges Scelle, 'La Fin d'un système', *PD* 47/4–5 (Apr.–May 1937), 169–72.

condemned public opinion for lethargically accepting the remilitarization of the Rhineland. Spain however was the big crisis and still no
action was forthcoming from either the British or the French governments. Important parts of French public opinion, he wrote, were
blinded to the real issues of legality, freedom, civilization, and
pacification—all of which remained very much in the background
—because of the ideological divisions caused by the Spanish Civil
War. The whole policy of non-intervention was wrong-headed, he
believed, based as it was upon a misconception of what law and
justice were really about. He remained 'profoundly convinced that if
the governments of Paris and London had had the energy to oppose a
categorical veto to the intrigues of the totalitarian governments while
there was still time, these governments would have withdrawn . . .'.[8]
The governments hid behind what they claimed to be public opinion,
an opinion which refused to envisage the slightest risk. This 'infant-
ile' public opinion, he wrote, now needed to be guided towards
accepting the fact that no more could possibly be conceded to
totalitarian threats. The line had to be drawn, and for Scelle it had
become necessary to affirm a slogan which he had hoped as a pacifist
to see banished forever from human political discourse: *Si vis pacem,
para bellum.*[9]

Scelle returned to the attack in an article written just before the
Anschluss in which he castigated the 'defeat of the democracies', a
defeat which 'annihilated almost completely the results so dearly
bought in the war of 1914–1918'.[10] This defeat existed on three
levels. First, there had been a juridical defeat. The League of Nations
was dead because it had lost what Scelle considered to be the three
essential components of the Covenant: 'the guarantee of the governmental and territorial competence of its members (Art. X), the
principle of respect due the treaties and rules of international law;
and finally, the principle of the abrogation of the right to wage war,
and the obligatory recourse to pacific procedures'.[11] Flowing out of
the juridical defeat was the diplomatic defeat, essentially the failure
of collective security. Finally, there was the moral defeat, and the
prime example of this was the policy of non-intervention in Spain.[12]

[8] Scelle, 'La Paix . . . et le droit', 10.
[9] Ibid. 10–12.
[10] Georges Scelle, 'La Défaite des démocraties', *PD* 48/4 (Mar. 1938), 129.
[11] Ibid. 130.
[12] Ibid. 130–1.

The big question was whether or not it was too late to limit the damage done and save the situation. The choice seemed to lie between the policies of Eden or Chamberlain, firmness or continued pliability in the face of threats. For Scelle, the choice was clear, but he feared that it would not be taken:

The virile choice would be the choice of the immediate danger, compensated by an energetic attitude and feverish effort at armament. We persist in believing that this would be the lesser risk.

But we are under no illusions. The democracies will choose the long-term peril, even if it be the peril of death.[13]

When the Anschluss finally did occur in March 1938, Charles Rousseau wrote that it had proved easier to accomplish than the formation of a French cabinet.[14] Perhaps the worst aspect of the crisis was the incredible extent of French disunity which it showed up; the intransigence of the so-called 'national' parties was most to blame in his view, and he darkly concluded that 'a 1938 Sadowa has occurred. Between Sadowa and Sedan there were but four years.'[15]

The Fiftieth Anniversary Congress held in Nîmes from 19–21 April 1938 was thus a time of reflection on a glorious past combined with debate on a depressing present.[16] The question of colonialism and the economic bases of peace continued to figure largely in the Association's deliberations, the former topic being covered in a report by Hubert de Monbrison, and the latter by Edgard Milhaud, professor of political economy at the University of Geneva.[17] But undoubtedly the core of the Congress was a discussion of the 'present tasks of pacifism'. This essential topic was covered in a report by Jacques Lambert, a *professeur agrégé* and the holder of the chair of peace at the University of Lyon, and in Ruyssen's report on 'Peace through Justice'.[18] The tone of both reports and indeed of the

---

[13] Scelle, 'La Défaite des démocraties', 133.

[14] Ch. Rousseau, 'La Politique internationale de la SDN', PD 48/5 (Apr. 1938), 187. [15] Ibid.

[16] See Jules Prudhommeaux and J. Lahargue, 'L'Assemblée générale et le Congrès du cinquantenaire, Nîmes, 19–21 avril 1938', PD 48/6–7–8 (May–June–July 1938), 209–99.

[17] See 'Les Colonies, terrain de lutte ou de collaboration entre les peuples (rapport présenté par M. Hubert de Monbrison)' and 'Sur la réorganisation économique du monde, condition de la paix future (rapport présenté par M. Edgard Milhaud)', ibid. 278–89 and 293–7.

[18] See Lambert's report, the ensuing debate, and the two resolutions, by Lambert and Ruyssen, ibid. 230–9. For Ruyssen's report on 'La Paix par le droit', see ibid. 256–68.

resolutions springing from them was the bitter-sweet mixture of pessimism and optimism—pessimism for the immediate future, but clearly optimism in the long-term success of the APD's goals for building a better world.

Lambert emphasized in his report that it was not the League of Nations which had failed, but rather the governments which had broken with the Geneva institution and the moral obligations which it represented. The doctrine of collective security remained a sound idea, but its implementation had failed. He insisted that the famous trilogy—arbitration, security, disarmament—was still valid and the day would come when it would impose itself on international politics.[19] The extent to which the pacifist debate had subconsciously accepted many of the Nazi/Fascist arguments about the nature of post-Versailles Europe was once again demonstrated by Lambert's musings on the need for conciliation even in 1938. Sadly he chose Czechoslovakia as his example and argued that while it would be 'odious' to abandon it, nevertheless the Czechs themselves had to admit that their state contained many internal contradictions which required the moral disarmament of its ethnic minorities.[20] This was the Achilles' heel in an otherwise excellent report. Lambert's resolution spoke of preparing the public for the acceptance of the necessity of a temporary policy of rearmament.[21] Ruyssen's resolution remained firmly attached to the League and collective security and declared itself willing to defend these principles by force if necessary.[22] Needless to say, there was tremendous debate both on the reports and the resolutions which arose from them. One speaker declared that fear was at the basis of French pacifism, but saw the greatest danger of the present hour in the continued blood-letting in Spain, rather than in the danger posed by Italy and Germany. Another speaker, Émile Giraud, condemned French pacifism's 'incoercible terror' of war, but Mme J. Prudhommeaux sharply defended the principle of not accepting any war until it was actually upon the nation:

Let us remain loyal to our past; let us refuse today any declaration implying acquiescence, even conditional, to war. The day on which the methods of law fail, the war will be inevitable, and may each one of us act according to his conscience. But until then, let us not proclaim that the next 'last' will be a

---

[19] Ibid. 230.   [20] Ibid. 231.
[21] Ibid. 239.   [22] Ibid. 238.

'war of justice'. We thought so, we said so for four years, from 1914 to 1918. And we received, in recompense, these nefarious Treaties of 1919 which created more injustices than they repaired. And since we are speaking of 'fear', she concluded with emotion, the mother that I am rebels against the ignoble realities of today's aerial warfare: yes, I have the right, I would say even that I have the duty, to be afraid *for my children!*[23]

Paul-Marie Masson, a professor at the Sorbonne, proposed an amendment to the resolution which would have seen an active preparation undertaken in French schools against the eventuality of war. This provoked in the audience what was 'discreetly called in parliament *"des mouvements divers"'*, and the idea was quickly rejected.[24] It is clear from all of the above, then, that the last pre-war Congress of the APD was rent with the same divisions as usual when faced with the question of pacifist tactics. Undoubtedly, the majority of the members present remained true to the Ruyssen conception of the Association's task, that is to say, of the necessity of peace being laboriously constructed *in justice*, and if that proved impossible, the necessity of fighting to defend it. But it is also clear that many members—the Prudhommeaux foremost amongst them—were terribly unwilling to grasp the nettle before them. No doubt they would have been horrified at the idea of 'peace at any price', but in their unwillingness to see that the Europe of Versailles was dead and that even the cadaver was threatened by Hitler, they unwittingly came close to the *intégralité* they professed to combat. It is clear from the account of the Congress that there were other subtle currents representing variations on these two main themes as well, but the majority sense of the deliberations and vote was certainly in favour of the national defence against any further affronts by the Fascist states.

There remained but one more major crisis in European affairs before the outbreak of war: the two-step dismemberment of Czechoslovakia. The APD's response to the Czech crisis can hardly be characterized as wholeheartedly *munichois*. Once again, the Association seemed to revolve around two fixed reference points: Ruyssen's hardline anti-*munichois* attitude and Prudhommeaux's softer approach. The official pronouncements made by the Association condemned outright the attack on Czech territorial sovereignty.

---

[23] Prudhommeaux and Lahargue, 'L'Assemblée générale', 234.   [24] Ibid. 236.

A press communiqué welcomed the initiative taken by Paris and London to resolve the problem peacefully, but bitterly attacked these same governments for 'imperiously' putting aside the attempt made by the Czech government to arbitrate the situation according to the 1926 Germano-Czech Treaty. It nevertheless congratulated the Czech government for its 'sagacity' and sense of sacrifice in putting the European good before the Czech.[25] The title of Ruyssen's article on the crisis, 'Peace outside the Law', said it all—he saw nothing but further trouble coming out of the Munich débâcle.[26] Prudhommeaux took the opposite view, however. He defended the government's actions at the Ligue des droits de l'homme and in the pages of the *PD*.[27] The divisions within the APD were further underscored by the publication of two essentially *munichois* articles by Maurice Lacroix and Henri de Man in the review.[28]

The end was definitely now in sight. The January number of the review contained three articles all of which presaged the war which was only eight months away. P. Teissonnière enumerated the failures of collective security over the past twenty years and argued that justice had to have force on its side.[29] Ruyssen was already addressing an article to 'our friends of tomorrow', in which he rejected categorically the four main political developments pacifism had made in the interwar period: conscientious objection which, while to be respected on the genuine and individual level, in no way resolved the social problem of war; non-resistance to war; the purely negative and sentimental pacifism based merely upon a horror of war; and finally, unilateral disarmament.[30] The most important of the three pieces, though, was that by A. Bloch, on the 'necessary adaptations pacifism must make' in the wake of Munich and the ideological upheavals it had suffered.[31] Since 1933 events in Europe had succeeded in turning the world of ideologies and politics upside down.

[25] Théodore Ruyssen, 'Notre effort pour la paix', *PD* 48/11 (Oct. 1938), 338–9.

[26] Théodore Ruyssen, 'La Paix hors du droit', *PD* 48/11 (Oct. 1938), 341–50.

[27] Jules Prudhommeaux, 'La Ligue des droits de l'homme et la paix en péril', *PD* 48/11 (Oct. 1938), 359–63.

[28] Maurice Lacroix and Henri de Man, 'Les Lendemains de Munich: Faisons la paix!', *PD* 48/13 (Dec. 1938), 404–10.

[29] P. Teissonnière, 'Faut-il résister aux violents?', *PD* 49/1 (Jan. 1939), 12–14.

[30] Théodore Ruyssen, 'A nos amis de demain', *PD* 49/1 (Jan. 1939), 1–3.

[31] A. Bloch, 'Adaptations nécessaires de la doctrine pacifiste', *PD* 49/1 (Jan. 1939), 4–7. See also the suggestive essay on the ideological changes occurring within pacifism: Joseph Folliet, *Pacifisme de droite? Bellicisme de gauche?* (Paris: Éditions du cerf, 1938).

Right and left seemed to have lost their traditional meanings as French nationalists supported Munich and refused to fight, while what he called the 'pacifists of the resistance' found themselves in general agreement with the Communists (who had always castigated pacifism as a 'petit bourgeois' ideal), and some renegades from the right.[32] He, too, examined the mistakes of the past twenty years, but insisted that the time was not for recriminations, but rather for new ideas. Disarmament and even the League of Nations were now mere cadavers. What had to be recognized was that the League had always been an instrument, a means to an end, and not the end in itself. In this sense, the APD was undoubtedly in a stronger position morally than the groups which had the support of the League as their sole reason for being. For the APD the ideal could and would live on. For the moment, he argued in favour of energetic rearmament as a first measure, followed by an attempt at a European agreement, disarmament, and a return to the principles of collective security if possible as long-term goals.[33]

The final dismemberment of Czechoslovakia in March 1939 put the last nail in the lid of the APD's remaining optimism. Georges Scelle informed readers that from a purely logical point of view, no one could now say that war was not inevitable. The final capitulation of the Czechoslovakian republic meant war in the long or short term. The only hope was that the coming of war would in the long run bring about the downfall of the dictatorships.[34]

---

[32] Bloch, 'Adaptations nécessaires', 4.

[33] Ibid. 7. Cf. Georges Scelle, 'Péril de mort', PD 49/3–4 (Mar.–Apr. 1939), 81–6 in which the author described the European situation in terms similar to those of Bloch. Scelle's article also contains the seeds of the *épuration* mentality in its search for someone to blame for the mess France found herself in. He said that Munich ought never to have taken place (82), and blamed a 'certain pacifisme idéologique et passif qui nous a menés où nous sommes' (81).

[34] Scelle, 'Péril de mort'.

PART II

PACIFISME NOUVEAU STYLE, OR THE POLITICS OF DISSENT

6. The Origins of the New Pacifism

Part I showed how traditional pacifism developed within French political society from the end of the Great War onwards. This evolution followed an ascending curve in terms of pacifist commitment, culminating in the early thirties with the debate between Ruyssen and Challaye on the latter's contentious thesis in favour of 'peace without reservations'. Having reached this high-water mark, *pacifisme ancien style* began a retreat into a defence of justice and law as opposed to peace—a retreat which coincided with, and indeed was largely shaped by, the Nazi seizure of power and the succession of European crises which followed it down the decade to September 1939. The new pacifism which superseded it was integral or absolute, one which rejected and condemned all foreign wars. It was not synonymous with conscientious objection, nor with absolute non-violence, although these elements were certainly prominent within it. On the contrary, it occasionally espoused violence, or at least accepted it in cases of civil as opposed to international conflict. The new pacifism did not pretend to homogeneity either, but rather sought to group together all those who were opposed absolutely to any external war, and who were prepared to fight against such wars with a variety of means. In broad terms, it emerged from three types of dissent: historical dissent about the origins and nature of the First World War, a deepening divorce from French political society, and finally a growing conviction that modern warfare had become unthinkable by virtue of the magnitude of the destruction it could wreak upon society.

HISTORICAL DISSENT

Mathias Morhardt, in a letter to Georges Demartial in the spring of 1936, wrote that

For the past twenty-two years, you and I have suffered an unspeakable moral and intellectual martyrdom. The atmosphere of imposture in which we live has poisoned all our joys. And we no longer have before us the hope of seeing the fog of hatreds dissipate, in which minds and spirits are so furiously agitating. This is because we are expiating the honour of belonging to a class of Frenchmen that is far too small. We are those, in effect, who suffer more from an injustice committed by France than from an injustice committed against her.[1]

This 'moral and intellectual martyrdom' of which Morhardt wrote was the *fons et origo* of the new pacifism. While the pacifists of the Association de la paix par le droit had accepted the need to fight the Great War, held it to be a just war which had been forced upon an unwilling France, and saw much good in the Versailles Treaty and the new Europe which it founded, the fundamental tenet of the new pacifism was a complete rejection of post-Versailles Europe and of all the premisses upon which it was built.

A decade before *pacifisme nouveau style* finally emerged in the French body politic as a corpus of coherent and developed ideas, its foundations were laid in what was perceived by a small group of intellectuals to be the lies of the Great War. The primary critique was a rejection of Article 231 of the Versailles Treaty and the thesis of unique war guilt. This was followed closely by a rejection of the political and demographic nature of post-war Europe. In the minds of the new pacifists, the second flowed logically out of the first. If Europe continued to seethe with political problems which might lead to war, this was precisely because of Versailles and the war-guilt 'lie'. As René Gerin (1892–1957)[2] wrote in the introduction to a brochure he published in 1933: 'The question of responsibilities for the war has not ceased to be current since the end of hostilities; it is

---

[1] M. Morhardt, 'Le Respect des traités' (letter to Demartial dated Capbreton, 19 Mar. 1936), *Le Barrage*, 91 (26 Mar. 1936), 3.
[2] See James Friguglietti, 'René Marius François Léon Gerin', in Harold Josephson (ed.), *Biographical Dictionary of Modern Peace Leaders* (London, Westport: Greenwood Press, 1985), 317–19.

becoming increasingly so because on it depend all of the present problems in world politics.'[3]

The foundations of historical dissent were laid in Paris in January 1916 when a small group of men met together to discuss the origins of the War as they could then be known. This group, known as the Société d'études documentaires et critiques sur les origines de la guerre, quickly discovered discrepancies in the French government's case against the Central Powers as the breakers of the peace.[4] The Society included in its number eminent men such as the economist Charles Gide, professor at the Collège de France, Mathias Morhardt, formerly secretary-general of the Ligue des droits de l'homme, and Georges Demartial, a former under-secretary of state in the colonial office. None of these men was a political extremist, but they all shared a passionate desire for truth and justice, and they were appalled at what they saw happening around them in France as men and women of all political hues threw themselves into the *union sacrée*. With the war over, the group continued to publish harsh criticism of the Versailles Treaty and French foreign policy, especially with regard to their insistence on the total guilt of the Central Powers.[5]

In 1925 Georges Demartial published an article in the American journal *Current Affairs*, contesting the Poincaré version of events in 1914. For his pains, he was expelled for five years from the Légion d'honneur for having brought the French nation into disrepute.[6] He joined Victor Margueritte in the ranks of the victims of the Legion's purges. René Gerin, a former *normalien*, an infantry captain mentioned in dispatches in the Great War and decorated with the ribbon of the Légion d'honneur himself, was scandalized by the treatment

[3] René Gerin, *Les Responsabilités de la guerre de 1914* (Paris: Éditions de la LICP, 1933), 3. See also Georges Demartial, 'Les Responsabilités de la guerre: Une réponse de G. Demartial à M. Camille Bloch', *PH* 105 (2 Mar. 1934), 2. See also Félicien Challaye, 'Raymond Poincaré, René Gerin, et les responsabilités de la guerre', *Le Barrage*, 26 (8 Nov. 1934), 1–2. In late 1934 Challaye also published a series of articles in *Le Barrage* on 'Les Responsabilités russes et françaises', and beginning in No. 36 of *Le Barrage*, General de Montgelas began a series on 'L'Explosion de la guerre de 1914'.
[4] See the account in Félicien Challaye, *Georges Demartial: Sa vie, son œuvre* (Paris: A. Lahure, n.d. [1950]), 6–7.
[5] For a bibliography of Demartial's articles and books, see ibid. 28–54.
[6] For Challaye's account of the affair, see ibid. 14–15. For an account of the inquest and expulsion, see 'Le Dossier Demartial (défense, témoignages et plaidoirie)', in *Évolution*, 30 (June 1928), 34–50.

meted out to Demartial and began his own investigations into the origins of the war. As an *agrégé des lettres*, he was eminently well qualified to pursue these researches, which culminated in a book published in 1930 containing fourteen questions by René Gerin together with fourteen answers by Raymond Poincaré. This, together with his subsequent pacifist activities, earned Gerin, too, an expulsion from the Légion d'honneur.[7]

In 1926, Victor Margueritte, together with Armand Charpentier (1864–1949),[8] founded the journal *Évolution*, whose contents and subtitle (*Revue mensuelle des questions intéressant l'apaisement international et le rapprochement des peuples*) really underscored the developing nexus between the new pacifism and the question of war guilt and war origins. *Évolution* was one of the primary journals of comment in France on the question of war origins, and attracted not only French commentators, but also German and American scholars and journalists.[9]

By 1930, it was thus a well-established fact in the mental universe of integral pacifists that the Great War had been an unjust war, fought under false pretences, and that the peace which had resulted from it contained the seeds of a future conflict. It was the duty of pacifists to enlighten the public about these matters and in so doing put pressure on the French government to adopt different policies, primarily towards Germany. For right or wrong, this historical *Weltanschauung* provided the new pacifism with an anti-

[7] René Gerin, *Les Responsabilités de la guerre: Quatorze questions par René Gerin, ancien élève de l'École normale supérieure, agrégé des lettres: Quatorze réponses par Raymond Poincaré de l'Académie française* (Paris: Payot, 1930). On Gerin's expulsion from the Légion d'honneur, see René Gerin, *Honneur et patrie ou comment j'ai été exclu de la Légion d'honneur* (Paris: Éditions de la LICP, 1934).

[8] See James Friguglietti, 'Armand Charpentier', in Josephson, *Dictionary*, 160–1.

[9] It appears that the German Foreign Ministry attempted to influence Margueritte, and through him the French peace movement, at the time of the Geneva Disarmament Conference in early 1932. Dr Gerhard Köpke, the director of the West European division of the Ministry, wrote in April of that year, 'Der ehemalige französische Oberst und politische Schriftsteller Margueritte ist uns bekanntlich auf dem Gebiete der Abrüstung und auch sonst politisch nützlich. Margueritte war noch nicht in Deutschland und beabsichtigt nunmehr nach den französischen Wahlen hierher zu kommen, um aus eigener Anschauung an Ort und Stelle ein Bild von Land und Leuten zu gewinnen. Ich halte diesen Besuch für erwünscht und politisch zweckmäßig ... Ein Beitrag aus amtlichen Fonds ist aber unvermeidlich. 1500 würden genügen.' From US National Archives, T-120 microfilm series, Roll 2697, Frames HO 25099–HO 25100.

establishment political orientation which would last well into the Second World War.[10]

CAUSES OF THE PRESENT DISCONTENTS

The historical dissent over the question of war guilt and the origins of the Great War quite naturally manifested itself in the growing sense of estrangement which the nascent integral pacifists felt with regard to French political society. With the signing of the Kellogg–Briand Pact in 1928, integral pacifists tried to take governments at their word in their claim to have made war a crime. Conscientious objectors began to use this argument as one of the planks in their defence after 1928. By 1932, however, it had begun to become apparent that nothing much had really changed. The Geneva Disarmament Conference which opened in February of that year had been hailed by many pacifists as the one last chance they had of imposing their wills upon governments and of bringing national policies into line with the provisions of the Kellogg–Briand Pact.

It soon became clear, however, that nothing of the sort was happening in Geneva. In the four years from Kellogg–Briand to Geneva, the world situation for pacifists had swung sharply from one of optimism to one of pessimism. The deepening world depression combined with increased political turmoil in Europe conspired to wreck the hopes of many pacifists who began a retreat from participation in political society, and began to speak in extraparliamentary, if not anarchist, terms of peace being an issue which the peoples had to impose upon their governments. All hope seemed to be lost in governments which were increasingly viewed as corrupt, unrepresentative, and completely in the hands of the capitalist class.

There was thus very much a Socialist analysis of peace in the new integral pacifism, but it was coupled with a political anarchism which waxed and waned according to circumstances. In the 1933–4 period, French integral pacifists became convinced that the greatest danger to peace was an internal one, in the form of French Fascism. The conviction that Frenchmen had to 'sweep their own doorstep' grew and provided a mirror image in the domestic sphere of the ideas held with regard to the question of responsibility for the Great War.

---

[10] See for example Georges Demartial, *La Légende des démocraties pacifiques* (Paris: Rieder/Presses universitaires de France, 1939); and *1939: La Guerre de l'imposture* (Paris: Éditions Jean Flory, 1941).

The enemy was within. As Michel Winock commented recently, 'the French expended much talent and energy during the thirties in a cold civil war'; this produced a 'francocentric myopia' which permitted the temporary reconciliation of the irreconcilable: antifascism and pacifism.[11] But the antifascism was directed at an internal danger and not so much at the outward manifestations of Fascism in Italy or Germany. From the pacifist perspective, there were, initially at least, good reasons to be primarily concerned about the internal danger. Pacifist meetings were regularly the target for the excesses of right-wing thugs, especially in the period up to 1934, and integral pacifism was the subject of continual vilification by the organs of the right-wing press.

Integral pacifism was also squeezed from the extreme left. In the early years of the Ligue internationale des combattants de la paix, Victor Méric (1876–1933),[12] the Ligue's founder, often complained in the columns of the *Patrie humaine* of attacks by the Communists. The split became even more pronounced after the Laval–Stalin Pact of 1935 which once again made Communists patriotic Frenchmen by rehabilitating military service for them. Integral pacifism in France was, then, subjected to a pincer movement between an extreme left

[11] See Michel Winock, 'Le Fascisme passera ... Pourquoi?', *Le Monde aujourd'hui*, Supplement to No. 12852 of *Le Monde* (Sunday 25–Monday 26 May 1986), v.

[12] James Friguglietti writes that Victor Méric was a 'rebel with a cause' all his life. He came from a politically active family. His grandfather had been imprisoned in 1851 for his ardent republicanism by the government of Louis Napoleon, and his father, Victor Sylvain, was a Radical-Socialist senator from the department of the Var. Méric's three years in the army made him a convinced antimilitarist. He arrived in Paris in the 1890s and eked out a bare existence as a proof reader and petty thief. He was gradually drawn to anarchism and formed a life-long friendship with Sébastien Faure, to whose newspaper *Le Libertaire* he contributed regularly. From 1906 Méric was a member of the SFIO. In the pre-war years he contributed regularly to Gustave Hervé's *La Guerre sociale* which he helped to found. He also collaborated with Henri Fabre in the creation of *Les Hommes du jour*, to which he remained a regular contributor. He was active before the war in the Association internationale antimilitariste which was founded in 1904; he took part in extensive speaking tours across France on behalf of the AIA. Despite his strong antimilitarist views, Méric spent the Great War in the trenches as a military engineer. At the Congress of Tours in 1920 Méric threw in his lot with the new French Communist Party. He rose quickly within the party and twice ran unsuccessfully for office. Méric's anarchist inclinations soon drove him from the party, however. In 1923 he returned to the SFIO. During the 1920s he was a regular contributor to *Le Merle blanc* and *La Nouvelle Revue socialiste*. See Philippe Robrieux, *Histoire intérieure du parti communiste, 1920–1945* (Paris: Fayard, 1980); and James Friguglietti, 'Victor Méric', in Josephson, *Dictionary*, 622–4.

and a virulent proto-Fascist right which is probably unparalleled in the history of other modern peace movements. This was partially due to the extreme polarization of Third Republic political society, but also to the political nature of much of French pacifism. Thus, paradoxically, while appearing to reject French political society, French integral pacifists were actually intimately bound up in it in an antipolitical movement which expressed itself in uniquely political terms. The result was that, shunned by the *bien pensant* middle, attacked by the extreme right and vilified by the extreme left, French integral pacifism had nowhere to go. By 1939, the politics of dissent had become in France the politics of utter marginality—the politics of no man's land.

FRAÎCHE ET GAZEUSE: FEARS OF A COMING WAR

The third strand in the origins of the new pacifism was the increasing sense that another war could destroy civilization because of the progress made by science and technology since the end of the Great War. The 'bombing aeroplane' and gas warfare constituted the atomic weapons of the 1920s and 1930s. Writers were convinced that they spelled the end of civilization if ever they should be released upon an unsuspecting humanity. Professor Paul Langevin provided the Ligue internationale des femmes pour la paix et la liberté with his considered scientific opinion that another war would be the last, given the progress made in the delivery of death by science and technology since 1918.[13]

In Paris, Victor Méric, a journalist on *Le Soir*, conducted an *enquête* on aero-chemical warfare in 1930 which led to the foundation of the Ligue internationale des combattants de la paix. He published a book on his findings the following year with the evocative and darkly amusing title *Fraîche et gazeuse*.[14] The theme of terrible destruction was a common one in the editorials of Méric and others in his newspaper *La Patrie humaine*. It is also to be found in the LICP's more official newspaper, *Le Barrage*, from 1934 onwards. In fact, *Le Barrage* carried a citation from Bertrand Russell on

---

[13] Langevin's 'Déclaration', together with the accompanying petition organized by the LIFPL and a list of the original signatories, are to be found in BDIC/DD/FΔRés. 235/4/3.

[14] Victor Méric, *Fraîche et gazeuse! La Guerre qui revient* (Paris: Éditions 'Sirius', 1932).

its masthead which gave utterance to the deep belief of pacifists that
war could never be justified because of the destructive forces it would
unleash: 'Not a single evil that one should like to avoid by war, is
greater than the evil of war itself.' This is what Martin Ceadel has
called the single important moral or philosophical advance of interwar pacifism: the enunciation of an apparently value-free rejection of
war based purely on humanitarian or utilitarian grounds.[15]

It is difficult to say whether the impetus for this development in
France came from abroad or not. It seems likely that the same train of
thought was being followed by pacifists in several European countries at the same time. Whatever the case, fears of the next war
allowed the integral pacifism of some intellectuals to be broadened
into a pacifist campaign attracting mass support. If people were
sometimes unwilling or unable to understand the complexities of the
historical arguments about war origins, or to take sides in the politics
of dissent with regard to late Third Republic political society, they
most certainly were able to understand the inflammatory rhetoric of
the propagandists of the LICP who fanned out across the length and
breadth of France beginning in the winter of 1930–1. This *croisade
de la paix*, as it was called, brought home to hundreds of French
towns and villages the pacifist message that the next war would be
the last. It is probably true to say that it was this fear which
contributed largely to the initial successes of integral pacifism at a
time when it was manifestly clear that not much could be expected of
governments at the Geneva Disarmament Conference.[16]

---

[15] Martin Ceadel, *Pacifism in Britain, 1914–1945: The Defining of a Faith*
(Oxford: Clarendon Press, 1980), 13–15. Ceadel cites Bertrand Russell's adage in
slightly different and later form: 'Modern war is practically certain to have worse
consequences than even the most unjust peace.' This version is taken from Russell's
1936 book *Which Way to Peace?*, cited ibid. 216.

[16] The government was particularly concerned at the spread of ideas relating to
conscientious objection. The LICP was singled out as the organization having the
most impact across France in the spread of integral pacifist ideas. A report dated 19
Apr. 1933 in the files of the Ministry of the Interior reads: 'La propagande pour la
reconnaissance légale de l'objection de conscience et pour la libération des objecteurs
de conscience emprisonnés a pris en France un grand développement depuis quelques
mois, sous l'impulsion des associations pacifistes, en particulier de la Ligue Internationale des Combattants de la Paix. Non seulement les manifestations pacifistes se
multiplient mais encore elles réunissent des auditoires de plus en plus nombreux. Elles
attirent couramment plusieurs centaines de personnes et il n'est pas de ville de quelque
importance qui n'ait été le siège d'une de ces manifestations.' See report entitled 'La
Propagande pacifiste et le mouvement en faveur de l'objection de conscience en
France', in AN F7/13352.

To summarize this brief introduction to the new pacifism, it was based upon three lines of thinking which began to converge around 1928 and were united in a fairly coherent way by about 1931. The first was the continuing sense that the Great War had been fought under false pretences in France, and that the peace which flowed out of it was iniquitous and furthermore based on the lie of the unique war guilt of the Central Powers. Secondly, there was a growing feeling of divorce from French political society; the new pacifism embodied a belief in the efficacy of direct action by the masses upon corrupt parliamentary governments. Finally, the realization by the end of the twenties of the terrible destruction the next war would bring acted as the humanitarian/utilitarian catalyst necessary, in company with the other two factors, to give birth to a new type of pacifism. Part II will examine the growth and development of this new type of pacifism in France from 1928 to the outbreak of war.

PRECURSORS OF INTEGRAL PACIFISM

Integral pacifism emerged as a coherent, developed movement in the period from 1928 to 1930, but its origins go back much further than that. Isolated individuals and numerically insignificant groups were precursors, voices crying in the wilderness, proclaiming the advent of a new pacifism which would respond to the growing aspirations of many people for a categorical rejection of war.

Probably the most important precursor in the French context was Romain Rolland, who in the dark days of the Great War defined almost single-handedly the nature of the new French pacifism already gestating in the minds of a generation marked in the trenches of northern France. Because of his courageous, albeit essentially élitist, stand during the war, Rolland was viewed as the grand old man of French, if not European, pacifism in the twenties. But his political evolution away from absolute non-violence, his flirtation with and then gradual embracing of a Soviet-orientated view of peace and pacifism, gradually left behind many of the people who had seen in him the John the Baptist of the new pacifism.[17] For all that, his influence remained strong throughout most of the period

---

[17] See Norman Ingram, 'Romain Rolland, Interwar Pacifism and the Problem of Peace', in Charles Chatfield and Peter van den Dungen (eds.), *Peace Movements and Political Cultures* (Knoxville, Tenn.: University of Tennessee Press, 1988), 143–64.

under discussion, and it was with sorrow that French integral pacifists in the mid-thirties felt themselves obliged to leave behind the man who had been their spiritual guide for much of the pacifist pilgrimage.

There were, of course, other precursors to the new pacifism. One such was Marianne Rauze (1875–1964)[18] who published a number of small books and brochures on pacifism in the twenties. In one of these she defined the essence of the new pacifism as follows: 'Antimilitarism—real antimilitarism—can only be achieved through absolute pacifism. It is in order to cause war to disappear immediately and definitively that the antiwarrior is antimilitarist. To be an antimilitarist is to work towards the total suppression of all the institutions that are instruments of death.'[19] Rauze prefigured many of the concerns of pacifists in the thirties. She underlined, for example, that antimilitarism must be collective and active. 'Emotions and feelings are nothing', she wrote, 'action is everything.'[20] Isolated, individual gestures were of little value; but they could become effective if they were organized into a mass movement. This concern for collective action was a predominant theme in all of French interwar pacifism. The individual gesture was usually respected but not recommended if it could not play a part in a larger collective movement.[21] Finally, Rauze argued that in order for antimilitarism to be effective, it had to be international. Antimilitarism on the national level would be 'foolishness' because, far from being an obstacle to war, it would encourage the covetousness of neighbouring nations which had not disarmed.[22] This latter insistence on international action gradually gave way in the thirties to an emphasis on unilateral national pacifism, even in the face of Nazism.

Another theme in Rauze's book which was to become a commonplace of integral pacifism was her view of the League of Nations. She had nothing but scorn for people who expected general disarmament from this 'powerless' body. She also attacked the old-style pacifists

---

[18] Marianne Rauze was the pseudonym of Marie-Anne-Rose Gaillarde. She was married to an army officer, Captain Léon Comignan, who died in 1916 from wounds received in the war. She was active before the Great War in the SFIO and at the Congress of Tours she joined the newly formed Communist Party. See Albert S. Hill, 'Marianne Rauze', in Josephson, Dictionary, 793–4.

[19] Marianne Rauze, L'Anti-guerre: Essai d'une doctrine et d'une philosophie de l'antimilitarisme en 1923, Suivi d'une post-face de Romain Rolland, Préfaces de W. Wellock et Dr Stoecker (Niort: Imprimerie du progrès, 1923), 3.

[20] Ibid. 4.   [21] Ibid.   [22] Ibid.

who continued to believe in defensive wars; and interestingly, she condemned the new 'revolutionary' pacifism which sought to justify a war fought for revolutionary reasons. The only real pacifism, she proclaimed, was that which refused all wars.[23]

Conscientious objection, which was a subset within interwar French pacifism, also began to attract its exponents and defenders in the twenties. Paul Bergeron founded a Ligue pour la reconnaissance légale de l'objection de conscience in Lyon in 1924, which, after publishing a few tracts, seemed to lapse into lethargy. The twenties also saw the first of the rather spectacular trials of objectors in France which sent men of varying religious or political persuasions to prison for terms of six months to a year. Conscientious objection in France initially drew much inspiration from the example set in Britain during the First World War. Only in the thirties did it begin to find its own theoreticians in France, such as René Gerin. The connections between anarchism, libertarianism, and conscientious objection were always strong. For example, *Le Semeur*, a libertarian newspaper published in the Calvados, supported COs from at least 1924 onwards.

Integral pacifism also had its Christian voice in France in the 1920s. The French branch of the International Fellowship of Reconciliation began publishing its *Cahiers de la réconciliation* in the mid-twenties. Some of the most famous COs of the period, including Philippe Vernier and Jacques Martin, came from its ranks.[24]

The Kellogg–Briand Pact provided much of the impetus to the development of *pacifisme nouveau style*. Many pacifists, and certainly not only the least educated amongst them, wanted to take the pact at its word and declare war a crime. Thus, for example, Francis Delaisi could declare at the annual general meeting of the rather staid APD in 1928, that forced to choose between his mobilization papers and the Kellogg–Briand Pact which made war a crime, he would not hesitate to choose the latter. It was this kind of independent thinking which worried the authorities.[25]

---

[23] Ibid. 9–10.
[24] See for example *Procès de Jacques Martin* (Aubervilliers: 'La Réconciliation', 1932); and *Procès de Philippe Vernier* (Aubervilliers: 'La Réconciliation', 1933).
[25] See Francis Delaisi's report, 'Les Garanties intérieures de la paix, conséquence du Pacte Kellogg', in J. Prudhommeaux, 'L'Assemblée générale de la Paix par le droit, Bordeaux, 2 et 3 novembre 1929', in *PD* 39/12 (Dec. 1929), 458.

La Volonté de paix, the organ of the peace movement of the same name, started by Madeleine Vernet (1878–1949)[26] in 1928, took much the same view. In its manifesto it demanded that war be declared a crime, that immediate and total disarmament take place, and that all war *matériel* be destroyed and the public or private production of arms abolished. This manifesto gathered 10,000 signatures in France and 3,000 in Belgium by the late summer of 1928, but these numbers paled into insignificance beside the results obtained by similar petitions in England and Germany. By early 1931, the Volonté de paix was claiming 30,000 signatures for this petition—still not an impressive number over a three-year period.[27] Madeleine Vernet and the Volonté de paix are important as examples of the nascent integral pacifism, but the movement never really became very large and its influence was limited accordingly. The group's organ appeared regularly at first, and then more and more intermittently, until finally, in 1936, the Volonté de paix folded up and merged with the larger and more influential Ligue internationale des combattants de la paix.[28]

But that is in the future. What is important is the fact that the Volonté de paix was one of the first examples in France of the new-style pacifism, albeit in rather limited and sentimental form. Probably its most important act over the course of its existence was the organization in Paris in 1932 of two Conférences libres du désarmement, which brought together people who despaired of ever seeing anything significant come of the Geneva process.[29] The V.d.P.'s pacifist experience was, in effect, bounded by the two formative experiences of Kellogg–Briand and the Geneva Disarmament Conference. In 1928, the Pact had given it the tremendous boost of optimism it needed to proclaim an end to all wars. By 1932,

---

[26] Vernet was a feminist in the sentimental mode. She believed that women ought to be pacifists because of their motherhood role. Her pacifist and feminist activity were consequently closely intertwined. In addition to founding the Volonté de paix, Vernet was also the director of another journal entitled *La Mère éducatrice*. See Albert S. Hill, 'Madeleine Vernet', in Josephson, *Dictionary*, 986–8.

[27] See 'Manifeste de la Volonté de paix', *La Volonté de paix* (Aug.–Sept. 1928), 4. See also 'Lettre ouverte aux 30.000 signataires de notre manifeste', *La Volonté de paix* (Jan.–Feb. 1931), 1.

[28] 'Volonté de paix et L.I.C.P.', *Le Barrage*, 99 (28 May 1936), 1.

[29] There is some material on the two Conférences libres du désarmement in BDIC/DD/FΔRés 273/8. For the report on the first one, see *Pour un désarmement réel: Compte-rendu de la Conférence libre du désarmement tenue à Paris les 23 et 24 avril 1932* (Levallois-Perret: Édité par la Commission de la Conférence, 1932).

however, it was clear how little had really changed in the world situation and the V.d.P. sank into lethargy after one last burst of pessimistic activity in organizing the independent disarmament conference.

By the beginning of the thirties, the hope expressed by the German pacifist Kurt Hiller to Edmond Vermeil at the 1925 Universal Peace Congress in Berlin, that the two 'tendencies' within pacifism might continue to work together towards their common goal, was becoming manifestly impossible to sustain.[30] The means began in essence to define the end—the type of peace envisaged by the different strands of pacifism. Thus, for the old-style pacifists, peace and pacifism were functions of law and justice. Later on in the thirties, the integral pacifists would also have to refute the arguments of those who sought to make peace a function of the social revolution. What was new and exciting in integral pacifism was its insistence on peace as the ultimate end. This ultimate end was to be achieved either through an individual rejection of war—conscientious objection in one form or another—or through concerted collective action which might involve the use of civil violence. The clearest nexus for the multifarious strands of thinking which defined it, and the most important new-style pacifist group in interwar France, in terms of numbers, intellectual depth, and certainly of radical commitment, was the Ligue internationale des combattants de la paix, to whose examination we now turn.

---

[30] For Hiller's comment to Vermeil, see Edmond Vermeil, 'Le XXIIIème Congrès international de la paix de Berlin', *PD* 34/12 (Dec. 1924), 454.

7. Years of Growth (1930–1934)

The Ligue internationale des combattants de la paix was the most important and influential of the new-style pacifist groups in interwar France. This significance was based upon a variety of factors. First, the LICP was a numerically large pacifist group by French standards. Two and a half years after its creation, Victor Méric claimed that it had almost 20,000 members.[1] Secondly, the LICP was important because it provided a consistently high standard of comment on French political affairs for the nine years immediately preceding the Second World War. Thirdly, it was a remarkably heterogeneous group composed of people from varying political, philosophical, and religious traditions, although the anarchist and Socialist elements were always strongest within it.

In some ways, Méric was the Dick Sheppard of French pacifism. The LICP was his creation, the response to his series of articles on the dangers posed by aero-chemical warfare. He almost single-handedly founded the Ligue in October 1930[2] and, some four months later, the *Patrie humaine*, which was the Ligue's semi-official newspaper until 1933. Like Dick Sheppard and the Peace Pledge Union, Victor Méric and the LICP relied initially on an emotional response from a population preoccupied by rising political unrest in Central Europe and fears of a coming war. The LICP sought to group together all those people who were resolutely prepared to fight against the fatality of war. But there the similarities end because Méric's Ligue was essentially secular in character and was not explicitly non-violent in nature.

---

[1] Figure cited in Victor Méric, 'Pour tuer la guerre', PH 54 (4–11 Feb. 1933), 1.
[2] See Victor Méric, 'Rapport moral', PH 59 (11–18 Mar. 1933), 5.

In his book *Fraîche et gazeuse*, written between November 1930 and February 1932, Méric described the formation of the LICP. He elaborated the reasons behind the creation of yet another pacifist league in France. There was certainly no lack of pacifists, he wrote. There were those who remembered the horrors of the Great War; there were others who condemned war through a sort of sentimentality, still others based their rejection of war on a 'cold' rationality which detested the periodic and criminal massacres which humanity inflicted on itself. His purpose, he wrote, was to 'gather together all of these scattered energies, to assemble them in a solid bundle and throw them irresistibly against war . . .'.[3] There were certainly many other pacifist groups in France. But they acted in isolation one from another, and 'the battle is carried out in dispersion'.[4] What he wanted to create was a 'vast movement, a powerful association, brimming over onto the international level, capable of imposing its will on politicians and diplomats'; this organization remained still to be created.[5] Méric's desire in creating the LICP had been to found a group which would draw together pacifists of all origins, inspirations, backgrounds, and political persuasions. The Ligue's first appeal called for the union of 'all energies, *with no concern whatsoever for political, philosophical, or religious creeds.* Believers or atheists, socialists or bourgeois, revolutionaries or conservatives, *whosoever is determined to fight for peace* is one of ours. No distinctions of class or of caste . . . Only one thing counts: *Peace.*'[6]

The LICP sought therefore to group together pacifists from all backgrounds. But Méric laid down one condition which he viewed as essential to the new group. The LICP was only interested in absolute pacifists, integral pacifists. Méric recognized that 'pacifism can be a vague aspiration towards peace' and in this sense, 'everyone is pacifist and it is the eminent Clément Vautel who is right'.[7] But Méric rejected out of hand this vague pacifism which at the first call to arms would collapse in the heat of nationalist fervour. In contradistinction to an insipid pacifism, Méric defined integral pacifism as follows:

One is really, thoroughly, pacifist only on condition of having rejected, once and for all, the extravagant nonsense with which we have been brainwashed. I suggest in principle that for the true pacifist: 1. *There is no national defence*

---

[3] Victor Méric, *Fraîche et gazeuse* (Paris: Éditions 'Sirius', 1932), 239–41.
[4] Ibid. 241.   [5] Ibid.   [6] Ibid. 246.   [7] Ibid. 247.

and *2. peace is only possible and lasting by total and rapid disarmament, without concerning oneself about the neighbour.*[8]

Méric underlined the disaffection from the official diplomatic and political worlds of Paris and Geneva felt by the new pacifists. The tone of pessimism in his conclusion was paramount. Asking rhetorically what tomorrow would bring, he wrote that despite all the pacific palaver and talk of 'Guerre hors la loi', war still went on around the world. His view of political society was scathing in its denunciation of the abdication of leadership in France and elsewhere. 'Our leaders are mediocrities', he wrote, 'and the leaders of all nations are mediocrities.'[9] But he provided no concrete answers to the problems he raised. The pessimism of his approach to peace and politics was overwhelming. The vague calls to undefined action, the continual anathemas pronounced against war, gave voice to a pacifist nihilism of despair. In the early years of the LICP this cry was sufficient to rally thousands of people across France to the pacifist cause, but under the cold douche of post-*Machtergreifung* reality, the angry rhetoric began to appear slightly sterile and empty. Practical, well-thought-out approaches to integral pacifism became necessary and were increasingly formulated within the LICP from about 1934 onwards. But in this chapter we shall be primarily concerned with the House that Méric built, the LICP in the years of growth from 1930 to 1934.

The LICP's first Appeal spoke in apocalyptic terms of the approaching catastrophe hovering over everything, of 'cities destined to incendiary bombs, deadly gases, and annihilation', in which the population would succumb to 'mortal panic, terror, and misery'.[10] The choice open to people was that between 'Devastation, Ruin, and Madness' on the one hand, and Life on the other—all capitalized in shades of the religious tract. In political terms, the Appeal called for an individual response couched in antipolitical terms: 'We must rise up against the Masters and those Responsible, against the bellicist Insanity, against the Hatreds which throw the Peoples against one another.'[11] Méric ended with a call to pacifist militant action. Peace had to be *imposed*, and readers were invited to join the 'combat formation' of the LICP. A complete break was

[8]   Méric, *Fraîche et gazeuse*, 249.   [9] Ibid. 254.
[10] Cited ibid. 244.
[11] Ibid. 245.

needed from sterile political debates, from the games that egos played, from the 'human intelligence which is spinning aimlessly, and applying itself desperately to a masturbation as conscientious as it is infinite'.[12]

Méric's appeal seems to have struck a responsive chord in France. The LICP grew quickly, as did the readership of *La Patrie humaine*. A financial statement for the year 1 December 1930 to 31 December 1931 showed a total income for the Ligue of 135,199 francs, of which some 61,000 francs had come from memberships, a further 18,000 had come from a voluntary subscription, and 39,500 francs were raised at meetings across France[13]—these are impressive sums for so young an organization. By issue number eleven, the *Patrie humaine* had become a weekly, and in early 1932 it was reported that 6,200 membership cards for the Ligue had already been distributed for that year.[14] A report about the LICP's first Congress in Angers later in 1932 claimed that 200 delegates took part in the debates. This included representatives of sixty-five sections numbering 7,000 Ligue members, as well as the mandated representatives of a further 5,000 individual leaguers.[15]

The local sections grew rapidly, too—especially those in the provinces. In February 1932 the Avallon section reported that it had 200 members, and at Limoges during a demonstration for peace, the section seemed disappointed to have collected only fifty new members.[16] Two months later, the Saintes section numbered 200 members, and at a meeting held on 2 April at which Marcelle Capy (1891–1962),[17] Rudolf Leonhard, and Roger Monclin spoke, there were 400 people present. This was exceeded at St Jean d'Angely, where 1,200 people heard the Ligue's propagandists speak in a converted hangar.[18] These meetings were not without their troubles.

---

[12] Ibid. 245 and 255.

[13] 'Comité central de la Ligue', *PH* 10 (30 Jan.–14 Feb. 1932), 8.

[14] A note on p. 4 of *PH* 12 (20–6 Feb. 1932) gives this information.

[15] '200 délégués participent aux débats', *PH* 31 (2–9 July 1932), 1.

[16] 'La Vie de la Ligue', *PH* 12 (20–6 Feb. 1932), 4.

[17] Marcelle Capy was educated at the University of Toulouse, and then began a career as a journalist, novelist, and public speaker. She was also one of France's most ardent feminists. During the First World War she broke with her colleagues on *La Bataille syndicaliste*, and identified herself with the pacifism of Romain Rolland who contributed a preface to her book *Une voix de femme dans la mêlée*. See James Friguglietti, 'Marcelle Capy', in Harold Josephson (ed.), *Biographical Dictionary of Modern Peace Leaders* (Westport, London: Greenwood, 1985), 141–3.

[18] 'La Vie de la Ligue', *PH* 19 (9–16 Apr. 1931), 4.

At Poitiers, the Camelots du roi tried to prevent Leonhard from speaking but were given a thrashing instead by the pacifists and had to retreat to a local pharmacy to plaster their wounds.[19]

By the time he wrote his New Year's editorial in 1933, Méric was claiming that the LICP had almost 16,000 members. The *Patrie humaine* had a readership of about 20,000, of whom 6,000 were subscribers.[20] A year later, after the trauma of the schisms between the LICP and the *Patrie humaine*, further exacerbated by Méric's death in October 1933, Robert Tourly noted with satisfaction that all of that notwithstanding, the paper had increased its print run from 18,000 in January 1933 to 22,000 copies in 1934.[21] And a year after the schism, the LICP still claimed a membership of 12,000.[22] As has already been noted, Méric had claimed in early 1933 a membership of just under 20,000.[23]

Clearly the numbers game is a dangerous one, but the LICP was indubitably a numerically important group in the first four years of its existence at least. As a rather alarmed report in the files of the Ministry of the Interior put it in May 1933: the LICP 'estimates at 300,000 the number of mobilizable men who, touched by the propaganda of this organization in France, are liable to return their mobilization papers or destroy them in the event of a direct threat of armed conflict'.[24] Another, slightly earlier, report from an informer who appears to have been present at the LICP Congress in early March 1933 reported that the LICP estimated its membership at 40,000 across France, although the money for only 5,000 memberships had so far been received by the Paris office.[25] The latter point highlights the organizational confusion which attended the LICP's early development. Perhaps because of lack of staff, but more likely because of Méric's inherent distaste for organizations and centralized control, the LICP in its early years showed astonishing growth and an equally amazing capacity for self-immolation and disintegration which came to a head at this same 1933 Congress. More will be said about that in due course. Suffice it here to say that

[19] Reported in *PH* 19 (9–16 Apr. 1931), 4.
[20] Victor Méric, 'Nos souhaits', *PH* 49 (31 Dec. 1932–7 Jan. 1933), 1.
[21] R. Tourly, 'Bilan et souhaits', *PH* 97 (5 Jan. 1934), 1.
[22] 'Précisions nécessaires', *Le Barrage*, 13 (9 Aug. 1934), 1.
[23] Figure cited in Méric, 'Pour tuer la guerre', 1.
[24] 'D'un correspondant', Paris, 2 May 1933, J./5 A-3870 in AN F7/13352.
[25] 'D'un correspondant', 25 Apr. 1933, A/3624 GB5 in AN F7/13352.

the LICP was a major pacifist organization by French standards in terms of the size of its membership. It had grown very rapidly and spawned a newspaper which had quickly become a weekly and was being distributed across France by Messageries Hachette.

For all that the LICP began life as a Paris-based organization in which Parisian intellectuals played a preponderant role, it quickly developed a large base of support in the provinces. As the Interior Ministry report mentioned above made clear, by 1933 there was hardly a village of any importance in France which had not been the site of a pacifist meeting for which the LICP was held largely responsible.[26] The provinces began to outstrip Paris in importance, and this was probably one of the factors which led to the effective seizure of power by a group of provincial pacifists at the 1933 Congress. The most important regional federations were undoubtedly those of the Calvados, Angers, and Algeria. All three of these regional federations were strong numerically, and their leaders —Émile Bauchet, Marcel Fouski, and Édouard Lemédioni respectively—played important roles in the development of the Ligue after 1933. But that is to jump ahead somewhat.

The organizational weakness of Paris became apparent in the communiqués from the Paris sections in 1932. Parisians could be depended on to turn out for a mass meeting at the Salle Wagram or the Palais de la mutualité, but the week by week work in the sections seemed difficult to sustain. Perhaps, as Camille Drevet remarked in 1938, the rural masses were more easily organized than the highly politicized urban populations.[27] For whatever reason, Paris seemed to provide the head to the organization (although even this was disputed), and the rest of France the body. Thus, for example, the section in the 11th and 12th *arrondissements* in Paris somewhat bitterly complained in the autumn of 1932 that 'for almost a year now, we have tried to unite all of the *Ligueurs* in our *arrondissement* into a section, . . . Unfortunately, our efforts have not been a great success, since at our meetings we scarcely gather forty comrades, even though some 250 are on the books'.[28] The reporter from the section in the 7th and 8th *arrondissements* echoed this criticism

---

[26] See the report entitled 'La Propagande pacifiste et le mouvement en faveur de l'objection de conscience en France', in AN F7/13352.

[27] See Camille Drevet, 'Rapport moral', *Le Barrage*, 125 (17 Mar. 1938), 3.

[28] 'La Vie de la Ligue: 11e et 12e arrdt.', *PH* 40 (29 Oct.–5 Nov. 1932), 4.

when he wrote that there was too much 'carelessness' in the section.[29]

What is clear is that the LICP organized a very effective propaganda campaign across France in the winters of 1931–2 and 1932–3. It is impossible to ascertain the aggregate number of Frenchmen who heard the Ligue's speakers, but the number must run into the tens, if not hundreds, of thousands. For example, in June 1932, the *Patrie humaine* reported that more than 3,000 people attended a public meeting in Saint Étienne at which Pierre Scize, Méric, and Georges Pioch spoke on behalf of the Ligue. Henri Jeanson (1900–70),[30] 'toujours fantaisiste', was also supposed to speak but missed his train and arrived at midnight. At Morlaix, in the Finistère, 1,000 people turned out to hear Méric, Leonhard, and Robert Tourly on 4 June.[31] In early 1932, Marcelle Capy spoke for the Ligue at meetings in Hamburg, Munich, Berlin, and elsewhere in Germany and Switzerland, and the *Patrie humaine* reported that 'despite the Hitlerians' all of these meetings were successful demonstrations of fraternity between the two peoples.[32] Georges Pioch spoke before 30,000 people at the Palais des projections in Barcelona, and later before an audience of 5,000 people in the small city of Geronne. As a result of his Spanish tour, a Spanish section of the LICP was formed.[33] In Angers, Méric, Maurice Gilles, and Louis Loréal spoke before 3,000 people in the Cirque-théâtre. Méric was clearly elated at the growth in the Angevin region; two months before, Angers had been completely ignorant of the Ligue's existence, but now there was a section of 400 members active in the city.[34] In Brest on 19 February 1932, Marcelle Capy addressed 1,500 people in the Salle Peloutier of the Maison du peuple; the same edition of the *Patrie humaine* reported meetings of eighty people in the small village of Sainte-Lazaigne (Indre), 250 people at a meeting held by Roger Monclin at Meudon, 600 present for a meeting at Quimper, and 1,700 attending a meeting at Lorient.[35]

Clearly something extraordinary was happening. Sections and federations were springing up across France and growing rapidly.

---

[29] 'La Vie de la Ligue', *PH* 38 (1–15 Oct. 1932), 4.

[30] See James Friguglietti, 'Henri Jeanson', in Josephson, *Dictionary*, 467–8.

[31] 'Notre agitation', *PH* 28 (11–18 June 1932), 4.

[32] 'Marcelle Capy en Allemagne et en Suisse', *PH* 10 (30 Jan.–14 Feb. 1932), 2.

[33] See short report in *PH* 10 (30 Jan.–14 Feb. 1932).

[34] Victor Méric, 'La Paix est en marche', *PH* 10 (30 Jan.–14 Feb. 1932), 2.

[35] Figures given in 'La Vie de la Ligue', *PH* 13 (27 Feb.–4 Mar. 1932), 4.

One of the fastest areas of growth seems to have been the Calvados. A report in the *Patrie humaine* in March 1932 on the *Grande Semaine de manifestations pacifistes internationales* outlined how quickly the Calvados federation had grown. The first LICP section in the department was formed on 3 January 1932. Twenty-four members contributed 45 francs for a propaganda campaign. With this small sum as seed money, 400 posters and 20,000 prospectuses were printed and distributed across the department. The Ligue's speakers were shuttled around in one of Bauchet's motor coaches, and although the whole campaign cost some 3,000 francs, the outlay was recovered by voluntary collections at the meetings. The result was that from being a section of forty-seven leaguers in January, the Calvados had grown to over 1,000 members by March.[36]

The Algerian federation also recorded spectacular growth. By late 1932, after a speaking tour by Pioch, Capy, and Lemédioni during which a profit of 2,000 francs was made, the federation reported that it now numbered fifteen sections. The speaking tour had seen fifty-three public meetings held, and the writer claimed that the LICP's propaganda had reached more than 200,000 people in Algeria. This might well be one of the reasons for which Gerin later in 1933 was forbidden by the authorities in Algiers from preaching the pacifist message to the indigenous population there.[37]

Normally one might well be rather sceptical about the strict veracity of these figures, but they seem to represent a realistic assessment of the LICP's initial development. It will be remembered that the police and Interior Ministry reports cited above all came to the conclusion that the new pacifism, and especially the LICP, was making tremendous headway in towns and villages all across the Hexagon. The period 1930–4 was one of growth for the LICP, but its flowering was to be short-lived. It remained an important organization right down to 1939, but it began to shrink in size from about 1934 onwards.

At the time of the schism at the 1933 AGM, Méric claimed that the Ligue had 18,000 members and the *Patrie humaine* about 6,000 subscribers; this he contrasted to the Ligue's first winter (1930–1)

[36] R. Henry, 'Un bel exemple à suivre', *PH* 16 (19–26 Mar. 1932), 3.

[37] See 'La Vie de la Ligue: Alger', *PH* 47 (17–24 Dec. 1932), 4. See telegrams of 10, 28, 29, and 31 May 1933 from the Governor-General of Algeria to Minister of the Interior. See also telegraphed response of 'Intérieur Affaires Algériennes à Gouverneur Général et Sécurité Générale Alger', 11 May 1933, all in AN F7/13352.

just a little over two years previously, during which the organization had grown from nothing to about 2,000 members.[38] Of these numbers only 10,056 Ligue members were represented at the Congress by 253 mandates.[39] By the following year at the Montargis Congress, René Gerin reported that the number of leaguers was only about 11,000—although it was difficult to be more precise because of some sections' unreliability in reporting their membership figures to the office in Paris. In any case, it was a far cry from the figure of 18,000 quoted the previous year at the Paris Congress.[40]

These figures were called into question by the Ligue itself only two years later at its 1936 Congress when Émile Bauchet revealed in his *rapport moral* that in 1933 the LICP had had 7,868 members, 7,617 in 1934, and 7,481 in 1935. He had arrived at these figures by the only effective means, that of counting the francs which arrived at the Paris office as the percentage of the membership subscription that was its due.[41] While these figures are doubtless accurate, they probably do not reflect the total number of LICP members across France. It is clear from the reports published in *Le Barrage* and elsewhere that one of the perennial problems faced by the organization was the unreliability of its local sections in the matter of sending the Paris headquarters the requisite percentage of the membership subscriptions they received. The 1938 Congress did not provide global membership figures, but only fifty-eight sections containing 2,560 members were actually represented when the meeting opened in Arras.[42] To give some idea of the magnitude of the decline, at least in terms of the numbers of Ligue members and sections represented at the congresses, it is worth noting that in 1936 at the Congrès de Bernay, 107 sections comprising 5,728 Ligue members had been represented.[43]

If not an entirely accurate representation of the Ligue's size, these

---

[38] Victor Méric, 'Rapport moral', *PH* 59, 5. Robert Tourly, in his report on 'L'Activité de la Ligue', ibid., claimed 'almost 20,000 members' and 'hundreds of thousands of sympathizers' in France.

[39] 'Congrès national de la LICP, 16–17 avril 1933', *Le Combat pour la paix*, 1 (May 1933), 5.

[40] René Gerin, 'Rapport moral sur l'activité de la Ligue de Pâques 1933 à Pâques 1934 qui sera présenté au Congrès de Montargis', *Le Combat pour la paix*, 10 (Mar. 1934), 4–5.

[41] Emile Bauchet, 'Rapport moral', *Le Barrage*, 87 (5 Mar. 1936), 4.

[42] Cited in 'Les Travaux du Congrès d'Arras', *Le Barrage*, 127 (28 Apr. 1938), 4.

[43] Reported in 'Les Travaux du Congrès de Bernay', *Le Barrage*, 94 (23 Apr. 1936), 3–4.

figures nevertheless give some indication of the downward trend it was experiencing. Given the political situation, the 1939 reports on the Ligue's health are surprisingly optimistic. Camille Drevet reported that there had been a surge in membership following the Munich crisis and most of the new members had remained loyal to the Ligue. She believed that the number of members would exceed that for 1938, but unfortunately gave no precise figures.[44] In the report on the 1939 Congress, however, it was reported that only forty-three sections or federations were represented, and these contained a total membership of only 2,023 leaguers.[45] Once again, it is clear that these numbers do not indicate the full extent of the LICP's membership because not all sections or individual members would be represented at any one congress. But it is equally apparent that the general trend in terms of membership was downwards from about 1934 on.

Further indications about the size of the Ligue can be gained from an analysis of the number of sections, public meetings held, and subscribers to the *Barrage* reported every year. In 1933, Roger Monclin claimed that more than 600 meetings had been held across France, Algeria, and Morocco since the previous congress. In the process some 500 cities or towns had been visited, and 200 LICP sections created.[46] In 1934, Gerin noted that there were 180 active sections with a further twenty or so which had fallen dormant. Six sections had been dissolved for a variety of reasons. There were also approximately 120 localities in which small groups of leaguers existed which had not yet been able to consolidate themselves into proper sections.[47] The following year showed a slight increase in the apparent level of activity with 191 active sections, and a further hundred in the process of formation. The year ending in February 1935 had also been a good one for the Ligue's propaganda; Bauchet reported that some 300 public meetings had been held. In this same period the LICP had also distributed some 100,000 copies of its Tract/Programme, 3,000 copies of its brochure, *Programme, tactique et moyens d'action*, 30,000 copies of the tract 'Enfants, ne jouez pas à la guerre', 20,000 copies of the tract 'Aux travailleurs', and a large number of propaganda posters and postcards. In addition

[44] Camille Drevet, 'Rapport moral', *Le Barrage*, 145 (16 Mar. 1939), 4.
[45] 'Les Travaux du Congrès de Marseille', *Le Barrage*, 147 (20 Apr. 1939), 4.
[46] Roger Monclin, 'L'Activité de la Ligue', *PH* 59 (11–18 Mar. 1933), 5.
[47] Gerin, 'Rapport moral', 4.

Bauchet estimated that about 400,000 copies of the *Barrage* were circulating in the country.[48]

1936 produced another strong showing on the propaganda front with about 180 lectures or meetings held over a five-month period in forty or forty-five departments. 150,000 copies of the Ligue's tract 'Nos principes' were distributed. The number of sections seemed to have fallen, though. It will be remembered that 1936 marked the beginning of a slump in the membership figures. It also saw the number of sections decrease to 158 with an additional twenty-nine in either dormant or embryonic stage. In 1938 no global figures are given, but apparently the Ligue had lost five sections, while gaining seven. Having said that, Camille Drevet acknowledged that the work was more difficult in the highly politicized urban areas than in the countryside. The Paris office had organized more than 200 lectures or meetings, though, in the period ending March 1938. The number of subscribers to the *Barrage* was slipping, however; in 1937–8, only 2,300 Ligue members held subscriptions, along with about 300 non-leaguers.[49]

Because of the Munich effect, the 1939 Marseille Congress was vaguely optimistic about the Ligue's future. Although only forty-three sections comprising 2,023 Ligue members were represented at the Congress, Gerin reported that Munich had created a great upsurge in subscriptions to the journal which now stood at approximately 3,000 Ligue members, and a further 350 non-Ligue members. If nothing else, the last figures show that the number of sections represented at the congresses had little bearing on the aggregate number of Ligue members, at least not in the latter half of the decade.[50]

The above figures give some impression of the numerical size of the LICP and the extent of its propaganda. The growth of its financial side was also rapid. In the financial year ending 28 February 1934,

---

[48] Émile Bauchet, 'Rapport moral', *Le Barrage*, 43 (7 Mar. 1935), 4. Bauchet listed the departments which were 'relatively untouched' by the LICP's propaganda as: Manche, Morbihan, Vendée, Eure-et-Loir, Oise, Ardennes, Meuse, Seine-et-Marne, Aube, Cher, Nièvre, Sâone-et-Loire, Creuse, Allier, Cantal, Aveyron, Pyrénées-Orientales, Var, Basses-Alpes, Hautes-Alpes. All other departments had been reached.
[49] Camille Drevet, 'Rapport moral', *Le Barrage*, 125, 3. See also René Gerin, 'Rapport sur le "Barrage"', *Le Barrage*, 125 (17 Mar. 1938), 4.
[50] Figures cited in 'Les Travaux du Congrès de Marseille', 4; and René Gerin, 'Rapport sur le "Barrage"', *Le Barrage*, 145 (16 Mar. 1939), 4.

the LICP had receipts totalling 137,132 francs.[51] The following year at the Agen Congress, the Ligue itself had receipts totalling 117,127 francs; the separate *Barrage* account had an income that year of 106,525 francs.[52] By 1936, the LICP's financial outlook was once again improving. The Ligue account showed a surplus of 25,000 francs on an income of 151,214 francs. The *Barrage* took in some 110,000 francs but had an outlay of 118,000; the situation for the *Barrage* was actually much worse because it was carrying a deficit of about 106,000 francs.[53] The 1938 financial report does not distinguish between Ligue and newspaper; total receipts of 166,063 francs are recorded.[54] The 1939 Congress reports gave no financial details whatsoever aside from the impressionistic claims mentioned above about the Ligue's membership rising substantially after Munich.[55]

The composite picture, then, is one of an organization which experienced enormous initial growth, in terms of membership, subscribers, financial returns, and in the extent to which its ideas were spread across France. This was followed by a levelling off from about 1934 to 1936, followed by a gradual downward spiral thereafter, only partially off-set by the Munich effect in late 1938 and early 1939. Even at the end, though, the LICP probably had claims to being the largest and most influential pacifist group in France—either old-style, or new.

THE NATURE OF THE LICP'S PACIFISM

The preceding pages have given some idea of the extent of the LICP's propaganda campaigns during the thirties in France. But what of the intellectual content of these campaigns? What sort of pacifism was the LICP propounding, and what sort of tactics did it envisage in its fight against war?

The answers to these questions are complex, especially for the initial period (1930–4) under discussion here. In the general intellectual effervescence in which the Ligue appeared there were many apparently contradictory approaches to integral pacifism, for all of

[51] Émile Bauchet, 'Rapport financier', *Le Combat pour la paix*, 10 (Mar. 1934), 5–6.
[52] Louis Léger, 'Rapport financier', *Le Barrage*, 43 (7 Mar. 1935), 4.
[53] Émile Bauchet, 'Rapport financier', *Le Barrage*, 87 (5 Mar. 1936), 4.
[54] Y. Dandieu, 'Compte-rendu financier', *Le Barrage*, 126 (31 Mar. 1938), 4.
[55] See Camille Drevet, 'Rapport moral', *Le Barrage*, 145, 4.

which the LICP tried to provide a home. The spectrum spanned everything from absolute non-violence to a revolutionary pacifism which, while eschewing external war, was not at all averse to a little civilian blood-letting now and again. The predominant elements within the LICP were those of Socialism and anarchism. There was also a minority of Communists, but they were discouraged by their party from having too much to do with *petit bourgeois* pacifism like that of the LICP. As far as the Christian community is concerned, the LICP did attract a variety of Catholic and Protestant members, but the marriage between the political avant-garde and the churches was always rather uneasy.

Méric had originally envisaged the Ligue as a haven for all forms of absolute pacifism. In his mind, the sole qualifying characteristics of the integral pacifist were a complete rejection of the idea of the national defence, and a commitment to working towards total, rapid, and, if need be, unilateral disarmament.[56] Within this very broad framework, anything was possible. There were thus LICP members who advocated absolute non-violence, those who believed in armed insurrection, advocates and opponents of civil war, proponents of judiciously planned assassinations of those 'responsible', and the list goes on.

By early 1932, Méric had expanded the two first principles of the LICP into four: (1) negation of the idea of the national defence; (2) struggle against war by all means; (3) pacifism to be placed above the political parties and governments; and (4) the struggle for the union of the Peoples.[57] The Appeal disclaimed any interest in creating an organization of 'followers'—LICP members were to be free individuals making a collective statement against war. It also underlined the eclectic nature of the LICP and its willingness to consider a very broad spectrum of tactics under the general rubric of pacifism:

If some lunatic were to take no account of the popular desire for peace, and were to let loose the massacre, it would be up to the peoples to resist the fact of war by all possible means: general strike, individual or collective revolt, passive or violent, according to the free decision of each man placed before his duty and his responsibilities . . . We must teach men to be MEN.[58]

---

[56] Méric, *Fraîche et gazeuse*, 239–41.
[57] 'Appel', *PH* 20 (16–23 Apr. 1932), 6.
[58] Ibid.

The propensity to consider anarchist tactics and revolutionary violence as legitimate pacifist methods is one of the distinguishing characteristics of French absolute pacifism which sets it apart from the primarily ethically inspired pacifism of the Anglo-Saxon world. There were certainly those pacifists in France who were integrally pacifist in the British sense of the word (the members of the small Mouvement international de la réconciliation spring to mind). These pacifists existed within the LICP as well. But what is interesting is the juxtaposition of non-violent and violent elements in mainstream French integral pacifism.

Largely under the influence of Méric, the LICP in its first few years of activity embodied this eclectic approach to the politics of peace. Under the effects of the pincer movement from left and right discussed briefly above, the LICP developed a 'rhetoric of violence' in its discussion of pacifist tactics and political problems. In so doing, it created a semantic reflection of the violent abuse of which it was itself the object—primarily at the hands of the extreme right-wing press. No doubt some of this rhetoric of violence was due to the anarchist analyses underpinning much of the LICP's world view, but equally one could argue that it is yet another example of the extent to which the fabric of late Third Republic political society was frayed, and the political temperature rising. The vitriol which was so liberally splashed about in the course of the pacifist debate was in some respects a prelude to the *épuration* mentality.

Examples of this rhetoric of violence abound in the LICP's language of political discourse. In early 1932 the LICP held a large rally at the Salle Wagram in Paris at which Pioch, back from his Spanish tour, and Marcelle Capy, back from Germany, were the featured speakers. Pacifist meetings, in the Paris area especially, had been the target of attacks by right-wing extremists[59] and at this meeting at Wagram all of the leaguers who had been wounded in clashes with the Camelots du roi and their ilk were collectively made the honorary chairmen. Maurice Gilles, who chaired the meeting, warned the 'gigolos du Roy', 'Taittinger's little boys', and the 'Croix du feu in the pay of Coty' that interruptions and an uproar would not be tolerated. Méric was more explicit, warning that 'we are determined, if

---

[59] See a note on p. 2 of *PH* 12 (20–6 Feb. 1932) in which is described the setting up of a 'Caisse de solidarité' of leaguers wounded or hospitalized in fights with right-wing thugs. To date 1,570 francs had been raised, of which 891 had been disbursed.

need be, to get rid of those responsible'.[60] Demonstrating his essentially non-conformist, antipolitical stance, Méric wrote in the same number of the *PH* that honest, ordinary people were in a state of legitimate self-defence *vis-à-vis* the government: 'We shall draw up a list—the red list. . . . We, too, will have our "Carnet B" . . . we will take our precautions and pillory them, . . . while waiting to line them up against the wall.'[61]

A few weeks later, Méric urged LICP members to examine their consciences and prepare themselves for any eventuality. He said it was absolutely essential to know where the embassies of the imperialist powers were located, so that action could be taken in an emergency. The implication was clear enough.[62]

The direct link in rhetorical style between Méric's editorials and those of some of the right-wing papers was made startlingly clear in June 1932 in a review of the press in the *Patrie humaine*. Commenting on an article in *L'Ami du peuple* in which François Coty fulminated against the 'financiers who run the world', and darkly threatened that names and addresses were known and thus would be called to account, the *PH* responded that 'this time . . . the masses know where to find those responsible. We know their names, where they live . . . The "red list" has been drawn up and on it is the name of the Coty of Cotys.'[63] And in January 1933 when the conscientious objector Gérard Leretour lay dying in a hunger strike in prison in Paris, Méric threatened that 'we will not let one of ours be assassinated with impunity. If, through inertia, cowardice, even through ignorance, they let Leretour die, pacifists will know how to establish responsibilities. And they will move on to other options.'[64]

The above examples indicate how the LICP rather carefully and ambiguously raised the possibility of reprisals against those whom it considered responsible for the problem of war. In a broad sense, this meant envisaging attacks on those members of the capitalist, governing political class who might embroil France in a war. It also meant, in a more immediate way, responding by threat of violence,

---

[60] 'Notre meeting à Wagram', *PH* 12 (20–6 Feb. 1932), 1. The abusive epithets are, of course, references respectively to the Action française, Pierre Taittinger's Jeunesses patriotes, and the right-wing veterans' organization, the Croix de feu.

[61] Victor Méric, 'Du bon travail', *PH* 12 (20–6 Feb. 1932), 1.

[62] 'Pacifistes, tenez-vous prêts!', *PH* 21 (23–30 Apr. 1932), 1.

[63] 'Ce que disent les autres', *PH* 28 (11–18 June 1932), 3.

[64] Victor Méric, 'On assassine un homme!', *PH* 52 (21–8 Jan. 1933), 1.

or even violence itself, to the provocations and attacks of right-wing zealots. To this end, the LICP established what it called the 'Young Pacifist Guard' in early 1932 which was termed a 'combat group *par excellence*', designed to protect LICP meetings and 'if necessary to pass to the offensive'.[65] The Camelots du roi and 'Taittinger's boys' had thus found their pacifist equivalent.

The fact that the latent violence of the LICP remained ambiguously camouflaged most of the time in no way lessened its importance as an undercurrent of values in the new pacifism. Occasionally, however, the 'rhetoric of violence' became abundantly transparent. This occurred just before the fractious 1933 Congress in an editorial in which Méric enjoined pacifists to 'remember the days when dynamite brought fear to bourgeois stomachs and sowed the "green terror". Science in the service of the powerful sets itself against the individual. It is up to the individual to use science against the masters and the assassins.'[66] On a motion from the Algerian federation, the Congress of the LICP unanimously underlined that this article represented Méric's personal views and not those of the whole Ligue.[67]

Méric's pacifism was essentially negative. It did not attempt to provide positive answers to the problems of peace, but contented itself instead with increasingly sterile anathemas hurled at French political society. He balanced on the fine line between total despair —announcing that war was imminent and inevitable—and calling the French to resist its fatality. Méric's negative pacifism was incapable of envisaging action in the event of war, however. He called for resistance to war in the peaceful *hic et nunc*—once war began it

---

[65] 'Une jeune garde pacifiste', PH 10 (30 Jan.–14 Feb. 1932), 2.

[66] Cited in 'Congrès national de la LICP, 16–17 avril 1933', 8.

[67] Ibid. See also Roger Monclin, 'Violence . . . ou soumission?', PH 21 (23–30 Apr. 1932), 3. Monclin raised the question of violence as a means of legitimately reacting to the violences of society and the attacks of the nationalist camp. He listed three cases of pacifists either beaten up by the police or harassed, and concluded: 'Devant la répression fasciste qui s'abat sur les meilleurs militants, nous n'avons plus le droit de rester inactifs. Nous comprenons très bien que nombre de nos amis, tolstoiens, gandhistes, objecteurs de conscience (encore que tous les objecteurs ne soient pas des non-violents), des chrétiens, entendent lutter par les moyens qui leur semblent les meilleurs. Mais nous leur demandons de ne pas considérer tous ceux qui n'ont pas exclu la violence de leurs moyens commes des fanatiques de la bagarre. Il est des moments où il est nécessaire, il est des iniquités scandaleuses qui nous tracent notre devoir: il est normal qu'à la violence on oppose la violence.'

would be too late, and he did not have a coherent plan to offer his followers. As he wrote in August 1932:

How many times will it be necessary to repeat that what matters is to fight war—*while it is not upon us*—by every means: the spoken word, the written word, demonstrations, education, violence . . . and to create a coalition of people across borders, across the nations. Afterwards, it will be too late. When war is upon us, it will become vain to seek the best way of avoiding it . . . The day that war falls upon us, despite all our exhortations, our bleatings, and our bellowings, knowing that we can do nothing and that we are irredeemably condemned, we will suffer our fate.[68]

But, he added menacingly, 'before falling victim to human stupidity and bloody covetousness, we will settle a few scores'.[69]

Méric seemed to see no contradiction between the veiled anarchism of these statements and his position against all wars, including civil wars. Discussing the Einstein declaration in April 1932 and the fact that too many people were trying to water down the *intégralité* of their pacifism, he declared that 'for the convinced pacifist, there can be no pretext, no excuse for war, whatever form it might take, even if its apostles baptize it "civil". War is the enemy which must be killed. War must not only be outside the law, but be vomited by real pacifists.'[70] This pacifist *prise de conscience* had to be achieved by a complete rethinking of how society operated. Pacifists had to see that there were occult forces as well as human weaknesses at play in the creation of wars, but once rid of their old 'prejudices', pacifists could begin to see clearly.[71] Having just rejected the idea of civil war, however, Méric concluded that pacifist tactics must include 'if events permit it and if our skin is in danger, *violence* and *reprisals*, exercised against the assassins'.[72] A few months later, he had arrived at the point of admitting that for the integral pacifist either his life or his liberty might have to be lost in a war.[73] This reflected the position already taken by Félicien Challaye that a foreign occupation of France was more desirable than war.[74]

Fortunately, there were more nuanced analyses of what constituted integral pacifism in the pages of the *Patrie humaine*. Pierre

[68] Victor Méric, 'Celle d'hier, celle de demain', *PH* 23 (6–19 Aug. 1932), 1–2.
[69] Ibid.
[70] Victor Méric, 'Le Véritable Pacifisme: Le Postulat d'Einstein', *PH* 19 (9–16 Apr. 1932), 1.   [71] Ibid.   [72] Ibid.
[73] Victor Méric, 'Pour tuer la guerre', 1.
[74] See the discussion of Challaye's thesis in favour of peace without reservations in Part I.

Cuenat discussed the problem in an article in late 1932, taking as his point of departure the postulate that everyone in France was a pacifist.[75] He distinguished two broad categories of inspiration for pacifism: fear, and philosophical or political conviction. There was nothing the matter with fear, but a constructive pacifism needed to be based on more than that. He thought that one could divide the population up into three categories on the question of peace. First, there were those who found war exalting and beneficial—these people were mercifully getting rarer. Secondly, there were those who accepted war through 'amorphism', naïveté, and fatalism. Cuenat believed this category to be the most ripe for pacifist propaganda. Thirdly, there were the pseudo-pacifists, those who accepted the idea of defensive wars. Recognizing the difference between the LICP's brand of pacifism and this latter form of pseudo-pacifism, Cuenat wrote that 'the only pacifism is a total pacifism'.[76] As far as methods and tactics were concerned, he distinguished two tendencies. The first was the 'democratic' tendency which believed people had a duty to elect pacifist governments, support the League of Nations, and so on. Their method of propaganda was education. Secondly, there were revolutionary pacifists who offered a 'little more variety', but who shared a belief in the total rejection of war. Revolutionary pacifism could be further broken down into two strands: on the one hand, there was 'individual revolt' or conscientious objection which had tremendous propaganda value, but which was weakened and strengthened paradoxically by its very individuality. Finally, there was revolutionary pacifism based upon the belief that peace was a function of economic and social considerations.[77]

There were certainly also those who saw the need to elaborate specific tactics for avoiding war. Sébastien Faure (1858–1942),[78] to take one example, subscribed to the Einstein declaration but argued that pacifism needed to go beyond it to the *prevention* of war by all suitable means. The most efficacious of these he believed to be total and unilateral disarmament.[79] The Geneva process represented the opposite of this unilateral disarmament, and was viewed with a

[75] Pierre Cuenat, 'Du pacifisme à la paix', *PH* 46 (10–17 Dec. 1932), 2.

[76] Ibid.

[77] Ibid.

[78] See Albert S. Hill, 'Sébastien Faure', in Josephson, *Dictionary*, 274–6.

[79] S. Faure, 'Avant tout et à tout prix il faut empêcher la guerre', *PH* 20 (16–23 Apr. 1932).

jaundiced eye by the LICP. The desire for general disarmament was certainly not strong enough in the men charged with representing France in Geneva; moreover, general disarmament was well-nigh impossible in the European situation created by the Versailles Treaty. Pulling together the themes of disarmament, treaty revision, and fears of an international armaments cabal, the *Patrie humaine* concluded in 1932 that 'it is perfectly clear that the road to Geneva must pass through Versailles. For the moment, it passes through Le Creusot.'[80] Another writer in the *PH* declared that the world situation was like that of 1912 all over again. He demonstrated the militaristic character of the French government and said that Michelet's dictum about France declaring peace to the world was a sham.

When our officials perorate, they never fail to speak about the true face of France; they give us credit for intentions which the facts put the lie to. We are wasting our resources in armaments, we are provoking war through our attitude, and through our own example we allow our neighbours to justify their armaments. As Delaisi says, we give 'the strange spectacle of peoples who arm because they scare themselves, and who scare themselves because they are armed.' The true face of France does not appear crowned with the laurel wreath on which the symbolic dove comes to rest; our features are those of the old trooper, our face has the sinister mouth of Militarism.[81]

The LICP's integral pacifism thus embraced a broad spectrum of ideas about what constituted pacifism. In terms of the Ligue's orientation towards French society, one can only term it non-conformist, anti-establishment, and antipolitical. The LICP incarnated the politics of dissent in the pacifist debates of the thirties. As opposed to the old-style pacifists of the Association de la paix par le droit, those of the LICP had no faith whatsoever in the slow march of juridical and social progress. As one commentator in the *Patrie humaine* put it in early 1932, with regard to the Kellogg–Briand Pact and the League of Nations:

They promise us a juridical organization of the peace; but we don't want scholarly texts, we want facts. It is vain to dream of legislating Peace —before having created peace in fact and having sculpted it in social reality, before having disorganized the administrative, economic, and military

---

[80] 'Ce que disent les autres', *PH* 12 (20–6 Feb. 1932), 3.
[81] Bernard André, 'Désarmement', *PH* 10 (30 Jan.–14 Feb. 1932), 7.

apparatus of war and having eliminated its essential and fundamental causes.

Facts always precede the law ... We have a Bastille to storm and to destroy: it is Capitalism which creates wars. Afterwards we will legislate ...[82]

Gabriel Gobron was even more caustic in his attack on the old conceptions of pacifism and, by clear implication, on the APD later in 1932. He referred to the 'good untroubled bourgeois, official and decorated,' whose organization is 'reconnue d'utilité publique' and who enjoins his fellow countrymen to reject wars of aggression. Such a suggestion in 1932 was enough to make one laugh. Those who advocated such beliefs were 'intellectual crustaceans'.[83]

The LICP's pacifism in this initial period from 1930 to 1934 was thus largely a negative one. It contented itself with verbal polemics against war which contained an implicit critique of capitalist society, but little in the way of concrete prescriptions for peace. There were some exceptions to this rule; the advocacy of unilateral disarmament is one. Generally speaking, one can say that the LICP was initially an organization incarnating an unstructured, sentimental revolt against the threat of a coming war. It balanced on the knife edge between total despair which could produce no effective results, and calls to resistance against the fatality which it came close to proclaiming itself. To the extent that tactics and methods were envisaged in this initial period, the spectrum of the possible embraced everything from the most violent attack on those held to be responsible, to complete non-violence. Only with the passage of time, as the rhetoric began to appear a little empty and worn, did the Ligue begin to evolve specific policies for action. It did this largely as a result of challenges to its view of pacifism and as it became necessary to respond to specific political issues.

The first of these challenges to the LICP's world view came in the form of the Amsterdam Congress against Imperialist War which convened in August 1932 on the initiative of Romain Rolland and Henri Barbusse. In an appeal to the LICP, Romain Rolland laid out three steps to peace as he saw them: individual refusal of war, collective refusal, and finally collective action. Collective action meant 'taking Bastilles' and he recommended to the LICP the

[82] Jean Tempête, 'Propos incisifs: Législation', *PH* 15 (12–18 Mar. 1932), 3.
[83] Gabriel Gobron, 'Les Crustacés intellectuels', *PH* 44 (26 Nov.–3 Dec. 1932), 3.

forthcoming world Congress.[84] The question of whether or not to attend the Amsterdam Congress greatly divided the Ligue, although Méric's negative view eventually prevailed at the LICP's first Congress in Angers in late June 1932.[85]

Méric's primary reason for wanting the LICP to steer clear of the Amsterdam Congress was that the latter seemed to have been taken over entirely by 'our old friends' the Communists. It was therefore not merely 'a question of Barbusse and Rolland ... In reading L'Humanité we note that it is all a question of defending Soviet Russia against imperialist aggression, and also that they are preparing to debunk the *false pacifists*.'[86] He took great exception to the notion that the LICP was comprised of false pacifists. He reminded Ligue members of the nefarious campaign conducted against the LICP by L'Humanité when the Ligue was still struggling to establish itself. In three or four 'copious articles', it had been explained that the LICP was composed of 'bourgeois pacifists, sold to the government and playing the game of Fascism, duping the masses'.[87] The Ligue could not forget that Communist speakers would arrive at its meetings to spread these lies, causing an uproar and fights. All of that could perhaps be forgiven, but Méric underlined that an even greater obstacle remained. The LICP had been founded on very strict

[84] Romain Rolland, 'Appel de Romain Rolland aux Combattants de la paix', PH 31 (2–9 July 1932), 1–2. This appeal is also reprinted in Romain Rolland, 'Appel à la Ligue des combattants de la paix', in *Par la révolution, la paix* (Paris: Éditions sociales internationales, 1935), 31–6. Rolland's original appeal for the Amsterdam Congress, dated 1 June 1932, is also in this collection. See Rolland, 'Contre la guerre: Rassemblement!', in *Par la révolution, la paix*, 29–30.

[85] See reports on the Angers Congress of the LICP in PH 31 (2–9 July 1932), 1. The LICP Congress decided after a long discussion that the Ligue would send a message to the Amsterdam Congress expressing its point of view, principles, and methods and that members would be free to participate on an individual basis. In the wake of the Angers Congress, there was much discussion however in the pages of the *Patrie humaine* about the LICP's decision not to attend. See PH 32 (9–23 July 1932) and 33 (23 July–6 Aug. 1932).

[86] Victor Méric, 'Nous n'irons plus au bois . . .', PH 30 (25 June–2 July 1932), 1–2.

[87] Ibid. See also PH 33 (23 July–6 Aug. 1932), 4, on which is reprinted an article from L'Humanité which attacked 'le verbalisme stérile des pacifistes à la Victor Méric et Georges Pioch' as well as 'l'action paralysante des individualistes et anarchistes qui croient lutter contre la guerre par "l'objection de conscience" et autres fadaises impuissantes'. The PH pointedly asked what Romain Rolland thought of these 'autres fadaises impuissantes' of which conscientious objection formed a part, and it concluded emphatically that 'on ne peut collaborer avec des gens qui non contents de nous insulter, tentent de jeter le discrédit sur des actes qui prouvent, tout de même, la conscience des hommes qui les accomplissent'.

principles: 'negation of the national defence, repudiation of *all ideas of fatherland*, and *war against all wars*'. But the upcoming Congress was trying to establish the idea of a necessary defence of the 'patrie socialiste'. This was a dangerous illusion which would lead straight to the Just War, War-to-end-all-Wars mentality of 1914. There was thus a definitional problem involved in the Ligue's repudiation of the Amsterdam movement. The LICP was against all wars, and not just against imperialist wars. Furthermore there was a fundamental question of tactics to be considered. Méric wrote that the methods

envisaged by the Communists for fighting against war are really completely fantastic. These pacifists, who are not *petit bourgeois*, invite their militants in times of peace to go to the barracks and take up their rifles. It seems that in the barracks, under the sympathetic eye of Adjutant Flic, they will do some excellent propagandizing. In time of war, they will ask their militants to join their regiments. There, they will wait patiently for the hour to arrive when the foreign war can be transformed into a civil war. And, in waiting for that to happen, they will fire their rifles, shoot their cannons, and use their machine-guns against other partisans of the same civil war.[88]

Romain Rolland finally intervened directly in the debate within the LICP in his role as honorary president. In a letter of 12 July 1932 to Méric, he wrote that it was agreed that he and the LICP sought the same goal: the achievement of peace by efficacious means. Having said that, there remained three questions which required further clarification. First, he wanted to know what Méric would do if asked to contribute, either directly or indirectly, to war. Would he refuse absolutely, even to the point of facing the firing squad? Romain Rolland was prepared for this possibility, but was Méric? Secondly, Rolland argued that it was all well and good for intellectuals to refuse to fight because they had little to lose in so doing. But what about the working class? In Rolland's view, it was *only* the working class that was capable of stopping the outbreak of war. But if the working class revolted or refused service, it could instantly be declared part of the national defence structure and therefore in mutiny. Romain Rolland called that civil war. What did Méric call it? Finally, Romain Rolland wrote that war had become internationalized to the point that it might well not occur in Europe in future, but rather might be fought by proxies hundreds of miles away. What did Méric plan to do to prevent such transplantation away from French foyers? What did the

[88] Méric, 'Nous n'irons plus au bois'.

LICP say to its members who were part of the 'infernal machine'? Rolland saw civil war at the end of every path. The origins of the debates later in the thirties over collective security and the idea of an indivisible peace are clearly to be seen in this letter. Rolland concluded that he was horrified by the idea of civil war, but saw no other hope in the West:

I know of only one great tactic of non-violence which might be capable, maybe, of bringing war to its knees. It is that of Gandhi and of his people in India. But we still don't know how that experiment will end.

I should be ready to use it in the West. But who is interested in it here? Who is concerned about any tactic at all? Words, words . . . What will remain on the day of battle? . . . We must achieve social justice without which war is perpetual. Whatever the bridge may be—non-violence or violence—it must be crossed.[89]

In his response to Rolland's questions, Méric replied that he was personally willing to face execution for his beliefs. As far as conscientious objection was concerned, he agreed with Rolland that in itself it was not enough, despite its great moral value. The coming war would make no distinction anyway between combatants and non-combatants, so in some respects the question was irrelevant. He agreed that the people who had to be reached were the working class, those who produced the chemicals and armaments necessary for modern warfare. The working class needed to be ready to prevent war by sabotaging equipment, going on strike, and refusing to participate in the crime. Hundreds of thousands of workers needed to be committed to this action, but that would mean civil war or insurrectional violence. Méric thought Rolland was in contradiction with himself on the possibility of violence having to be used, but this merely indicated the direction Rolland's thought was travelling away from absolute non-violence. As far as the massacre of distant peoples in surrogate wars was concerned, Méric was as opposed to this as Rolland. But he categorically rejected the Communist tactic of preparing civil war by sending young Communists to the barracks to do their military service:

Romain Rolland accepts civil war with a sort of fatality. He goes so far as to doubt the efficacy of the Gandhian movement. And he proclaims his dislike for the aforementioned civil war which, as Georges Pioch has rightly

---

[89] Romain Rolland, 'Le Combat pour la paix: Romain Rolland intervient dans le débat', *PH* 33 (23 July–6 Aug. 1932), 1.

commented, exists already in fact. If it is a question, as the Communists demand, of joining the army, taking up a rifle, fighting, while waiting for the right moment, we will not march. Our entire difference is there. A civil war with cannons, machine guns, tanks, airplanes, bombs, gas, officers, and soldiers? No. It would be too like the other.[90]

Returning to his anarchist theme, Méric asked what Rolland for his part thought of the individual violent gesture, that is to say of the violent act of doing away with one of those responsible for war should it ever break out? And on a larger scale, what did Rolland think of the idea of organizing pacifists to commit reprisals in self-defence against the criminals who caused wars?[91]

Georges Pioch, who had decided to attend the Amsterdam Congress, took pains to explain why he did so and how his conception of pacifism differed fundamentally from the crude Leninist view that an imperialist war could be turned into a civil war and hence lead to the revolution. Pioch ridiculed those old-style pacifists who still believed that a coherent pacifist doctrine could be erected on shifting national ideas of what constituted justice. He believed that capitalism could cause wars, but equally that war was the result of the 'lies and megalomania of certain men', the 'apathy, obedience, and submission of the peoples', and that 'cupidity was not the monopoly of one social regime only'. There existed therefore the possibility of wars other than of capitalist origin. And in this sense, he attacked the Communist notion of turning imperialist wars into civil wars. He accused the Leninists of attempting a social experiment; pacifists on the other hand just wanted to live. He revolted against the idea that war could be inevitable; the whole core of his pacifist belief was incarnated in an 'intelligent and certain . . . Non-Acceptance'.[92]

The debate dragged on into 1933 and beyond. Romain Rolland resigned his position as honorary president of the LICP at the Ligue's Easter Congress in 1933.[93] In the meantime, the Amsterdam Congress came and went. Its final manifesto condemned conscientious objection among other things, and provoked even a negative

---

[90] Victor Méric, 'Le Combat pour la paix: Réponse de Victor Méric', *PH* 33 (23 July–6 Aug. 1932), 1.   [91] Ibid.
[92] Georges Pioch, 'Paix dans notre Ligue, d'abord!' *PH* 33 (23 July–6 Aug. 1932), 1–2.
[93] His resignation speech is contained in Romain Rolland, 'Le Pacifisme et la révolution (adresse du 15 mars 1933 au Congrès national de Pâques de la Ligue internationale des combattants de la paix)' in *Par la révolution, la paix*, 119–23.

response from Romain Rolland himself who had been prevented from travelling to Amsterdam because of illness.[94] Gustave Dupin (1861–1933),[95] writing in the *Patrie humaine* shortly thereafter, attacked the *étatisme* and the negation of individual values and action contained in the Amsterdam manifesto which he called a *phantasme verbal*.[96] Méric for his part had already rejected out of hand the accusation that the LICP was composed almost entirely of anarchist elements:

We are not followers. And don't let anyone say that the anarchist spirit reigns in the Ligue. Lies! There were many anarchists who wanted to participate in the Communist practical joke in Geneva [the originally intended site of the Amsterdam Congress]. Those who understood were the 'Party-less', the 'outsiders', professors, teachers, intellectuals, *petits bourgeois*, civil servants, all opposed to war—against all wars—and who have put their trust in us to lead the battle.[97]

In his message to the LICP's 1933 Congress, Rolland rejected the notion contained in the Ligue's statutes that pacifism was to be placed above all other considerations and that Ligue members should commit themselves to working towards the unique goal of peace. He also attacked Méric's strange affirmation that the LICP's statutes were intangible; more will be said about that in due course. The thrust of Rolland's message was that revolutionary concerns and the righting of injustices were just as important as pacifism, and indeed defined the essence of the longed for goal of peace. Pacifism in Rolland's view had to be social and not exclusively individual and introspective. He wrote,

I will not admit that the Ligue should limit its preoccupations to the salvation of the individual, under whatever form it may be conceived, whether it be in the most noble form of Conscientious objection for moral or

---

[94] Romain Rolland, 'Lettre à Henri Barbusse sur la place qui doit être faite aux objecteurs de conscience et aux Gandhistes, dans le mouvement révolutionnaire, issu du Congrès d'Amsterdam', in *Par la révolution, la paix*, 61–4.

[95] Gustave Dupin was a glassmaker before the Great War and a journalist and polemicist thereafter. His pacifist *prise de conscience* was occasioned by the death of his only son in the Great War. He was a founding member of the Société d'études documentaires et critiques sur la guerre, but he held himself aloof from joining any particular pacifist group, preferring to maintain his independence. He published numerous articles and several books, usually under the pseudonym Ermenonville. See James Frigulietti, 'Gustave Dupin', in Josephson, *Dictionary*, 234–5.

[96] Gustave Dupin, 'L'Individu et l'état', *PH* 47 (17–24 Dec. 1932), 2.

[97] Victor Méric, 'Précisions', *PH* 32 (9–23 July 1932), 1.

religious reasons, or whether it be in the lowest form of the save-your-own-skin egoist. I find it natural that these preoccupations exist and that account should be taken of them. But if they claim to be exclusive and divorce themselves from the social salvation, from the protection of the human community, they would be shamefully insufficient and I should tax them with indignity.[98]

But the LICP declined to follow Rolland in his evolution away from his former pacifism as an ethic of ultimate ends. In a manifesto published after the Congress, the LICP rejected Rolland's questions as outside the Ligue's competence. It reaffirmed that the LICP had been formed 'outside and above the political parties, to fight against war by all means, and to struggle for peace with no reservations'.[99] The questions posed by Rolland and the connections he made between peace and the struggle for political and economic social justice were the province of political parties, labour unions, and philosophical or revolutionary groups, but not of the Ligue. The LICP did go some way to answering his criticism, however. It changed its statutes to eliminate the old formula of 'Pacifism above all else' and 'against all wars' to read 'Against wars imposed by governments on the peoples, in the name of a so-called National Interest'.[100] This was done in order to realize a greater unity between those pacifists who rejected the notion of the national defence, and those elements which considered themselves revolutionary within the Ligue.[101]

Méric contributed his views to the debate in an article published in late April 1933 in which he sought also to defend his own conceptions of the pacifist struggle which had been partially censured by the Congress. Responding to what he called Rolland's 'sort of message' to the Congress, Méric wrote that Rolland was 'bolshevizing' himself more and more.

This is his right. It is also ours not to follow him. And if he wants to drag us into what he calls a 'civil war' (one needs to define one's terms) and the defence of the oppressed, it is understandable that we should hesitate.

[98] Rolland, 'Le Pacifisme et la révolution', 121. For an analysis of Rolland's changing conception of pacifism see Norman Ingram, 'Romain Rolland, Interwar Pacifism and the Problem of Peace', in Charles Chatfield and Peter van den Dungen (eds.), *Peace Movements and Political Cultures* (Knoxville, Tenn.: University of Tennessee Press, 1988), 143–64.
[99] 'Manifeste du Congrès', *Le Combat pour la paix*, 1 (May 1933), 3.
[100] Ibid.   [101] Ibid.

In this paper we have always said that we are against all wars, by whatever means, and we accept no excuse for them. We shall no more march in a war against Hitlerism or Mussolini than in the social war of the proletariat. All of these wars are prepared by the profiteers of cannons and munitions who leave it to their bought press to create and develop the indispensable psychosis and to agitate one people against another.[102]

In terms of pacifist methods in peacetime, Méric recognized the most passive to the most violent. But what about in time of war? He responded to the criticism he had faced at the Congress in the form of the motion from the Algerian section condemning an overtly anarchist leader he had written a few weeks previously. The pacifist despair of his position came through clearly. For Méric there were no effective means of fighting against a war once it had started—and he included the whole spectrum of pacifist tactics from conscientious objection to insurrection. Nothing would be effective. And so, in the last resort, in the event of war, the only course open to the pacifist was that of individual action, carefully left undefined.[103]

There to all intents and purposes the debate ended. Romain Rolland returned, as he put it, to his place amongst the rank and file, although to 'the extreme left of action', and the Ligue went its separate way. The friendly divorce between the LICP and its former honorary president marked the first of the significant challenges to the integral pacifist position which the Ligue was to fight off before 1939. Rolland, and to an even greater extent the Amsterdam movement, had tried to make pacifism and the achievement of peace a strict function of other social goals—economic change, social revolution, and one specific sort of political outlook. Despite all protestations to the contrary, it is clear that the type of pacifism espoused by the Amsterdam movement was a very limited one whose parameters were defined by the exigencies of the Soviet world view. The LICP rejected this consequentialist definition of pacifism and clung tenaciously to the view that the achievement of peace was an end in itself.

Having said that, it is clear from the discussions within the LICP that its conception of pacifism was far from an exclusively non-violent one. At one end of the spectrum there existed within the Ligue men who were quite prepared to envisage the most violent tactics as

[102] Victor Méric, 'Nos moyens de lutte', PH 66 (29 Apr. 1933), 1.
[103] Ibid.

methods of preventing war. Even in the case of its libertarian elements, the definition of pacifism within the LICP seemed to take on overwhelmingly political overtones which masked the ethical point of departure for many of these pacifists. This is probably one of the major differences between Anglo-Saxon and French absolute pacifism. It is perhaps an extension of the dichotomy already noted by Pierre Cot (see Part I) with reference to old-style pacifism. The distinction between the British old-style pacifist's Bible and the Code Napoléon of his French counterpart was mirrored in the new pacifism of the thirties by the continued insistence of the French integral pacifists on the political aspect of pacifism. Once again, it is probably a comment on the deeply divided nature of French political society in the thirties that the question of peace should take on such fiercely political colours in an antipolitical movement which expressed such deep-seated resentments against the recent course of French political history.

The paradoxes within the LICP's integral pacifism abound. The extent to which the Ligue sought to provide a refuge for both non-violent and violent pacifists has already been observed, as has its propensity to define itself as an antipolitical movement in uniquely political terms. Its rejection of Amsterdam-Pleyel was largely based upon its refusal to define pacifism in purely collective terms according to just one view of political society. But the opposite position was not necessarily true within the LICP; it did not embrace conscientious objection wholeheartedly as a means of resisting war. Officially, the LICP supported COs and applauded their moral courage but did not see in objection an effective way of preventing war.

1932 and 1933 saw a great upsurge in conscientious objection in France which elicited both a governmental response and a tactical response from the LICP. Despite the fact that some French dictionaries date the entry of the expression *objecteur de conscience* into the French language as 1933, there is little doubt that it was a known quantity, both as a political instrument of resistance to war, and as a philosophical, moral, or religious position, in the fairly immediate post-World War I period. We have already noted how the problem posed by objection was dealt with by the representatives of old-style pacifism. During the 1920s and early 1930s a number of small books discussing the merits and disadvantages of conscientious objection as an instrument of war resistance were published. Certain newspapers of anarchist tendencies discussed the subject from their own particular perspective from about 1924 onwards. And, in the late 1920s, a bona fide pacifist press appeared and began to include reports on objection in its pages.[104]

Michel Auvray mentions several groups either promoting or supporting objection in the early twenties in France: *inter alia* the War Resisters' International and the International Fellowship of Reconciliation, the latter known in France as the Mouvement international de la réconciliation. He has discovered the first French support group for COs, the Comité de défense de l'objection de conscience, in existence as early as 1920. It counted in its Comité d'honneur writers such as Henri Barbusse and Georges Duhamel.[105] The earliest trace of CO activity in the files of the Ministry of the Interior, however, is the Ligue pour la reconnaissance de l'objection de conscience, founded in Lyon in 1924 by Paul Bergeron.[106] This Ligue, despite a Comité d'honneur counting in its number a great proportion of the future leaders of the French pacifist movement of the late twenties and thirties, seems to have become rapidly moribund. The late twenties and early thirties also saw the first of the rather pitiful public trials of conscience which sent men of various political, religious, and philosophical persuasions to prison for terms of a year or more; in the case of two Protestant theology students, Philippe Vernier and Jacques Martin, these were but the first in a series of sentences they would receive for their convictions until the chaos of June 1940 finally released them into the dangerous world of

[104] For examples of the development of this genre, see: Manuel Devaldès, 'Les Objecteurs de conscience anglo-saxons', in *Mercure de France*, 166 (15 Sept. 1923), 642–69; Manuel Devaldès, 'L'État mondial de la question de l'objection de conscience', *Mercure de France*, 198 (15 Aug. 1927), 100–22; Marceline Hecquet, *L'Objection de conscience devant le service militaire* (Paris: Éditions du groupe de propagande par la brochure, 1924); René Valfort, *L'Objection de conscience et l'esprit maçonnique*, Préface de Édouard E. Plantagenet (Paris: Collection des documents maçonniques de *La Paix*, n.d. [1930]); Madeleine Vernet, *De l'objection de conscience au désarmement* (Levallois-Perret: Éditions de la Volonté de paix, 1930); see also the newspapers and journals *Le Semeur*, *La Patrie humaine*, *Les Cahiers de la réconciliation*, amongst others for a continuing discussion of conscientious objection in the late 1920s and early 1930s in France.

[105] Michel Auvray, *Objecteurs, insoumis, déserteurs: Histoire des réfractaires en France* (Paris: Stock/2, 1983), 174–5.

[106] Archives nationales, Paris. F7/13352. See report entitled 'Le Mouvement en faveur de l'objection de conscience en France' (Paris, 16 Feb. 1933); see also *Tract 1* (Christmas 1923) of the Ligue pour la reconnaissance de l'objection de conscience in F7/13352. *Tract 3* of the LROC is in Bibliothèque nationale, Paris, 8° Wz 3636.

Vichy.[107] The essential point then is that for those who had ears to hear and eyes to see, conscientious objection was no wildfire malignancy which, in a spasm of bad timing, contrived to make its appearance in the body politic at almost the precise moment that events across the Rhine were riveting French eyes on the spectre of post-Versailles *revanche*. Far from it. Conscientious objection existed in France throughout the interwar period, although always very much as a minority movement, if one can call it even that. But it was only in January 1933 that the French government suddenly perceived that it had a 'conscientious objection problem'.

The governmental response to this problem took the form of a ministerial circular sent out by Camille Chautemps, the Minister of the Interior, to the prefects of the French departments in January 1933 asking that they investigate the problem and take appropriate action. It was accompanied by a parallel circular from the Minister of War, Édouard Daladier, to the commanding generals of the various military regions. Chautemps's circular of 26 January 1933 emphasized that conscientious objection represented something new and dangerous to the French state precisely because it constituted such a radical departure from the usual brand of revolutionary defeatism with which French governments had long been acquainted. As Chautemps wrote, his attention had been 'particularly drawn to the development of a campaign presently being conducted in France in favour of conscientious objection, that is to say, young people who refuse to submit to the military laws for apparently moral motives'.[108] He wrote dismissively of the usual 'propaganda conducted for several years by the Communist Party', thereby recognizing that

[107] A few examples of men who were condemned in the late twenties and early thirties are: Georges Chevé, sentenced to six months' imprisonment on 7 Oct. 1927 (see report on Chevé's case in *Le Semeur*, 108 (19 Oct. 1927)); Eugène Guillot, condemned to one year in prison on 10 Jan. 1930 (see 'L'Objection de conscience et l'Affaire Eugène Guillot' in *La Volonté de paix* (Spring 1930)). For Romain Rolland's reaction to the affair consult Romain Rolland, 'L'Objection de conscience doit être, non individualiste et libertaire, mais sociale', in *Par la révolution, la paix*, 91–2. See also 'Textes du Comité de défense Eugène Guillot' in Bibliothèque de documentation internationale contemporaine (BDIC) Fonds Duchene FΔRés 273/6; for the trials of Camille Rombaut, Jacques Martin, and Philippe Vernier, see *Procès de Camille Rombaut* (Aubervilliers: 'La Réconciliation', 1932); *Procès de Jacques Martin* (Aubervilliers: 'La Réconciliation', 1932); *Procès de Philippe Vernier* (Aubervilliers: 'La Réconciliation', 1933); Martin and Vernier were also interviewed by the author on 16 and 17 Sept. 1983.

[108] AN F7/13352. 'Le Ministre de l'Intérieur à Monsieur le Président du Conseil, Ministre des Affaires étrangères, même lettre à Ministre Guerre', Paris, 9 Jan. 1933.

conscientious objection differed in style and intent from the more ideologically motivated and politically opportunistic antimilitarism which was part and parcel of the traditional mythical baggage of sizeable portions of pre-war Socialist and post-war Communist militancy.[109] In January 1933 the danger seemed to lie elsewhere. Chautemps and the Sûreté were particularly concerned at the spread of the moral contagion to other social classes, in short, at its apparent, albeit nascent, generalization across class barriers.

Most of the prefects eventually reported some activity or sympathy for conscientious objection in their departments. For some, it was an easy case of enumerating those who had refused their reserve mobilization papers and would therefore be serving short sentences in the local army garrison gaol. Other prefects reported genuine cases of young conscientious objectors, refusing all military service for the first time. The vast majority, however, were preoccupied by propaganda in favour of conscientious objection. One is struck by the scrupulous detail of the reports which made their way to Paris. It seemed that every insignificant primary school teacher, postman, or shoemaker who held seditious views, or had merely expressed sympathy for the plight of men and families caught in the trap of conscience, was carefully noted down and sent to the Ministry. An example of this is a report on a Professor Choski of the *lycée* in Oran, Algeria, who had delivered a lecture dealing with conscientious objection in a favourable light to his mathematics class on 29 March. Jaurès, Einstein, and the Oxford Union debate all figured in the notes of a schoolboy's *cahier* which formed the basis of a report written by the Oran Division Commanding General and passed on to Chautemps through the Governor-General of Algeria in mid-May.[110]

The LICP played a key role in the campaign in support of conscientious objection, despite the fact that it had no official policy on the matter and its membership was divided on its efficacy, of which more will be said shortly. That notwithstanding, several of its key speakers and organizers, notably Georges Pioch, René Gerin, Marcelle Capy, and Jeanne Humbert, were of great concern to the authorities because of their extreme views on the subject. A lecture

[109] AN F7/13352.
[110] Ibid. 'Le Général de Division Guedeney, Commandant la Division d'Oran à Monsieur le Général commandant le 19e CA Alger', Oran, 31 Mar. 1933. Forwarded to the Minister of the Interior only on 12 May 1933 by the Governor-General of Algeria.

by Pioch on conscientious objection, scheduled for February, was cancelled by the prefect in Strasburg on the advice of the Interior Ministry which feared, it seems, the spread of this idea in border areas, especially Alsace-Lorraine. Pioch spoke nevertheless, two weeks later, but on a thinly disguised different topic: 'Poets against War'.[111]

René Gerin was probably the most indefatigable and dangerous of the LICP propagandists, however. He was certainly the most visible exponent of conscientious objection in the higher echelons of the LICP. This Parisian journalist, Chevalier of the Legion of Honour, an *ancien normalien*, and *agrégé en histoire*, covered most of France in the winter and spring of 1933 in his campaign for peace, speaking regularly before crowds of 250 to 1,000 people. He paid for his commitment to this form of pacifism in several disciplinary sentences of short duration and one long sentence passed on him by virtue of the newly strengthened law of July 1934 on conscientious objection. Gerin was careful, however, to emphasize to his audiences that he advised no one to become a CO. On 13 March 1933 Gerin and Henri Guilbeaux spoke before an audience of 2,500 people at Limoges, and in a circumspect tone, Gerin said that he would not advise young people to refuse their military service, but if they did so nevertheless, he would support them. Above all, it was to the men of his own generation, to the men of 1914, that Gerin addressed his comments. He urged these men to refuse their military papers, to return them to the War Ministry, and he assured them that having done so they would be no more troubled than he.[112]

Pioch, too, when asked directly in public whether he counselled conscientious objection would only say that it was a delicate question which had to be answered by each person individually since the consequences were potentially very serious.[113]

Some LICP groups debated collective objection as a means of resistance to war, but seemed chary of actually putting match to tinder. On 4 March the Caen section of the LICP discussed the question after one member suggested a massive, organized return of all members' mobilization papers. According to the police report, the

[111] AN F7/13352. 'Rapport de l'Inspecteur principal Léonard sur la conférence faite à Strasbourg par M Georges Pioch', Strasbourg, 22 Feb. 1933. See also 'Rapport', Commissariat spécial, Strasbourg, 22 Feb. 1933.

[112] AN F7/13352. Report from the Commissariat spécial de Limoges, 14 Mar. 1933.

[113] Léonard report, Strasburg, 22 Feb. 1933.

president of the section replied that 'the number of conscientious objectors is not yet strong enough for that, and he feared that the result obtained might be the complete opposite of that hoped for'.[114] His conclusions were put to the vote and adopted unanimously; the return of mobilization papers was put off until a later date. Small consolation for the government, though, which could only see that the LICP was organizing a most effective and widespread pacifist propaganda campaign which touched all corners of the Hexagon.

Two position papers in the Ministry files make clear that it was not the *number* of objectors which worried the government, but rather the latent effects objection might be having on the national morale; even in the case of war, it was not thought that the number of conscientious objectors would increase significantly. Nevertheless, one report writer noted, 'the campaign in support of conscientious objection in France has taken a not negligible development over the past few months', and he commented most disapprovingly that it made the citizen 'judge of his own opinions'. But if the danger did not lie in numbers, where did it lie? The report writer saw two great dangers in the CO movement. The first was 'the fact that, under the influence of the anarchists and Communists the idea of simple non-resistance, which is that of pure objectors, is being replaced little by little by that of rebellion'. Rebellion was, of course, envisaged differently by the anarchists and the Communists. For the former, it was the individual gesture; for the latter, it was the mass movement. But according to the report writer, whether it be under one form or another, thoughts of rebellion were winning the world of objection. The second fear was that of defeatism, the destruction of national morale by a moral disease, and here, too, the anonymous writer believed there was cause for grave concern. The efforts of the COs had not been in vain. Several reserve officers had already given their support to the cause. It was possible, if not probable, that the movement was not sufficiently strong to create disorder in a mobilization, but the CO propaganda might bear its fruit in the aftermath of a mobilization. In the words of the report writer, 'this campaign sows doubts in minds poorly placed to see and to understand'. Of even more concern was the fact that objection could serve as a cover for cowardice, and could thus contribute to a feeling of defeatism in the first weeks of a

[114] AN F7/13352. 'Le Préfet du Calvados à Monsieur le Ministre de l'Intérieur', Caen, 6 Mar. 1933.

war. If the war were prolonged, this defeatism could have very serious consequences. It was the writer's conclusion that there was 'here a disease capable of destroying the morale of the nation and weakening the force of its resistance'.[115]

Two months later another report merely strengthened these basic observations. The writer pointed out that in the interval, the number of objectors and sympathizers identified had doubled from 95 to 183. Still, this was enough to qualify as a 'great development'. Much of the credit for the expansion of the movement was given to the LICP which regularly attracted large crowds to its meetings. Not a single city of any importance in France had not been the site of an LICP meeting. The writer detected a growing current of selfishness in the expanding CO movement:

. . . the attitude of the greater part of the pacifists is evolving. As their 'public' expands, they become more aggressive, and in their speeches, the 'right of not endangering oneself' takes the place of the 'duty not to shed blood'. They are less attached to exalting a noble ideal than they are to awakening and strengthening sentiments of utility and individual preservation. There is here a danger for the morale of the Nation of a potentially grave nature.[116]

Thus, of immediate concern to the government was the threat of nascent defeatism, incipient rebellion, and a growing selfishness which denied national values. Notes such as one dated 2 May 1933 from an informer with good contacts in the LICP could still be a trifle shocking. According to this source, the LICP estimated that 300,000 Frenchmen might very well ignore a mobilization order in the event of a political or military crisis.[117]

Whilst the Interior Ministry files fall almost silent on the problem of conscientious objection after May 1933, in the wake of publication of the circular in the press, there continued to be much interest in the subject in the rue Saint Dominique. A note of 26 December 1933 indicates that the matter was discussed at a meeting of the Council of Ministers and that subsequently a working party from the Ministries of Justice and War agreed to submit amendments to the law of 31 March 1928 on recruitment to the army to the next sitting of the Chamber of Deputies. Whereas the old law had only penalized

---

[115] AN F7/13352. See, 'Le Mouvement en faveur . . .' (report dated 16 Feb. 1933).
[116] AN F7/13352, short report dated 19 Apr. 1933, 'La Propagande pacifiste et le mouvement en faveur de l'objection de conscience en France'.
[117] AN F7/13352, PJ/5 A-3870, 'D'un correspondant', Paris, 2 May 1933.

people who were convicted of actually materially impeding a mobilization, the proposed amendment to Article 91 extended the offence to anyone found guilty of 'provoking disobedience or the return of mobilization papers', whether or not this propaganda or provocation actually led to the act in question—in effect creating a *délit d'opinion*. The penalties envisaged for recalcitrant reservists were harsher by several degrees of magnitude. Whereas previously purely disciplinary penalties of four or eight days in the local garrison gaol were provided for men who could not produce their reserve or mobilization papers, the amended version of Article 92 laid down penalties of between six months and three years with a fine varying from 100 to 3,000 francs and the potential removal of one's civic rights for five years attached for good measure.[118]

Daladier submitted these amendments to the Minister of Justice in early January 1934. The government wanted to slip this bill through the Chamber with as little fuss and debate as possible, 'having as its sole object the stopping of the most dangerous manifestations of the systematic propaganda which appears to have been organized for some time against the fulfilment of their military duties by French citizens'. The harshness of the penalties envisaged was justified by the Ministry's fear that CO propaganda could conceivably compromise a mobilization order.[119]

The events of 6 February intervened, however, and removed Daladier from office. Not surprisingly, the new War Minister, Marshal Pétain, was equally interested in stamping out the effects of the CO 'movement', as a note from him to the president of the Army Commission in the Chamber makes abundantly clear. The Army Commission agreed with the government's analysis of the situation and the proposed amendments in a report dated 21 February. On 2 March the Chamber's Civil and Criminal Legislation Commission recommended that the penalties suggested in the amendments be reduced to between one month and one year. The government and the Chamber's Army Commission agreed with alacrity, such was the desire to see the amendments become law. Despite the opposition and counter-amendments of the deputies Armand Chouffet and

---

[118] Service historique de l'armée de terre (hereafter cited as SHA), Château de Vincennes, 6N468/Dossier 4, 'Note pour le Secrétariat général travaux législatifs', 26 Dec. 1933.

[119] Ibid., 'Le Ministre de la Guerre à Monsieur le Garde des sceaux, Ministre de la Justice', 8 Jan. 1934.

Camille Planche,[120] both of them pacifist sympathizers, the amendments were finally passed by the Chamber on 30 June, by the Senate on 5 July, becoming law on 8 July 1934.[121]

All of this seems to coincide with Pétain's thinking on the nature of French education and military preparedness. The army was concerned about the direction of events in Europe and France's ability to 'enforce respect for a state of peace which she herself would not disturb'. As Pétain wrote in a memorandum of 26 March 1934, 'the education of the race is too much neglected. Youth and children are not educated with a view to their duties: this is what must be remedied first of all, through a better pre-military preparation of youth and by a primary system of education which guarantees health of body and mind to the child. We ought to draw inspiration on these two levels from what is happening in Germany and Italy.'[122]

So much for the governmental response to the conscientious objection crisis in 1933. What of the LICP? Within the Ligue three currents of opinion on objection could be distinguished. The first, represented by Méric, was that objection was inefficacious as a means of fighting war but that objectors should be honoured for their moral courage. The second, epitomized by René Gerin, was that

[120] Camille Planche (b. 1892) was deputy for the department of the Allier from 1928 to 1942. In 1931 he joined the SFIO. He took an active part in Chamber debates, particularly on foreign affairs. He was a member of the Chamber's foreign affairs commission, and in 1936 and 1937 he was one of the French delegates at the League of Nations. He was a member of the Central Committee of the Ligue des droits de l'homme and was the president of the Ligue des anciens combattants pacifistes. See the entry on Planche in the *Dictionnaire des parlementaires français, 1889–1940* (Paris: Presses universitaires de France, 1972), vii. 2709. Armand Chouffet (b. 1895) was the deputy from the Rhône from 1928 to 1942. He was a lawyer who lent his support to the pacifist cause on several occasions. See the entry on Chouffet in ibid. iii (1963), 1050–1.

[121] SHA, Château de Vincennes, 6N468/Dossier 4, 'Philippe Pétain à Monsieur le Président de la Commission de l'armée de la Chambre de députés', 16 Feb. 1934; 'Rapport no. 3086 (annexe au procès-verbal de la 3e séance de la Chambre des députés du 21 février 1934) fait au nom de la Commission de l'armée . . . par M Albert Forcinal'; 'Avis (no. 3157, annexe au procès-verbal de la séance de la Chambre des députés du 2 mars 1934) présenté au nom de la Commission de la législation civile et criminelle par M Georges Pernot'; 'Rapport supplémentaire (no. 3286, annexe au procès-verbal de la séance de la Chambre des députés du 15 mars 1934) au nom de la Commission de l'armée . . . par M Albert Forcinal'; 'Note sur l'amendement de M Chouffet, député' (29 June 1934); and 'Rapport fait par M Jean Taurines, Sénateur (No. 496, Annexe au procès-verbal de la séance du 3 juillet 1934 du Sénat)'.

[122] SHA 5N577(2). 'Notes du Maréchal Pétain pour le chef de l'État-major général de l'armée sur "les idées maîtresses qui doivent inspirer l'organisation de la défense national"', 26 Mar. 1934.

objection was a personal decision made by the individual pacifist; because of the nature of the penalties for conscientious objection by young recruits, Gerin would only go so far as to advise older men like himself, who had fought in the Great War, to return their mobilization papers, thus incurring only short disciplinary sentences in the local gaol. The hard line position was that taken by Eugène Lagot[123] and Gérard Leretour who wanted the LICP to organize a massive homecoming of deserters and objectors from abroad and the concerted return of mobilization papers to the Ministry.

Thus, to take an example in the first category, in late 1932 Victor Méric saw repression coming for pacifists because of the great increase in conscientious objection. As long as pacifism had remained 'bleating', governments had had little to fear, but it was now becoming active. Men were showing their resolve to reject war by a variety of means and this brought disquiet to the authorities. Conscientious objection was one of these means and Méric wrote that 'we accord a high moral value to these acts. [But] we do not believe they have any practical value, given the form the next war will take against civilian populations . . . we do not believe we have the right to give advice to our younger brothers which will put them gravely at risk . . .'[124] There was thus much respect for objection in the Ligue, but little belief in its practical effects. In view of the coming debate with Leretour over generalized conscientious objection, it is important to note that Méric was against advising young men to become objectors because of the much severer penalties imposed on those who had not yet fought in a war.

Armand Charpentier expressed this duality explicitly in an article on Leretour in early 1933. He had met Leretour just before Leretour turned himself in to the authorities and had been most impressed. But he thought that despite the moral grandeur of the objector's act, it would remain essentially sterile because of the complete indifference of the press and the more important fact that modern warfare meant that both civilians and military would be attacked and annihilated in

---

[123] Eugène Lagot apparently died in Panama in early 1945, having spent most of the war as a representative of the War Resisters' International working on its 'South American Refugee Settlement' project in Colombia. See WRI International Council Communication No. 336 (8 June 1945), and letter of 7 June 1945 to Madame Lagomassini (Lagot's mother) in WRI archives, now housed in the International Institute for Social History in Amsterdam.

[124] Victor Méric, 'Vers la répression', PH 40 (29 Oct.–5 Nov. 1932), 1.

a few short hours. Conscientious objectors would not even have time to show themselves 'before being asphyxiated and roasted with the rest of the citizens'. Given these conditions, Charpentier argued that the 'struggle for peace must pass from the individual level of conscientious objection to the collective level of non-resistance', and this in turn meant directing the LICP's propaganda 'more and more in the direction of making the unsuspecting masses understand that with aero-chemical warfare all of the armaments and all of the armies are completely useless'. Thus, in Charpentier's view, the only way a nation could defend itself was by disarming totally.[125]

Gerin placed before his public the various options open to pacifists and left them to make up their own minds. As he pointed out in a 1934 editorial, the Comité directeur of the Ligue refused to counsel conscientious objection to young men of 20 years because they believed it to be an *individual* question eliciting a very personal answer. Perhaps more to the point, they believed along with Gerin that those who advised objection should be the ones to pay for it.[126] Having said that, Gerin was a very successful propagandist with the *anciens combattants* and it was to this group that he held up the example of his own successful objection at least until the change in the law in 1934. To these men who had shared the trench experience with him, Gerin showed the possibility of making a pacifist statement at relatively little personal cost. In an open letter to Édouard Daladier in April 1933, Gerin reckoned about 100 men had so far followed his example; just over a year later, he put the number in the hundreds if not thousands. To the veterans he said, 'To begin with, we want the legal recognition of conscientious objection, and we believe that it is above all the veterans who should be fighting for the realization of this first point in our programme'.[127]

In the summer of 1933 Gerin also recommended a way around the problem of the long prison term for young men who nevertheless wanted to affirm their integral pacifist beliefs. Rather than becoming one of the 130,000 Frenchmen who had either left France or assumed a false identity in order to avoid military service, Gerin suggested a third alternative. He advised young men to do their military duty in time of peace, but before joining their regiment for the first time, to

[125] Armand Charpentier, 'Un héros de la paix: Gérard Leretour', *PH* 53 (28 Jan.–4 Feb. 1933), 1.

[126] René Gerin, 'Une nouvelle loi scélérate', *Le Barrage*, 8 (5 July 1934), 1.

[127] René Gerin, 'Lettre ouverte à M Daladier', *PH* 63 (8 Apr. 1933), 1–2.

send a letter to their regimental commander and to the Minister of War outlining their conscientious objection and making it clear that they would not serve in time of war.[128] But this tactic raised the ire of Alphonse Barbé, sometime editor of the libertarian newspaper *Le Semeur* in the Calvados, who protested that Gerin as an ex-officer could not imagine what a young recruit 'deuxième classe' writing such a letter would be put through. Gerin completely underestimated the brutal stupidity and sadism of the non-commissioned officers if he thought such a plan would work. For Barbé it was better to affirm an all-or-nothing stance: either declare oneself an objector and take the consequences or else do one's military service as quietly as possible. In Barbé's view, the more honest and effective approach was that taken by Leretour: the organization of a massive return of deserters, objectors, and *insoumis* from abroad and from internal exile in an attempt to paralyse completely the army's judicial system.[129]

Leretour and Lagot advocated the creation of a vast collective movement of conscientious objection which would force the French government to change the law on conscription. The publication of the Chautemps circular in the press in early May 1933 had convinced them that the government was weakened and the time had come to strike while the iron was hot. They attempted to persuade the LICP to back them in this campaign, but the Ligue's Comité directeur refused, prompting Lagot to respond in a scathing article that the LICP did not have the courage of its pacifist convictions.[130] Instead, Lagot and Leretour created a Ligue des objecteurs de conscience and appealed for COs, deserters, and *insoumis* to come forward in droves, go to prison, and begin a hunger strike.[131] Later that summer, Leretour wrote that the main reason for its creation had been the almost total incomprehension faced by COs within the wider pacifist movement in France. He underlined that he wanted to create a collective movement of objection and was tired to death of hearing that objection had no practical impact—one had only to look at the Chautemps circular to see that it did.[132] But in the generally received opinion of the LICP that would be to assume a collective responsibil-

---

[128] René Gerin, 'A ceux qui doivent bientôt "partir"', *Le Combat pour la paix*, 4 (Aug.–Sept. 1933), 5–6.

[129] A. Barbé, 'A ceux qui doivent bientôt "partir"', *PH* 83 (15 Sept. 1933), 4.

[130] Eugène Lagot, 'Sous le signe de la peur', *Le Semeur*, 232 (22 July 1933), 1.

[131] Gérard Leretour, 'Debout, les objecteurs!', *PH* 71 (2 June 1933), 2.

[132] Gérard Leretour, 'Pourquoi le manifeste?', *PH* 81 (18 Aug. 1933), 4.

ity of conscience which by definition had to remain the decision of each man. What the Ligue did promise was to remain faithful to those who rebelled and this it did.[133]

The first three years of the LICP's life saw, therefore, major definitional debates on the nature of the new pacifism. Méric had sought to create an organization which would be as broad as possible in its intake; political, social, and religious preferences were to be left in the vestibule, as he liked to say. Thus began an uneasy marriage of different strands of absolute pacifism. The most difficult dichotomy to be bridged was undoubtedly that between the partisans of non-violence and violence. Amsterdam-Pleyel highlighted some of these contradictions but the Ligue was able to maintain its organizational independence by insisting on the purity of its pacifism and its application to all wars. Conscientious objection provided the next challenge to the Ligue's position but was easily accommodated within the LICP's world view. The third and final *crise de croissance* came at the Ligue's second national Congress in 1933.

By 1933 it was clear that more was needed than sterile anathemas hurled at the spectre of a war which Méric proclaimed imminent, almost inevitable, and impossible to resist once it had arrived. Pacifist despair undoubtedly succeeded in grouping together the thousands of men and women who joined the LICP in its first three years, but increasingly it became necessary to offer these leaguers specific policies for fighting war. A further problem was the deepening perception within the Ligue, especially in the provincial sections, that the LICP was being run like a tin-pot dictatorship by Méric and a few friends in Paris. The Ligue's accounts were mixed up with those of the *Patrie humaine*, and were in a state of considerable chaos. There was also the question of the *Patrie humaine*. Many people thought that an organization like the LICP ought to have its own independent organ. The question had been raised at the Angers Congress in 1932 and Méric had explained that the '*PH* is completely at the disposition of the Ligue but does not belong to it'.[134]

All of these issues came to the boil in the Congress which convened at Easter 1933 in Paris. It is clear that Méric felt control of the Ligue

[133] Robert Jospin, 'Précisions nouvelles', *Le Combat pour la paix*, 4 (Aug.–Sept. 1933), 2. The Ligue's position was supported by Professor Pierre Doyen, the president of the French section of the War Resisters' International. See Pierre Doyen, 'Deux lettres du Professeur Doyen', ibid. 4.

[134] See the account of the Angers Congress in *PH* 31 (2–9 July 1932), 2.

slipping from his grasp; there was a violent altercation between him and Émile Bauchet, president of the Calvados federation and chairman of the commission charged with organizing the Congress, over what would and would not be published in the *Patrie humaine* concerning the Congress.[135] As the writer of a report on the Congress quite rightly pointed out, Méric's *rapport moral* was more an exercise in self-exculpation and justification of past errors than a report as such.[136] Méric spoke at length about the origins of the LICP and about the complete intangibility of both the Ligue's structure and its statutes. The Ligue under Méric had a committee of patronage at the top, composed of eminent writers, professors, and intellectuals. This committee designated a president and a secretary-general. Méric also outlined the Ligue's principles—and it was these, or rather their wording, which prompted Romain Rolland's intervention as we have seen. What is clear is that Méric viewed the LICP as akin to the law of the Medes and the Persians. This dogmatism asserted itself even down to the section and federation level where no dissent would be brooked: 'It has never been a question of the sections and federations intervening in the general propaganda of the Ligue or of claiming to modify in the slightest its directives.'[137] It is unclear from all this exactly what the members, sections, and federations of the Ligue were supposed to do if they were barred from any active role either in policy formation or in spreading the good word. In a man of such obvious anarchist inclinations as Méric, there was a surprising degree of *étatisme* when it came to the running of 'his' Ligue. Undoubtedly, part of the reason for the grass-roots revolt in 1933 was due to financial mismanagement. Méric referred in his report to the Odéon Incident; Pierre Odéon had been taken on to help run the Ligue after his release from prison for conscientious objection. Without going into the sordid details and defending Odéon's probity, Méric nevertheless acknowledged that a debt of some 70,000 francs had been run up before Odéon had finally been let go. Méric ascribed the subsequent 'malaise' in the Ligue to this incident.[138]

With regard to the *Patrie humaine*, Méric refused to give it up, ostensibly to protect it from becoming the journal of just one

---

[135] See 'Bulletin officiel de la LICP: Autour du Congrès de Pâques', *PH* 61 (25 Mar. 1933), 5.
[136] See Bauchet's comments in 'Congrès national', 4.
[137] Méric, 'Rapport moral', 5.   [138] Ibid. See also 'Congrès national', 5.

tendency within pacifism. He was also afraid that it would quickly collapse if not run by professional journalists like himself. All of this was probably just a smokescreen for Méric's real desire to hold on to a paper which despite its debts was increasingly widely read in France. It also guaranteed him a continued voice in French pacifism.[139]

Finally, Méric argued vehemently against the idea of registering the LICP at the Préfecture de police, a move which would have the advantage of giving the Ligue legal status. He foresaw problems because of the Ligue's potential advocacy of illegal means in the fight against war.[140] Marcel Fouski of the Angers section, who had written the report in favour of declaring the Ligue, said that such fears were groundless. Instead, declaration would protect the Ligue financially, permit it to sue those who defamed it, and protect individual members from the effects of a lawsuit.[141]

René Gerin read a report on the Ligue's propaganda which sought to define the LICP's position within the peace movement and in relation to the political parties. The LICP had no doctrine as such, and was neither a movement (like Amsterdam), nor a political party. Gerin defined it rather as simply a *league*—a society of study, propaganda, and information. Having said that, it was necessary to delimit those parts of the political spectrum with which the LICP could have nothing to do. On the right, this meant rejecting all persons or groups who accepted the idea of a national defence through arms. On the left, he admitted that definition was much more difficult because the Ligue's formula 'Against war by all means' implied an acceptance of revolutionary tactics. Given the problems the Ligue would face at the time of Munich over the question of the neo-pacifism of the *munichois* extreme right, it is worth noting that as early as the 1933 Congress, the LICP seemed unprepared to share its political bed with just anybody.[142]

When the Congress closed, it was clear that the House that Méric built had been redecorated, if not redesigned, from top to bottom. He had been censured in a resolution from the Algerian section for

[139] Méric, 'Rapport moral'. See also André Dumas, 'Ligue, "*Patrie humaine*" et Librairie', *PH* 58 (4–11 Mar. 1933), 4. See also 'Congrès national', 7.

[140] Méric, 'Rapport moral'. See also 'Congrès national', 5.

[141] Marcel Fouski, 'Rapport sur la déclaration de la Ligue', *PH* 58 (4–11 Mar. 1933), 3. See also 'Congrès national', 5.

[142] René Gerin, 'Rapport provisoire sur la déclaration de la Ligue', *PH* 58 (4–11 Mar. 1933), 3–4. See also discussion of this report in 'Congrès national', 6–7.

advocating violent anarchist tactics, the Ligue had decided to register itself officially at the Préfecture de police, a paid treasurer (Bauchet) had been designated, the Comité directeur was henceforth to be elected, and the old committee had been turned into a Comité d'honneur. Individual leaguers were to be attached obligatorily to a local section. The *PH* remained Méric's property. The Ligue's statutes were also changed to reflect a more nuanced definition of the type of pacifism espoused; henceforth the LICP was to fight against wars 'imposed by governments on peoples in the name of a so-called national interest'.[143]

In the debate on Romain Rolland's message to the Congress and in the continuing discussion on adherence to the Amsterdam move-ment, the amazing spectrum of pacifist values within the LICP was once again evident. Méric was censured, as has been seen, for his overtly anarchist prescriptions for a violent approach to peace. But Pioch agreed with Rolland that in the coming struggle 'conscientious objectors, organized non-violents, and the armed proletariat' should coalesce in the LICP. In almost the next breath, however, Victor Margueritte announced that the Ligue agreed with Romain Rolland but was in favour of non-violence. Han Ryner and Armand Charpen-tier both thought that no distinction should be made between civil and foreign wars. Sébastien Faure was against the Gandhian method and announced himself a partisan of violence every time one was a victim of it. The Toulouse group wanted to draw up lists of those responsible for wars as future 'hostages for peace' and was in favour of armed resistance to any war. The Toulouse resolution was approved by a majority of the Congress. Gerin continued to believe that if the masses knew what the LICP knew about the origins of the Great War, they would flock to pacifism—an indication that the question of war responsibilities continued to be important in the pacifist debate. Even on the question of conscientious objection there was incoherence. A motion from the Saint-Denis section demanding that the Comité directeur officially support the 'movement of collect-ive conscientious objection proposed by comrade Leretour' was adopted; but strangely a resolution from the section in the 14th *arrondissement* demanding a collective return of mobilization papers was rejected.[144]

---

[143] 'Chez les Combattants de la paix: Le Congrès de Pâques', *PH* 66 (29 Apr. 1933), 4. See also 'Congrès national', 4–10. See also 'Réunion du comité directeur', *Le Combat pour la paix*, 1 (May 1933), 10–11.   [144] See 'Congrès national', 8–12

The 1933 Congress was important, therefore, because it marked a break from the Méric-dominated past of the Ligue, which, while fecund in membership growth, had increasingly come to be seen as undemocratic and imbued with a sterile nihilism incapable of developing specific policies for pacifists. 1933 also reaffirmed the Ligue's position on the Amsterdam movement and began a debate on conscientious objection which would broaden into a discussion on pacifist tactics generally. That said, the Congress continued to show up the divisive nature of the Ligue and the uneasy alliance which existed between its disparate constituent parts. A police report on the Congress underlined the 'great doctrinal confusion' as well as the 'strong personal rivalries' which existed within the Ligue, mostly between Méric and Pioch, and concluded, 'To sum up, no precise policy directives given, no political line laid down. Each section and each member of a section is left free to act as he pleases. This is anarchy.'[145]

The anarchy evident in the Ligue as a whole was apparently even more extreme in the Paris federation. It led finally to the resignation of three early members, J. Bardin, A. Dumas, and O. R. Monod. These three published a manifesto explaining their decision to leave the Ligue in November 1933. They castigated the LICP's inability to put its house in order. They thought that the Easter Congress had succeeded finally in clarifying the Ligue's principles and providing it with a sound and democratic administration. But the situation in Paris was even worse where the 'vast majority' of the Paris sections, 'under the direct influence of anarchist elements, declared themselves against the majority of the Ligue, represented by the provinces, and for the continuation of the "methods" and the fantasies of the old administration'.[146] The manifesto writers criticized the sterile gesture of Leretour and Daunay in decapitating the statue of Déroulède, and the folly of the armed attack made on a meeting of the Amis de la patrie humaine. In response to these criticisms, Gerin had apparently

---

[145] See the report 'D'un correspondant', 25 Apr. 1933. A/3624 GB5 in AN F7/ 13352. The chronology in this report is a little ambiguous. It refers to a 'congrès fédéral' taking place in the first fortnight of March in Paris. The dates of the national Congress were 16–17 April. However, from the context of the report, it is clear that the informant or the person taking down the report was confused about the dates, and it must refer to the national Congress, rather than a meeting of the Paris federation.

[146] J. Bardin, A. Dumas, O. R. Monod, 'Pourquoi nous quittons la Ligue internationale des combattants de la paix'. Copy in BDIC/DD/FΔRés. 235/4/7.

said that the Paris region was of little interest to the Ligue because of the minimal possibilities for action there. Part of the problem for the Ligue as a whole was its attempt to be all things to all men:

We know now that it is vain and sterile to gather together in the same pacifist league, *for action*, Tolstoyans and revolutionaries, individualists and social-ists, religious pacifists and Marxists. In order for such a *unity, based on confusion* to continue, it is necessary for each tendency to renounce the enunciation of its own points of view, it is necessary for the most active elements to take a vow of immobility.[147]

This the minority refused to do. Since action within the LICP was proving impossible, they had decided to leave. They rejected the sterile, inflammatory rhetoric of the Ligue and opted instead for a 'methodical documentation and systematic education of the masses' on the causes of war and how to fight it. They insisted on the need to maintain a close unity between *study* and *action*. The Paris federa-tion seemed to be interested in nothing more than the 'action' of 'the demagogues of the "green terror"', the fanatical monument attackers, and the professional hunger strikers'.[148]

Thus ended 1933 for the LICP. Méric died of a stomach cancer in early October, leaving the running of the *Patrie humaine* to Robert Tourly and Roger Monclin.[149] With Méric gone, French integral pacifism had undoubtedly lost one of its greatest visionaries and leaders, a man who had almost single-handedly created the largest French integral pacifist group whose influence was being felt by the government. Méric represented the politics of dissent to his core, but his vision and work were tragically flawed by an unwillingness or inability to see beyond the increasingly sterile polemics which had caused thousands to flock to him initially, but which were incapable of keeping them at his side without the inducement of sound pacifist policies. Méric the anarchist finally triumphed over Méric the pacifist to the detriment of the LICP. 1933 marked the revolt of clear-thinking, democratic forces imbued with just as much vision as Méric, but with organizational sense as well.

---

[147] Bardin, Dumas, and Monod, 'Pourquoi nous quittons la Ligue'.
[148] Ibid.
[149] See Robert Tourly, 'L'homme qui s'en va . . .', *PH* 86 (13 Oct. 1933), 1; Robert Tourly, 'Sa vie, son œuvre', *PH* 86 (13 Oct. 1933), 1–2; Roger Monclin, 'Adieu', *PH* 86 (13 Oct. 1933), 1; and Robert Tourly, 'Les Obsèques de Victor Méric', *PH* 87 (20 Oct. 1933), 1.

8. Challenges to *Intégralité* (1934–1938)

The LICP's pacifism in the period 1930–3 was largely negative. Its rejection of war owed more to sterile anathema than to sound and practical policies. In the period from 1934 to Munich it began, however, to develop an intelligent approach to pacifism which was reflected in a deeper analysis of internal and external political problems, and in the discussion of pacifist tactics.

If the LICP under Méric had been slow to come to grips with concrete political reality, this was not the case in the post-schism Ligue. In May 1933, immediately after the tumultuous Easter Congress, the Ligue created its own journal, *Le Combat pour la paix*, which was published monthly until April 1934, after which it was replaced by the weekly and then bi-weekly newspaper *Le Barrage*. Both of these publications contained more in the way of political analysis than had the *Patrie humaine* under Méric.

GERMANY

The primary political problem of the thirties was undoubtedly that of Germany. The LICP was consistently in favour of a revision of the Versailles Treaty in order to arrive at a more equitable European situation. Before the Nazi *Machtergreifung* the Ligue's propagandists defined the danger posed by Hitler purely in terms of internal German politics. Thus, for example, Rudolf Leonhard, a German *émigré* and a member of the Gruppe revolutionärer Pazifisten, propagandized tirelessly in 1932 and 1933 for the LICP to which his organization was twinned in an amicable accord. Leonhard argued that 'It is not you who have to fear this imbecile Hitler, but I. Hitler isn't war, he is civil war. He is the white terror. If he comes to power—and this may well come to pass and the other States will tolerate him there—Germany's foreign policy will not change.'[1]

This analysis found its echo in that other indefatigable propagandist of the first hour, Marcelle Capy, who along with Pioch and Leonhard traversed France in two successive peace crusades in the winters of 1931–2 and 1932–3. Capy, who knew Germany well but apparently spoke little German, shared Leonhard's prognosis on the political situation there and what it might mean for France. Hitler represented 'not an exasperated chauvinistic Germany showing its teeth to France, but instead big German capitalism—and behind it big international capitalism—showing its teeth to working people and to German republicans'.[2]

Before 1933 there were also those within the LICP who did not believe that Hitler would be successful in his bid for power, or if he was, that he would be able to retain it. Robert Tourly, writing in March 1932, thought that it 'was impossible, despite the crazy excitations of the passions, so strangely helped until now by events, to believe in the decisive and durable victory of a party, or rather a movement, whose ideology is nothing but a bric-à-brac of puerile demagogies'.[3]

Méric, writing a few weeks later, saw nothing surprising in the Nazi election gains; they were almost inevitable given Hitler's financial backing. He seemed unconcerned at the thought that the Nazis might succeed in taking power, and, in a portentous miscalculation of the nature of Nazism, wrote that 'Hitler in power, will do neither worse nor better than the others'. Méric not only underestimated Hitler, but also showed no small amount of political naïveté in equating Nazism with other political systems. He placed his hope in the 'other Germany' which was pacifist and wanted neither Hitler nor war. Méric thought that this other Germany would succeed in keeping Hitler in his place. The bottom line was that Hitler represented no more than a passing crisis on the lines of the Boulanger or Dreyfus affairs, crises 'which bring Democracy within a hair's breadth of disaster'. But he insisted that the trouble would pass and the German people would return to calm reason.[4]

---

[1] Rudolf Leonhard, L'Allemagne et la paix (Paris: Éditions de la LICP, 1932), 12.
[2] Marcelle Capy, 'Retour d'Allemagne', PH 13 (27 Feb.–4 Mar. 1932), 1.
[3] Robert Tourly, 'Le Programme de Hitler', PH 17 (26 Mar.–2 Apr. 1932), 3.
[4] Victor Méric, 'L'Aventure hitlérienne', PH 22 (30 Apr.–7 May 1932), 1.

Obsessed as they were with the perceived threat from an internal Fascist foe in France, the pacifists of the LICP seemed unable to conceive of the danger posed by Nazism in any other terms. This view seemed to prevail within the Ligue from top to bottom. A grass-roots pacifist, one comrade Dumont, returned from a trip to Germany in 1935 to announce to his local section that Germans, like people anywhere, were pacifist. He concluded that while the Hitler regime was a danger to the internal situation in Germany, it posed no threat to the outside world. Those who argued otherwise were playing the game of French chauvinists and should be denounced.[5]

A note of anti-Semitism crept into some of these analyses of the new Germany. Gustave Dupin attacked the 'Jewish press' for contributing to the war psychosis which was being fostered by the French General Staff after the Nazi seizure of power. He likened the horror stories coming out of Germany to the atrocity propaganda of all belligerents during the Great War, and rejected the fears being whipped up through 'the exploitation of Dictatorship (in other nations), Fascism and the bluff of anti-Semitism'.[6]

Pierre Cuenat addressed the question directly in October 1933 when he asked whether in fact Hitler had changed anything. French public opinion seemed to have swung round dramatically to acceptance of the potential for another war. Cuenat wrote that he was under no illusions about the dangers to peace represented by Hitler —he, unlike some subsequent writers in the *Barrage*, did not believe in Hitler's pacific disposition—but he posed the essential question, 'has anything changed for the integral pacifist?' His answer was that for integral pacifism any notion of legitimate wars of defence had to be rejected. Frenchmen would perhaps have hesitated to give their lives for the post-Versailles system, but Hitler seemed to be providing a *casus belli*. It was now once again possible to speak in terms of a war to defend liberty and democracy against barbarism and Fascism. But this was a false trap:

Frenchmen need these metaphysical hoists in order to accept a war. Hitler has allowed war to be disguised under this mask. Against this brainwashing, our duty is to proclaim loudly that nothing has changed; French imperialism against German imperialism doesn't interest us. We will not defend this

---

[5] See anonymous report in 'L'Activité de la Ligue: Montargis', *Le Barrage*, 40 (14 Feb. 1935), 4.

[6] Gustave Dupin, 'La Revanche de la caste', *PH* 79 (28 July 1933), 1.

cause no matter what label is attached to it. . . . We denounce those who identify French hegemony with peace and proclaim the French army the only guarantor of peace, those who (*Revue des deux mondes*, etc.) make of internationalism a treason against peace, and of French nationalism the only internationalism.[7]

The position taken by most writers in the LICP's newspaper in 1933 and 1934 was that Hitler was an unsavoury character but that for the good of world peace one had to do business with him. Thus, for example, Gérard de Lacaze-Duthiers (1876–1958),[8] reviewing Challaye's brochure *Pour la paix désarmée, même en face de Hitler*, was of the opinion that Hitler should be taken at his word in his stated desire for peace 'whatever' the atrocities committed by the Nazi regime. Thus, while condemning the actions of the Nazi regime—'this medieval night which has rung the knell of an entire civilization'—Lacaze-Duthier argued that 'we must have confidence in such a language [of Peace] and try to respond with something other than a complete rejection'.[9]

The idea was also prevalent that Nazism and Hitler were not really that much different from the capitalist ruling classes in the democracies. The notion that there was little to choose from between Hitler and some representatives of the Western liberal democracies was evident in an article written later that year by Gerin. He compared a speech made by Churchill demanding more armaments for Britain and denouncing the Nazi menace with an interview with Hitler published in *Le Matin* of 18 November 1934. Hitler came off much the better of the two. According to Gerin, every time Hitler had gone to the German people, plebiscite in hand, it had been on the question of peace: 'He could not have imposed himself without this policy of renunciation of war; he is only obeyed because he declared that he has rejected a bloody settling of accounts . . .'[10] Thus, although Gerin recognized that Hitler's regime was odious and that

---

[7] Pierre Cuenat, 'Depuis qu'Hitler est là . . . qu'y a-t-il de changé?', *PH* 88 (27 Oct. 1933), 1.

[8] See James Friguglietti, 'Gérard de Lacaze-Duthiers', in Harold Josephson, *Biographical Dictionary of Modern Peace Leaders* (Westport, London: Greenwood Press, 1985), 533–4.

[9] Gérard de Lacaze-Duthiers, 'Livres, revues, journaux' (review of Félicien Challaye, *Pour la paix désarmée, même en face de Hitler*), *Le Barrage*, 1 (17 May 1934), 3.

[10] René Gerin, 'Un discours et un entretien', *Le Barrage*, 28 (22 Nov. 1934), 1.

Germany was rearming, he refused to believe that Nazism was any more dangerous than Italy, France, or Britain.[11]

Sylvain Broussaudier, a member of the Ligue's Comité directeur, former *normalien*, and a professor at the *lycée* in Oran, wrote in 1935 that he did not understand why it was no longer possible or correct to seek a *rapprochement* with Germany. Paul Faure had recently criticized in the pages of the *Populaire* the creation of a Franco-German society under the patronage of important Nazis and the French ambassador in Berlin. Yet, just a few years previously, Faure had been the first to castigate the French government for its consistently anti-German policies. For Broussaudier, whatever repugnance one might feel for Nazi Germany, he thought it 'infinitely preferable' to make peace with Hitler rather than war with Germany. And this was not just because 'peace is infinitely preferable to war, but also because all danger of war reinforces at one and the same time both German and French Fascism'.[12]

At its most basic, then, the LICP's general position on the danger posed by Nazism and Fascism was that these were internal problems which needed to be resolved by the countries concerned, however much one might sympathize—and there was much sympathy—with the victims of atrocities and oppression in Germany and Italy. Hitler was a political fact and the LICP argued that France needed to do business with him. The desire for peace with Hitler, rather than war with Germany, was an overriding concern. This did not mean that the Ligue was oblivious to the external dangers posed by Nazism. On the contrary, it was very aware that Hitler could spell war. But what it sought to do was underline the need for a *modus vivendi* with Hitler, a defusing of potential conflicts. And because in the integral pacifist *Weltanschauung* France and the Allied powers bore a share of unexpiated and unconfessed guilt for the present European situation, that meant agreeing to many of the revisions of the European political map first demanded and then taken by Hitler. There was no question of sympathy for the ideas and methods of Nazism in the LICP. It is true that a rhetoric of violence did insinuate itself into the Ligue in the period 1930–4. It is also true, as we shall see, that the Ligue at times spoke an antiparliamentary language in its analysis

---

[11] Ibid.

[12] Sylvain Broussaudier, 'Nous demandons à comprendre', *Le Barrage*, 72 (21 Nov. 1935), 3.

of French politics. It is also the case that it saw *rapprochement* with Nazi Germany in the *foreign* sphere as the best policy for France to follow. But it is completely false to suggest that the LICP was in any way 'soft' on Nazism. The Ligue consistently condemned without reservation the atrocities committed by the German regime. What it can be accused of is political naïveté, myopia, and a distorted historical vision. But for all the world-weariness with which the LICP viewed the decay of Third Republic society, it never separated the struggle against Fascism from that against war. It is the tragedy of its vision that all of this goodwill directed against a perceived Fascist threat found its expression almost solely in the internal political domain.

Thus, Pierre Cuenat, writing soon after the Nazi seizure of power, condemned utterly the idea that war was inevitable, and that responsibilities for this situation lay unilaterally with the Nazis. It was too easy to say simply that Hitler was responsible for everything. That allowed Frenchmen to forget 'the unjust Versailles system, France's policy of hegemony after the war, to say nothing of the economic system which had caused the present collapse which gave rise to conflicts and Fascism'.[13] Harking back to 1914, Cuenat asked whether the responsibilities were in fact one-sided. He believed that Hitler had come to power essentially on a platform of bastard Socialism; the nationalism in his programme was still in the larva stage, but would certainly emerge if the policy of encirclement of Germany did not stop. Peace with Hitler did not mean, therefore, remaining silent about Fascism, but it did mean realizing that any foreign intervention would only strengthen the Nazi regime. Cuenat defined instead the task for French pacifists as follows: 'For us, the task which is incumbent on us, is to struggle against our own Fascism, against our own nationalism. "Sweep our own doorstep". No *union sacrée*, even against Hitler, if we wish to spare ourselves another 1914.'[14]

PACIFISM AND ANTIFASCISM

All of this points back to the idea that the enemy was 'within'. French pacifists were antifascist and opposed to the Hitler regime, but they

[13] Pierre Cuenat, '1914, deuxième édition?', *PH* 71 (2 June 1933), 3.
[14] Ibid.

clung firmly to their belief that for the overriding good of inter-national peace they had to concentrate on fighting the perceived Fascist menace in France and leave Nazism to the German anti-fascists. The enemy in France was at various times described as the capitalist governing class, the military caste, or simply the politicians of the Third Republic. In its latter form, the idea carried with it definite antiparliamentarian connotations. Gerin, for example, writ-ing in December 1934 about what he perceived to be an improved international situation, wrote that the real enemies of peace were inside France. They were the parliamentarians, 'the pikes and swind-lers of the present ministerial team', who were 'ready to do anything, even to declare themselves men of the "left" and even to dishonour Fascism, in order for their plots to succeed'.[15]

The notion that there was something rotten at the very core of Third Republic democracy is a resonant chord in much of the LICP's political analysis during the thirties. In general—and there were exceptions—the Ligue's position was not so much antidemocratic as one of dissent, opposed to what it viewed as the machinations and corruption of the Third Republic. Thus, for example, when plans were mooted in 1934 for a reform of the constitution, Gerin wrote that the 'parliamentary regime is worth what it is worth, that is to say, little. Such as it is, sold as it is to the economic and financial powers, it allows, nevertheless, an opposition to make itself heard, if not to be victorious. It justifies, in any case, the great word "republic".'[16] He said that men of the 'left', revolutionaries and pacifists, were indiscriminately accused of working towards dis-order. 'Order' must not be confounded with subjection or servitude, though. Gerin believed that it was not the product of tyranny or the complementary resignation in the governed that this required. Rather, he thought, it was liberty and a search for progress on the part of both governments and governed.[17]

The LICP nevertheless enjoined its members to put the pacifist case before the public at the time of elections. In 1935, Gerin wrote that pacifists, and Frenchmen generally, had been terribly disappointed at the lack of progress made towards peace in the Chamber elected under the 'sign of peace' with Briand at the helm in 1932. In the

---

[15] René Gerin, 'Détente?', *Le Barrage*, 31 (13 Dec. 1934), 1.
[16] René Gerin, 'Un dictateur?', *Le Barrage*, 24 (25 Oct. 1934), 1.
[17] René Gerin, 'Les "Mentalités obstinées"', *Le Barrage*, 21 (4 Oct. 1934), 1.

upcoming elections, candidates had to be forced to take positions on the question of peace, and if possible straw candidacies should be run in order to give the Ligue access to the French electoral billboards. Having said that, Gerin held no illusions about the success of pacifist propaganda in the present state of French democracy: 'In the LICP we do not have great confidence in the elected to maintain the peace. We count much more on the governed rather than on the governors to kill war.'[18]

In 1937, just before the Congress of the Ligue des droits de l'homme which had as its theme 'how to defend both democracy and peace', Gerin addressed the question directly in *Le Barrage*. He began by emphasizing that not all members of the Ligue were democrats in the 'present, unfortunately precise meaning' of the word. But, if one were to restore 'to the word democracy its broader sense, which is the liberation of individuals, equality of rights, justice, etc. . . . there is no doubt that we all aspire to the same idea, because this means to aspire at the same time to peace'.[19] It seemed to be increasingly the case that friendship between nations was a function of similarity of their regime, a fact which made it difficult for pacifists to urge peace with all peoples. The LICP did not condone dictatorship, but it did seek peace with the dictators, believing that nations must have the right to manage their own affairs. With regard to France and the other democracies, the LICP did not confuse their pale reflections with the higher ideal of true democracy. Nor did it confuse the totalitarian regimes with the democracies. In this sense, Gerin wrote that it would be preferable for the world political situation, if all nations were 'democratic'. At least in the democracies a sufficient level of freedom existed for people to express themselves. He envisaged the possibility of war between democracies and the Fascist states. Hitler had said on 30 January that no further disputes between Germany and France were 'humanly' possible. For Gerin, the word 'humanly' was the key. It was precisely because the French and Germans were equally pacific, 'but unequally free, above all unequally concerned about freedoms, in a word unequally democratic, that there will perhaps continue to be disputes between them'.[20] But the distinction which Gerin admitted existed between democracies and the Fascist states in no way implied an acceptance of war

[18] René Gerin, 'Bientôt, des élections', *Le Barrage*, 47 (4 Apr. 1935), 1.
[19] René Gerin, 'La Démocratie et la paix', *Le Barrage*, 113 (24 June 1937), 1.
[20] Ibid.

as the means to resolve these differences. To defend peace, it was necessary to defend democracy such as it existed in France after centuries of struggles, but it had to be done by example and not by force.[21]

It has already been noted that the LICP was convinced from the outset of the danger posed by Fascism in France. In the first years of its existence, this was often the result of personal experience since LICP meetings were frequently the target for the excesses of right-wing thugs. The crisis of 6 February 1934 in France, however, served to convince the Ligue even more of the danger posed by indigenous Fascism. It strengthened its belief both that France's sickly parliamentary democracy had to be defended and that the first duty of integral pacifists was to fight the war psychosis by fighting French Fascism.

In a press communiqué of 10 February 1934, the LICP called for unity against French Fascism: 'More than ever, an end to political discussions. Accept, and even advocate the organization of a common struggle of all of the popular masses against the Fascist hordes!'[22] Edouard Lemédioni, a barrister at the Court of Appeal in Algiers, wrote shortly thereafter that 'peace is less threatened today than is liberty'. He said that the present situation in France 'resembles, alas, only too much that of Italy and Germany a little before the advent of Fascism and Nazism'.[23] He laid a large part of the blame for the crisis precisely at the feet of the democrats, Socialists, pacifists, Communists, syndicalists, and libertarians, none of whom had reacted early enough to the situation. The problem with the parties of the left was that they spent too much time tearing one another apart and too little time fighting the real foe. Lemédioni could not overstate the seriousness of the situation: 'The proletariat, and with it the democrats and pacifists, has just suffered a redoubtable setback. The so-called Ministry of National Union or of the party truce is making a bed for the Fascists if we do not know how to react.'[24] He called for the creation of local antifascist committees across France and with them the establishment of militias designed to defend Republican France by force of arms.[25]

[21] Ibid.
[22] 'Notre mot d'ordre', *Le Combat pour la paix*, 9 (Feb. 1934), 4.
[23] Édouard Lemédioni, 'Rapport sur la tactique que la Ligue doit adopter afin de rendre efficace l'action qu'elle mène contre la guerre', *Le Combat pour la paix*, 9 (Feb. 1934), 4.   [24] Ibid.   [25] Ibid.

In the wake of the events of 6 February, the LICP reviewed its statutes and revised its goal to include the fight against Fascism as well as war. A manifesto read to the Ligue's 1934 Montargis Congress and passed unanimously condemned Fascism and war in equal terms, but suggested that the more immediate danger came from Fascism. In the LICP's view, Fascism in France, which was defined as the triumph of capitalist, military, clerical, and police reaction, greatly aggravated the dangers of war. The signatories of the manifesto were careful, however, to define the Ligue's struggle as against *internal* Fascism and *external* wars, the conjunction of these two phenomena being the paramount danger.[26] The position taken by the manifesto writers was enshrined in a rewording of the Ligue's goal so that it now read:

[The Ligue] will use all means of action (lectures, publications, demonstrations) against wars imposed by governments on the Peoples in the name of a so-called national interest, and against Fascism which, destroying our liberties, leads inevitably to war. Against Fascism and against war by all means, that is our motto.[27]

Six months later, Gerin declared, however, that Fascism had failed in France, and was in retreat in the rest of Europe. In his view, France had never really known Fascism; instead there were only the usual reactionaries who sought to exploit social problems in an attempt to create a 'renovating' regime on foreign lines. The two forces which had coalesced in creating Italian and German Fascism had been a strong need for national unity and the misery created by economic collapse. With regard to the first, it had proved impossible to resuscitate the nationalist passions in France necessary for the creation of an indigenous Fascism. As for the second, France had mercifully been spared the full effects of the Depression. In Gerin's view, the events of 6 February had in the final analysis merely shown the impotence of French Fascism.[28]

The LICP remained committed to this policy of internal antifascism right up to 1939. It also continued to condemn the atrocities of the Nazi regime but increasingly, as the thirties drew to a close, the

---

[26] 'Paix et liberté (manifeste adopté au Congrès de Montargis)', *Le Combat pour la paix*, 11 (Apr. 1934), 1–2.

[27] 'Compte-rendu du Congrès de Montargis', *Le Combat pour la paix*, 11 (Apr. 1934), 4.

[28] René Gerin, 'Le "Fascisme" a fait faillite', *Le Barrage*, 17 (6 Sept. 1934), 1.

LICP became concerned that antifascism 'for external use' might lead to war. The Ligue's insistence on the somewhat paradoxical need to take a moral position on Nazism—and at the same time to eschew any unnecessary stirring of troubled waters with the Nazis —is the hallmark of the LICP's approach to the problem posed by the external threat of Fascism. In this sense, the LICP drew its historical inspiration from Robespierre.[29] Georges Michon (1882–1945),[30] for example, writing about Robespierre's position on the external, essentially imperialist wars of the French Revolution, compared Robespierre's opponents with their latter-day equivalents:

May our little politicians draw inspiration from this great example of civic virtue. But they do not like the Incorruptible who would have nothing to do with a *République des camarades*. They prefer Danton. One understands how M. Herriot not long ago sharply criticized the idea of erecting a statue to Maximilien, and that. he afterwards figured at the head of an honorary committee constituted to commemorate the centenary of Napoleon I (1921). Do we not also see the Communist party celebrating the centenary of Rouget de l'Isle, and waxing lyrical on posters about Danton—whose venality was proven many times—without even mentioning Robespierre or Babeuf?[31]

Félicien Challaye expanded this view eighteen months later in a review of Michon's book *Robespierre et la guerre révolutionnaire (1791–1792)*, arguing with Michon and Robespierre that war does not serve the interests of the masses. He denounced the 'criminal and anti-revolutionary character' of war; 'we shall repeat that war is incapable of sowing a love of liberty; because "no one likes an armed missionary"'.[32]

This historical position easily translated itself into a justification of the Ligue's opposition to external antifascism and its views on German refugees in France. In early 1936 Challaye expressed concern at the actions of 'certain refugees' in France who seemed to be pushing towards a war with Germany. He had all the sympathy in

[29] It is interesting to note that Albert Mathiez, the historian of Robespierre, was one of the first members of the old Comité directeur of the LICP under Méric. See James Friguglietti, *Albert Mathiez, historien révolutionnaire (1874–1932)*, translated from the English by Marie-Françoise Pernot (Paris: Société d'études robespierristes, 1974), 226–7.

[30] See James Friguglietti, 'Georges Michon', in Josephson, *Dictionary*, 634–6.

[31] Georges Michon, 'Robespierre et la guerre révolutionnaire', *Le Barrage*, 80 (16 Jan. 1936), 1.

[32] Félicien Challaye, 'Robespierre et l'actualité', *Le Barrage*, 116 (30 Sept. 1937), 1.

the world for the victims of Nazism who were in France—the Jews, Communists, Socialists, and democrats—but he was alarmed at the anti-German, or pro-war, propaganda being spread by these people. It was essential in his view that the ire of these refugees not be allowed to be added to the traditional hostility already existing between the French and German peoples. The refugees must not be allowed to foment a war that would enable them to return victorious to Germany on the backs of the French army. Connecting present events with historical antecedent, Challaye drew his conclusion: 'the action of the German refugees of 1935 calls strangely to mind that of the foreign refugees of 1792, pushing France into a so-called war of liberation of the nations'.[33] This general position on the dangers of an antifascism directed exclusively at external threats was echoed by Gerin, who at the same time recognized the tactical discomfiture felt by integral pacifists in defending a political position shared only with the right in France:

We must warn our comrades against the possible excesses of antifascism, however legitimate it might be; we remind them forcefully that our hatred is directed against the tyrants and not against the people, and we regret that it should be only the French Right today which is favourable to ideas of Franco-German *rapprochement*.[34]

The LICP thus trod a very narrow line at times between an ethically acceptable, left-wing pacifism and ideas which seemed on the surface to be more at home on the extreme right in France. The Ligue was consistently antifascist *within* France but tended to limit its external antifascism to condemnations of Nazi racial attacks in Germany. As far as the claims of the Nazi regime to a complete restructuring of the European political map were concerned, the LICP was often acquiescent, believing these claims to be justified by the 'mistakes' made at Versailles. The LICP condemned anti-Semitism both in France and in Germany, but equally attacked those Jews it felt were pushing France towards another *guerre du droit*. The fundamental tenet of its belief was that one could be both a convinced antifascist and a pacifist at the same time.

Thus, for example, Victor Méric in April 1933 wrote that there

[33] Félicien Challaye, 'La Préparation de la guerre et l'action de certains réfugiés allemands', *Le Barrage*, 78 (2 Jan. 1936), 1. See also Félicien Challaye, 'Antifascisme et pacifisme intégral: Réponse à Bernard Lecache', *Le Barrage*, 81 (23 Jan. 1936), 1.

[34] René Gerin, 'Bilan 1935', *Le Barrage*, 78 (2 Jan. 1936), 1.

were 'Jews and Jews'. He condemned those who sought to embroil France in a war with Germany by rushing to the aid of German Jews. He warned them not to 'be more royalist than the King himself'; instead he called them to align themselves with their natural friends, the Socialists, revolutionaries, and pacifists. Together they would defeat the enemy within France.[35]

In 1934 an anonymous writer warned readers of *Le Barrage* against what it considered the extremist position of the Ligue internationale contre l'antisémitisme (LICA). There was a great danger that the heightened campaign against anti-Semitism would only serve to increase the chauvinism and Germanophobia which the writer thought the French government was trying to encourage.[36]

Having said that, the LICP consistently condemned the attacks on Jews both in France and in Germany. Gerin, writing in the wake of the assassination of the German diplomat Von Rath in Paris in 1938, said that the Ligue and the *Barrage* 'condemned with the greatest indignation the persecutions and diverse acts of anti-Semitism in which the German government is indulging, in the wake of the assassination, odious in itself, of Counsellor Von Rath'.[37]

The LICP's insistence on a division between its internal and external antifascism, coupled with its essentially non-interventionist view of European politics based on Robespierrist principles and a conviction that many of the political claims of Nazism in the European sphere were either justified or understandable, led in 1936 to the final break with Romain Rolland. In the period from the Amsterdam Congress to 1936 Rolland had become increasingly convinced of the need for what he called an 'indivisible peace' which basically meant collective security.[38] This was rejected categorically by the ideologues of the Ligue. Rolland had argued that the most pressing danger was that from without; he had called for a moral and material resistance to Nazism. Georges Pioch agreed with the idea of a moral resistance but wondered whether material resistance did not mean war. Nations, like people, could no more be forced to be free than to be happy. Italy and Germany had to free themselves from the

---

[35] Victor Méric, 'Lettre ouverte aux Juifs de France', *PH* 64 (15 Apr. 1933), 1.

[36] 'Prenons garde!', *Le Barrage*, 20 (27 Sept. 1934), 1.

[37] René Gerin, 'Décrets-lois', *Le Barrage*, 137 (17 Nov. 1938), 1. Similar views were expressed by Nadia Gukowski in 'Racisme et nationalisme', *Le Barrage*, 138 (1 Dec. 1938), 1.

[38] Romain Rolland, 'Pour l'indivisible paix', *Le Barrage*, 83 (6 Feb. 1936), 2. This article was reprinted from *Vendredi* of 24 Jan. 1936.

tyranny of Fascism. He did not personally believe that a Franco-German *rapprochement* was likely but if one were possible he believed that for the cause of peace pacifists would have to swallow their disgust of the Nazi regime.[39]

The differences in approach to the problem of external Fascism were largely due to the different perspectives held about Nazi Germany and Hitler's intentions. Félicien Challaye protested that Romain Rolland could not possibly know what Hitler's future plans were or that he was lying—to claim the contrary was simply not logical. Much of the dispute seemed to centre around the anti-French passages in *Mein Kampf* and whether a book written during the Ruhr crisis should be taken seriously in 1936. Challaye argued that it should not. It was understandable that it was widely distributed in Germany where it helped to 'create a maximum of national cohesion' and also that it was not freely available in the West where in Challaye's view it would merely risk 'increasing the hostile incomprehension of which Germany is the victim'.[40] Instead of a 'material resistance' to Nazism, Challaye proposed general disarmament. If that failed and war broke out between Germany and the Soviet Union, then France should attempt to localize it and not get involved. If Germany should attack France, then the true interests of the French people lay in avoiding participation in such a war. The only sane strategy, according to Challaye, was to avoid the destruction of war at all costs and wait for the internal revolt against Nazi rule to begin.[41]

In a further analysis of Rolland's evolution away from integral pacifism, Challaye wrote that the author of *Liluli* and Stalin's friend were fighting within Rolland, 'just as Jesus and Dionysus fought within the soul of Nietzsche'.[42] The ambiguity of Rolland's position was obvious to Challaye. He was clearly no longer in agreement with Bertrand Russell that war was the ultimate evil. Instead, the worst evil had become the debasement of a people. Challaye disagreed, arguing that social justice was a necessary goal but that it could not emerge from a war. Secondly, Challaye challenged the assumption that Nazism was, in fact, the ultimate evil. He pointed out that

[39] Georges Pioch, 'Questions à Romain Rolland', *Le Barrage*, 82 (30 Jan. 1936), 1.

[40] Félicien Challaye, 'A propos de "l'indivisible paix": Réponse à Romain Rolland', *Le Barrage*, 83 (6 Feb. 1936), 1.   [41] Ibid.

[42] Félicien Challaye, 'Seconde réponse à Romain Rolland', *Le Barrage*, 90 (19 Mar. 1936), 2.

concentration camps existed in Italy, and indeed that France used them in Tunisia and Indochina. And what about the Soviet Union under Stalin? His third point was that Rolland's desire to see treaty revision negotiated from a position of strength for the Western democracies was ridiculous; for fifteen years after the Great War the West had enjoyed this superiority and had not used it wisely. Germany would never agree to negotiating on such a basis. Finally, Challaye distinguished yet again between external and internal antifascism:

The struggle against internal and external Fascism presents, despite every-thing, very different characteristics. The struggle against internal Fascism is the civil battle which we accept. Idea against idea, truncheon, against truncheon. The fight against Hitler and Mussolini is, for a Frenchman, the fight against the Colonel-Count de la Rocque and against Charles Maurras. This is the national front which we must occupy in the international struggle against Fascism. But the struggle against external Fascism takes on neces-sarily the aspect of a war. We want nothing to do with war, even that which is baptized antifascist and revolutionary. We are convinced, moreover, that one does not bring freedom on the tip of a sword, nor democracy in foreign troop carriers [fourgons de l'étranger].[43]

PACIFIST TACTICS

The preceding pages have attempted to define the diversity of the LICP's approach to pacifism, and to describe the Ligue's position on violence, antifascism, anti-Semitism, and French parliamentary democracy. We have also shown how the Ligue developed an approach to the problem posed by the Nazi seizure of power. As will no doubt be clear from the above, the LICP was an intellectually amorphous organization comprising many different strands of thought on pacifist definitions and tactics. The one underlying theme common to all of these different orientations within the Ligue was a complete rejection of foreign wars.

At its yearly congresses from 1934 to 1939, the LICP debated a series of reports which defined its views on the nature of pacifism, the causes of war, its political orientation within French society, and the ever-present dilemma for pacifists of effective tactical responses to the problem of war.

At its third annual Congress in 1934, and the first since the schism

[43] Ibid.

with the *Patrie humaine*, Edouard Lemédioni prepared a lengthy report on the tactics which the LICP should adopt in its fight against war. The time had come to elaborate specific policies and to attempt to create a truly mass organization drawing members from both the working class and the middle class. Lemédioni, perhaps referring to Méric's style, wrote that demagogy was worthless; what was needed was propaganda and education. In his view there were three essential points which had to be made to the public. First, the Ligue had to demonstrate to its audiences the shameful reality of the munitions trade, before, during, and after the Great War, a question 'which engages the crowds' and which Lemédioni considered essential. Secondly, the LICP must emphasize the horrors that another war would bring with the advances since 1919 in military science. And finally, it was important to remind audiences of the responsibilities for the war of 1914, thus proving to the masses 'that the peoples are always fooled by the governments which are dominated by the powers of money, and that it is impossible to designate an aggressor when a conflict breaks out'.[44] With regard to the League of Nations and a 'certain pacifism' which sought to establish peace through purely juridical means, Lemédioni believed that the LICP had to put the masses on their guard; the League of Nations was nothing more than an association of imperialist governments, some of them under the thumb of heavy industry. On conscientious objection Lemédioni believed strongly that the LICP could not recommend it as a tactic because it was an individual act with such personal consequences; however, the Ligue had an obligation towards COs to aid them materially and morally. Fascism had to be opposed, but he underlined that it was not the only regime which practised a policy of expansionism; he believed that imperialism could be just as great a danger to peace as Fascism or Nazism. In any case, the Ligue had to reject any notion of a preventive war of the democracies against Germany. With regard to economic sanctions against German goods, he argued, together with the minority group on the Central Committee of the Ligue des droits de l'homme, that these sanctions were ineffective and would only accentuate the hatred between the peoples and 'weld the German people more closely to its government'.[45]

---

[44] Édouard Lemédioni, 'Rapport sur la tactique que la Ligue doit adopter', 1–2.
[45] Ibid. 2–3.

Having outlined his position on the above matter, Lemédioni proceeded to elaborate a series of steps towards what he called a positive pacifism. This positive pacifism had to be supple and capable of responding even to half measures in the political sphere. As a first measure, he suggested demanding clarification of positions from politicians at election time and support for a bill giving freedom of conscience to conscientious objectors. Secondly, he pressed for the nationalization of the armaments industry. Thirdly, he demanded the abrogation of the anti-anarchist 'lois scélérates' of 1893 and 1894. Finally, he thought the Ligue should press for the abrogation of the law of 31 July 1920 which punished anticonceptional propaganda —a law of which several of the LICP's speakers had fallen foul already. In the wake of the crisis of 6 February, he also went on to prescribe a series of measures to respond to the perceived Fascist threat which has been discussed above.[46]

Lemédioni's report was passed almost unanimously by the Montargis Congress, and the Comité directeur of the Ligue was charged with drafting a programme which would reflect concrete policies for pacifists. It should be stressed, though, that in the wake of the events of 6 February, the Congress took the position that the most pressing danger was that posed by Fascism which had to be fought on the domestic level.[47]

The 1935 Agen Congress was another fractious one for the LICP. Lemédioni, Marcelle Capy (who was president of the Ligue in 1934–5), and Henri Guilbeaux all left the Ligue for reasons which are not entirely clear. Guilbeaux had been writing a weekly column for some time on international affairs and had been charged with the drafting of the first edition of the Ligue's brochure, *Programme, tactiques et moyens d'action*. He also prepared a report for the 1935 Congress on the idea of a Franco-German-Soviet union and the struggle against Fascism. This report was printed in the *Barrage*, but strangely appears never to have been presented or discussed at the Congress; Guilbeaux resigned from the Ligue in an apparently discourteous letter before the Congress opened.[48] From the Congress proceedings it appears that part of the reason for these multiple departures was the Ligue's consideration of a report by Sébastien

---

[46] Ibid. 3–4.
[47] 'Compte-rendu du Congrès de Montargis', 4. See also 'Paix et liberté', 1–2.
[48] See 'Les Travaux du Congrès d'Agen', *Le Barrage*, 50 (2 May 1935), 4.

Faure on unilateral disarmament. Lemédioni attacked it as a 'chimerical idea', 'inoperative', and liable to 'upset public opinion'. He accused Faure of making an 'anarchist profession of faith' in arguing for unilateral disarmament.[49]

Guilbeaux's report, which was never voted on, was a logical continuation of his column in the pages of the *Barrage*. He argued against any policy of encirclement of Germany which could only lead to war. He was opposed to the League of Nations because it was an association of imperialist powers which 'by definition' could only foster wars. On the other hand, he was in favour of the nationalization of war industries as a useful first step towards eliminating war. Undoubtedly, Guilbeaux's favourite project, though, was the idea of a Franco-Soviet-German union. He declined to call this an alliance or a bloc, because these all led inevitably to war, and denied that the idea had an anti-British flavour to it. The logic behind his thinking, difficult though it is to conceive, was that the three powers that mattered in continental Europe were France, Germany, and the Soviet Union. Any other constellation was likely to be dangerous because the ideological dimension might create friction; but in the arrangement proposed by him, liberal democracy, Fascism, and Communism would, supposedly, harmoniously cancel one another out. He also wanted the Ligue to differentiate between imperialism and Fascism which were both dangerous for peace, but in different ways.[50]

Lemédioni's report on an obligatory popular referendum before any declaration of war was not presented to the Congress. A report by Robert Jospin (1899–) on the nationalization of the armaments industry was passed by the Congress. It seemed to contradict the conclusions reached the year before which had been favourable to such a move. Jospin argued that while nationalizing weapons manufacture could perhaps be interpreted as a first step, in reality such a move would change little or nothing for the integral pacifist. A nationalized arms industry was no guarantee of peace, although it would undoubtedly cut off a source of funding for the 'bought' press. Nevertheless, the weapons would remain instruments of death. A further problem was the incompleteness of such a proposal. To be truly effective, nationalization would have to include all the raw

[49] 'Les Travaux du Congrès d'Agen'.
[50] Henri Guilbeaux, 'Rapport sur le programme, l'union France–Allemagne–URSS, et la lutte contre le fascisme', *Le Barrage*, 43 (7 Mar. 1935), 4–5.

materials industries—the iron, potash, petroleum, and colonial markets—which contributed to the manufacture of arms. But perhaps more importantly, Jospin saw a potential trap for integral pacifists in this proposal. Pierre Cot had already suggested in the Chamber that if nationalization occurred it would remove one of the biggest arguments for pacifism. Jospin concluded: 'We have been fairly warned. Our total submission would be the ransom, the payment in a sense, for the nationalization of arms.'[51]

The Congress also passed by a large majority the report by Sébastien Faure in favour of unilateral disarmament; this report really summarized Faure's thinking on a subject on which he had already published.[52] Maurice Weber's report on nationalist ideologies was also passed but it implied nothing for the Ligue's tactics and was more a critique than a call to action.[53] In another report, though, Robert Jospin addressed the question of what to do if war actually broke out. He wove a narrow line between laying down specific recommendations and avoiding the entrapment of the 'lois scélérates' by saying little that was precise. His emphasis, though, was on the *hic et nunc*. War had to be opposed before it erupted and this meant education and having the courage to take individual positions. 'We will reap what we have sown', he said, '. . . let us promise ourselves, and that will suffice.' His report was passed by the largest majority, thus giving it claim to being the method of fighting war most favoured by the LICP.[54] The Comité directeur had wanted to establish a sort of hierarchy of pacifist tactics at the Agen Congress. At the same time, it was careful not to exclude any and to leave the choice of tactics up to the individual sections. In order of preference, the LICP had therefore pronounced itself in favour of Jospin's educative approach with the latent suggestion that individual acts of resistance would be called for in the event of war;

[51] See Édouard Lemédioni, 'Rapport sur le référendum populaire', *Le Barrage*, 44 (14 Mar. 1935), 4. Lemédioni's report was not presented to the Congress or voted on. See 'Les Travaux du Congrès d'Agen'. See also Robert Jospin, 'Rapport sur la nationalisation des armements', *Le Barrage*, 44 (14 Mar. 1935), 4.

[52] S. Faure, 'Rapport sur le désarmement unilatéral', *Le Barrage*, 44 (14 Mar. 1935), 5–6. See also 'Les Travaux du Congrès d'Agen'. See also S. Faure, *Nous voulons la paix* (Paris: chez l'auteur, 1932), in which Faure argued the case for unilateral disarmament.

[53] Maurice Weber, 'Rapport-critique sur les idéologies nationalistes', *Le Barrage*, 44 (14 Mar. 1935), 4–5.

[54] Robert Jospin, 'Rapport sur la question: Si la guerre éclatait?', *Le Barrage*, 44 (14 Mar. 1935), 6. See also 'Les Travaux du Congrès d'Agen'.

secondly for the idea of unilateral disarmament; and thirdly against the idea of a simple nationalization of the armaments industry only. The popular referendum and Guilbeaux's political report were never discussed.

The following year at the Bernay Congress, the Ligue continued its examination of pacifist tactics; Bauchet said in his *rapport moral* that while all methods were acceptable, the Ligue needed to continue its attempt to establish a hierarchy of values.[55] Aside from the theoretical questions, there were also practical issues to be considered. In the previous Congress, at Agen, Bauchet had presented a report on the practical organization of the Ligue, especially as it pertained to propaganda.[56] The following year at Bernay, Gerin ran through the many excellent suggestions made by Bauchet and found that hardly any of them were being followed. The Ligue was in danger of failing in its mission because of lack of organization.[57]

The 1936 Congress saw two main doctrinal reports presented and discussed. The first of these, by Jeanne Humbert, dealt with overpopulation as a cause of war. Humbert argued an essentially Malthusian case, saying that there were natural or biological reasons for war as well as social and psychological ones. Overpopulation and scarcity of food and raw materials caused wars, and she demanded in conclusion an end to the restrictive laws on anticonceptional propaganda and sex education. Humbert's report was adopted with near unanimity, although Challaye reacted strongly against the suggestion that overpopulation led *inevitably* to war.[58]

POLITICAL PARTIES, THE POPULAR FRONT, AND PACIFISM

The 1936 Congress also discussed a substantial report on 'The Political Parties, the Popular Front, and Peace', drawn up by Robert Jospin and Maurice Weber.[59] They underlined the differences between the LICP's viewpoint and those of all political parties. Their

[55] Émile Bauchet, 'Rapport moral', *Le Barrage*, 87 (5 Mar. 1936), 4.

[56] See Émile Bauchet, 'Rapport sur l'organisation pratique', *Le Barrage*, 44 (14 Mar. 1935), 2.

[57] René Gerin, 'Rapport sur l'organisation de la propagande', *Le Barrage*, 87 (5 Mar. 1936), 4.

[58] Jeanne Humbert, 'La Surpopulation et la guerre', *Le Barrage*, 87 (5 Mar. 1936), 5. See also 'Les Travaux du Congrès de Bernay', *Le Barrage*, 94 (23 Apr. 1936), 3.

[59] Maurice Weber and Robert Jospin, 'Rapport sur les partis politiques, le Front populaire et la paix', *Le Barrage*, 87 (5 Mar. 1936), 5–6; and *Le Barrage*, 88 (12 Mar. 1936), 4.

distinction between political party and pacifist movement is important to our definition of what is under discussion in this study. For Jospin and Weber, the essential characteristic of political parties was a preoccupation with the organization of society and the state. 'All parties, however excellent may be their intentions, claim to create man's happiness in spite of him if necessary: they resign themselves sometimes to sacrificing a great number of men in order to guarantee the salvation of those who are left.'[60] Thus, in the authors' view, the masses were but the instruments which the parties used to further their own external and internal political views. The LICP, on the other hand, had a completely different conception of the role of the state; it placed the 'interests of the governed, not those of the governors' first.[61] The distinction reduced itself fundamentally to one between an individualist and a collectivist view of the state. The LICP believed fervently that the individual was the most important social unit, while still taking account of the needs of the larger social group. The problem in France was that the needs of society had begun to take precedence over those of its units, with the unfortunate result that society had become an oppressive creature periodically demanding the sacrifice of the individual to its 'higher' needs. The LICP was not arguing for unbridled individualism; Weber and Jospin believed that individualism must be limited in its expression, but that equally society had to attempt to assure the maximum amount of happiness and prosperity for the greatest number in the greatest liberty. In France it seemed that there was an inevitable drift towards forgetting this principle; that was why the slide towards absolutism had to be constantly checked by, to borrow Alain's expression, 'the citizen against the authorities'.[62] The important concept in the report was that *all* political parties in France were infected with varying degrees of the same mentality.

With regard to the parties of the right in France, Weber and Jospin demonstrated that they were torn between conflicting ideas and tendencies. The political situation had become even more complicated with the Nazi accession to power because the right was now split between those who favoured a pact with Hitler and those who advocated the Laval–Stalin Pact because they continued to conceive of Germany as the principal and traditional enemy. A pseudo-

---

[60] Weber and Jospin, 'Rapport' (5 Mar. 1936), 5.
[61] Ibid.   [62] Ibid.

pacifism had thus insinuated itself into the right, a pacifism based not on conviction but on political opportunism. Weber and Jospin thought that the LICP should find encouragement in this without being under any illusions about the temporary nature of the conversion of these 'unexpected neophytes'; the right remained camouflaged bellicists, interested only in the maintenance of France's conquests and colonial domains.[63]

As far as the Radicals were concerned, the report concluded that they had always been infected with nationalist and patriotic ideas. Some Radicals, it was true, professed a vague pacifism based purely on juridical principles—'genre "Paix par le Droit"'—but their pacifism was based on too many mistakes from the past. The idea that peace could be achieved through the League of Nations or an armed international force was 'the policy of sanctions pushed to the point where it could provoke a war'.[64] The LICP rejected a repetition of this tragic vision from recent history.

The position of the Communist Party created special problems for the Ligue. Weber and Jospin wrote that they were 'profoundly convinced of the need to defend the USSR', but the 'essential question' was precisely to know by what means this could be achieved. As far as the LICP was concerned, methods of force and violence were not the way to go about this. The Stalin declaration had turned the world of pacifism upside down. Part of the blame for the situation lay with the Allies' failure to disarm according to the provisions of the Versailles Treaty. This had helped to prepare the way for Hitler. But they rejected out of hand any notion of a Communist-inspired crusade against the Fascist dictatorships. For real pacifists the challenge and the duty were clear:

It is up to pacifists to affirm, despite all individual weaknesses, the convictions that are theirs, and to resist with all their force the bellicist contagion. They must maintain the distinctions which are necessary, and not permit the confusion of the necessary fight against the Fascist regimes with a crusade which would be transformed into a holy war . . . The danger is so great that one can perhaps after all consider the existence of a part of French public opinion favourable to Hitlerism—as long as it remains a sufficiently weak minority—as a useful counter-weight. For it is good that a government does

[63] Weber and Jospin, 'Rapport', Cf. Joseph Folliet, *Pacifisme de droite? Bellicisme de gauche?* (Paris: Éditions du cerf, 1938), which examines the pseudo-pacifism of the right at the time of Munich.
[64] Weber and Jospin, 'Rapport' (5 Mar. 1936), 6.

not have behind it an overly unanimous public opinion; that helps to make it more prudent and wise.[65]

Because of this view of international politics, Weber and Jospin could only warn Ligue members to stay away from the Rassemblement universel pour la paix, as well as Soviet front organizations like the Amsterdam-Pleyel movement.[66]

Unlike the situation within the PCF, the Socialist Party was completely divided on the question of peace and how best to attain it. The party contained a number of different *individual* attitudes which did not worry the LICP as much as those of other parties. This was not to say that they all gave complete satisfaction—far from it. The writers singled out Zyromski and his faction, in particular, for attack. They praised the SFIO for always having refused to condone the Versailles Treaty and for its condemnation of the Ruhr occupation. Léon Blum was lauded for his personal stand against war and for unilateral disarmament, but he was too constrained by his position as party leader. Paul Faure was praised. There was also support for Marceau Pivert's Gauche révolutionnaire which seemed to be evolving towards the sort of pacifism espoused by the LICP.[67]

The programme of the Front populaire came in for serious criticism as much for what it did not say, as for what it said. Weber and Jospin provided a critique of the seven points of the programme of the Popular Front which related to the defence of peace. The first of these was an appeal for the collaboration of the masses in the work of the organization of the peace. But as the writers acerbically remarked, if peace was indeed so threatened and in such a precarious state, it was certainly not the fault of the masses, but rather of governments. It was these same governments which had created the Versailles system which was the origin of so many of Europe's troubles.[68]

The second point of the programme demanded national collaboration within the context of the League of Nations, and collective security through the definition of the aggressor and the automatic application of sanctions. The LICP rejected this idea almost in its entirety. Its confidence in the L.o.N. was very limited anyway, and the notion that military sanctions could be called for under Article XVI of the Covenant was completely unacceptable.[69]

[65] Ibid.
[66] Ibid.
[67] Weber and Jospin, 'Rapport' (12 Mar. 1936), 4.
[68] Ibid.
[69] Ibid.

The third point spoke of an 'incessant effort to move from a state of armed peace to one of disarmed peace', through the negotiation of an accord first on the limitation, and then on the reduction, of armaments through gradual, controlled, and simultaneous disarmament. The LICP praised the good intentions, but criticized the method. Governments did not have the courage to set an example through unilateral disarmament.[70]

Fourthly, the programme called for the nationalization of the armaments industry and the suppression of free trade in arms. The LICP report saw this as a positive demand but one which was far from capable of assuring peace. Jospin and Weber wrote, 'to say that war is due to the will of the arms merchants is really to minimize and make puerile a terribly complex question'.[71] But it would not do away with the problem of war and pacifists should not be lulled into thinking that it would.

The Popular Front's fifth point was a 'repudiation of secret diplomacy', coupled with an attempt to reintegrate into the League of Nations those countries which had left it, whilst at the same time reaffirming the ideas of collective security and an indivisible peace. Weber and Jospin rejected the notions of collective security and indivisible peace and stressed that the programme did not mention the denunciation of the secret treaties already in force. This had to be done in order to clean up international affairs.[72]

The sixth point dealt with the 'peaceful adjustment of those treaties which were dangerous for the peace of the world'. It is interesting to note that the LICP view of what constituted a dangerous treaty was any treaty which 'was not in accord with the political, economic, and moral realities of the moment, and which was dictated to the vanquished by force, instead of being freely negotiated between equals'.[73]

Finally, Weber and Jospin criticized the seventh point of the programme which pressed for an extension of the open pact system in Central and Eastern Europe along the lines of the Franco-Soviet Pact. They rejected the idea that these pacts were in fact open to everybody; they could not be because they were based upon a vision of Europe which had its origin in the Versailles Treaty and was therefore inimical to the desires and views of the defeated nations of 1918. The Franco-Soviet Pact was in danger of becoming anything

[70] Weber and Jospin, 'Rapport'   [71] Ibid.   [72] Ibid.   [73] Ibid.

but 'an instrument of pacification' in their view. If further pacts were to be signed, it was essential that they contain no military clauses, but the reticences of the programme on the specific point of secret treaties caused Weber and Jospin great concern.[74]

These specific concerns were relatively minor alongside Jospin and Weber's main worry about what the Popular Front programme did *not* say. There was nothing in it about imperialism which the authors called the idea that nations enjoyed an absolute sovereignty in their own affairs. This was the real cause of wars. Harking back to 1918, Jospin and Weber strongly criticized the programme for remaining frozen in the past and refusing to embrace the still untried ideas of Wilson, 'the only ones which can lead to a real peace'.[75] The indispensable revision of the treaties could never occur in a moral and political climate so opposed to it. They concluded that the Popular Front's peace programme was 'insufficient for the creation of peace'; furthermore, despite the admitted 'goodwill of its authors', the programme was unlikely to preserve France from war, and might even bring war closer.[76]

Having criticized at great length the policies of both the Popular Front and the main political parties in France, the authors passed to an examination of what they considered the fundamental question, the conditions of a genuine Franco-German *rapprochement*. With regard to recent events, such as the remilitarization of the Rhineland and the abrogation of the Locarno Treaty, Jospin and Weber 'dared' to write that they found the new situation 'more encouraging' because clearer. They cited Paul Faure in an article of 8 March in the *Populaire*, who wrote that 'everything remains to be done, everything remains to be re-begun, or rather everything must now begin'. As far as the internal atrocities of the Nazi regime were concerned, these undoubtedly constituted a 'difficult psychological obstacle to be overcome'. In a biting criticism of what they perceived to be the essentially anti-German, rather than specifically anti-Nazi, orientation of recent French foreign policy, they wrote,

In reality, the argument about the internal regime is really just a bad pretext; those who would move against it confound the necessary struggle against Fascism within each country with an anti-German crusade. These are not real pacifists. These people did not seriously protest against the formation of the 'Stresa Front', and they continued to view Mussolini's Italy as a pacifist

[74] Ibid.   [75] Ibid.   [76] Ibid.

nation right up to the outbreak of war in Ethiopia. They also find it completely normal to have military alliances with the little Fascist countries of the Balkans.[77]

Thus, while reserving the legal and moral right to criticize, Jospin and Weber argued that the only logical and sane approach to the dilemmas posed by Nazism was to follow religiously the old diplomatic rule of 'taking no account of our preferences or repugnances for any particular regime'.[78] To do otherwise required a constantly high level of military preparedness and constituted what the authors called 'the revolutionary deviation of 1792' which led 'us to foreign wars, militarization, and Bonapartism'.[79] They rejected the idea that by refusing an alliance with the USSR, France would be opening herself up to the possibility of an aggression which would finally rebound on to her. They supported Guilbeaux's idea of a Franco-German-Soviet union which had not actually been discussed at the previous year's Congress.

Weber and Jospin concluded their report with a plea for a measure of historical transcendence; Europe urgently needed to forget the history of which she was the victim, and to unite. If this did not occur, they foresaw instead a new war of religion between the latter-day faiths of Fascism and Communism. They accepted Hitler's principal prescriptions for a peace with Germany: equality of rights, bilateral and reciprocal treaties, simultaneous demilitarization of zones on both sides of the border, the return of all European nations to the League of Nations, this time on an equal footing, and a thorough revision of the Treaty of Versailles. In order for much of this to be accomplished, the League's Covenant would have to be separated from the treaty, and a rapid and total disarmament would have to occur.[80]

In the discussion of the report at the Bernay Congress, it was stressed that while the Ligue disagreed with many aspects of its programme, it did not want to do anything to harm the Popular Front in terms of domestic politics. Jospin indicated the point of disagreement with most Socialists on the question of peace: the pacifists of the LICP could not support the reservation 'in a capitalist regime' inherent in the traditional Socialist rejection of war. As he said, 'our refusal of war is absolute', and that was what distinguished integral pacifism from all other shades of antiwar feeling. The Congress also decided not to mount a public campaign against the

[77] Weber and Jospin, 'Rapport'.   [78] Ibid.   [79] Ibid.   [80] Ibid.

policies of the PCF, but merely to continue its comments in the pages of *Le Barrage*. The Weber–Jospin report was passed unanimously.[81]

The Bernay Congress came at the mid-point of the LICP's trajectory *vis-à-vis* the Popular Front. The Ligue had originally supported the idea of a Popular Front, not so much as an organization of parties, but as a powerful manifestation of popular feeling on a range of issues, including peace.[82] By early 1936 many of the reservations discussed above had already begun to make their appearance. Jospin attacked the insufficiencies more than the defects of the Front's programme. It had nothing to say about the two-year military service law, the swollen war-budget, repealing the Daladier–Forcinal law on conscientious objection, or about creating a statute for COs.[83] After the election victory of the Popular Front, however, Gerin expressed the optimistic euphoria of the Ligue in what he hoped would be the pacifist orientation of the new government. He declared that the victory of the Front meant the defeat of Fascism in France, and the creation of a left-wing government a sign of hope for pacifism because 'it is always on the left, among the exploited, that world peace is wished for most ardently and prepared the best'.[84] The hopes he placed in the Popular Front—especially as regards the liberation of conscientious objectors and a separate statute for them—were almost bound to be dashed. He spoke of the 'guaranteed vote' of an amnesty of COs, and the failure of Fascism in France. In the longer term, Gerin demanded a real disarmament, 'supported by a policy of sincere *rapprochement* with all peoples'.[85] These hopes invested in the Popular Front were great, and it is easy to see how disappointments followed. Gerin had in fact put his finger on one of the reasons for this. He wrote of the opportunistic hypocrisy of the Communists who, in order to attract middle-class votes, had 'noisily accepted the need to guarantee the national defence and the defence

---

[81] 'Les Travaux de Congrès de Bernay', 4.

[82] Initial positive reactions to the Popular Front idea can be found in René Gerin, 'L'Espoir, enfin, change de camp', *Le Barrage*, 52 (16 May 1935), 1; Le Barrage, '14 juillet 1935', *Le Barrage*, 60 (18 July 1935), 1; 'A propos du Front populaire', *Le Barrage*, 67 (17 Oct. 1935), 4.

[83] Robert Jospin, 'Le Rassemblement populaire et la paix: A propos d'un programme', *Le Barrage*, 84 (13 Feb. 1936), 2. Cf. Charles Boussinot, 'Le Salut n'est qu'en nous-mêmes', *Le Barrage*, 86 (27 Feb. 1936), 1; Édouard Rothen, 'Avec la peau des autres', *Le Barrage*, 92 (2 Apr. 1936), 1; Maurice Weber, 'Fermeté et vigilance', *Le Barrage*, 86 (27 Feb. 1936), 1.

[84] René Gerin, 'Les Élections et la paix', *Le Barrage*, 95 (30 Apr. 1936), 1.

[85] Ibid.

of "democratic" liberties'.[86] He thought that this sudden conversion had undoubtedly profited them in parliamentary terms, but would have little impact on the revolution. The world of French politics was rapidly changing in the face of threats from within and without; and as integral pacifists were to learn in the next few years, the presence of a left-wing government in the Palais Bourbon was no guarantee of the implementation of pacifist policies.

There was no lack of warnings in the pages of the *Barrage* of the disappointments likely to be in store for pacifists who put too much faith in the political process. Armand Charpentier welcomed the Popular Front, but warned that pacifists ought not to have the 'naïveté' to believe that much would change. Relatively few members of the Popular Front parties were in any sense integral pacifists.[87] Sébastien Faure echoed these fears in even more precise form. He predicted that the Blum government would very quickly make concessions on two capital points: the League of Nations, and support for the national defence. He claimed that Blum had never considered disarmament outside the bounds of the League of Nations, and in order to retain power it would be necessary to arrive at a *modus vivendi* with the military establishment. He wagered that the Popular Front would not change to any appreciable extent the foreign policy of France, that the length of military service would not be diminished, the size of the army and its budget would not decrease, and if they persisted in talking about disarmament, it would be a very official and gradual one.[88]

Disenchantment was not long in making its voice heard, quietly at first and then in increasingly strident tones. At the end of May 1936 Gerin urged the Popular Front to embrace a real antimilitarism which would move beyond the anodyne nationalization of the arms industries to real disarmament. He criticized the Socialists for following the evolution of the Communists towards the idea of defence of the Soviet fatherland as well as of France. This was all a result of the Franco-Soviet Pact, and he noted that the closer a party got to the reins of power, 'the more it is willing to compromise with the militarism which will be its protector'.[89] This was why the Socialist

---

[86]   Gerin, 'Les Élections et la paix',

[87]   Armand Charpentier, 'Heureuses victoires et joyeux échecs', *Le Barrage*, 96 (7 May 1936), 1.

[88]   Sébastien Faure, 'La Sauvegarde de la paix', *Le Barrage*, 98 (21 May 1936), 2.

[89]   René Gerin, 'Antimilitarisme d'abord!', *Le Barrage*, 99 (28 May 1936), 1.

Party had sworn in the recent elections to support the necessary credits for the War Ministry. Léon Blum wanted disarmament, but he was now constrained by the realities of holding power. Gerin hoped fervently that at least the minimum programme of controlled, simultaneous, and progressive disarmament would be achieved.[90]

The wave of strikes in June 1936 provided an object lesson for pacifists. Gerin wrote that they proved that if the people had the courage to follow Mirabeau's dictum—'the people would be powerful if they knew how to remain immobile'—they ought to be able to prevent any war from breaking out. No mobilization was possible without the active consent of the mobilizable. This was the antithesis of the Communist approach which preached the creation of the revolution from within the army in time of war. The militarism and uncertainty of this method were reason enough to reject it. Gerin enjoined his Communist comrades to 'meditate instead on the lesson of these past days; and for the maintenance of peace, as well as moreover for the triumph of the revolution, to draw the necessary conclusions'.[91]

There was tremendous initial goodwill towards Léon Blum within the LICP. At the outset of the Popular Front, the Ligue often criticized its failures and shortcomings while at the same time making clear that it believed in Blum's commitment to peace. Thus, Georges Pioch announced in June 1936 that he was 'playing the Léon Blum card'.[92] At the same time Challaye addressed an open letter to Blum which was full of affection and faith in what Blum was trying to achieve. He clearly considered Blum to be 'one of us', but he was most concerned that Blum's government break with the past and with those advisers who were urging continuity in French foreign policy. Blum also had to contend with those within his own coalition who were partisans of revolutionary wars. Challaye enjoined him to remain true to his convictions. There were serious lacunae and ambiguities in the government's programme, but Challaye demanded that these be transcended and that France declare 'peace to the world' through moral disarmament, revise the treaties of 1919, and proceed to a material disarmament as well. The latter point Challaye recognized would be difficult, if not impossible, even for the

---

[90] Ibid.

[91] René Gerin, 'Une leçon à méditer', *Le Barrage*, 100 (11 June 1936), 1.

[92] Georges Pioch, 'Je joue la carte Léon Blum', *Le Barrage*, 100 (11 June 1936), 1–2.

Popular Front government to achieve, so as a first measure of good faith, he advocated the reduction of military service to one year.[93]

By July 1936, the LICP's disillusionment with the Popular Front was palpable. In a second letter to Blum, sent on behalf of the Ligue's office-bearers, Challaye expressed his disappointment that there was no mention of conscientious objectors in the bill being prepared on an amnesty.[94] Georges Michon was far more caustic. He wrote that the first sitting of the new Chamber exclusively devoted to questions of foreign affairs, had been a 'demonstration of an anti-German union sacrée'.[95] The ministerial statement had 'affirmed . . . the continuity of French policy', making no mention at all of the rather 'timid' hints of a complete revision of the unjust treaties which had been contained in the Front's programme. Instead, there had been the familiar insistence on the need for a strong defence and the prevailing length of the military service had been reaffirmed. From right to left there seemed to be unanimity on the fact that Hitler was the great danger to peace. Rather than revise the treaties, the government was preparing to follow the Moscow line and recommend regional treaties within the context of the League of Nations. Michon concluded:

These are the consequences of the Blum speech. In truth, Poincaré and Tardieu could not have done better. Did the electors of the Popular Front want that? On top of this, there are the stupefying reversals of the Communists, and the apotheosis by the extreme left of the *Marseillaise*, the flag, Joan of Arc (who will remain the symbol of religious mysticism and monarchical faith), and of the national union in all its forms. These manifestations create in some a demoralizing effect, and in others a nationalistic and pseudo-revolutionary state of mind which recalls Boulangism, both of which are essentially favourable to Fascism and above all to the acceptance of war.[96]

The criticism of the Popular Front continued, even into 1939 with post-mortem comments on why it had all failed to give satisfaction to the great desire for peace. Having lost its political virginity, the Popular Front seemed unable to move beyond quiescence and lack of

[93] Félicien Challaye, 'A bas les deux ans! Lettre ouverte à Léon Blum', *Le Barrage*, 101 (25 June 1936), 1.
[94] Félicien Challaye, 'Lettre à Léon Blum', *Le Barrage*, 102 (9 July 1936), 1.
[95] Georges Michon, 'Union sacrée', *Le Barrage*, 102 (9 July 1936), 1.
[96] Ibid.

daring in everything from its foreign policy to what Pioch considered to be its unworthy attitude towards the Moscow Purge Trials.[97]

We have already noted the affinity felt for Blum within the LICP. There was also initially a tremendous feeling of communion of thought with the Socialist Party as a whole. But by 1937, the LICP was becoming very concerned at the evolution the SFIO seemed to be taking on questions of peace. Maurice Weber and Sylvain Broussaudier took opposing views of whether the Socialists could be counted on as a force for pacifism. Weber, who in 1936 had written that he could see no incompatibility between membership of the SFIO and the LICP,[98] wrote the following year that the situation seemed to be changing as the party moved steadily away from its old, admittedly vague, but deep-seated antimilitarism, in the face of German rearmament. Weber concluded that the next party congress would probably see the end of pacifism within the SFIO.[99] Broussaudier disagreed with Weber's conclusions about the direction the Socialists seemed to be taking. Instead, he thought that while the SFIO could not be described as integrally pacifist, it would continue to represent a 'minimum pacifist programme, realizable in the short term, and able to exercise a positive influence on the government'.[100]

But it was perhaps left to René Gerin in early 1939 to sum up the feelings of disillusionment experienced by many pacifists, in an article in which he referred to Blum as a simpleton. After the Montrouge Congress of the party, it was clear that Blum must henceforth be placed among the LICP's adversaries. He was perhaps not even still a Socialist because he seemed to put little stock in the concerted action of the international proletariat against war:

[97] For developing disenchantment on the Popular Front, see Maurice Weber, 'Ce n'est pas par la guerre qu l'on fera la paix', *Le Barrage*, 102 (9 July 1936), 2; Félicien Challaye, 'Un terrible lapsus', *Le Barrage*, 109 (29 Apr. 1937), 1; Adrien Duthu, 'Ange ou démon?', *Le Barrage*, 110 (13 May 1937), 1–2; Georges Pioch, 'Rougeur sur le Front populaire', *Le Barrage*, 111 (27 May 1937), 1–2; Madeleine Vernet, 'La Paix et la politique', *Le Barrage*, 113 (24 June 1937), 2; Pierre Nézelof, 'Le Front populaire ruiné pas ses chefs', *Le Barrage*, 150 (8 June 1939), 2.

[98] Maurice Weber, 'Pacifisme et socialisme', *Le Barrage*, 78 (2 Jan. 1936), 1.

[99] Maurice Weber, 'La Situation des pacifistes dans le Parti socialiste', *Le Barrage*, 109 (29 Apr. 1937), 2.

[100] Sylvain Broussaudier, 'Les Pacifistes dans le Parti socialiste', *Le Barrage*, 110 (13 May 1937), 2. See also Maurice Weber, 'Les Pacifistes et le Parti socialiste', *Le Barrage*, 111 (27 May 1937), 3; Régis Messac, 'Lettre à Sylvain Broussaudier', *Le Barrage*, 111 (27 May 1937), 3; Sylvain Broussaudier, 'Brève réponse à R Messac', *Le Barrage*, 111 (27 May 1937), 3.

If one renounced the union of the world working class, in order to participate *totally and without reservation* in the defence of the fatherland; if, in
spite of all denials, one became an imperialist, under the grossly false pretext
of pacifism, then one could certainly still lay claim to the title of Statesman,
but it would be an imposture to call oneself a socialist.[101]

Gerin also asked whether Blum was any longer a democrat, because
he had recently expressed support for the 'exaltation of all energies'
and the 'effort of national stimulation'. Citing Paul Valéry's *bon
mot*, Gerin charged that since coming to power, Blum had become a
petty politician, practising the art of 'preventing people from involving themselves in the things which concern them'.[102] Finally, Gerin
asked whether Blum could be considered a pacifist any longer. The
answer was a categorical no, because he 'no longer believes in peace';
instead, Blum had become an 'evangelist for the policy of blocs', a
man who wanted '*his* peace and not *the* peace'.[103]

WARS AND RUMOURS OF WARS

The positions taken during the thirties by the LICP on questions of
foreign policy were consistent with its general outlook and activity in
the domestic sphere. In both domains, the LICP's stance was a
reflection of its general dissenting attitude outlined at the beginning
of this section. In the period from 1934 to 1938, the Ligue's pacifism
was challenged by events outside France. The most important of
these were the outbreak of the Italo-Abyssinian War, the Saar
plebiscite, the remilitarization of the Rhineland, the Franco-Soviet
Pact, and the Spanish Civil War.

With regard to the Saar, Gerin wrote in late 1934 that if Paris was
worth a mass, then peace was certainly worth the Saar. He was in
favour of negotiations with Hitler, and approved Blum's statement
that he was prepared to shake the bloodiest hand for peace.[104]

There was dissension, however, within the Ligue. Rudolf
Leonhard, the German propagandist who had been an active member of the LICP's Comité d'honneur almost from its inception,
disagreed entirely with the Gerin analysis. He put his case in a
two-part article published in late December 1934 which was printed
with the disclaimer that the views expressed therein were those

---

[101] René Gerin, 'Blum-Gribouille', *Le Barrage*, 140 (5 Jan. 1939), 1.
[102] Ibid.   [103] Ibid.
[104] René Gerin, 'Si Paris valut une messe . . .', *Le Barrage*, 30 (6 Dec. 1934), 1.

neither of the *Barrage*, nor of the LICP. Leonhard wrote that for some time now, German *émigrés* had been receiving a bad press in France; it was almost as if they, rather than Hitler, were to blame for preventing an *entente* with Germany. He attacked a recent article in *La Paix par le droit* which sought to minimize the atrocity stories coming out of Germany; on the contrary, Leonhard retorted that he 'could show the pacifist review *La Paix par le droit* and Georges Demartial the unhealed wounds which our comrades have brought back from the Hitlerian hell'.[105] As to the argument that the *émigrés* were fomenting war, Leonhard underlined that not only did they not believe in the efficacy of a 'war of liberation', but that each time the opportunity presented itself, they spoke out against any notion of a preventive war as well. Coming finally to the question of the Saar, he wrote that it was false to assume that Hitler had a united German people behind him. Leonhard claimed to be speaking as a German on the Saar issue, and as such, it was his considered opinion that the status quo should prevail in the Saar. Why? 'Because the Saar is German, without the slightest doubt. We want it to remain German, and not become Nazified.'[106] The problem of the Saar was not so much a Franco-German one as an international one. It ought to be seen in European terms and the Saar should remain independent until Germany herself became so once again.[107]

Georges Demartial responded by insisting that the only course for French pacifists was to respect the internal affairs of Germany and avoid meddling in them.[108] Henri Guilbeaux took the same line, castigating Leonhard for supporting the point of view of the Saar Communist Party which received its orders from Moscow.[109] When the vote finally went in Hitler's favour, Guilbeaux thought it entirely predictable—and not just the fault of the Nazis, but also of the incompetence of the Social Democrats and Communists. He did not want to see the Saar become a further point of friction in Europe, but

[105] Rudolf Leonhard, 'Le Problème de la Sarre du point de vue allemand', *Le Barrage*, 32 (20 Dec. 1934), 2. The article in *La Paix par le droit* would seem to be 'Lettre à M. Charles Rousseau à propos de "l'Allemagne contre le droit": Lettre du 20 novembre 1933 de Mlle Hélène Lhoumeau, licenciée en droit et fonctionnaire des services de la Société des nations', *PD* 44/1 (Jan. 1934), 18–21.

[106] Leonhard, 'Le Problème de la Sarre', 2.

[107] Rudolf Leonhard, 'Le Problème de la Sarre du point de vue allemand (suite)', *Le Barrage*, 33 (27 Dec. 1934), 2.

[108] Georges Demartial, 'L'Hitlérisme et la France', *Le Barrage*, 34 (3 Jan. 1935), 1.

[109] Henri Guilbeaux, 'La Sarre et les rapports franco-allemands', *Le Barrage*, 34 (3 Jan. 1935), 3.

argued that it could instead evolve into a sort of bridge between France and Germany, perhaps through an economic and customs accord.[110]

Gerin tried to demonstrate that the massive vote in favour of attachment to Germany proved that the war-guilt issue, which transcended party political lines, was one which *all* Germans wanted to see expunged. The vote in the Saar was the 'consequence of all of the stupidly inhumane policies of France in the last fifteen years'.[111] Hitler had said that there now remained no more territorial problems between France and Germany. Gerin thought that the time had now come to try to resolve the *moral* issues which remained between these two countries.[112]

The LICP also took a very measured view of the remilitarization of the Rhineland which conformed with the general position it had taken on the Saar. Gerin wrote that people from the extreme left to the extreme right were asking what Hitler really wanted. The answer was simple: 'the suppression of Article 231 of the Versailles Treaty, which gratuitously and stupidly dishonours a great people, [and] equitable revision of the treaties'.[113] He expressed no surprise at the remilitarization of the Rhineland: 'Germany has a habit of presenting her adversaries with a *fait accompli*. And it is to be expected, too, that our rulers, after having for so long refused a policy of open hands, will be forced, one day, to accept the *fait accompli*.'[114] The exculpation of Hitler's moves in the present was thus justified by the LICP's view of the past. As the Ligue officially stated in a front-page communiqué, 'bellicists and belli-pacifists obstinately continue to close their eyes to the injustices of the past, and dream of a war to resolve the conflict'; integral pacifists, on the other hand, 'proclaim that it is time to have recourse to a genuine peace policy: a policy that is frank, loyal, and courageous. It is time to recognize the errors and the faults of the past which are at the origin of the present conflict.'[115] The apparent insouciance with which the LICP viewed the remilitarization of the Rhineland might well be summed up in the

---

[110] Henri Guilbeaux, 'La Sarre est allemande', *Le Barrage*, 36 (17 Jan. 1935), 3.
[111] René Gerin, 'Ce que signifie le vote des Sarrois', *Le Barrage*, 37 (24 Jan. 1935), 1.
[112] Ibid.
[113] René Gerin, 'Que veut l'Allemagne?', *Le Barrage*, 88 (12 Mar. 1936), 1.
[114] Ibid.
[115] 'Nous ne marchons pas!', *Le Barrage*, 88 (12 Mar. 1936), 1.

headline of that fount of irony, *Le Canard enchaîné*, at the time: 'L'Allemagne envahit . . . l'Allemagne'.[116] In taking such a position, the Ligue seemed to ignore that more was at stake than simply the Versailles Treaty. In remilitarizing the Rhineland, Hitler had also torn up the Locarno accords as well—an agreement which had been fairly negotiated with Republican Germany. This point was passed over in silence by the *Barrage*.

It is interesting to contrast the above two incidents with the reaction of the Ligue to the outbreak of the Italo-Abyssinian conflict. The LICP found it much easier to condemn Italian aggression and atrocities in Ethiopia than to castigate Germany for the Rhineland episode. Undoubtedly there were good reasons for this. Ethiopia was, after all, a real war. But one wonders if the ability to censure more easily in the case of Italy might have been due to the fact that the LICP always saw the German problem as the major difficulty which had to be resolved in French foreign affairs. Its resistance to post-war French policy, its politics of dissent, created an inbuilt need in its political analysis to criticize French policy towards Germany. Having said that, the Ligue did maintain a pacifist position on the Ethiopian affair while criticizing the Italian government very sternly for its aggression.

The received opinion within the LICP was that the developing conflict in Ethiopia was more about colonialism and imperialism than about Italian Fascism. Henri Guilbeaux claimed to see the occult hand of British imperialism in the matter, with a supporting role being played by Japan.[117] Challaye echoed this view, and denounced the spurious Italian argument that they were performing a 'civilizing' task in Ethiopia where slavery still existed; better to have black man exploiting black man, than to have the wholesale proletarianization of the nation under the imperialistic boot of the white man, according to Challaye.[118] Two months later, in September 1935, he analysed what the Italo-Ethiopian conflict meant in terms of the principles of the LICP. People who called themselves pacifists were currently making two sorts of comments on the

[116] Cited in Michel Winock, 'Le Fascisme passera . . . Pourquoi?', *Le Monde aujourd'hui*, Supplement to No. 12852 of *Le Monde* (Sunday 25–Monday 26 May 1986), 7.
[117] Henri Guilbeaux, 'Le Conflit italo-abyssin', *Le Barrage*, 33 (27 Dec. 1934), 3.
[118] Félicien Challaye, 'A propos du conflit italo-éthiopien: Guerre et colonisation', *Le Barrage*, 60 (18 July 1935), 1.

conflict. There were those who argued that sanctions led to war and should therefore be avoided. And there were others, like the British TUC, who advocated the imposition of all sorts of sanctions, including military ones if necessary. In Challaye's view, the latter position was not 'pacifist' at all. So, was the choice between doing nothing and going to war? He argued that on the contrary, the Ethiopian people should fight foreign oppression by means other than war, which would have as its only effect the destruction of their country. Challaye suggested Gandhian non-violent resistance, strikes, individual acts of terrorism, insurrections, and so on. As for the other nations of the world, it was incumbent on them not to get involved at almost any price. He rejected the idea of an indivisible peace and argued that wars must be localized, not generalized. The methods to use were a diplomatic, moral, economic, and financial boycott, universally applied. Sanctions did not automatically mean war because their application could be limited to one's own national territory. There was no suggestion of using gunboat diplomacy to erect naval blockades around the belligerent countries.[119]

Challaye's prescriptions for peace were reiterated by the Ligue as a whole which published a manifesto on the Ethiopian crisis. It condemned Fascism and Mussolini's incursion into Ethiopia but advised the Ethiopian people that it 'would defend itself more effectively and bring honour to itself in not having recourse to the means of war'.[120] The Ligue also condemned in anticipation any attempt on the part of other powers to get involved in the conflict. The political anarchism of the LICP, or its politics of dissent, came through baldly in its statement that for both the Italian and Ethiopian peoples, their primary enemy was to be found in their own governments. The LICP recommended the breaking-off of diplomatic relations with Italy, a freeze in all arms trade with both countries, and the refusal of all bank credits to the aggressor. The important task was to halt the spread of the conflict.[121]

The Ethiopian War had as a further interesting result the significant emergence for the first time of what the LICP chose to call, somewhat incongruously to the Anglo-Saxon ear, the pseudo-

[119] Félicien Challaye, 'Le Conflit italo-éthiopien et les principes de notre Ligue', *Le Barrage*, 64 (12 Sept. 1935), 1.
[120] 'L'Affaire d'Éthiopie et nous', *Le Barrage*, 65 (26 Sept. 1935), 1.
[121] Ibid. These demands were repeated in the following number as well. See 'Honte aux assassins!', *Le Barrage*, 66 (10 Oct. 1935), 1.

pacifism of the French right. This was to appear in even more evolved and virulent form at the time of Munich. But 1935 gave a foretaste of things to come. The *Barrage* of 10 October catalogued the anti-interventionist views of a number of right-wing newspapers and the anonymous writer concluded that this 'pacifism' was all well and good. The LICP would remember it the next time when it was no longer a question of fighting 'Uncle Mussolini' but instead of going into battle against 'our German, Russian, or Patagonian brothers'.[122] Gerin denounced Mussolini's aggression and French Fascists for supporting him. He also condemned the League of Nations for not doing anything to stop the conflict and Laval for tacitly supporting the Italians.[123]

Gerin had nothing but scorn for the 'patriots' who had the 'audacity to cry "down with war"', not because they want peace, but because they want a victory for external Fascism'.[124] Challaye tackled head on the issue of what the Ligue viewed as the opportunistic pseudo-pacifism of the right in an examination of the manifesto 'Pour la défense de l'occident', drafted by the royalist Henri Massis. He recognized that the intellectuals who had signed it agreed with the LICP on several points. Should the Ligue reject or accept this apparent convergence of views? Challaye recalled La Rochefoucauld's maxim that 'hypocrisy is a praise that vice gives to virtue'. It was clear that this so-called pseudo-pacifism of the right was ephemeral. The signatories of the manifesto were not against all wars like the LICP. With no inkling of what lay in store at Munich, Challaye concluded with an attack on the right in which he assumed its Germanophobia as a constant value: 'If it so happens that a government approved of by the signatories of the manifesto wants one day to throw us into a war against Germany, we shall turn back on these gentlemen the weapon of their own declarations.'[125]

Throughout the rest of 1935 and until Addis Ababa fell, the LICP continued to press for the application of economic and financial sanctions against Italy, and a complete boycott of war *matériel* to both belligerent countries. The Ligue did not want to see the Italian people die of hunger, but it was profoundly disappointed that the

---

[122] 'Échos', *Le Barrage*, 66 (10 Oct. 1935), 2.
[123] René Gerin, 'Honte aux assassins!', *Le Barrage*, 66 (10 Oct. 1935), 1.
[124] Ibid.
[125] Félicien Challaye, 'Un manifeste d'intellectuels', *Le Barrage*, 66 (10 Oct. 1935), 2.

sanctions which should automatically have come into play under Article XVI of the League of Nations Covenant never did. But even with the apparent end of the war, the Ligue still expressed its certainty that Mussolini would one day pay for his African adventure. One writer in the *Barrage* expressed the hope that the atrocities committed by the Italian army would not simply be forgotten.[126]

The LICP viewed the Laval–Stalin Pact and the general evolution of the French Communist Party on the question of peace with a very jaundiced eye. It has already been noted above that there was much friction between the early Ligue under Méric and the PCF. This increased in the wake of the Amsterdam Congress with which the LICP would have little to do, at least officially. There was therefore a long tradition of hostility to the opportunistic antimilitarism—not pacifism—of the Communists. The Ligue could never agree with the Communist distinction between just revolutionary wars and unjust imperialist wars, nor with the notion of sending young Frenchmen to the *casernes* to learn the military art in the hope that some day this knowledge could be used against the bourgeoisie. For the LICP external war could never be justified.

It is no surprise therefore to learn that the Ligue condemned the Laval–Stalin declaration and the nascent anti-Nazi nexus which seemed to be developing between Paris and Moscow. Sacred alliances spelled holy wars, and the LICP wanted to avoid this at all costs. The Franco-Soviet Pact marked the end of the hopes of integral pacifism in the peaceful outlook of the Soviet Union.[127] Hubert Gilbert wrote that the pact brought France full circle back to the situation of 1894 and the defensive military alliance with tsarist Russia.[128] Gerin condemned the Pact without reservations, but had seen it coming for some time. In the course of the Ligue's speaking tours across France, they had been 'constantly asked to take a position for the defence of the USSR which was confused with the defence of peace'.[129] But the Ligue's position had been and remained one of opposition to all alliances. The Franco-Soviet Pact had

---

[126] René Gerin, 'Sanctions', *Le Barrage*, 73 (28 Nov. 1935), 1; 'Addis-Abéba est prise: A bas Mussolini!', *Le Barrage*, 96 (7 May 1936), 1; Pierre Nézelof, 'Une enquête', *Le Barrage*, 100 (11 June 1936), 1.

[127] René Gerin, 'La Nouvelle Alliance franco-russe est-elle une étape vers la paix?', *Le Barrage*, 51 (9 May 1935), 1.

[128] Hubert Gilbert, 'Le Pacte Laval–Potemkine', *Le Barrage*, 51 (9 May 1935), 3.

[129] René Gerin, 'Le Coup de Staline', *Le Barrage*, 53 (23 May 1935), 1.

changed definitively the LICP's view of Soviet Russia. It would continue to support the economic and social work of the revolution, but the Soviet leadership was now to be placed in the same camp as that of other nations. He underscored that the LICP rejected all military alliances, even with the land of the revolution, and refused all foreign wars. The Ligue also 'rejected all civil wars—which in no way means that we do not accept the revolution; but we want a clean revolution, and if this revolution becomes bloody, it will not be we who have wished it so'.[130] Gerin's rejection of civil war is here more absolute than it was to become at the time of the Spanish Civil War of which more will be said presently.

The Pact occasioned the departure of Challaye from the Cercle de la Russie neuve, of which he had been one of the founders.[131] It also created one of the fissures within integral pacifism which would slowly lengthen into the attempt to split antifascism from pacifism in the wake of Munich. But it is instructive for what was to follow that Félicien Challaye rejected in 1935 any suggestion that such a divorce was necessary or desirable from the pacifist point of view. What was good was that people were now being forced to think about political choices that related to peace. As Challaye concluded, 'one might well be tempted to thank Stalin for having, involuntarily, provoked this vast outpouring of pacifist sentiments—just as Leibniz praised God for having allowed the fall of Adam because it occasioned our redemption through Jesus Christ'.[132]

Léon Emery attacked the Pact as a danger to peace because, despite its pretentions to being open to Germany, it was in fact directed solely against her. It was a one-way treaty, and destroyed the symmetry of Locarno which envisaged, theoretically at least, an attack by either France or Germany. To say that such a treaty was open to Germany was 'really to abuse the elasticity of the language'.[133] No one could take this type of formula seriously.

For Gerin, the Franco-Soviet Pact represented a lack of faith in the Revolution and in the ability of the masses to carry it through. The

[130] Ibid.
[131] 'Au cercle de la Russie neuve', *Le Barrage*, 56 (13 June 1935), 2.
[132] Félicien Challaye, 'Pour l'union des adversaires de toute guerre', *Le Barrage*, 58 (27 June 1935), 1.
[133] L. Emery, 'Le Pact franco-russe et la paix européenne', *Le Barrage*, 95 (30 Apr. 1936), 2. This article is an extract from Emery's article published in the 15 Apr. 1936 number of *Europe*.

Russians were simply afraid of Nazi Germany; but fear led to massacres as much as did ambition. He had always felt that Communist comrades did not put enough stock, enough faith in the feeling of revolution, the desire for revolution. This desire was only temporarily asleep in Germany—and he begged the Communists not to compromise the world revolution by lowering themselves to the level of reaction, that is to say the battlefields on which it preferred to fight.[134]

The Saar, the Rhineland, Ethiopia, and the Franco-Soviet Pact were all important stages on the pacifist journey in the thirties. But no event so shook the world of the integral pacifist as the Spanish Civil War. Spain caused French pacifists to reflect deeply on the problems posed by international Fascism. Should one resist and if so how, and on what level? These were the issues which Spain raised and which were debated within the LICP. The LICP had certainly never proclaimed itself against civil wars in principle. In August 1934, for example, Gerin had explained that there were many in the Ligue who believed in the necessity of the revolutionary struggle. If this struggle became violent and blood was shed, it would not be the pacifists who would strike the first blow. The non-violence of the civil struggle was therefore to be the responsibility of capitalist society; if the Rubicon of bloodshed were crossed, it alone would bear the responsibility.[135]

It is not surprising, then, to find that with the worsening situation in Spain, Gerin and the LICP took the position that the Spanish conflict must be prevented from becoming an arena for imperialist rivalries—be they black or red—and also that there was nothing preventing an integral pacifist placed in a situation similar to that of Spain from responding to social violence with violence. In an editorial in early August 1936 Gerin reiterated the Ligue's opposition to both civil and foreign wars. 'We are against *all* wars, including *civil* wars', he wrote. 'We believe, in effect, that to shed the blood of one's "fellow citizens" is just as abominable as to shed that of "foreigners".'[136] One of the differences, though, between civil and foreign wars, was that in the former one generally knew why and against whom one was fighting. Integral pacifists would never

[134] René Gerin, 'La Politique extérieure de l'URSS', *Le Barrage*, 96 (7 May 1936), 1.

[135] René Gerin, 'La Joie mauvaise', *Le Barrage*, 14 (16 Aug. 1934), 1.

[136] René Gerin, 'Guerre étrangère et guerre civile', *Le Barrage*, 104 (6 Aug. 1936), 1.

foment a civil war, and they did not confuse civil war with revolution. Having said all that by way of preamble, Gerin nevertheless admitted that if he were Spanish, he would have taken up arms to fight for Azaña and the Republic against the rebels. The reasons for this were threefold. First, Azaña represented democracy (for what it was worth), freedom, and some measure of the social revolution. Even the 'anarchists' who fought with him agreed on this. Secondly, the civil war in Spain had been forced upon the Azaña government. The Spanish government, the Popular Front, was thus in a state of legitimate self-defence against its own internal Fascism. Finally, Gerin wrote that this internal Spanish Fascist enemy was completely comparable to an individual enemy. Only Tolstoyans would refuse to fight such an enemy. The Spanish state had become a collection of internal police forces which were fighting a domestic foe. It was the occasional duty of the citizen to aid his police force.[137]

Gerin's position on the conflict in Spain is interesting. It points out the rather artificial dichotomy which existed in the LICP's view of international versus civil conflicts. The Ligue believed that only in cases of civil conflict could the aggressor be reliably determined. The problem reduced itself to one of the fight against internal Fascism and the propensity for Fascist reaction inherent in the institution of the army itself. In Gerin's view, armies served merely as hotbeds of reaction which provided the means for a Fascist *coup d'état* and hence civil war. If one got rid of the army, the potential problem would disappear as well. But the important aspect of Gerin's position on civil war is his insistence on the need for violence only in cases where civil conflict has been imposed upon a pacifist population. In general, he continued to affirm that the revolution could and should occur without recourse to violence, even if only by means of the general strike.[138]

It was clear, though, that Gerin's views were far from being the unanimous position of all Ligue members. There must have been a sizeable minority who were opposed to civil war as well as foreign wars, because Gerin and Challaye both responded to criticisms in the next number of the *Barrage*. For Challaye it was important to point

---

[137] Ibid.
[138] Ibid. For a more complete analysis of the problem posed by civil war, see René Gerin, *Pacifisme 'intégral' et guerre civile* (Paris: Ligue internationale des combattants de la paix, 1937).

out that the LICP's pacifism extended only to 'wars imposed by governments on the peoples in the name of a so-called national interest'. He argued for mutual indulgence within the Ligue so that revolutionaries and Tolstoyans could continue to live and work together.[139]

Adrien Duthu was one such leaguer who refused to admit the rectitude of civil wars. He begged to differ with Gerin's and Pioch's statements that if they were Spanish they would be fighting. For Duthu, there was nothing intrinsically different about civil as opposed to international conflicts. The LICP had made much of the idea that any modern war would be so costly in terms of the destruction it would bring that it must be avoided at all costs. Duthu asked why a civil war would be any less destructive. He suggested that the LICP should make disarmament its condition of support for the left. In no case, however, should the masses consider taking on the army. Technology would quickly slaughter vast numbers, and that was what was happening in Spain.[140]

The general impression gained from the *Barrage*, however, is one of non-interventionist moral support for the Spanish government coupled with the implicit or even explicit warning to reactionary forces within France, that if the Republic were attacked, integral pacifists would be found amongst those who defended it by force of arms. The general principle of separation of internal antifascism from external pacifism found its expression clearly in the Spanish Civil War. Régis Messac, for example, wrote of accepting the battle 'on class frontiers, but not on capitalist frontiers'.[141] Maurice Weber also thought that the events in Spain were producing a profound reorientation in pacifist thinking. It had long been part of pacifist mythology that it was governments which often caused or declared wars. This had now been shown to be false in Spain, where the legitimate government had been attacked by the rebels, and more recently in France where only the sang-froid of the Popular Front had prevented France from becoming embroiled in the Spanish war. Paradoxically, both the Communist Party and the CGT advocated

[139] Félicien Challaye, 'Pacifistes, tolstoiens ou révolutionnaires', *Le Barrage*, 105 (20 Aug. 1936), 1. See also René Gerin, 'Union sacrée et lutte de classes', *Le Barrage*, 105 (20 Aug. 1936), 1.

[140] Adrien Duthu, 'Une leçon à tirer des événements d'Espagne', *Le Barrage*, 108 (22 Oct. 1936), 2.

[141] Régis Messac, 'Que chacun reconnaisse les siens!', *Le Barrage*, 106 (3 Sept. 1936), 1.

this intervention. Weber congratulated Blum and Delbos for having resisted the interventionist temptation. While it was tragic to have to put the Madrid government on the same moral footing as the rebels, imposing sanctions was a necessary step in order to prevent the conflict from spreading. He saw the hand of Moscow behind all of the formerly pacific forces which were trying to get France involved in the Spanish war—the Communists, the CGT, some parts of the Socialist Party, and the Amsterdam-Pleyel movement. In 1936, Weber believed the greatest danger came from what he called 'red Fascism' as opposed to 'black Fascism'.[142]

In official pronouncements on Spain, the LICP tried to emphasize that it remained an organization for all types of integral pacifists, while acknowledging that there were some pacifists who would fight in a civil war. The Ligue declined therefore to take a position on the legitimacy of the Spanish Civil War, although its sympathies were with the government. It approved the French government's decision to impose an embargo on Spain, and drew from the Spanish tragedy the justification for one of its standard theses. If Spain had been disarmed, the aggression of the rebels—and hence civil as well as international war—would have been impossible.[143] A year later, the Ligue was still holding to this official position of strict non-interventionism coupled with the belief that if the Spanish situation were to be replicated on French soil, many Ligue members would take up arms.[144]

Guernica seemed to provide another striking proof of the rectitude of the Ligue's long-held position against war. 'Think . . . what the effects would be of a war brought over great cities by, not just fifteen or twenty aeroplanes, but hundreds and thousands.'[145] In this situation it was a nonsense to speak of passive defence.

Thus, while it is true that the LICP hardly presented a unanimous face to the world regarding the Spanish Civil War, it is nevertheless the case that the majority of Ligue members seem to have taken the

---

[142] Maurice Weber, 'Excitations guerrières', *Le Barrage*, 106 (3 Sept. 1936), 3. Armand Charpentier also attacked the Communist support for armed intervention in Spain. He argued that this was one of the effects of the Franco-Soviet Pact. See Armand Charpentier, 'Ce que coûtent les alliances franco-russes', *Le Barrage*, 107 (1 Oct. 1936), 1.

[143] 'Résolution sur les événements d'Espagne', *Le Barrage*, 108 (22 Oct. 1936), 1.

[144] 'Réunion du comité directeur', *Le Barrage*, 113 (24 June 1937), 3. See also René Gerin, 'A propos d'un incident', *Le Barrage*, 114 (22 July 1937), 1.

[145] René Gerin, 'Guernica . . .', *Le Barrage*, 110 (13 May 1937), 1.

line consistently presented by Gerin, namely that civil wars could be justifiably fought by pacifists but only within their own national context. Even in Spain, where the conflict had quickly become internationalized, one could still speak of an essentially civil affair in which the men fighting knew for whom and for what reasons they were laying down their lives. There was thus a fundamental distinction of scale and of orientation between civil and international wars. What integral pacifists outside Spain had to do was ensure that the conflagration did not spill over the Pyrenees to the rest of Europe. As Gerin wrote in 1937, 'the most clear-sighted and effective pacifism in these troubled times is undoubtedly not that which refuses all wars, but rather that which refuses to transform localized civil conflicts into universal butchery'.[146]

The period from 1934 to the beginning of 1938 ended for the LICP on a worried note. The Saar, the remilitarization of the Rhineland, the Italo-Abyssinian conflict, the Franco-Soviet Pact, and the continuing development of Nazism in Germany had all provided in different measures a challenge to the LICP's pacifism. Through it all, the Ligue had remained true to its initial premises that external wars and internal Fascism could and must logically be fought together. Spain began the slow process of doubt that perhaps integral pacifism could ill afford to be so absolute in its prescriptions. In the final two years of the interwar period these doubts manifested themselves in two opposing lines of thought. Some pacifists began to express serious reservations about the extent to which pacifism could claim to be absolute, while for still others, it became finally necessary to argue the primacy of pacifism over antifascism. These challenges to the LICP's carefully elaborated world view came in 1938 and 1939, and it is to this final stage that we turn now.

---

[146] René Gerin, 'Défense de libertés et "défense nationale"', *Le Barrage*, 111 (27 May 1937), 1.

9. Munich and all that (1938–1939)

It is strange that while the events of 1938–9 seem to have challenged the LICP's view of pacifism, there is nevertheless no single moment which can be selected as the point at which the Ligue's world view changed. No line was drawn that could not be crossed. In terms of the Ligue's comments on the issues raised by the crises of this eighteen-month period, there was little apparent dissent over its policies. The debates which did occur seem almost to have taken place in a vacuum. The Anschluss did not produce a *crise de foi* and neither did Munich. March 1939 and the final agony of Czechoslovakia occasioned no *prise de conscience* and in August, the Ligue was still most unwilling to die for Danzig. So what happened? There is no doubting that fundamental changes were occurring in the Ligue's thinking. The *intégralité* of its pacifism was brought into question, and there was an attempt to separate antifascism from pacifism. In other words, major debates took place in the immediate pre-war period, but they did so in some isolation from real political events, on which the LICP maintained a steady pacifist doctrinal outlook.

In the first crisis of 1938, the Anschluss of Austria to the Third Reich, there was little surprise and certainly no breast-beating within the Ligue. Gerin sanguinely commented that the treaties were being revised and it was in that light that the Ligue saw the annexation of Austria. He seemed to take roughly the same position as that of the *Canard enchaîné* at the time of the remilitarization of the Rhineland: Germany was invading part of Germany. He stressed that the Anschluss had been effected without war, that it did not seem to affect too many Austrians who had been living under a dictatorship already anyway, and that, citing the expression of La Fourchardière, 'what happens between Austria and the Reich is *pure politics*'.[1] Moving from the particular to the general, Gerin also considered the question of the other *Auslandsdeutsche*. He thought that, as a democratic principle, they should be allowed to join the Third Reich if they wanted to. This begged the question of whether democratic principles were involved at all, but Gerin seems to have passed this problem over. As an interesting backdrop to what was to follow, Gerin attempted to refute the argument that Hitler would turn on the other peoples of Europe once the German minorities had been reintegrated into the Reich. In a stupendous miscalculation of the nature of Hitler's plans, he wrote that 'if the Sudeten Germans, at least in part, desire to be reattached to Germany, the Czechs, for their part, will never want to submit to the yoke of the Reich. Hitler is not so stupid as to compromise the advantages he has justly won through an attempt at an imbecile conquest.'[2] In any case, the whole problem was the fault of the 1919 treaties and of French policy, and he foresaw that France still had more to pay in penance for the errors of its ways at Versailles:

We have several moral kicks up the backside still to receive—unless—better late than never—our rulers decide to substitute the policy of the extended hand [de la main tendue] for that of the presented posterior, and understand that peace will only result from an international economic and political negotiation, openly and generously offered to everyone, to the Germans as well. And to the Germans of 1938 since we did not want to deal with those of 1928 who were still in a republic.

All mistakes are paid for. And the longer one waits to pay for them, the more expensive they are.[3]

The important thing was to prevent these mistakes being paid with the blood of 20-year-old young men.

Henri Jeanson expressed the complete sense of disillusionment and alienation from the Third Republic felt by some pacifists at the time of the Anschluss. For Jeanson, the enemy was within. In response to the cries for an anti-Hitlerian *union sacrée*, he wrote,

So be it.
I want to fight for the Republic.
I want to defend democracy.
I want to sacrifice myself for freedom.

[1] René Gerin, 'On revise les traités...', *Le Barrage*, 125 (17 Mar. 1938), 1.
[2] Ibid.
[3] Ibid.

But first, give me a Republic, give me a democracy, and restore my freedoms.

The Republic is a trust, democracy is a business, and freedom is a monopoly.

. . . Our real enemies are not outside.

They are within.[4]

Instead of looking outside France for the battle to come, he invited readers to begin the fight amongst Frenchmen. The old class struggle had been waylaid, but in the interests of defeating Fascism once and for all, Jeanson declared that it was necessary to defeat the General Staff, the industrialists, and the 'petty politicians'.[5]

The LICP's 1938 Congress was held in the city of Arras. Three important reports were debated dealing with the economic and political aspects of the fight against Fascism and war, and also with the colonial problem. Probably the most important of the three was Sylvain Broussaudier's report on the political aspects of the fight against Fascism and war. Since the Nazi seizure of power, this question had been debated with increasing urgency and frequency. Broussaudier took it as given that everyone within the LICP was as equally committed to antifascism as to pacifism, but many old friends were beginning to renounce their pacifism in favour of antifascism pure and simple. Pacifism was slowly becoming a dirty word and pacifists were accused of doing Hitler's work. This idea was current amongst Communists and a growing number of Socialists. As for the Radicals, 'their jacobinism is strangely allied with the anti-Hitlerism of the extreme left'.[6] The Popular Front had now more or less abandoned its antimilitarism and accepted the preparation of war with either enthusiasm or resignation.

The crux of the question was to determine whether or not Fascism inevitably meant war. Broussaudier reminded LICP members that

---

[4] Henri Jeanson, 'À bas l'union sacrée!', *Le Barrage*, 125 (17 Mar. 1938), 1.

[5] Ibid. For further comment in much the same vein on the Anschluss, see Louis Trégaro, 'À la croisée des chemins', *Le Barrage*, 125 (17 Mar. 1938), 1. Trégaro argued that France must follow Chamberlain in the policy of appeasement, or rather 'accompany him'. Negotiating did not mean capitulating. See also Félicien Challaye, 'Pas de guerre pour l'Autriche!', *Le Barrage*, 126 (31 Mar. 1938), 2; A. Duthu, 'Autriche–Tchécoslovaquie', *Le Barrage*, 127 (28 Apr. 1938), 2; Louis Trégaro, 'Aragon-Autriche', *Le Barrage*, 131 (7 July 1938), 1; Jean Carrère, 'L'Autriche depuis l'Anschluss', *Le Barrage*, 135 (20 Oct. 1938), 3.

[6] Sylvain Broussaudier, 'Comment lutter à la fois contre la guerre et contre le fascisme? Rapport sur l'aspect politique de la question', *Le Barrage*, 124 (24 Feb. 1938), 3.

after the events of 6 February, the Ligue had included a line to this effect in its statutes. But in 1938, he rejected the fatalism of this view for a number of reasons. First, there had been many wars before Fascism appeared, and even the most democratic of countries had many of them on their consciences. Secondly, France bore heavy responsibility for the emergence of German Fascism. Thirdly, it was clear that France did not hesitate to ally herself against Germany with regimes which were 'clearly Fascist', such as those of Poland, Romania, and Yugoslavia. Fourthly, and perhaps more importantly, because it revealed the dissenting nature of much of the LICP's thinking on internal versus external politics, Broussaudier wrote that,

> Our democracy is often only distinguishable from Fascism by differences of degree and not of nature. The administration of the country is overrun with Fascists, and our politics are subject to economic forces which have nothing in common with the will of the people, but on the contrary are in solidarity with capitalism and external Fascism.[7]

Finally, Broussaudier argued that if Fascism did, indeed, bring with it an increased danger of war, it did not mean that war was inevitable. In either a democracy or a Fascist dictatorship, war was only possible with the active consent of the population.[8]

Two possible approaches to the problem of Fascism presented themselves. One was the policy of firmness or even of force. This entailed engaging in an arms race with Germany in the belief that the structural weaknesses of the Nazi regime would cause a collapse in its economy thus making war impossible. This was a pernicious argument, though, because it required in the democracies an abdication of all hope for social progress through lack of public funds, and therefore, in reality, a 'progressive Fascization'. It was an illusion to think that the democratic economies were immune to this same sort of dislocation anyway. Secondly, he argued that economic hardship in the Fascist countries would not necessarily bring about their internal collapse; it was equally possible that it might exacerbate the political situation to the point where in a moment of desperation, these countries threw themselves into a war as a way out of their difficulties.[9]

At the opposite end of the spectrum, there was the policy of peace. Broussaudier argued for a policy of concessions to the dictators

---

[7] Broussaudier, 'Comment lutter à la fois'.   [8] Ibid.   [9] Ibid.

so that wounded national feelings could be healed, and the psychological reason for war thereby removed. In the process, the political rug might be pulled from underneath the dictators. If the protestations of peace of Hitler and Mussolini were shown to be false, this hypocrisy would 'explode' in the eyes of their own people. What is important here, though, is the fact that Broussaudier stressed that the LICP did not at all agree with a policy of simple capitulation. Capitulation, instead, had been the hallmark of the policies of French governments. 'The absurdity of the policies followed until now by France in particular, is that they combined imprecatory bravado (verbal energy) and retreats (practical weakness), adding therefore the dangers of the one to the dangers of the other, without drawing any benefit from either.'[10] In Broussaudier's view, the hope for peace lay in a resolution of the economic conflicts in the world. This would remove the primary propaganda weapons from the dictators and at the same time strengthen the democracies morally, politically, and economically.[11]

If war should break out anyway, Broussaudier underlined that the course of action to take was an entirely individual decision. But he believed that it was naïve to think that one could defend one's liberties by fighting Fascism. His report makes clear that even at the eleventh hour in 1938, the LICP still placed its primary emphasis on preventing war and had nothing to say about the tactics to be employed once war had broken out; this decision was left entirely to the personal appreciation of the individual leaguer. The problem of civil war was necessarily beyond the purview of the LICP, but he believed that it could be prevented from occurring through essentially the same policy of reforms which would weaken Fascism.[12]

Broussaudier's conclusions contain the seeds of the debates which would erupt later in the year in the wake of the Munich crisis. He believed that it was possible to reconcile the struggle against war and the fight against Fascism 'as long as the catastrophe has not occurred'. But, and here lay the crux of the future dilemma, 'pacifism can only be opposed to antifascism if, all our efforts having failed, we are thrown into a war, that is to say, when all other acceptable solutions are impossible'.[13] Broussaudier's report was passed unanimously by the Congress.[14] Later that spring, the Ligue's statutes

[10] Ibid. [11] Ibid. [12] Ibid.
[13] Ibid.
[14] See 'Les Travaux du Congrès d'Arras', *Le Barrage*, 127 (28 Apr. 1938), 4.

were also amended so that Article 1 on the Ligue's goals now read that it was 'against Fascism which, destroying our liberties, aggravates still more the dangers of war'. This resolved the problem posed by the phrase in the 1934 version of the statutes that Fascism led 'ineluctably to war'.[15]

Gaston Pauthe's report on the economic aspects of the same question was full of statistics which gave credence to the idea of 'nations repues' and 'nations affamées'. It was a report larded with Leninist citations and analysis, and Pauthe envisaged the use of revolutionary violence in certain situations. The hour was desperate; he believed the current was pulling France ever closer to Fascism, the *union sacrée*, and war. The Popular Front had failed, and it needed to be recreated at the grass-roots level. As far as the external danger was concerned, Pauthe thought that the French people had to speak directly to the Germans, over the heads of both sets of rulers. When the Congress debated his report, it unanimously passed the first section dealing with the analysis of the economic situation, but declined to express its views on the conclusions arrived at by Pauthe because of their tendentious support for civil war and revolutionary violence. The Ligue was, after all, supposed to be a home for pacifists of all persuasions, violent and non-violent.[16]

Léon Emery's report on colonialism condemned it in principle, but equally rejected the Communist notion of wars of liberation and armed insurrection. He considered this method to be either utopian or catastrophic in its practical effects. It entailed allying oneself with indigenous nationalist parties, and this led to increased national isolation and not internationalism. Emery rejected nationalism for Frenchmen and also for their colonial subjects. He criticized the parties of the left for having done precisely nothing in the colonial field; the Popular Front was too preoccupied with questions of defence. What did Emery recommend as a solution to the problem posed for peace by the existence of colonies? He argued for an 'internationalization of the colonial regime' within the context of a peace policy. This meant giving Nazi Germany colonies. For Emery, justice and peace demanded a new division of colonies:

[15] 'Modifications aux statuts', *Le Barrage*, 130 (9 June 1938), 4.
[16] Gaston Pauthe, 'Comment lutter à la fois contre la guerre et contre le fascisme? Rapport sur l'aspect économique de la question', *Le Barrage*, 124 (24 Feb. 1938), 3–4. See also 'Les Travaux du Congrès d'Arras', 4.

... it is annoying that we have allowed Hitler to be right; in the area of colonial demands, he is right ten times over ... You say that we cannot possibly make a negro from the Cameroon a subject of Nazi Germany; start at least by asking him if he prefers that we turn him into a cadaver dressed up in horizon-blue ... But naturally, the transfer, pure and simple, of a colony must be considered as the last possible solution, only war being more abominable. What must be attempted is the creation of a system which will provide the greatest amount of international control ... the mandate system of the League of Nations was an appreciable progress. We must take inspiration from this system and perfect it.[17]

Emery's report was passed unanimously, too.[18]

The Arras Congress manifesto, which was written by Challaye, reaffirmed the LICP's implacable opposition to Fascism but stressed that Fascism could only be fought inside one's own country. The Ligue declared itself against the idea of any foreign war for freedom. 'In the city of Robespierre, we reiterate his formula: "Liberty cannot be found at the tip of a bayonet. The peoples do not like armed missionaries".'[19] On the Anschluss, the manifesto expressed the disgust of the Ligue at the excesses of militarism which had accompanied it, but underlined that it had long been the desire of the Austrian people to be joined to Germany. Looking ahead to the coming Czech crisis, the LICP 'rejected in advance any idea of war for Czechoslovakia'. Challaye turned around the phrase in vogue, to express the LICP's belief that war would mean the suppression of all liberties in favour of a military dictatorship: we know, he declared, that 'War is Fascism'.[20]

With the worsening international situation and especially, perhaps, with the experience of the Spanish Civil War, some parts of the LICP began to express doubts about the use of the word *intégral* to describe the Ligue's pacifism. Gerin gave voice to these concerns in two articles in early 1938 in which he argued that it was time to abolish the term 'integral' because it was 'incorrect, inexact, and even pretentious'; it was abstract and evoked the absolute. Gerin thought that it was enough to affirm that 'we are pacifists as much and as well as we can be. That is already not so easy! Let us reject all verbal outbidding.'[21] The LICP contained pacifists of many

[17] L. Emery, 'Le Problème colonial et la paix', *Le Barrage*, 125 (17 Mar. 1938), 3.
[18] 'Les Travaux du Congrès d'Arras', 4.
[19] 'Manifeste du Congrès d'Arras', *Le Barrage*, 127 (28 Apr. 1938), 1.
[20] Ibid.
[21] René Gerin, 'Pas de surenchère verbale!', *Le Barrage*, 122 (20 Jan. 1938), 1.

tendencies but what united them was their opposition to wars between peoples. To imply more in a word such as *intégral* only gave ammunition to the Ligue's opposition, and confused 'our friends and comrades'. The clinching argument for abolishing the word 'integral' was that it allowed people to assume that the LICP espoused absolute non-violence, according to Gerin. But there was no 'catechism' in the Ligue. He could not come up with a word to replace 'integral' however; nothing seemed to capture fully the essence of the Ligue's pacifism, which he defined in largely dissenting terms: 'Our pacifism is antinationalist, antifascist (in a sense which the next congress will define), anticolonialist, antimilitarist ... and anti- many other things. But it also wishes to construct peace in a positive way by multiplying efforts towards justice on both the national and international levels.'[22] In any case, the Arras Congress declined to follow Gerin in his apparent evolution away from an absolute expression of pacifism, deciding instead to retain the use of the word 'integral' because no other word seemed to come close to expressing the Ligue's position.[23]

If the Spanish Civil War and the generally worsening international situation proved to be major trials for the LICP's pacifist vision, Munich and the two-step dismemberment of Czechoslovakia provided the major crisis of the period under discussion here. Paradoxically, as has already been noted, Munich also occasioned an upsurge in the Ligue's membership.

Beginning in the spring of 1938, writers in the *Barrage* began to comment on the impending Czech crisis. They rejected the idea of fighting a war for Czechoslovakia in part because they viewed the Czech state as the bastard creation of Versailles. Adrien Duthu, for example, argued that in 1919 when the Czech state was created, Austria advised against including the Sudeten German minority, but it was to satisfy the demands of the Czechs for their 'natural' frontiers and the heavy industry of Bohemia that the Sudetenland was included. He did not believe that France was in any way compelled to come to the aid of Czechoslovakia in the event of an attack because the Locarno Treaty, to which the accord with the Czechs had been linked, had fallen by the wayside. This was a

[22] René Gerin, 'Pas de surenchère verbale!', See also Gerin, 'Pas de surenchère verbale: (II) Réponse à Robert Tourly', *Le Barrage*, 123 (3 Feb. 1938), 1.
[23] 'Les Travaux du Congrès d'Arras', 4.

convenient euphemism for France's abdication; strangely, it seemed that Duthu was arguing that one abdication was worth another. Because the German minorities were apparently oppressed by the Czechs after the war, he believed that they ought to be given self-determination. In short, Czechoslovakia was not worth going to war for.[24]

Léon Emery was even more radical in his prognosis for the future of Europe, a future which he saw quite naturally dominated by Germany. He attacked the 'pacifists' who would have France defend the territorial integrity of Czechoslovakia. Instead, he proposed a referendum along the lines of those held in Upper Silesia and the Saar. If this idea were refused, he suggested that Czechoslovakia should be assimilated into the Swiss federation. Whatever happened, the Czechs must renounce their alliances with France and the USSR, and give up all ideas of collective security, which were nothing but a smoke-screen for an anti-German coalition. The Czech affair was not about principles in Emery's mind, but about the defence of a political system in which the Czech state played an important role—in other words, the old balance of power. According to this view, then, Europe needed to adjust peacefully to the historically determined rise of a German hegemony:

Any real pacifism presupposes that one believes in the possibility of changes in the organization of the world, changes which are made inevitable by the play of natural forces which need not entail war. We do not see how it is possible to prevent Germany becoming the economic and demographic power called, by virtue of its size and its workforce, to colonize Danubian Europe.

Did not the Versailles Treaty prepare this victory in the long run? All that we can hope is that this evolution will take place in peace. The only chance this has of happening is through a global negotiation with Germany, including the Czech problem, in a search for a just equilibrium of the resources and vital needs of everyone. It is necessary for the democracies —and this is their supreme chance to avoid the catastrophe—to take the initiative of this revision of the treaties, in the broadest possible sense, in thus using the last possibility they have to undertake a new and generous policy, that is to say one that offers a new colonial partition capable of leading to a moral *détente* and to disarmament. May each one take his responsibilities here, and know, in himself, if he really wants peace.[25]

[24] A. Duthu, 'Tchécoslovaquie', *Le Barrage*, 129 (26 May 1938), 2.
[25] L. Emery, 'Encore la Tchécoslovaquie', *Le Barrage*, 130 (9 June 1938), 1.

When the September crisis finally broke, Gerin declared that it was the beginning of peace. War would not break out over Czechoslovakia because neither Hitler nor the German people wanted war. Secondly, no one anywhere else either wanted war, with the possible exception of what he called some 'communistes exaltés'. The French government did not have the nerve to declare war, he thought, and even if it did, it was doubtful whether there would be the required unanimity either in Parliament or in the country as a whole. No one wanted war. He seconded Alain's declaration that the September crisis was in fact the beginning of peace. It was beginning with the wholesale destruction of the iniquitous treaties of 1919. He said that a sort of 'immanent justice' was repairing the damage of Versailles, and if that process went against France it was because France was too proud to have done it herself. 'Am I exaggeratedly optimistic?', he asked,

I am convinced that we have just won the peace: at the hour in which I write these words, English and French are in the process of trying only to save face, in *accepting the inevitable*.

Courage, comrades! The treaties are being revised *without war*! This is indeed what we have been demanding in our propaganda. But we never dared to hope that we would be listened to so soon.[26]

There certainly seem to have been few tears shed in September 1938 in the pages of the *Barrage* for the truncated Czech state. Armand Charpentier attacked it as a totally artificial creation which should not exist, this 'proscenium arch called Czechoslovakia'. He proclaimed 'eternal glory to Neville Chamberlain'.[27]

At the beginning of October Gerin reiterated his belief that peace was just beginning. War had been impossible in September because circumstances were not at all comparable to July 1914. None of the diplomatic, military, social, moral, or psychological conditions were favourable to the explosion of a war. 'We knew that in 1914 *all* of the rulers and all of the peoples had to some degree *wanted or accepted* the massacre; and that in 1938 no people, no government even, envisaged it with a light heart.'[28] The 'peace of the peoples' had thus

[26] René Gerin, 'Alain a raison: C'est la paix qui commence', *Le Barrage*, 133 (22 Sept. 1938), 1.

[27] Armand Charpentier, 'Similitudes: 1914: Iswolsky—1938: Bénès', *Le Barrage*, 133 (22 Sept. 1938), 1.

[28] René Gerin, 'Au travail, pour la paix des peuples!', *Le Barrage*, 134 (6 Oct. 1938), 1.

emerged from the Munich crisis. For the first time the masses had shown their pacifism and there had been a collective rejection of war which made a mobilization impossible. He claimed victory for the pacifist cause. This peace was their peace. It was a peace 'conceived before the war', and a 'revision of the treaties *without war*'. He went further and called it the 'birth of a . . . peace psychosis'. But he warned against complacency. 'Real peace, that which will last, because it is just, has not yet been made. It is only starting to be made. We are at the dawn of a new day, *at the first hour*. Everyone to work!'[29]

If the LICP was *munichois*, it was so from pacifist conviction and a (perhaps misguided) historical *Weltanschauung*, not from philo-Fascism. In late October 1938, Gerin returned to the question of Munich to underline that there were still at least two dangers to beware of. The first was a misplaced confidence in Hitler. Gerin did not believe that Hitler wanted a war, but equally he stressed that the *paix hitlérienne* in no way represented the LICP's ideal. He blamed the European situation on 'French idiocy' which had allowed the *gars de Berchtesgaden* to reign in Europe. On the domestic level, it would be criminal to express the slightest admiration for Hitler's man in France, Flandin. If Flandin had served the cause of peace in September, the LICP was only 'moderately thankful' to him. In any case, the Ligue rejected German hegemony in Europe, as indeed it rejected all hegemonies. He warned leaguers to have nothing to do with what he termed an ideology as dangerous as that of Stalinism, that is to say, the wave of anti-Semitism which had been sweeping across France in recent months.[30]

The second big danger was that of rearmament. Chamberlain had returned to London to announce a major armaments programme and the same thing was happening in France, Germany, and the USA. An understanding had to be reached. The peoples had made it very clear three weeks previously that they wanted nothing to do with a war. They must now refuse to pay for the armaments which their governments wanted. For the first time, Gerin laid down a test for Hitler: '*Disarmament and negotiations*—in the order that one wishes or is possible—this is, this must be our programme. If, now, Hitler and his disciples, German and French, accept this programme,

[29] Ibid.
[30] René Gerin, 'Écueils', *Le Barrage*, 135 (20 Oct. 1938), 1.

may they say it *and prove it*. Then—and only then—will we be able to reach an agreement with them.'[31]

March 1939 and the annihilation of the rump Czechoslovakia occasioned a partial *prise de conscience* in Gerin. The scales seem at least partially to have fallen from his eyes. He recognized the odious threat posed by Hitler, but refused obstinately to modify 'one iota' of the Ligue's principles. He rejected the solutions of force proposed by others, and called instead for the immediate convocation of an international conference. He did not specify, however, exactly what this conference should discuss. As far as economic sanctions were concerned, these he rejected 'in principle', at least until such time as all attempts at economic collaboration with the Reich had failed. Instead, he suggested moral sanctions which he thought the Reich feared most. He proposed a propaganda campaign by radio to enlighten the German people to the point of revolt. But even this method was to be used only in the last resort, because it was in essence an attack on the territorial integrity of another country. So, in Gerin's view, the situation, while serious, had not reached the point where this type of moral sanction ought to be imposed.[32]

Robert Jospin was also in favour of some sort of international conference to sort matters out, although the title of his article —'force or collaboration'—was an unfortunate semantic example of what was to come. He thought that Hitler had made an enormous mistake in taking the rest of Czechoslovakia, but he also ran through the usual litany of Allied faults running back almost twenty years, as if the sins of the sons were justified by those of the fathers. He could see no way to stop the expansion of Germany into south-eastern Europe. The peoples of the Balkans needed German markets and vice versa. Germany had no choice but to expand. It was either that or disappear. From this (and indeed from many other articles in the *Barrage*), it is clear that the Ligue had accepted the Nazi arguments about *Lebensraum*. 'Collaboration' with Nazi Germany was thus the only possibility which did not lead straight to unparalleled

---

[31] Gerin, 'Écueils'. For further comment on Munich, cf. Madeleine Vernet, 'Protestation', *Le Barrage*, 134 (6 Oct. 1938), 1; Pierre Nézelof, 'Aux innocents les mains vides', *Le Barrage*, 135 (20 Oct. 1938), 1; Robert Jospin, 'Maintenant, bâtissons l'Europe', *Le Barrage*, 135 (20 Oct. 1938), 1; Fernand Gouttenoire de Toury, 'Désarmement, ou catastrophe final', *Le Barrage*, 135 (20 Oct. 1938), 1; Sylvain Broussaudier, 'Le Repli impérial', *Le Barrage*, 142 (2 Feb. 1939), 1.

[32] René Gerin, 'Pour un appel aux peuples', *Le Barrage*, 146 (30 Mar. 1939), 1.

slaughter, although to give Jospin his due his article was vague about what he actually meant by this term.[33]

By the spring of 1939 it was clear that support for the LICP was falling off as the international situation worsened. In early May the Ligue commented that 'we receive only a very few communiqués from the Sections [and] the requests for speakers are less numerous . . .'.[34] Claude Jamet, writing a fortnight earlier, noted that pacifism was once more in retreat as a minority belief: 'We are alone in a world, in a country, almost unanimously gone crazy. It doesn't matter. Truth is often in the minority.' And referring to the departure of the pseudo-pacifists of the previous September, he said, 'here we are once again by ourselves, few but pure'.[35]

The moment seemed to have arrived when political pacifism had become virtually untenable. Gerin wrote in May that he considered the annexation of Czechoslovakia 'both a mistake and a crime'. He did not see how anyone could be convinced of the rectitude of Germany's cause by Hitler's speech of 28 April. But the speech did appear to open the way to further negotiations. Hitler's tone was more moderate and diplomatic than previously, and he seemed to be renouncing the ideological demagogy which had been his stock-in-trade. His demands were also becoming more precise and his support for Mussolini was on the wane. In the short term, Gerin thought that the pacifist policy of disarmament was dead in the water. What remained was the fight to prevent war from breaking out and that had not yet been lost. He foresaw the policy of 'firmness' towards the dictators continuing for many months or even years. Hitler was fooling himself if he thought he could separate the two Western democracies, but France and Britain were deluded if they believed it possible to throttle Germany economically. Gerin believed firmly that only negotiation could save the day. It had started already, but the road would be long and hard, and pacifist nerves would be truly frayed before its end was reached.[36]

Gerin's moral revulsion at what had finally happened to Czechoslovakia was not echoed by all Ligue members, however. One of the original architects of historical dissent, Georges Demartial, could not

[33] Robert Jospin, 'Force ou collaboration', *Le Barrage*, 146 (30 Mar. 1939), 1.

[34] 'L'Activité de la Ligue', *Le Barrage*, 148 (4 May 1939), 4.

[35] Claude Jamet, 'La Paix inévitable', *Le Barrage*, 147 (20 Apr. 1939), 1–2.

[36] René Gerin, 'La Négociation aura lieu', *Le Barrage*, 148 (4 May 1939), 1.

see the difference between the German duplicity in overturning the Munich accords, and the history of French and British double-dealing in Egypt and Morocco. Try as he might, he could not attune himself to the 'general diapason', as he put it, he could not 'share the indignation of which Germany was the object'.[37] If Germany had been able to lay its hands on Austria and Czechoslovakia without firing a shot, without shedding blood, this was 'incontestably because of the anarchy into which these two States had fallen which was leading them to civil war'.[38] He saw the Nazi armies almost as liberators. Both peoples either accepted or desired their inclusion in the Third Reich; the Austrians had ratified it in a plebiscite, and the civil and military authorities in the Czech Republic had quickly put themselves under German protection.[39]

NI DROITE, NI GAUCHE?—OR PACIFISM VERSUS ANTIFASCISM

The extent to which the LICP was prone to equate the failings of the Western democracies with those of Nazism and Fascism has already been noted. Because of its peculiar historical vision and dissenting stance with regard to French political society, the Ligue was apt to justify the Nazi reshaping of the map of Europe for historical, as opposed to moral or present-day political, reasons. Even near the end, when Hitler's designs were at last becoming apparent to all and sundry, there was still debate within the LICP about the rectitude of Nazi expansionism.

The Ligue was also concerned with the internal threat posed by Fascism in France. Taking historical inspiration from Robespierre, it was convinced that France must look inward on itself and deal with its own political open sores rather than busying itself with the affairs of others. As the thirties progressed, this political introspection finally succeeded in isolating the Ligue from the rest of political society. It also led in the first months of 1939 to an attempt to separate the fight against Fascism from that against war.

The origins of the Ligue's isolation go back well into the mid-thirties. Georges Pioch, for example, as early as 1935 wrote that 'the time has come when the criers of the *Union sacrée*, whether they be of

---

[37] Georges Demartial, 'Le Problème tchèque et la paix', *Le Barrage*, 148 (4 May 1939), 1.
[38] Ibid.
[39] Ibid.

left or right, will soon have only one enemy . . . the conscious pacifist who desires a complete peace'.[40]

Having said this, the LICP had to deal with the gradual emergence in the thirties of an extreme right-wing pseudo-pacifism which seems to have become confused in the public mind at the time of Munich with the genuine pacifism of groups like the LICP. For example, as early as 1935 once again, at the time of the Italo-Abyssinian War, the *Barrage* was complaining of what it regarded as the opportunistic conscientious objection of Charles Maurras. With regard to the situation in Ethiopia, Maurras had written, 'We do not say: down with war. We say: down with *this* war. It would be vain, empty, iniquitous and a folly! Down with war against Italy. Down with a war for London and for Geneva. Down with war for the Covenant . . .'[41] The sea-changes occurring in the old right–left boundaries on the question of peace left the pacifists of the LICP somewhat confused. In early 1936, one militant had written quite simply, 'we do not understand anymore',[42] and in April of that year the *Barrage* commented on a piece by Albert Thibaudet in the *Nouvelle Revue française* which had argued that the danger of war now came more from the left than from the right. 'The war of religion for or against Moscow is replacing the war of religion for or against Rome.'[43]

By early 1938 it had become apparent to Gerin that the *union sacrée* was rejected only by integral pacifists and some parts of the right. But he stressed that the motives and ideals of the right were not at all those of the LICP. The right rejected the idea of a *union sacrée* with the left 'because they wanted to rid themselves of the representatives of the proletariat' and because 'they admire, at the end of the day, both Hitler and Mussolini'.[44] The attitude of the right was therefore completely ephemeral and opportunistic. Its rejection of war was based upon internal political antipathies and external political sympathies which transcended national boundaries. Gerin wrote that he rejected the notion of the *union sacrée* because he was opposed to Fascism, dictatorship, and nationalist reaction, and

[40] Georges Pioch, 'Quand Brid'oison se double de Basile', *Le Barrage*, 61 (1 Aug. 1935), 2.

[41] Cited in 'Échos: Distinguo', *Le Barrage*, 76 (19 Dec. 1935), 2.

[42] 'Une politique maladroite', *Le Barrage*, 87 (5 Mar. 1936), 3.

[43] 'Une prédiction d'Albert Thibaudet', *Le Barrage*, 94 (23 Apr. 1936), 1.

[44] René Gerin, 'Pourquoi nous refusons toute union sacrée', *Le Barrage*, 126 (31 Mar. 1938), 1.

because he desired justice and peace. These reasons were very different from those of the right. And he rejected the idea that integral pacifism could find an ally in this passing pacifism of the Vautels, Doriots, Maurras, and their ilk:

Let there be no equivocation! We are not two-faced. We reject and will always reject, *in all cases*, any national union, any sacred union . . . One would have to be terribly naïve not to understand the hypocrisy of the Right. It would be the most vulgar stupidity to consider as allies, even temporarily, the neo-conscientious objectors of the *Journal*, *Gringoire*, or the *Action française*. They are just as pacifist as the malignant Muscovites.[45]

This was the somewhat confusing backdrop, then, to the debate which broke on the Ligue in January 1939. Félicien Challaye published an important article in which he questioned the linkage between pacifism and antifascism which had until then been one of the cardinal tenets of the LICP's system of belief. It was the Spanish Civil War which had caused him to begin to revise his ideas on the acceptability of civil war. He described how the old political divisions of left and right seemed to have become blurred. The warmongering spirit seemed to lie more to the left than to the right now, 'in the sole interest of Stalinist policies'.[46] For Challaye, the choice was simple. 'If one had to choose, it would be better to save the peace with the right than to throw oneself into war with the left or extreme left.'[47] Happily, though, he did not think it would be necessary to make this choice. There was a right wing in France which 'remained true to itself', the right of Tardieu, de Kerillis, and Pertinax. The great dividing line had been the events of the past September. Munich, which caused Challaye 'not the slightest humiliation', had occasioned a great political effervescence which had not yet settled. On the question of peace, however, the route to take was clear for Challaye:

Certain of our comrades are not wrong to say that neither Chamberlain, nor Daladier, nor Bonnet is a pacifist in the sense that we give to the word, because we demand a disarmed peace and they are for over-armament. But the 'Anti-Munichois' too, the Thorezes, the Léon Blums are in favour of over-armament. Between these over-armers, whose common thesis I reject, I ask permission to prefer those who have wanted and who want peace, to those who have wanted and want war.[48]

---

[45] Gerin, 'Pourquoi nous refusons toute union sacrée'.
[46] Félicien Challaye, 'Pacifisme et antifascisme', *Le Barrage*, 140 (5 Jan. 1939), 2.
[47] Ibid.   [48] Ibid.

Challaye argued that his new position did not change one iota his fundamental opposition to Fascism. He remained a convinced anti-fascist, which he defined as the 'will to protect in our country those of the union, political, and daily freedoms which still exist', the will to reconquer those which had been lost, the will to liberate the workers in a capitalist society, the immigrants who were the subjects of police harassment, and the peoples suffering under the yoke of colonialism.[49] He also called antifascism the struggle against war, because he believed that once war had broken out, it spelled the end of all liberties and the imposition of a form of Fascism, through military dictatorship. Here lay the essential distinction in Challaye's mind. He distinguished between what he called an 'antifascism of peace' and an 'antifascism of war'. Because of recent events, he thought it would be wise to dissociate antifascism from pacifism in the Ligue's propaganda.[50]

Gerin replied to Challaye in the next number of the *Barrage*. He insisted that he, too, supported an 'antifascism of peace', not of war. But he was equally insistent that all Ligue members were resolutely opposed to Fascism; Challaye's article contained the seeds of 'grave disagreements' within the Ligue if the issues it raised were not dealt with quickly. For his part, Gerin rejected any idea of separating antifascism and pacifism, for four main reasons. First, he argued that just because certain antifascists deported themselves like 'bellicose imbeciles' was no reason in itself to renounce one's own antifascism. The Ligue was not obliged to follow them in 'their criminal deviations'. In his view, it sufficed to distinguish as they had always done between antifascism for internal use and antifascism for external use. This usage, consecrated by time, was also easier to understand than Challaye's rather nebulous construct 'antifascism of peace'. If antifascism were removed from the Ligue's programme, Gerin said he would resign from it immediately.[51]

Secondly, he pointed out that the Ligue had been officially anti-fascist since its Congress at Montargis in 1934, that is to say two years before the arrival of the Popular Front in power. If the Popular Front had subsequently deviated from its original programme, that was of no immense concern to the LICP which ought to remain true to its own ideals. Thirdly, Gerin argued that to accept Challaye's proposition would actually mean taking a step in the direction of a

---

[49] Ibid. [50] Ibid.

[51] René Gerin, 'Pacifisme et antifascisme', *Le Barrage*, 141 (19 Jan. 1939), 2.

union sacrée with the very political elements that were the natural enemies of pacifism. *Le Matin, Le Temps, Gringoire*, and the *Action française* had none of them ever genuinely worked for peace between the peoples; what he called their pseudo-pacifism was opportunistic and ephemeral, and they represented moreover an attack on the same freedoms which the Ligue was trying to protect. If these pseudo-pacifists of September 1938 had rejected war with Germany, this was all well and good, but Gerin was certain that given half a chance they would support a war against Soviet Russia. He urged the Ligue not to be admirers of either *Le Matin* or *L'Humanité*, but to remain true to itself.[52]

Finally, Gerin recognized that the Ligue had perhaps been wrong in 1934 to call 'Fascism' in France what was in reality merely the most recent manifestation of an old, and deeply rooted, French right-wing reaction. But this reactionary force in French politics was becoming increasingly 'Fascist' in the proper sense of the word—in the same way that Stalinism had evolved towards a sort of left-wing Fascism. Gerin believed that Fascism could be found on the left or the right, and he declared that it was the thing that the LICP hated the most because it implied nationalism, militarism, racism, and totalitarianism. He wondered aloud whether any Combattant de la paix could be found who could say he was a Fascist.[53]

Gerin disagreed with Challaye about other things as well, such as the use of the word 'integral' to describe the Ligue's pacifism. He continued to believe that this was meaningless and furthermore dangerous. He also disagreed about the unacceptability of fighting a civil war should it be forced upon one. Unlike Challaye, he thought that to fight back in a civil situation was legitimate. In the troubled days of early 1939, he defined the kernel of pacifist truth to which the LICP as a whole adhered:

We are agreed not to prepare or start a foreign war, or even a civil war, on the pretext of antifascism. Fascism, we have always affirmed, can only be effectively fought inside a country. But we must also be agreed neither to give arms to our own Fascists, nor to those outside. Let us condemn Fascism *wherever it exercises its ravages*. Let us sweep our own doorstep first; but let us retain the right, indeed let us fulfil the duty, of pointing out that the doorstep of our neighbour can be just as dirty, if not more so, than our own.[54]

---

[52] Gerin, 'Pacifisme et antifascisme'.   [53] Ibid.   [54] Ibid.

It was necessary to put Tardieu, Kerillis, Pertinax, Péri, Aragon, *Le Matin*, *Gringoire*, the *Action francaise*, Flandin, Hitler, Mussolini, Franco, and even Daladier and Bonnet, all in the same bag, because each one was as much in favour of an arms race as the other. The LICP was not in the business of choosing between *surarmeurs*. Gerin concluded that '*we cannot do otherwise*. To act differently would be to betray our programme and peace itself.'[55]

The problem did not seem to disappear, however. A month later Gerin was writing as if the number of Combattants de la paix prepared to do business with the French Fascists was larger than he had first suspected.[56] Pioch, too, roundly attacked the notion that real peace, 'our peace', 'this peace which makes us not non-resistants, but the only real resistants to war—that this peace could have anything in common *avec ça*'.[57] It was an 'impossible promiscuity'.[58]

The debate bubbled on into late March. Louis Trégaro attacked the tendency of some LICP members to support the extreme right following Munich. He insisted that in order for pacifism to be viable, it had to be allied to antifascism, and also anticapitalist in orientation. Since Munich, it had been in crisis. Pacifists had been lumped together with Daladier and anyone else supporting the accords, for whatever reasons. He was particularly concerned at the position taken by Challaye, Léon Emery, and the Ligue des femmes pour la paix.[59]

Léon Emery replied to Trégaro's article in the next number, arguing that pacifism could no longer be assumed to be uniquely a left-wing position. As far as the temporary and 'fortuitous' alliance with the right at the time of Munich was concerned, it had changed nothing in the basic pacifist credo. Recent history seemed to give the lie to the assumption that pacifism was necessarily of the left. Blum was in favour of a policy of armaments, and the Communists had become just as bellicose as the right had ever been. What he called this 'parliamentary and electoral geography' was no longer of the

---

[55] Ibid.
[56] René Gerin, 'Union sacrée?—Non, jamais!', *Le Barrage*, 143 (16 Feb. 1939), 1.
[57] Georges Pioch, 'L'Impossible Promiscuité', *Le Barrage*, 144 (2 Mar. 1939), 1.
[58] Ibid.
[59] Louis Trégaro, 'Casse-cou!', *Le Barrage*, 145 (16 Mar. 1939), 1. See also Part III below for a brief analysis of the dissensions within the French section of the Ligue internationale des femmes pour la paix et la liberté which finally led to the creation of the schismatic Ligue des femmes pour la paix.

slightest interest to pacifists. The defence of liberty was no longer, any more than the defence of peace, a reliable criterion of political judgement. He argued that the left, for twenty years and in twenty different countries, had often been just as authoritarian and militaristic as the right. Emery argued that pacifism had to remain above and outside the political parties—it was no longer even nominally a party issue. Instead, it had taken on almost mystical proportions. He rejected the idea that it was the preserve of Socialism, or even any particular class. By extension, there was also no reason why pacifism should necessarily be revolutionary or anticapitalist. If that were the case, and orthodoxy had been important, the LICP would never have been formed, and the fight for peace, such as it was, would have remained the preserve of the political parties.[60]

Emery stressed instead the mystical nature of pacifism, and argued that pacifists had to be prepared to place their doctrine above party and political considerations. One could no longer deny that large sections of the working class, for example, now advocated an ideological war against Fascism. So, it was a nonsense for pacifists to feel obliged to fight both war and capitalism, and to refrain from choosing, if hard choices for the higher ideal of peace became necessary. He firmly believed that Fascism was only aided by the bureaucratic and military demands of war, and that it was as likely to come from the left as from the right. He rejected completely the charge that he and his friends were the dupes of international Fascism, however: 'What man of good faith could possibly contest that a programme which goes completely in the individualistic, anti-State direction, is therefore intrinsically antifascist?' From all points of view, Emery believed that his pacifism was 'diametrically opposed to Nazi doctrine'; in fact, much more so than many of the present manifestations of Socialism. The Fascist states thrived on international tension and economic competition. Take this away and they would slowly crumble. He concluded that 'the most fecund and certain revolution is the establishment of peace'.[61]

[60] Léon Emery, 'Le Pacifisme et la doctrine révolutionnaire', Le Barrage, 146 (30 Mar. 1939), 1.

[61] Ibid. There were, of course, opponents within the Ligue of the idea that pacifism had to be placed above all else. In December 1938, for example, Jospin had argued this case, saying that 'la résistance au fascisme demande des mains propres' (R. Jospin, 'Au dessus de la paix', Le Barrage, 139 (15 Dec. 1938), 3). But clearly what had changed in early 1939 was the insistence of Emery and Challaye on the potential need to separate antifascism from pacifism. It was this that so shocked Gerin who continued to

Challaye and Emery seem to have faded into the background after this debate. Given the importance of the issues it raised, it is surprising that it appears not to have been discussed at the Ligue's 1939 Marseille Congress which was, all things considered, a rather tired affair.[62] The only report of note was that by Jospin on economic problems and peace. He argued that the economic aspect of the present discontents was by far the most important. The dangerous ideologies of the hour had been erected on the substructure of economic malaise. There was a tremendous disequilibrium between the wealthy and the poor nations. The latter reacted to this situation by creating a powerful military apparatus which they used for territorial gain. Politically, they evolved into Fascism, trying to solve their problems internally through economic autarchy. Fascist ideology was therefore not that important according to Jospin; what mattered was the economic side of the question. 'The problem of peace and of war is entirely there.'[63]

MOURIR POUR DANTZIG?

A spirit of lassitude seemed to descend on the Ligue in the final six months before the outbreak of war. Régis Messac wrote that France had become a small country between two big power blocs: the Anglo-Saxon nations on the one hand, and Germany on the other. Her only hope was to become the *trait d'union* between them. He thought the fight had gone out of the French, and his description of the France of 1939 is dejected:

France already no longer belongs to the French, and the French are incapable of taking it back. Aside from the fact that they are no longer strong enough, either from the economic or the demographic point of view, their heart is no longer in it. We let things happen, even to us, but we are incapable of action or reaction.[64]

---

advocate an antifascism allied to pacifism, both of them conducted with 'clean hands'. In the summer of 1938 he had already embraced the formula of André Delmas who wrote 'je me refuse à choisir entre la servitude et la guerre. Je repousse les deux' (René Gerin, 'La Formule d'André Delmas', *Le Barrage*, 132 (11 Aug. 1938), 1).

[62] 'Les Travaux du Congrès de Marseille', *Le Barrage*, 147 (20 Apr. 1939), 4.

[63] Robert Jospin, 'Les Problèmes économiques et la paix', *Le Barrage*, 142 (2 Feb. 1939), 4.

[64] Régis Messac, 'Pour un esprit civique européen', *Le Barrage*, 147 (20 Apr. 1939), 1.

Poland was the final item on the European agenda before the shooting began. The LICP had not had much sympathy for Czechoslovakia, although it had certainly castigated the final dismemberment of the country in March 1939; it had even less sympathy for Poland, a country 'least worthy to be called a nation' in Gerin's words.[65] Poland was a mixture of different ethno-linguistic groups, largely illiterate, not at all liberal, but rather a country under the boot of a domestic Fascism. Furthermore, it was a nation in which anti-Semitism was as rife as in Nazi Germany. It was a 'still more artificial and stupid' creation of the 1919 treaties than Czechoslovakia but Gerin did not believe that France or Britain would be prepared to go to war for it. It was plain to Gerin that Danzig was a German city and the Corridor was still probably more German than Polish despite the expulsions. He agreed that Poland should have access to the Baltic, but this should naturally be the estuary of the Vistula. All of the territorial problems raised by the Polish question could be resolved without war, and Gerin predicted many more 'Munichs' to come.[66]

Even in the face of so obvious an external threat, the LICP continued to affirm that the primary foe was an internal one. In early June, Gaston Pauthe attacked a recent speech by Daladier in which he had said that 'the French belong to a privileged nation and their margin of happiness can only be preserved by a heroic resolution'.[67] Pauthe rejected categorically the idea that there was *one* nation of Frenchmen who must defend their privileges against an external foe. For him, the enemy was and would remain a class enemy: 'Yet again, let us state that *our enemy is above all here at home*, and Blum is worth no more than Daladier . . .'[68]

The desperate optimism of the Ligue remained right up to the end. In July, echoing the title of a play by Giraudoux, Gerin was proclaiming that the 'war for Danzig will not take place'.[69] He thought it was 'incontestable' that a certain *détente* seemed to be developing on the

[65] René Gerin, 'La Pologne et nous', Le Barrage, 149 (18 May 1939), 1–2.
[66] Ibid.
[67] Gaston Pauthe, 'Non! Monsieur Daladier, nous ne sommes pas dupes!', Le Barrage, 150 (8 June 1939), 2.
[68] Ibid.
[69] René Gerin, 'La Guerre de Dantzig n'aura pas lieu', Le Barrage, 151 (13 July 1939), 1. Jean Giraudoux's pacifist play was entitled La Guerre de Troie n'aura pas lieu and had been enthusiastically reviewed by Georges Pioch in 1935. See Le Barrage, 74 (5 Dec. 1935), 1.

international level. He asked whether it was but a truce in the war of nerves, and arrived at the conclusion that there would definitely be no war, at least not that summer. The situation had been 'serious' at the end of March after the 'crime' of the Nazis in invading Czechoslovakia. The *union sacrée* had begun to re-establish itself in France, the Anglo-French alliance became very close, and the encirclement of Germany was obvious. But the situation had improved since then for two reasons. First, the protests against the preparation of war had helped a lot. In particular, Déat's articles had provoked a good deal of discussion. Even the right-wing parties now seemed ready to consider negotiations rather than war. Secondly, and more importantly, the Anglo-Franco-Russian alliance did not seem to be coming together. The so-called 'peace front', the coalition of the 'pacific democracies', the organization of 'collective security' had all failed. This was a happy event for Gerin and the LICP. Tensions remained in the international sphere but pacifists would have to keep their sang-froid as they had done so far. 'The treatment for our nerves through a system of hot-and-cold shower-baths [la douche écossaise] is surely not over.'[70]

Seven weeks later, Europe was at war.

[70] Gerin, 'La Guerre de Dantzig'.

PART III

THÈMES ET VARIATIONS, OR FEMINIST PACIFISM IN INTERWAR FRANCE

10. Feminist Pacifism and the LIFPL

INTRODUCTION

One recent historian has written that opposition to the Great War among French women—feminists and otherwise—was 'almost negligible'.[1] But it is perhaps necessary to look behind this apparent inactivity on the part of feminists in the fight against the militarism of European society in the era of the Great War and afterwards. Jo Vellacott argues in a recent essay that far from being of no consequence whatsoever, women's peace efforts in the First World War and afterwards were important because by involving themselves in the peace movement, women were stepping outside their assigned social roles and thus making a powerful feminist statement. By implication, what matters according to Vellacott is not so much numbers as the mere essential fact of women's activity within a larger peace and protest movement. She writes:

Women's peace efforts are often dismissed as simply part of the general softness of women's nature, or as part of their motherhood role, with no serious import for the public sphere. This patronizing view has not only made it possible to disregard the content of what peace women have said, but at times even succeeds in making peace a suspect cause among feminists. Many First World War feminists believed, however, that pacifism was not only a logical development from feminism, but an integral part of it.

In a culture which strongly enforces gender inequality and the widely differentiated traditional roles of men and women, where women are relegated to the private sphere, and where they are not organized to reclaim equality or push back the frontiers, women do not emerge as forceful

---

[1] James F. McMillan, *Housewife or Harlot: The Place of Women in French Society 1870–1940* (Brighton: The Harvester Press, 1981), 112.

opponents of war, demanding to be heard. They fulfil, instead, their assigned role in war as in peace, sacrificing their sons and lovers without complaint (mourning, yes, but complaining, no), keeping the home fires burning, loving soldiers, being sexually available, bearing and nurturing cannon fodder for future wars, enduring hardships, taking on extra tasks for the duration and relinquishing them without a murmur when the men come home.[2]

Vellacott suggests that simply by stepping outside this traditional role *vis-à-vis* war, women were taking part in the larger feminist movement and it is in that context that their action must be seen. Although she is primarily concerned with the British example, her analysis is sufficiently broad in its theoretical implications to be interesting and useful here. Her statement that 'in the long run . . . making use of certain gender-based advantages, sisterhood made a stronger anti-war showing than brotherhood' is a provocative one.[3] Leaving aside the British case, one would have to agree with James McMillan that the Great War provided many examples of women active in the suffrage and feminist movement who supported the war effort *jusqu'au bout*.[4]

It is the purpose of this section to examine the putative link between feminism and pacifism in interwar France in the form of its clearest nexus, the French section of the Ligue internationale des femmes pour la paix et la liberté (LIFPL). There is no doubt that women played an important role in French pacifist groups of the twenties and thirties. Some women such as Madeleine Vernet (1878–1949) and Marcelle Capy (1891–1962) saw their role as little different from that of men, and organized and led important *nouveau style* pacifist groups from about 1928 onwards.[5] Both of these women were also active as pacifist and feminist journalists. Primarily though it is the French section of the LIFPL and its contribution to the pacifist debate at both the international and national levels which will be the focal point of this section.

[2] Jo Vellacott, 'Women, Peace and Internationalism, 1914–1920: "Finding New Words and Creating New Methods"', in Charles Chatfield and Peter van den Dungen (eds.), *Peace Movements and Political Cultures* (Knoxville, Tenn.: University of Tennessee Press, 1988), 106.

[3] Ibid.

[4] See McMillan, *Housewife or Harlot*, 105, 112, 114.

[5] See James Friguglietti, 'Marcelle Capy' in Harold Josephson (ed.), *Biographical Dictionary of Modern Peace Leaders* (Westport, London: Greenwood Press, 1985), 141–3. See also Albert S. Hill, 'Madeleine Vernet', 986–8.

The LIFPL was founded at the Hague in 1915 and was initially called the Women's International Committee for a Permanent Peace. It grouped together the cream of British, European, and North American avant-garde feminist women.[6] In France its leading lights were Gabrielle Duchene (1870–1954), Camille Drevet, Andrée Jouve (1884–1972), Léo Wanner, and Madeleine Rolland.[7] These five women served for much of the interwar period as members of the International Executive Committee of the LIFPL. Duchene was an international vice-president for a number of years and treasurer from 1935 to 1937. Camille Drevet was international secretary during the mid-thirties, and the others were so-called non-voting 'consultative' members of the executive.

In a broader sense, though, this section raises questions about the nature of the French feminist pacifist experience in the interwar period. For many feminist pacifists of the time (and indeed still today[8]), it was a self-evident axiom, as Vellacott mentions above, that feminism and pacifism *ought* to be linked. But it will be argued, unlike Vellacott, that it was not sufficient for women to emerge from their traditional sphere into the post-war political world in order to make a feminist statement for peace. As Vellacott herself admits, the *content* of women's peace ideas was important, and it was this content which distinguished women's efforts for peace from 'masculinist' pacifism. What was inherently new, exciting, innovative, and unique in the feminist contribution to peace in the immediate post-war world was lost in France by the thirties. In the process, the French section of the LIFPL became a shadow of what it might have been, its arguments a shell of what they once were, and the only genuinely avant-garde French feminist contribution to the pacifist

---

[6] For an account of the international work of the LIFPL see Gertrude Bussey and Margaret Tims, *Women's International League for Peace and Freedom* (London: Allen & Unwin, 1965). For a generalized overview of the French section of the LIFPL see Yvonne Sée, *Réaliser l'espérance* (Paris: Section française de la LIFPL, n.d. [1984]). See also *Gabrielle Duchene, 1870–1954: In memoriam* (Paris: Section française de la LIFPL, n.d. [1954]).

[7] See Albert S. Hill, 'Gabrielle Duchene', in Josephson, *Dictionary*, 226–8. Hill's short biography contains several elementary errors of fact. Duchene was born on 26 Feb. 1870 (not 1878), and died on 3 Aug. 1954 at her summer chalet in the Bernese Oberland in Switzerland. See also Yvonne Sée, 'Andrée Jouve', in Josephson, *Dictionary*, 481. Jouve was a *lycée* professor and the first wife of the French surrealist poet Pierre-Jean Jouve.

[8] See for example Pam McAllister (ed.), *Reweaving the Web of Life: Feminism and Nonviolence* (Philadelphia: New Society Publishers, 1982).

debate a mirror image of the ideologically divided world of main-stream French pacifism. Paradoxically this is in no way to denigrate the French feminist contribution to peace. Right up until 1939 women such as Gabrielle Duchene continued to play an extremely important role in the larger French pacifist movement, but they did this increasingly as pacifists in the male mould, rather than as feminists.

Thus, the feminist contribution to the pacifist debate in interwar France can be situated between the two extremes which have been examined in Parts I and II of this book. If the first two sections define the opposing poles of new- and old-style pacifism, then the pacifism of the women of the French section of the LIFPL constituted a sort of 'theme and variations' on the motif set in the world of 'masculinist' pacifism. The evolution of feminist pacifism in late Third Republic France followed a curve in opposition to the currents of the day. Thus, in the first decade of the predominance of *pacifisme ancien style*, the women of the LIFPL were representatives of integral pacifism before it became widely known by that name. And by the time the new pacifism had begun to emerge in the early thirties, the LIFPL, or at least its leadership, was beginning to evolve away from absolute pacifism towards a defence of justice and freedom. This led to an interesting *communion de pensée* between mainline bourgeois pacifists like Ruyssen and the once radical pacifists of the LIFPL.

INSIDE THE FRENCH SECTION

No French women were allowed out of France to attend the founding Congress of the LIFPL, or the Women's International Committee for a Permanent Peace as it then was called. Nevertheless, women in France followed the events at the Hague with great interest and founded a French section of the International Committee shortly afterwards. The French group's appeal to French women spoke of the 'special task' which fell to women in the struggle for peace: 'Women of all countries, mothers, hate the war with the same hatred. The deep reason, the real reason, for feminism is the will to conquer the means to prevent war.'[9] The evocation of motherhood as an

---

[9] See brochure entitled simply 'Section française du Comité international des femmes pour la paix permanente', in BDIC/DD/FΔ530/I, 1. On the creation of the French section of the LIFPL, see Sée, *Réaliser l'espérance*, 5–11; see also *Gabrielle Duchene, 1870–1954*.

inspiration, and the linking of feminism and pacifism, were therefore important facets of the original French feminist pacifism.

The French section was never one of the LIFPL's largest, either numerically or in terms of its financial influence. It was nevertheless a very significant one because of the breadth and variety of its programmes and because of its intellectual contribution to the life of the larger Ligue. In the mid-twenties it numbered some 500 members compared with Germany's 5,000, 4,000 in Britain, some 8,000 in the United States, and 10,000 in Denmark.[10] Out of an estimated total Ligue membership of about 35,000 members, it seems insignificant indeed. Likewise the financial contribution of the French section to the international work of the Ligue was minimal. In a statement of sums received for a six-month period in the mid-twenties, the French contributed the equivalent of twelve dollars compared with the two largest contributions of $3,000 and $542 from the American and British sections respectively.[11] However, by 1935 the French section was claiming a membership of about 4,500 women.[12] Whether this is an accurate representation of its size it is difficult to say. In 1931 Duchene had warned her colleagues on the International Executive Committee of the dangers of an international organization appearing too small numerically. She counselled prudence in whom these figures should be released to.[13] This might imply a certain elasticity in her approach to the truth in the matter of membership figures, especially given the French section's increasing isolation and its struggle to maintain its influential position internationally within the Ligue in the mid-thirties. It is impossible to be certain about this, but as a point of comparison, it should be noted that the total *maximum* membership of the fourteen groups present and voting at the 1936 French section National Conference was only 1,700 members.[14]

Broadly speaking one can say that the 1920s were marked by two parallel campaigns within the French section: that for disarmament

---

[10] Cited in typescript entitled 'Washington Object' in BDIC/DD/FΔRés. 205/5/5.

[11] Cited in 'Statement of Sums Received from National Sections within Six Months', Women's International League for Peace and Freedom, International Office, Geneva. In BDIC/DD/FΔRés. 205/5/4.

[12] Minutes, International Executive Committee Meeting, Geneva, 12–16 Sept. 1935, 39. In BDIC/DD/FΔRés. 206/Sept. 1935.

[13] Minutes, IEC Meeting, Geneva, 4–8 Sept. 1931, 3. In BDIC/DD/FΔRés. 206/Sept. 1931.

[14] Cited in Procès-verbal de la Conférence nationale de la section française de la LIFPL des 27 et 28 juin 1936, 6. In BDIC/DD/FΔRés. 208/17.

and that for peace education. Certainly it is true that at the beginning of the interwar period, Gabrielle Duchene and the French saw their role in much less dramatic and revolutionary terms than was the case in the thirties. For example, in her annual report for 1921–2, Duchene noted that 'it is above all the work of aid to children in which we have been able to act most effectively'.[15] At this stage, too, the section was much more closely allied to *pacifisme ancien style* in the form of the Délégation permanente des sociétés françaises de la paix, a group which represented the dominant strand of pre-war liberal, internationalist pacifism interested in the juridical approach to the problem of peace.[16] In 1921 they participated in the IXe Congrès national de la paix which was held in Paris and one of their members, the feminist journalist Séverine (1855–1929),[17] was asked to close the Congress. Duchene also noted that she and Séverine were both elected to the Délégation permanente, a move which constituted in her mind a sort of recognition of the importance of the French section within the larger scheme of French pacifism.[18] The fact that she placed such value on this recognition is perhaps an indication of the rather conventional, bourgeois starting-point from which the French section was to evolve under Duchene's leadership in the years ahead.

But if the Marxist overtones which were to characterize so much of the section's thinking in the thirties were absent in the immediate post-war period, the integral pacifism of Duchene was not in question. This is one of the paradoxes of early interwar French pacifism. In the immediate post-war period, the divisions and ideological differences of later years were not yet apparent. Barbusse, Rolland, Duchene, Ruyssen, and Prudhommeaux still believed that it was sufficient to desire peace. As has been shown in Parts I and II, it was only over the course of the twenties that the question of means began to take precedence over that of the end to be obtained. And, in fact,

[15] Extraits du Rapport sur l'action de la section française au cours du dernier exercice (1920–1921) adressé au comité central de la Ligue. In BDIC/DD/FΔRés. 208/2. [16] Cf. Part I above on *pacifisme ancien style*.
[17] Séverine was the pseudonym of Caroline Rémy. Séverine was a journalist and an activist in anarchist and pacifist circles. See Albert S. Hill, 'Séverine', in Josephson, *Dictionary*, 873–5. Once again Hill's biographical sketch contains errors and unwarranted generalizations. For example, he writes that Séverine, together with Madeleine Vernet and Marianne Rauze, founded the Ligue pour la reconnaissance de l'objection de conscience. In fact, the LROC was founded in 1923 in Lyon by Paul Bergeron.
[18] Mentioned in 'Extraits du Rapport ... 1920–1921', in BDIC/DD/FΔRés. 208/2.

the very notion of the goal began to be redefined by the mid-twenties as French pacifism began to define itself increasingly in terms of its position on what became integral pacifism. Thus, in the immediate post-war period, the LIFPL represented an integral pacifism *larvé* —hidden largely because of the unconsciousness of French pacifism generally of the differences which divided it.

Undoubtedly women did have an important role to play in the immediate post-war debates on peace, on *the* peace, and on how to pull Europe back together again after the cataclysm it had suffered. Not much positive action seemed to be forthcoming from the masculine world of French politics or pacifism; and, as during the days of wartime despair, it was the filling of this void which Duchene saw as the crucial role of the LIFPL. As she wrote in 1921:

The profound trouble of the present situation renders pacifist action very difficult whilst at the same time showing the urgent need of it. The divisions at the centre of the parties set at odds men whose goals are very often identical, and shows the necessity for pacifist action independent of all partisan questions. This has given birth to a current sympathetic to the independent feminist pacifist movement.[19]

Here lies the kernel of original, independent, feminist pacifist truth. There was nothing blindly idealistic about Duchene's 1921 report but in the passage cited above there is the recognition of the differences between masculine and feminist approaches to peace. Perhaps with the memory of the 1915 founding Congress relatively fresh in her mind, Duchene still adhered to Jane Addams's (1860–1935)[20] dictum that that which divided had to be set aside, and that which united, emphasized.

The French section defined its work in 1922 as twofold: first to exercise some form of political action to facilitate understanding between governments. Recognizing the minor political part played by French women, the report conceded that 'this action, pursued with zeal everywhere women have a political role, reduces itself in France, alas, to a few platonic demonstrations'.[21] Secondly, the French section strove towards a *rapprochement* 'of the peoples, giving

---

[19] Ibid.
[20] Jane Addams was an American social reformer and pacifist. She was elected president of the LIFPL at its first Congress at The Hague in 1915. In 1931 she shared the Nobel Peace Prize with Nicholas Murray Butler. See Nancy Ann Slote, 'Jane Addams', in Josephson, *Dictionary*, 5–8.
[21] See the untitled report, dated June 1922, in BDIC/DD/FΔRés. 208/3.

them the desire and the opportunity to get to know each other better and to help each other; to bring together the élite of all nations in a common struggle against prejudice, ignorance, injustice, and universal violence'.[22] It was especially this second part of the Ligue's work which the French section considered most fecund from its own perspective. In 1921–2 it had contributed to the 'work of human solidarity *par excellence*' which was the aid to infants stricken by famine and privation in other European nations. In particular the French section contributed 10,000 francs to the relief of children in Russia through the Union internationale de 'secours aux enfants' in Geneva.[23]

In this same year the French were also active in the pedagogy of peace. Andrée Jouve and Madeleine Rolland spoke at the summer school organized by the English section in Salzburg in 1921 at which some 300 students took part. Members of the French section also participated in summer schools organized in the English Lake District, at Bremen, and at Burg-Lauenstein. Not to be outdone, the French, in conjunction with the Italian section, held a summer school of their own in 1922 at Varese in Italy.[24]

Andrée Jouve was also the Ligue's representative to the Comité d'entente des grandes associations de coopération intellectuelle, with Camille Drevet as her substitute[25] from 1927 onwards. In that year the French section also organized a summer school directed by Félicien Challaye at which Dr Schweitzer was one of the lecturers. The school dealt with the question of relations between the races.[26]

In a report on summer schools delivered to the International Executive Committee in Lille in April 1931, Andrée Jouve tried to outline her philosophy for those for which she had been responsible. The underlying principle seemed to be one of openness. The Ligue had no desire to preach only to the converted, and accordingly looked for 'young people whom we hope to win for our ideas,

---

[22] Untitled report, June 1922. BDIC/DD/FΔRés. 208/3.   [23] Ibid.   [24] Ibid.
[25] See Minutes, IEC Meeting, 13 Sept. 1927, afternoon session, 2. In BDIC/DD/FΔRés. 206/Sept. 1927. For further information on the peace education movement during the interwar period, see Elly Hermon, 'Approches conceptuelles de l'éducation en vue de la compréhension internationale dans l'entre-deux-guerres', *Canadian and International Education*, 15/2 (1986), 29–52. See also Elly Hermon, 'The International Peace Education Movement, 1919–1939', in Chatfield and van den Dungen, *Peace Movements and Political Cultures*, 127–42.
[26] Minutes, IEC Meeting, 13 Sept. 1927, afternoon session, 2–3.

through presentation of the facts themselves and clear reasoning'.[27] In Jouve's philosophy of education it was 'best to guard against direct and dogmatic preaching of our doctrine, as that is a sure method of turning active and original minds away from us'.[28] The method seemed to produce results because a French section summer school held at Ribeauville in Alsace in 1930 dealing with the question of the Alsatian separatist movement resulted in the creation of Ligue sections at Colmar and Ribeauville.[29]

The section was also very active in the campaign for universal disarmament. Its efforts in this area were largely organized by Camille Drevet who, long after disarmament had ceased to be a popular pacifist issue in the mid- to late-thirties, was still campaigning for it both within and without the Ligue. The French section never attained the vast numbers of signatures on its petitions for disarmament that some of the other sections were able to achieve, but the campaigns did find a certain resonance within France. In the early thirties many French cities could boast a local peace cartel, one of whose goals would have been disarmament. The disarmament interest probably reached its apogee in 1932 at the time of the Geneva Disarmament Conference. The Grenoble peace cartel, for example, sent 21,918 signatures in favour of universal disarmament to Duchene in February of that year.[30]

It is important to note the degree to which the leading women of the French section were linked to other pacifist groups. Léo Wanner represented the LIFPL at the 1931 War Resisters' International Congress in Lyon. Camille Drevet was involved with the Rassemblement international contre la guerre et le militarisme in the late 1930s. Gabrielle Duchene was involved in literally everything: the RUP, the Comité d'entente des grandes associations internationales, the Amsterdam-Pleyel movement, and its subsidiary movement the Comité mondial des femmes contre la guerre et le fascisme. Marcelle Capy who had been closely involved with the French section during the twenties went on in the thirties to become a leading light within the Ligue internationale des combattants de la paix and finally its president. Madeleine Vernet was closely allied to Duchene and the

---

[27] Andrée Jouve, 'Summer Schools', report prepared for the IEC Meeting at Lille, 8–13 Apr., 1931. In BDIC/DD/FΔRés. 206/Apr. 1931.   [28] Ibid.

[29] Procès-verbal, Comité exécutif international, Amsterdam et Loenen, 11–15 Oct. 1930. Morning session, 11 Oct., 1. In BDIC/DD/FΔRés. 206/Oct. 1930.

[30] La Secrétaire du Comité de désarmement, secrétaire adjointe au 'Cartel de la paix', to Duchene, Grenoble, 5 Feb. 1932, in BDIC/DD/FΔRés. 208/24.

LIFPL for a time, but then founded her own pacifist group, La Volonté de paix, in 1928. She maintained close contacts however with Jeanne Challaye, and together with Jeanne Alexandre, they became the integral pacifist thorns in the French section's side in the late thirties. Rudolf Leonhard, the exiled German pacifist, propagandized for both the LICP and the LIFPL. And the list goes on.

One of the French section's more novel methods of propagandizing its views in the late 1920s was the use of the French general election campaign. Token candidates were fielded in the 1928 general election, a ploy which gave them access to the ubiquitous French election billboards as well as the right to have their 'candidates' speak at election rallies.[31] The campaign was centred in Paris where eight candidates ran in eight electoral districts. One of them was General Alexandre Percin (1846–1928)[32] who had experienced a 'road to Damascus' pacifist conversion a couple of years before his death and was only too willing to repent of his evil ways by helping the women of the LIFPL in their pacifist campaign. The eight *quartiers* were chosen with care as being the most likely to bear fruit for the cause of peace. Tracts, posters, and speeches at rallies were all used to put the pacifist message across. Teams of women, journalists for the most part, were deployed to distribute the tracts and to speak whenever the occasion presented itself. Marcelle Capy was often greeted with enthusiasm in the meetings in which she spoke. Andrée Jouve found it interesting that

almost the whole electoral campaign was conducted around the idea of Peace: internal peace, external peace. It was in camouflaging themselves and in supporting this programme that the majority of the candidates, even those of the Union nationale, were able to win their votes.

It is also to be noted that for their own electoral campaign the feminist groups borrowed a part of our programme. It was with these arguments ('give the vote to women, women's vote guarantees Peace, all women are against war'), often developed by the women who normally oppose us, that their propaganda was made.[33]

It is not our purpose here to examine this aspect of French political

---

[31] Andrée Jouve, 'Rapport sur l'activité de la section française relative aux actions décidées par le dernier comité exécutif', Sept. 1928. In BDIC/DD/FΔRés. 206/Sept. 1928.

[32] See Général Alexandre Percin, *Le Désarmement moral* (Paris: Delpeuch, 1925); Général Alexandre Percin, *Guerre à la guerre* (Paris: Éditions Montaigne, 1927). See also James Friguglietti, 'Alexandre Percin', in Josephson, *Dictionary*, 740–2.

[33] Jouve, 'Rapport' (Sept. 1928).

society, but it would seem possible to suggest that in the 1920s the mainstream of French politics saw fit to paint itself with the pacifist veneer, a veneer which had little to do with the genuine and radical pacifism of groups such as the LIFPL.

The question of the numerical size of the French section has already been dealt with briefly but it would be useful to consider here the extent to which the section grew from the twenties to the thirties. During the twenties the French section listed its membership officially as around 500 women. By 1935 this was claimed to be somewhere in the neighbourhood of 4,500 members, although the fourteen sections voting at the 1936 French annual general meeting had a maximum total membership of only 1,700 women. Examining the problem from the grass-roots level one can easily conclude that the section experienced substantial growth from about the late-twenties to the mid-thirties, but it is almost impossible to arrive at aggregate figures because the extant records simply do not support such an analysis.

That notwithstanding some insight can be gained into the size and distribution of the membership of the French section from the occasional comments and figures which exist in the correspondence between the various groups and the secretariat in Paris. Without doubt the Paris and Lyon sections were the largest numerically, which makes the purge of the Lyon section in 1934–5 all the more strange.[34] In 1936 the Lyon section still numbered some 300 members, but Paris was larger with 421 members, and perhaps another 200 at most in the suburbs. At the 1936 annual general meeting the following groups were present or represented although only fourteen of the sixteen are listed as having voted: Drôme-Ardèche, Le Havre, Rouen, Arles, Lyon, La Rochelle, Chalon-sur-Saône, Dijon, Chambéry, Nîmes, Roubaix, Troyes, Seine, Seine-et-Marne, Seine-et-Oise, Paris. The reason for the apparent irregularity in the voting procedure was that the meeting decided not to permit voting by proxy. To the above list was added the Montpellier section which voted, but subtracted from it were the Chambéry, Le Havre, and Nîmes sections which did not vote. In total, then, at the 1936 annual meeting some seventeen groups were represented if not all actually voting.[35]

[34] For the membership figures in 1936, see Procès-verbal de la Conférence nationale de la section française de la LIFPL, 27–8 June 1936, 6 in BDIC/DD/FΔRés. 208/17. The purge of the Lyon section is discussed more fully later in this chapter.
[35] Ibid. 1 and 6.

Other indicators give some credence to Duchene's 1935 claim of 4,500 members for the French section. Early numbers of *SOS*, the organ of the French section from 1930–4, had a print run which varied from 2,050 to 3,000 in 1930 and 1931.[36] Unfortunately figures for subsequent years do not exist. Not all French section members received *SOS* or its successor *En vigie* however. In 1931–2 for example the Grenoble section reported a total of 156 members only 49 of whom took *SOS*.[37] This figure for Grenoble shows considerable growth in the period since 1926 when the group seems to have been formed. In 1928 it had numbered only 27 members.[38]

The Auxerre group was another one which seemed to show remarkable growth in the early thirties only to die out in 1934. It included members outside the town itself and further afield in the department of the Yonne. In 1930 the group listed 73 members, half of them 'active', the remainder merely *adhérent*. In a list of members' occupations, one finds six *institutrices*, one woman school principal, a grammar school teacher (*professeur*), one hairdresser, a woman farmer, a lawyer, and a *voyageur*. Jean-Michel Renaitour, the mayor of Auxerre and the local deputy, was also a member.[39] Another undated list gave 99 members in the department. A list for the year 1931–2 gives some 150 members, and in 1933 the group claimed 220 active members and 70 *membres adhérents*. The group foundered in 1934 on the same issues which provoked so much dissension within the French section, and which will be discussed here shortly.[40]

The Le Havre group had some 55 members in 1934 but in late 1935 it became moribund due to pressures on the time of its local secretary, M. Noël. A meeting held in January 1936 to revivify the group produced a turnout of only 8 of the 70 members still on the group's books.[41]

The Caen group had 21 members in 1933, 27 in 1934 (of whom

---

[36] BDIC/DD/FΔRés. 208/11 contains bills for *SOS* Nos. 4 and 5 from the Association typographique lyonnaise.

[37] A membership list *c*.1931–2 gives these figures in BDIC/DD/FΔRés. 208/24.

[38] In BDIC/DD/FΔRés. 208/24 (report *c*.1931–2).

[39] Membership list, 1930, for the department of the Yonne, in BDIC/DD/FΔRés. 208/21.

[40] The undated list and the lists for 1931–2 and 1933 are to be found in BDIC/DD/FΔRés. 208/21. See also Duchene to Groupe d'Auxerre, 26 Dec. 1934, ibid.

[41] See 1934 report on the group's activity in BDIC/DD/FΔRés. 208/24. See also the letter of M. Noël to Duchene, 25 Jan. 1936, ibid.

several were primary school teachers, six were telephonists, and one was a *parfumeuse*), 35 members in February 1934, and 45 members in March of the same year. By 1937 it had 44 members, 5 having resigned that year. The membership list for this year seems to be the only one extant which provides some clues as to the origins of the women in a small provincial group. Of the 44 women in the Caen group, only 8 were unmarried. Not all of the names listed provide information as to occupation, political affiliation, or religious belief, but the majority do. The group contained two primary school teachers, one *commerçante*, one telephonist, the director of the local Catholic newspaper, *L'Éveil normand*, one landowner, one restaurant owner, and five women who worked for the Post Office. In terms of political affiliation, three women belonged to the Marc Sangnier movement, one was the secretary of the local Socialist Party, one was Communist, and eight others were listed as *gauche* or *très gauche*. The *commerçante* belonged to the Communist Party and was also the treasurer for the local RUP. The landowner had the additional failings of being bourgeois and Catholic but her saving grace was that she had two sons who were *nettement pacifiste*. There was one war widow who was described as a 'good pacifist'. Another woman was 'very afraid of war', while still another 'was afraid of her husband'. Jeanne Lenormand, the Caen group secretary, observed that four women had joined the LIFPL 'in order to please me', while a further ten names carried no annotation or were simply described as 'insignificant'. Four of the women had been drawn to the LIFPL through the newspaper articles written by Lenormand.[42] This very schematic overview provides the only insight into the origins and orientations of the membership of a small provincial group of the French section.

The Abbéville group reported 35 members by 19 November 1932. The Cannes section was constituted in the spring of 1931 and seems to have had around 40 members in 1933–4. By 1938 it had sunk slightly to 36 members. The Chartres section showed a membership of 35 in a report dated 22 April 1931; another undated (perhaps later) membership list gives 120 members. The Chambéry group

---

[42] See 'Adhérentes de la LIFPL—Caen' in BDIC/DD/FΔRés. 208/22. The date of this list must be 1937—it is referred to by Lenormand in her letter of 25 Jan. 1939 to Duchene (also in FΔRés. 208/20) in which she mentions having drawn up such a list giving comments on the group's members two years previously when she had resigned her office.

which was founded in 1931 had 19 members by November of that year; once again several of them were primary and secondary school teachers. The predominance of the teaching profession in the provincial groups was strong. The Bordeaux group, too, was composed largely of secondary school teachers with a large minority of *institutrices*.[43] The composite view then is one of groups gradually increasing in size in the early thirties with some fall-off in the mid- to late-thirties. The teaching element was strong in some of the groups while others displayed a more heterogeneous mixture of women from different social classes. In making the above comments one is very much aware of the lack of proper data on which to base a substantive analysis.

With regard to the activity of these local sections, diversity across the length and breadth of France is again the key. Some groups were much more Radical and left-wing in their orientation than others. Some were primarily middle-class in their outlook. Others viewed pacifism in a primarily moral, rather than political, light. Many local groups belonged to peace cartels in their cities or towns. Others had links with Marc Sangnier's Jeune République, while still others had close contact with local sections of the Ligue internationale des combattants de la paix.

A common problem for the peace women of the French section in the thirties was the attitude of right-wing elements of the population to their campaigns for peace. Not only internationally, but within France as well, the LIFPL became quite incorrectly associated in some minds with the Communist Party. This attracted the attention of the Camelots du roi and other right-wing militarist groups as much as did the Ligue's pacifism. From about 1930 onwards one begins to see references in the correspondence of the French section to the problems posed for peace women by the intimidation of these groups. Writing to Duchene in the early thirties, Louise Daudin of the Bordeaux group underlined two problems her section had faced in its campaign for the petition in favour of disarmament. First, the attitude of a large number of women revolted her, with their haughty, indifferent, and egotistical 'that-doesn't-interest-me' point of view. She added that it was hardly necessary to mention the second form of aggravation which consisted in the 'daily incidents' pro-

---

[43] See material on the Abbéville and Bordeaux groups in BDIC/DD/FΔRés. 208/21. Material on the Cannes, Chartres, and Chambéry groups is in FΔRés. 208/23.

voked around the group's stand at the local fair by the Camelots du roi.[44] The Auxerre group experienced similar difficulties in May 1933 at the local fair at which the LIFPL had a stand, manned by three of the group's women. The women were subjected to a diatribe by a passing officer, one Commandant Krazinski, who accused them of being in the pay of Germany. Apparently, similar incidents had occurred two years previously. The Auxerre women were not prepared to stand for this nonsense, however. They sent a report to the president of the local section of the Ligue des droits de l'homme demanding redress. 'It is inadmissible', the report read, 'in a country in which one is after all still free, that an officer in uniform should come and accuse women who are campaigning for peace, of being sold to Germany.' The incident only served to attract a sympathetic crowd and the supportive comments of the local Socialist newspaper, the *Réveil de l'Yonne*.[45]

These are but two instances recorded in French section correspondence of intimidation on the part of right-wing elements. The LIFPL certainly never had to deal with this sort of attack to anywhere near the same extent as the Ligue internationale des combattants de la paix as we have seen in the preceding section. However, it was intimidation such as this coupled with the French domestic political situation during the late twenties and thirties which undoubtedly fuelled Duchene's tendency to see Fascism lurking under every bed. As early as 1930 she told the International Executive Committee of the Ligue that 'the police reign in France and there is a very clear tendency towards Fascism'.[46] There was also opposition to the LIFPL at the official level. In order to be able to hold a public meeting at the Ligue's 1932 International Congress in Grenoble, Duchene had been obliged to ask the mayor of Grenoble to preside. It was only by cloaking themselves in the protection of the mayoral mantle that

[44] L. Daudin to Duchene, Bordeaux, undated (dated 30 June and from context early thirties), in BDIC/DD/FΔRés. 208/21.

[45] Rapport à Monsieur le Président de la fédération de l'Yonne de la Ligue des droits de l'homme et du citoyen par A. Pelcot, Présidente du groupe d'Auxerre de la LIFPL. Auxerre, 26 May 1933. In BDIC/DD/FΔRés. 208/21. See also 'Paix et désarmement: Glorieux exploit d'un Galonné!', undated clipping from the *Réveil de l'Yonne* in BDIC/DD/FΔRés. 208/21. See also the text of the nationalist poster attacking the LIFPL which appeared on the walls of Auxerre during the fair. It was printed in a local print shop whose manager was the Abbé Oudin. Contained in BDIC/DD/FΔRés. 208/21.

[46] See Duchene's comments in Procès-verbal de la réunion du Comité exécutif international, Geneva, 23–26 Apr. 1930, 3. In BDIC/DD/FΔRés. 206/Apr. 1930.

the Ligue could avoid the interdiction of the meeting by the prefect who was opposed to pacifist ideas.[47]

The intimidation felt by members of the French section led some of them to ask whether they should be setting up some sort of self-protection corps for Ligue events. Madame Perrin of the Besançon group proposed at the 1933 annual general meeting the creation of 'antifascist phalanxes' to protect meetings, and wondered if the Ligue had the right to organize such self-defence organizations. Perhaps indicating yet again the differences in outlook between the French section and the rest of the Ligue, Duchene responded that on the national level such a plan was possible, but that 'on the *international* level we could not do it because we would expose ourselves to criticisms and others might say that our method of action was a form of violence'.[48] This is a rather benign example of the way in which the rhetoric of violence insinuated itself into a pacifist group. In the LICP this tendency took on starker proportions with the creation of the so-called Jeune Garde pacifiste to protect LICP meetings from the ministrations of right-wing thugs. As the political fabric of the Third Republic continued to decay under the onslaught of competing antidemocratic forces (from both left and right) even the politics of marginality, the politics of dissent, were affected.

The events of February 1934 produced another paroxysm of paranoia in Duchene. She wrote in a circular sent out to the French groups that 'we have barely escaped a *coup d'état*'.[49] The fear did not dissipate. In her next circular she spoke of the preparations then in progress for the Rassemblement mondial des femmes contre la guerre et le fascisme to be held in the summer of 1934, and saw the great danger of the hour coming from the threat of a Fascist coup. 'Everyday incidents' and 'reactionary, arbitrary measures' were evidence of the attempts to 'implant' Fascism in France. A prime example of this was the decree-laws which Duchene thought were too easily accepted by Frenchmen. France remained under the threat of another *coup d'état*.[50]

[47] See Duchene's comments in Procès-verbal de la réunion du Comité exécutif international, Grenoble, 11–14 May 1932, 3, in BDIC/DD/FΔRés. 206/May 1932.
[48] Procès-verbal de l'Assemblée générale de la section française, 1933, 5, in BDIC/DD/FΔRés. 208/14.
[49] 'Circulaire no. 10 de la section française', 2. In BDIC/DD/FΔRés. 208/15. Undated (early 1934 from context).
[50] 'Circulaire no. 11 de la section française' (May 1934), 3. In BDIC/DD/FΔRés. 208/15.

The constantly changing international and domestic political situation demanded the rethinking of the shibboleths cherished by French pacifists. Some women such as Léo Wanner jumped on the ideological bandwagon and proclaimed that the place of women was on the side of the dictatorship of the proletariat where true feminist, pacifist freedom was to be found.[51] A more measured analysis of the political situation came from Andrée Jouve in a report prepared for the 1933 annual general meeting of the French section. In it she examined three key political terms which were greatly misunderstood and abused: revolution, Fascism, and class struggle. She underlined the falsity of the position taken publicly by the parties of the left that Fascism and Nazism were the 'last desperate attempts of capitalism to prevent its fall', and showed how in fact the Hitler and Mussolini regimes enjoyed waves of popular support, at least at the outset. If Marxism was the main enemy of Fascism it was precisely because it was internationalist, as opposed to nationalist. She rejected, too, the facile descriptions of class warfare which were the province of popular Marxism. She declared that 'bourgeois' and 'capitalist' were not synonymous, and those who confused the two did the 'greatest harm to the idea of a veritable revolution and economic reorganization'.[52] In her view the Fascist movement was unconcerned with class divisions and it was not from that perspective that one could combat a 'movement of unity' based on ideas of race and the nation, and which furthermore pursued economic ends very similar to those of the Marxists.[53]

The error was in trying to delimit the boundaries of these so-called opposing classes in a nation like France. At what point, she asked, did the bourgeois and the proletarian exchange places at the barricade? Was it a question of money or of *esprit*? She noted that it was supposedly the bourgeoisie which created capitalist wars, but from which social class, she asked, did most conscientious objectors come? It was a mistake in Jouve's eyes to try to limit the great pacifist experiment to any one class. Not all of the proletariat was pacifist by any means despite the claims of Marxist orthodoxy. She had equally measured comments about the word 'revolution' which had become

[51] See for example Léo Wanner, 'La Femme et les dictatures', *SOS* 16 (year 5) (1934), 1–2.
[52] See Jouve's report, 'Devons nous réviser quelques unes de nos idées?', attached to the Procès-verbal de l'Assemblée générale de la section française, 1933, in BDIC/DD/FΔRés. 208/14.   [53] Ibid.

a word without meaning in the political market-place. She made it clear that she detested revolutionary injustice and repression in Russia as much as in Italy or Germany. The LIFPL was a league for freedom, Jouve emphasized, but it was also for peace; and it was here that she thought the members of the Ligue would have to revise their ideas. The Ligue's belief that the causes of modern war were almost uniquely economic was true from several points of view, but it did not take sufficient note of the impact of ideas on men's actions. In her view the economic crisis the Western world was traversing could have led either to more internationalism or to the exacerbated nationalism it did produce. The reasons for the present unhappy political reality were to be found in 'national defeat, the humiliation of the treaties, the vindictive obstinacy of the allied policy which orientated the opposition in this direction'. All of this had produced the predictable result of a profound nationalist revival. For convinced pacifists and internationalists the crisis reduced itself in Jouve's view to an intellectual one:

It seems that the international idea, still lacking in mystique and traditions, is not meaty enough, not rough enough, not heated enough to inspire and raise up the masses which abstract ideas and . . . reason itself do not raise up . . .

A new mystique of peace must be born without which we will not be able to hasten its advent other than by our own personal faith. But I hope that it will be neither so blind, nor so demoniacal, nor so lacking in reason and good sense as the nationalist mystique.[54]

This measured and thoughtful tone was not always the norm of the political discussions within the French section. Léo Wanner of Lyon was a particularly hardline representative of the extreme left-wing orthodoxies within the Ligue which Jouve had argued against in her paper. There is little doubt that both within and without France, the French section presented a more left-wing face—at least officially —than did most other sections. With regard to the increasing duality of the Ligue's purpose—peace *and* freedom—and the difficulty from the early thirties onwards of reconciling these two ideas, Gabrielle Duchene prepared an important position paper for the 1936 French section annual general meeting on 'Les Deux Conceptions du pacifisme'. It mapped out her approach to peace for the remainder of the decade. The paper had its origins in her sad observation that at the moment when unity was most needed, pacifists were most

---

[54] Jouve, 'Devons nous réviser'.

divided. She did not believe that pacifists were at odds over the goals to be pursued, but only in tactics, and she wrote that 'the gravity of the situation imposes a tactic of unity which is as all-embracing as possible—with all of the sacrifices which this brings'.[55] In her view the defenders of the peace could be classified into two distinct categories: 'the pacifists who claimed to be *intégraux*, that is to say who wish to have recourse only to means which are *absolutely pacifist* and the *realists* who do not accept the questioning of *the "Absoluteness" of their desire for peace*, but who see the facts as they are and take account of them, in their choice of means for the action to pursue'.[56] The best of the former, she wrote, were doctrinaire and dogmatic, and erected systems of values and action which they expected the real world to conform to. They were the practitioners of a new religion, with all of the mysticism, fanaticism, and exclusivity that the word religion implies. She criticized their indulgence towards Hitler who was the enemy both of peace and of freedom. Perhaps indicating the extent to which the sterile Stalinist debates of the mid-thirties had made inroads into Duchene's thinking, she stated in a strange paragraph of her report that the 'pacifistes idéologues' were strange bedfellows of the Trotskyists who wanted a permanent revolution. Her claim that both of these groups could be found on the same side of the barricades is a perplexing one.[57] The pacifist realists had grouped together with other people from many walks of life in the Rassemblement universel pour la paix. Not all its members were pacifists—that much was certain—but Duchene asked whether anyone had the right to search hearts and establish a hierarchy of pacifist values. The realists were ready to do business with anybody, and in so doing to neutralize adversaries, and bring groups and individuals into the fight against war, whether from personal interest or out of idealism. The integral pacifists, on the other hand, denounced the RUP in *Le Barrage*, and in preparing a congress of *integral* pacifists committed the original sin of creating division.[58]

All of the above is interesting in view of Duchene's insistence in the twenties on principles. Means became blurred with ends in her mind somewhere along the road in the thirties. In her desire to support the Soviet Union, she, along with large swaths of French pacifism,

---

[55] See Duchene, 'Les Deux Conceptions du pacifisme', paper read at the Assemblée générale de la section française, 1936. In BDIC/DD/FΔRés. 208/17.
[56] Ibid.   [57] Ibid.   [58] Ibid.

allowed her previously principled pacifist action to become en-
meshed in the concepts of collective security. This collective security
was preached with equal vociferousness by both bourgeois, traditional statesmen and the denizens of a rightfully worried and still
somewhat politically isolated Soviet Union. In many respects her
analysis of the European political situation remained astute. In her
evolution from absolute pacifism to pseudo-pacifism, one should not
see a lessening of her desire for peace at all. But it is one of the
arguments of this study that for many French pacifists the *political*
nature of their pacifist experience was all important. What began in
the Great War and the twenties as an absolute revolt against the
militarism of French society had many echoes across a whole spectrum of European pacifist feeling. In the early years of the interwar
period, a *political* pacifist like Duchene (and indeed many other
French pacifists) could mistakenly assume that her convictions
sprang from the same source as that of the more ethically, if not
religiously, inspired British pacifism. But by the thirties this unconscious assumption was no longer tenable. The nature of French
pacifism was by and large very different from that of the British
experience, and by the mid-thirties this had become clear in the
rapidly widening rifts between the various French pacifisms. Arguably it was only some Christian pacifists and those in secular groups
like the Ligue internationale des combattants de la paix in France
who remained true to the purity of their pacifist principles. In so
doing they divorced themselves from political society, no matter how
much they might protest the contrary, and 'defined a faith', to
borrow Martin Ceadel's phrase. Not everyone who says, 'Lord,
Lord,' shall enter the kingdom of heaven.

By about the beginning of the thirties, the French section had
begun to be put on the defensive at the international level of the
Ligue, especially following the Amsterdam Congress against Imperialist War in 1932. The same phenomenon can be seen at the national
level within France, where the evolution of Duchene and the leaders
of the French section away from an absolute pacifism produced a
revolt in the ranks. This was in large part due to the close identification of the official level of the French section with the World
Committee against Fascism and War—or the Amsterdam-Pleyel
movement as it was more popularly known—in the post-1932
period.

On a theoretical level the issues at stake within the French section were non-violence and civil war; but in practical terms they were often expressed in terms relating either to the Amsterdam movement or to the policies of support for Soviet Russia.

Gabrielle Duchene was an important member of the World Committee against Fascism and War. She worked closely with Barbusse and Rolland, and indeed became the instigator and president of the offshoot organization, the Women's World Committee against Fascism and War. The politicization (in a Marxist direction) of the question of peace proved unacceptable to many national sections and the same was true within the French context. The Communist influence on the pacifist debate in France was thus extremely important. Gabrielle Duchene returned from the Amsterdam Congress convinced that an important step had been taken in the fight against war. She wrote in *SOS* of the unanimity which characterized the Congress and of the efforts made by all of the speakers to put aside inflammatory rhetoric and emphasize only that which united them all. This was due to 'the absolute desire of the organizers of the congress to keep it above all of the parties'.[59] Her only, and somewhat veiled, criticism was that the final manifesto passed by the Congress had been drawn up in too much haste and passed without discussion by the delegates. She and other members of the preparatory commission had made their feelings known to Barbusse but he had gone ahead and drafted the document as he saw fit anyway. Romain Rolland condemned it for its negative view of conscientious objectors and Gandhian pacifism.[60] Duchene concluded by emphasizing that in the work ahead a great deal of mutual respect, tolerance, and goodwill would be necessary. Unilateralism had to be avoided, as did discussions of doctrine, in order to arrive at the primary goal which was positive, practical action against war.[61]

But it was precisely this openness which seemed to be lacking almost immediately as a hierarchy of neo-Marxist, neo-pacifist values became implanted in the thinking and political discourse of Duchene and her colleagues within the Amsterdam movement. The

[59] G. Duchene, 'Congrès mondial contre la guerre, Amsterdam, 27–28 août 1932', in *SOS* 12 (1932), 5–6.
[60] Cf. Romain Rolland, 'Lettre à Henri Barbusse sur la place qui doit être faite aux objecteurs de conscience et aux Gandhistes dans le mouvement révolutionnaire issu du Congrès d'Amsterdam' (20 Dec. 1932) in *Par la révolution, la paix* (Paris: Éditions sociales internationales, 1935), 61–4.
[61] Duchene, 'Congrès mondial'.

new approach to peace was accepted with great difficulty, if at all, by many groups of the French section. On the question of adherence of local LIFPL groups to the Amsterdam committees which were supposed to be forming across France, Duchene wrote in October 1932 to the Grenoble group that it was possible to abstain from these, but only if this was done without any public displays of hostility. What, however, is more interesting is her comment in a letter to Grenoble that 'no one can refuse to fight against imperialist war, but if one wishes to fight against other wars that is a question of conscience'.[62] In that short statement can be summarized the problem for the next three or four years for the French section since some local groups continued to cling to the integral pacifist positions which Duchene condemned in 1936.

Goodwill and toleration seemed to be lacking as local Amsterdam-Pleyel committees were formed across France. Supposedly coming together in a struggle for the higher cause of peace, local groups found themselves rent by the same bitter political divisions as those of French political society in the latter years of the Third Republic. Because the Amsterdam Congress had been against *imperialist* war, it was impossible to separate political doctrine and ideology from the problem of peace, for all the goodwill in the world. As one British pacifist present in Amsterdam remarked, 'Lord, how the word "pacifism" stinks in the nostrils of most delegates'.[63]

Rosy unanimity about principle and practice certainly did not prevail within the French section. There was much discussion and dissension as to aims and methods in the fight against war; and it was the Amsterdam Congress and the movements flowing out of it which brought these issues to the fore and polarized the factions within the French section. Whilst it was true that the larger Ligue was officially non-partisan and apolitical, it quickly became clear that the French section was increasingly dancing to what Romain Rolland called the 'inevitable tempo of history',[64] in the form of a Marxist conception of war and peace. In the twenties Duchene had written about the difficulty of getting bourgeois women to join certain sections which were almost entirely working class; but in the thirties it became clear

[62] Duchene to Lucienne Leleu, Grenoble group, 21 Oct. 1932, in BDIC/DD/FΔRés. 208/24.

[63] Cited in Martin Ceadel, *Pacifism in Britain, 1914–1945: The Defining of a Faith* (Oxford: Clarendon Press, 1980), 114.

[64] Rolland cited in Eugen Relgis, *L'Internationale pacifiste* (Paris: André Delpeuch, 1929), 28–9.

that the middle-class sections resisted—in some cases fiercely—Duchene's attempts to force them to follow the doctrinaire Amsterdam-Pleyel line which she had laid down.

The Grenoble group provides a typical example of this sort of grass-roots revolt. V. Rancon, the local secretary, wrote to Duchene in August 1932 that 'the announcement of the world pacifist congress in Amsterdam has created some difficulty here'. The main problem—and this is a recurring theme across the length and breadth of France—was the role of the Communist Party in the Amsterdam movement. Rancon wrote that the local party was excluded from the Grenoble peace cartel because the latter organization, 'setting itself clearly against war, whether it be imperialist or revolutionary, cannot in principle admit a party of violence'. On a purely practical level, the local PC conducted a campaign against members of the cartel; and Rancon pointed out that it would therefore be most difficult for all concerned to have the Communists take a seat in its counsels. Later that autumn she wrote again to Duchene to announce that the local LIFPL had decided unanimously to maintain its own freedom and would not be joining the action committee formed in the wake of the Amsterdam Congress. These and similar concerns were voiced by sections in Chambéry, Le Havre, Caen, Nîmes, and Rouen.[65]

One of the clearest statements of principle and of dissent is that of the Colmar group during the spring of 1934. In a letter of 10 May the

[65] See V. Rancon to Duchene, Grenoble, 27 Aug. 1932; V. Rancon to Duchene, Grenoble, 10 Oct. 1932; and Duchene to Grenoble group, 21 Oct. 1932, all in BDIC/DD/FΔRés. 208/24. See also Margaret E. Dupont to Duchene, Chambéry, 3 May 1931 in BDIC/DD/FΔRés. 208/23, in which Dupont expressed her desire to found a centre for 'radical pacifism' in Chambéry after hearing Léo Wanner and Camille Drevet speak. In Mme Nicollet to Duchene, Chambéry, 27 Mar. 1933, the new local secretary asked what to respond to people who attacked the LIFPL as Communist inspired. She also mentioned the fact that in the Savoie the Ligue des mères et des éducatrices pour la paix had some 1,800 members whereas the LIFPL had only 28. Duchene responded (in Duchene to Nicollet, Paris, 4 Apr. 1933) that the LIFPL was independent of all parties, but that the public impression mentioned by Nicollet was probably due to the Ligue's adherence to the Amsterdam movement. As far as the Ligue des mères was concerned, Duchene stressed that it was not a genuinely radical pacifist group. Both of these letters are contained in BDIC/DD/FΔRés. 208/24. See also 'Rapport du groupe du Havre', 10 July 1934, in BDIC/DD/FΔRés. 208/15. See also Mme Noël (Le Havre group) to Duchene, 20 Aug. 1935 in BDIC/DD/FΔRés. 208/24. See also J. Lenormand (Caen group) to Duchene, 22 Apr. 1933 in BDIC/DD/FΔRés. 208/22. See also Groupe de Nîmes to Duchene, undated, in BDIC/DD/FΔRés. 208/16. See also 'Rapport du groupe de Rouen' by J. Decroix, secretary, 13 July 1934 in BDIC/DD/FΔRés. 208/15/10.

section threatened the probable resignation of the entire local committee and of a good portion of the membership if direct answers to direct questions were not forthcoming from Duchene and headquarters in Paris. The group said that for too long they had been kept in the dark about the policies of the Ligue and that they had received no answers to repeated enquiries. Of primary concern was what the group termed the fundamental principle of non-violence. 'Concessions seem to have been made in this area', they wrote. 'We have looked in vain in SOS and in the latest declarations of the French section for an absolute condemnation of civil war, which like any other war, renounces the solution of conflicts through conciliation and arbitration.' A further source of concern, flowing out of the question of non-violence, was the 'total adherence without restriction' of the French section to the committees issuing from the Amsterdam Congress. In the view of the Colmar group this was a betrayal of principle—indeed of the very principle which had attracted the sympathies of many of the members who were now prepared to leave.[66]

But the question of non-violence and the place of the Ligue within the larger Amsterdam-Pleyel movement were but the tip of the iceberg. The Ligue's entire political orientation of apparently blind support for Moscow was called into question. M. Burger, the Colmar group secretary, in a moment of some political insight, wrote plainly that in her view the Soviet regime was as intolerant and unjust as Fascism to those who sought liberty of conscience and of thought. She recognized that the Soviet Union had achieved tremendous success in bettering the social and economic side of life in Russia, but insisted that there were spiritual values in life which the regime did not uphold. It was the immediate, practical level of watching the local Communists in action which had been most revealing to her, however. She could not emphasize enough how much the activities of the great majority of Communist militants had harmed, and continued to harm, the cause of peace: 'They are a terrifying and disconcerting revelation of the spirit of violence which the "leaders" induce without scruple in the fanatical masses.'[67] The Colmar group felt that it could no longer support the principle of collaboration without conditions with a party which hated and persecuted everything that was near and dear to them. She complained that

[66] M. Burger to Duchene, Colmar, 10 May 1934 in BDIC/DD/FΔRés. 208/15.
[67] Ibid.

while *Pax internationale* (the international organ of the LIFPL) remained true to the principles of the Ligue, the French section seemed to have gone its own way. For Burger and the Colmar section the crisis which was rocking humanity was above all else a moral one, one which political and economic reforms alone would not solve. What was needed was a sort of moral revolution, in Russia as well as elsewhere. She warned Duchene not to misunderstand the motives behind her comments:

Do not think that all of this is greyness of formulas or dogmatism on our part. The principle of non-violence is a principle of life; if we abandon it in practice it will be the definitive failure of all action and of lasting reform . . . Do not think [either] that these criticisms formulated in our group come from capitalist *milieux*. Women who do not belong to the so-called bourgeoisie of our city are setting themselves against the pan-soviet tendencies of the French section.[68]

Duchene's response to this letter seemed to mollify the members of the Colmar group—at least temporarily. They adopted a wait-and-see approach in a subsequent letter to Duchene. Permanent damage had already been done, however. Burger told Duchene that she thought the whole incident had served to alienate, probably permanently, the practising Catholic women who had been part of the group. The group had decided to have nothing to do with the Amsterdam movement, which in any case was making very little headway in Colmar due to the lack of support for the Communists. Colmar left the issue open, deciding to wait and see what the outcome of the Zurich Congress would be. On her way back to France from Switzerland in the autumn of 1934, Duchene visited the Colmar group; and what she termed later to be an amicable divorce was decided upon. Some of the Colmar members remained attached directly to the Ligue on an individual basis; but Duchene thought that the rest of the group would be happier working with another organization more appropriate to local conditions, such as the Ligue des mères et des éducatrices pour la paix. A bloodless and friendly purge was thus effected, removing from the Ligue genuine pacifist elements who no longer viewed the world situation as Duchene did.[69]

[68] Ibid.
[69] M. Burger to Duchene, Colmar, 28 June 1934, in BDIC/DD/FΔRés. 208/15. See also Procès-verbal de l'Assemblée générale de la section française, Paris, 7 July 1935, in BDIC/DD/FΔRés. 208/16.

The Stalin–Laval Pact of 1935 provoked, not surprisingly, a similar crisis within the French section. The sudden about-face of the French Communist Party on the question of military service and support for the army provoked a great deal of consternation within the ranks of feminist pacifism. Camille Drevet, who had been the Ligue's international secretary, expressed surprise that Duchene placed before France only two alternatives, an *entente* with Hitler or one with Stalin. She asked whether in fact there was not a third, that of negotiating with 'everyone, including Germany, finally to begin the work of disarmament'. The Stalin–Laval Pact and with it Stalin's statement in favour of the French national defence constituted a crushing blow to the peace movement. As Drevet wrote, 'To see Marxists justify the national defence of a capitalist country really surpasses everything'.[70]

Whilst the Comité mondial des femmes was apparently prepared to accept the new directive, some parts of the French section of the LIFPL were not. Jeanne Petit of the Lyon group wrote to Duchene that 'the present marching orders of the World Committee concerning international politics are accepted with some difficulty here. The vast majority of the group wants to see the Ligue maintain the strictly pacifist position it has always had.'[71] And Petit promised to raise the matter at the AGM of the French section in July. The Lyon position was supported by the Saint Étienne group, whose secretary L. Leclerc wrote that they had been disappointed by a recent lecture given by Duchene. This had done nothing to help the local LIFPL section, but had given a great boost to the Saint Étienne group of the World Committee. The partiality of the Communist elements in the latter had provoked many negative observations but Leclerc said that her group would sort this problem out itself. More important was Duchene's support of the USSR's new international policy which Leclerc feared would 'one day force us into taking a position, and we do not want a war at any price, whatever it may be for'. Leclerc's letter made clear the sense of betrayal which the members felt: 'essentially', she wrote, 'we want to hold to the programme which converted us to the cause, and in this sense we share the view of the Lyon section completely'.[72]

Many of these views were summed up rather succinctly by Madeleine Vernet, the founder of the Paris pacifist group and

[70] Camille Drevet to Duchene, Claret-Toulon, 30 May 1935, in BDIC/DD/FΔRés. 208/16.   [71] J. Petit to Duchene, Lyon, 4 July 1935, in BDIC/DD/FΔRés. 208/16.   [72] L. Leclerc to Duchene, Saint Étienne, 5 July 1935. In BDIC/DD/FΔRés. 208/16.

newspaper of the same name, La Volonté de paix. She wrote to Jeanne Challaye in July 1935 asking her to voice her concern at the AGM of the French section which was to be held on the seventh. Vernet felt that she had come to the point of resigning from the Ligue, but had refrained from doing so because of her friendships with some members. But, she wrote,

I find that the attitude taken by the French section, reflected in *SOS*, simply does not befit the Ligue. To make the case for dictatorship and civil war cannot be the position of an organization which has for its name 'League for Peace and Freedom' ... Unfortunately divisions and political quarrelling have invaded everything. Since 1932 the Ligue has become the reflection of Amsterdam, thus losing all its personality. The fight for disarmament has fallen by the wayside. [Instead] anti-Hitlerian propaganda is pursued. Now this is not for us. We owe it to ourselves to seek appeasement first in order to arrive at peace later. I have no sympathy for Hitler, but his victory in Germany is the work of the governments of the allied countries of 1914.[73]

Not all groups objected to the evolving political orientation of the French section, however. The Marseille group was one which Duchene could count on to exceed even her own political trajectory. Lucienne Leleu, the local secretary, wrote to Duchene in 1934 concerning the approach to take in the face of the rise of domestic and international Fascism. In her view there was absolutely no place for neutrality and the Ligue needed desperately to delineate its doctrine. She saw its condemnation of violence during the Great War and after as an idea born of sentiment. She rejected the notion of neutrality in the case of civil war and declared that the Ligue must be with the workers:

The first confusion to clear up ... is above all that of refusing to see that violence is not something found only in war, but is at the base even of the present regime, and that it is not the unique, or even principal result of gunshots. The revolt against war which was the basis of the action of the Ligue, if it is conscious and not merely sentimental, if it is a revolt against violence in all areas ... must be a struggle against the present capitalist regime. A conscious pacifist must today be a revolutionary ...[74]

---

[73] Madeleine Vernet to Jeanne Challaye, 5 July 1935, in BDIC/DD/FΔRés. 208/16. This letter was read by Challaye to the 1935 annual general meeting of the French section. See the Procès-verbal de l'Assemblée générale de la section française, 1935, 1, in BDIC/DD/FΔRés. 208/16.

[74] Lucienne Leleu to Duchene, Marseille, 12 Apr. 1934 in BDIC/DD/FΔRés. 208/15.

She regarded the coming civil, partisan, class-based violence with astonishing equanimity, saying that Western Europeans were not saints 'à la façon de Gandhi'. The refusal of violence 'signified nothing' for Leleu.[75]

The ideological divisions within the French section described above were also manifestations of generational differences in the approach to the problem of peace. In a movement such as pacifism which seemed to be dominated by the pre-war generation (if subjective impressions are anything to go by in describing a movement which left such incomplete records), the French section of the LIFPL stands out as one group which seemed to recruit younger members. This younger membership contributed to the divisions within the French section, and between it and the rest of the Ligue. As early as 1932 for example Duchene declared that the Ligue Congress had 'disappointed youth because it had not adopted a radical manifesto'.[76] Lida Gustava Heymann thought then that youth must trace its own path in life[77] but three years later she admitted that the Ligue lacked 'young, energetic blood'.[78] There is no doubt that the LIFPL was an ageing organization. Even given the lack of eligible men in post-war France, the French delegation of eighteen unmarried and only six married women at the 1934 Zurich Congress of the Ligue must have seemed young in comparison with those of other national sections.[79]

The equation of youth and radicalism is perhaps a valid one. The youthful French delegation in Zurich was remarkably disappointed by what it heard and saw—to the point where the two representatives of the Marseille group actually walked out of the Congress in disgust.[80] Four other French delegates had already left the Congress by that point, disappointed too at their first contact with the International.[81] One of the delegates who remained, Germaine Baurez of the Ardèche group, wrote that those who stayed behind did so because Duchene was 'there to preserve the avant-garde spirit in

[75] L. Leleu to Duchene, Marseille, 21 June 1934. In BDIC/DD/FΔRés. 208/15.
[76] Procès-verbal, Comité exécutif international, Grenoble, 20–2 May 1932, 1. In BDIC/DD/FΔRés. 206/May 1932.   [77] Lida Gustava Heymann ibid.
[78] Lida Gustava Heymann in Minutes, International Executive Committee, London, 25–30 Mar. 1935, 4. In BDIC/DD/FΔRés. 206/Mar. 1935.
[79] List of Delegates, Zurich Congress, 1934. In BDIC/DD/FΔRés. 208/5/7.
[80] Mentioned in 'Intervention que voulait faire G. Baurez, déléguée de l'Ardèche (France) à la dernière séance du Congrès, VIIIème Congrès de la LIFPL', Zurich, 3–9 Sept. 1934. In BDIC/DD/FΔRés. 205/8/5.   [81] Ibid.

the French section'. She and the other remaining young French delegates left Zurich 'with a feeling of *disaffection* towards the Ligue and little confident in the future of an organization which no longer knows how to give satisfaction to the young'. And she commented sadly that some of the delegates present were opposed to any new ideas and could not or would not see things objectively.[82]

In another speech, Y. Paquet condemned the 'fetishism of words' which seemed to afflict the Ligue and its 'sterile formalism'. She said that the young had come to the Congress to learn, to receive directives for future actions, and that instead they had heard little to allow them to say 'now we know where we are going'. The question of violence and non-violence was all word play which had no bearing on reality. If youth could be damned for lacking in idealism, it was because it knew that 'real idealism is sometimes the sacrifice of idealism, an effort of living in the present, in reality with the oppressed of all nations'.[83]

Duchene recognized the danger inherent in allowing youth to distance itself from the struggle for peace. She told the Zurich Congress that organizations grow old more quickly than individuals, especially in a world evolving as rapidly as it was in the 1930s. And if these same organizations became immobilized in outdated formulas, they condemned themselves to a quick death. 'In order that they conserve their vitality,' she wrote, 'in order that they may renew themselves through the support of contact with youth, they must constantly maintain contact with reality and remain supple enough to evolve.'[84] But as we have already had ample occasion to observe, this suppleness was selective; and evolution tended towards revolution. In this same speech, Duchene defined the task of the 'true defender of Peace' as the preparation of minds for the acceptance of the 'idea that a transformation of society is *necessary, inevitable* and at the same time, to hasten this transformation by destroying the evil institutions which block human progress'.[85] That was the long-term goal but in the short term the present situation demanded a response based less on 'orthodox pacifist ideology' than on an 'effective practical, incessant struggle against war and Fascism'.[86]

---

[82] Ibid. See also 'Autour du Congrès de Zurich', *En vigie*, 1 (Oct. 1935), 4–5.

[83] 'Discours de Mlle Paquet, Congrès de Zurich', 1934, in BDIC/DD/FΔRés. 205/8/5.

[84] 'Intervention de G. Duchene, Congrès de Zurich', 1934, in BDIC/DD/FΔRés. 205/8/5.   [85] Ibid.   [86] Ibid.

The dissent expressed in letters to Duchene from across France began to make its appearance at the annual general meeting of the French section in 1934 in a discussion of a dispute between the La Rochelle group and the local Amsterdam committee.[87] But it is in July 1935 that the rifts within the French section became readily apparent at the annual meeting. Gabrielle Duchene protested to the assembled members that she could not understand where the impression had come from that the LIFPL had changed its philosophy or orientation. But changes there certainly were. Duchene spoke of the 'amicable divorce' which had been effected between the section and the Colmar and Mulhouse groups. Jeanne Challaye read a letter from Madeleine Vernet criticizing the present political line of the French section. These criticisms found their echo in a discussion on the Stalin communiqué and a report by Jeanne Alexandre which declared that in her view the Soviet Union had changed its foreign policy from 'one of peace to a policy based rather on force which repudiates disarmament as the Red Army grows, and that renounces revision of the Treaty of Versailles'.[88] The minutes record Alexandre's view that

the declarations of Stalin consecrate the traditional policy of the capitalists which is a policy of armed coalition, the re-establishment of the division of the world into two camps, etc.

She is certain that 'mutual assistance' with Russia is an assistance based on arms and that we have the right to raise doubts about the sincerity of Russia as regards peace. This pact that is supposedly open to Germany, do we know on what basis Germany will be asked to join it, . . .

Given the situation, she believed that the Ligue must take a position with regard to the policy of the USSR, with clarity and precision. If the Ligue wants to remain what it was in 1915—first and foremost a league for Peace—she demands that it pronounce itself for peace.[89]

And she concluded by demanding the *redressement* of the political line of the French section. This provoked a long and at times acrimonious debate, at the end of which Duchene asked for a vote on several policy questions. The Assembly passed a resolution (although

[87] Procès-verbal de l'Assemblée générale de la section française de la LIFPL, 14 July 1934, 2. In BDIC/DD/FΔRés. 208/15.

[88] Procès-verbal de l'Assemblée générale de la section française de la LIFPL, 7 July 1935, 5. In BDIC/DD/FΔRés. 208/16. See also Madeleine Vernet to Jeanne Challaye, 5 July 1935, in BDIC/DD/FΔRés. 208/16.

[89] Procès-verbal, 1935, 5.

with some negative votes), expressing its belief in 'the desire of the USSR for peace, as demonstrated by the Pact'. A resolution stating that the 'pacts of mutual assistance [were] a measure for the safeguarding of peace' was apparently also passed although with several abstentions, and a motion in favour of unilateral disarmament proposed by Camille Drevet was defeated.[90]

The dissent of 1933–5 became a full-fledged rebellion in 1936 and the most explosive challenge to Duchene's conception of the Ligue's work and her continued leadership of the French section. In an immediate sense the confrontations of 1936 can be linked to the expulsion of the executive committee of the Lyon group and all members sympathizing with it. But this incident, unparalleled in the history of the French section, also served to galvanize an entire body of opposition within the section which manifested itself at the 1936 annual meeting.

First, to deal with the purge of the Lyon group. It seems that trouble had been brewing for some time. In 1934 or early 1935 Léo Wanner of the Lyon group stopped production of the section's organ, *SOS*, for reasons which are unclear and refused to give up her proprietary rights to the title. This resulted in a long hiatus while Duchene searched for a new title, and also for someone to take over the job of editing and publishing it. The problem was finally resolved in 1935 and *En vigie* made its appearance.[91]

The immediate origins of the affray lie in what Duchene termed 'the ironical presentation of, or the attacks on, the actions of the national or international bodies of the LIFPL' in the Lyon group's new bulletin, *Rassemblement des femmes pour la paix et la liberté*.[92] The offending lines, ironical perhaps, but only mildly offensive, read:

The French section . . . thinks that in putting pressure on our rulers, these gentlemen will end up listening to us and will do something in favour of peace. (Our comrades no doubt have not heard of the Rome agreements). In this hope, the leaders [of the Ligue] are using their resources and their time to make representation to more or less important notables, to circulate petitions, etc. . . . Better yet, is it not a question of a forthcoming pilgrimage to the cemeteries of the Nord to protest against the war which is returning? The results of this action seem to us to go so much against the goal to

[90] Ibid.
[91] Report on the section's journal, ibid. 3.
[92] Procès-verbal de l'Assemblée générale de la section française, 27–8 June 1936, 17. In BDIC/DD/FΔRés. 208/17.

be attained that we have been dismayed at the thought of such an enter-prise . . .[93]

The French executive committee informed the Lyon group that it considered it inadmissible to make such comments in a journal sold to the public. Receiving no undertaking from the Lyon group that it would mend its ways, Duchene, L. Maréchal, and Gertrud Baer (1890–1981),[94] the international vice-president, descended on Lyon for a special general meeting on 26 February. They were 'very badly received', however, and the 'aggressive tension of part of the assem-bled audience did not permit the objective exchange of views that had been hoped for'.[95]

The real reasons for Duchene's annoyance become clear in a letter written to her by the Lyon committee in the wake of this meeting. She had apparently accused the Lyon group of being a 'branch of the Trotskyist party' because the group's new secretary, Berthe Joly, belonged to a Trotskyist minority group. Joly had only reluctantly accepted the position for fear that this very sort of confrontation might occur, but she had the support of the entire Lyon group. The Lyon committee charged that Duchene had made a tendentious interpretation of their doctrine, which they claimed was nevertheless in complete harmony with the fundamental principles of the LIFPL. By a large majority the Lyon group had decided to engage itself 'in the revolutionary work which seems to dismay you so much'. They were 'outraged' by Duchene's 'suffocating tone' at the meeting in Lyon and hoped for better things from the 'proven militant who in other times knew how to lead the fight for peace in complete independence'. They declared that they would continue to work loyally for the goals of the Ligue 'which the national office reminds us of constantly, but from which it deduces methods of action little in harmony with them'. They concluded by accusing Duchene and the Paris office of 'incoherence', 'sterile polemics', and an unwillingness to tolerate dissent and criticism.[96]

Andrée Jouve responded to this letter on the part of the executive,

---

[93] *Rassemblement des femmes pour la paix et la liberté* (Lyon), 1, cited ibid. 17.

[94] See D. v. Westernhagen, 'Gertrud Baer', in Helmut Donat and Karl Holl (eds.), *Die Friedensbewegung: Organisierter Pazifismus in Deutschland, Österreich und in der Schweiz* (Düsseldorf: ECON Taschenbuch Verlag, 1983), 35.

[95] Duchene in Procès-verbal, 1936, 17.

[96] Le Groupe de Lyon de la LIFPL à Gabrielle Duchene, secrétaire nationale, 18 Mar. 1936, cited *in extenso* ibid. 17–19.

quite rightly condemning the insulting tone of the Lyon group's attack, but leaving untouched the substantive questions it raised.[97] In a subsequent number of their journal, the Lyon group protested again against 'the abuse of power at the summit of our organization' and against the 'intolerable' participation of '"our" presidents and vice-presidents ... in the chauvinist campaign which has been unfolding across the country for several weeks, defending the policies of French imperialism in the Franco-German conflict'.[98] Extracts from the minutes of the special general meeting published by the Lyon group make clearer though what the dispute was all about. The Lyon group seemed to fear that the Popular Front was evolving into a *union sacrée* which they would never accept. This was why they were fighting against the Popular Front which in their view had 'no other goal, fundamentally, than to effect a coalition of the workers with a view to having them approve the policies of French imperialism under the cover of the "defence of the USSR" or of the "antifascist struggle"'.[99]

Joly declared that it was because the action of the Paris office was so sterile that the Lyon group had decided to throw itself into the genuinely revolutionary struggle. The wife of Léon Emery wanted to know why Duchene had 'done an about-turn' and was now supporting the Franco-Soviet Pact. She also wanted to know why the French section supported the Popular Front. Another 'comrade' demanded to know why the Ligue had suddenly stopped its campaign against the two-year military service law after the Stalin declaration. The Lyon group accused both Duchene and Baer of having no confidence in proletarian sanctions but of putting their faith instead in the bourgeois governments. The Lyon women remained 'convinced that the whole of the policies of the Popular Front, such as they are expressed, can only favour the war psychosis to the profit of the capitalists'.[100]

This was the straw that broke the camel's back. In a national executive committee meeting on 10 June, it was decided to purge the Lyon executive and all members of that group sympathizing with it.

---

[97] Jouve's response on behalf of the executive committee is given ibid. 20.
[98] *Rassemblement des femmes pour la paix et la liberté*, 4: 3, cited ibid. 21.
[99] Cited ibid. Cf. 'Extraits du Rapport d'Andrée Jouve "Nos tâches dans le Front populaire", présenté à la Conférence nationale, 28 Juin 1936' in BDIC/DD/FΔRés. 208/17.
[100] Cited in Procès-verbal, 1936, 22.

Duchene denied vehemently that she had changed her views on disarmament or working-class sanctions and repeated her by now rather sterile assertion that the LIFPL took orders from no political party.[101] It seems that she was perhaps reluctant to go through with the purge because the topic was again discussed at the AGM in July and the expulsions did not finally occur until November. To draw the whole affair out even further, it seems to have been raised yet again in a session of the International Executive Committee in a meeting closed to non-voting consultative members in Bruges in April 1937. No minutes exist for this meeting.[102]

The AGM of the French section in late June 1936 was thus an important one. It saw the most comprehensive attack yet made by the dissenters on the direction the Ligue seemed to be taking. Sixteen groups were represented;[103] and Clara Ragaz, the international vice-president, was also there. Duchene knew that the outcome of the meeting would determine the future course of the French section and her control of it. As she wrote in late June in one of a series of letters to people likely to support her view, 'we have alas in our Ligue, too, a struggle of opposing tendencies similar to that within the Comité de vigilance des intellectuels'; in her view the very future of the French section was at stake and she asked for the presence at the AGM, and support, of elements favourable to her position.[104]

Much of the meeting was taken up in a naked power struggle between Duchene and the Paris secretariat on the one hand, and a collection of provincial groups trying to effect changes in the French section's direction on the other. Their efforts bore little fruit; and indeed, the 'coalition' fell apart when the story of the Lyon group's imminent purge was strategically made public on the Sunday afternoon. The combined efforts of the Nîmes, Montpellier, Rouen, Le

[101] See text of two notes sent to the executive committee of the Lyon group by the national executive committee following its meeting of 10 June 1936. Both are contained ibid. 22–3.

[102] Copies of the form letter of exclusion addressed to members of the Lyon group are in BDIC/DD/FΔRés. 208/17. See the agenda for the closed special session of the International Executive Committee, Bruges, 5 Apr. 1937, in BDIC/DD/FΔRés. 206. See also Procès-verbal de la réunion du comité exécutif de la section française, 10 June 1936, in BDIC/DD/FΔRés. 208/17.

[103] The sixteen groups represented were: Drôme-Ardèche, Le Havre, Rouen, Arles, Lyon, La Rochelle, Châlon-sur-Saône, Dijon, Chambéry, Nîmes, Roubaix, Troyes, Seine, Seine-et-Marne, Seine-et-Oise, Paris.

[104] From a collection of copies of letters from Duchene to unspecified persons in BDIC/DD/FΔRés. 208/17. Quotation extracted from letter dated 25 June 1936.

Havre, La Rochelle, Lyon, and Arles groups effectively to disenfranchize the executive committee fell apart as the Lyon saga was revealed by an astute Duchene. One after another, groups distanced themselves from the affair, while struggling lamely to insist on the need for changes in the section's management and orientation.[105] There is no doubting the feeling of discontent within the membership of the French section. The minutes make abundantly clear the sense of alienation experienced by most groups. On substantive issues, too, there was hardly unanimity. The Montpellier group criticized the text of the letter sent to the president of the Assembly of the League of Nations, condemning the remilitarization of the Rhineland, which they did not believe was in conformity with the Ligue's principles.[106] Camille Drevet expressed her belief in the tremendous work of the English women for peace. Both of these statements reveal that the French section's confrontations at the international level of the Ligue did not represent the totality of the views of its membership.[107]

This was precisely the point. By 1936 it was apparent that Duchene had a very rigid idea of what constituted proper action for peace, and her attitude to the French section gradually became one of rule by fiat. As a disenchanted woman in Valence wrote to her later that year, 'if I had known that in such a Ligue the orders came "from above" and were given by an international executive committee, I should never have joined'.[108] This attitude was evident in the discussion provoked by Duchene's paper on 'Les Deux Conceptions du pacifisme' already mentioned above. She made it clear that she believed that in a political organization like the Ligue, only the barest minimum of dissent from its policies could be tolerated. She condemned the 'divisionniste' faction which she claimed was ruining the work of the LIFPL by its aggressive and violent opposition. In her opinion if members could not see their way clear to working within the Ligue, they should consider leaving it and joining a more amenable group such as the Ligue internationale des combattants de la paix. As for the others, they were quite welcome to remain in the Ligue as long as they did not hinder its action. The true pacifist, she

---

[105] Procès-verbal de l'Assemblée générale de la section française, 1936, 1–3, 6, and 12. In BDIC/DD/FΔRés. 208/17.
[106] This is most likely the letter strongly condemning the L.o.N.'s inaction in the face of Hitler's remilitarization of the Rhineland mentioned above. Mentioned ibid. 4.
[107] Ibid. 4.
[108] 'LM' to Duchene, Valence, 12 Oct. 1936. Typescript copy in BDIC/DD/FΔRés. 208/17.

claimed, must refuse to contribute to division within an organization which had already given so many proofs of its devotion to peace. She defined the Ligue for perhaps the first time as a body akin to a political party, with a doctrine which had to be imposed on the membership. In this she was both right and wrong, both reiterating an old Ligue principle and creating a new and dangerous precedent at the same time. The LIFPL had always insisted on genuine pacifist conviction in its members—this principle was at the heart of the 'aims' debates of the 1920s which will be discussed in the next chapter—but it had equally held itself above the level of party political strife. Duchene herself had often said at international meetings that if members disagreed on methods, they certainly did not on the goals pursued by the LIFPL. But at some time in the mid-thirties it is obvious that the question of means and ends, of goals and methods fused together in Duchene's mind and she found it increasingly impossible to brook contradiction. Here in the 1936 annual general meeting one can arguably see signs of the faint Stalinization of Gabrielle Duchene and the French section. As Camille Drevet tried in vain to make clear, the *real* question was not whether there were Trotskyists in the Ligue or not, but simply what policy the Ligue should adopt.[109]

The problem of the Lyon group did not disappear after the 1936 annual meeting. Rather it continued to rear its head for some time to come. The French section even went to the lengths of taking legal advice in order to recover section funds held by the Lyon group at the time of the purge.[110]

Having scored a somewhat Pyrrhic victory at the 1936 meeting, however, Duchene could afford to appear slightly more indulgent in her dealings with dissent. With the necessary political victory behind her, she reverted to the essentially generous and democratic spirit of former years. For example, in a meeting of the Paris region in November 1936, called to choose representatives to a special general meeting, Duchene supported the inclusion of Jeanne Alexandre in the group's delegation because she represented the minority tend-

[109] Procès-verbal de l'Assemblée générale de la section française, 1936, 7. BDIC/DD/FΔRés. 208/17.
[110] See Compte-rendu de la réunion du comité exécutif de la section française du 16/7/36 in BDIC/DD/FΔRés. 208/17. See also Procès-verbal de la réunion du comité exécutif du 13 avril 1937 in BDIC/DD/FΔRés. 208/18. See also 'Activités de la section française, Assemblée générale annuelle, 15 et 16 mai 1937' in *En vigie*, 6–7 (Oct.–Nov. 1937), 4–5.

ency. She also attempted to ensure that the French section's executive should contain a member from the 'opposition' and that groups interested in sending delegates to the Ligue's 1937 Congress should seek, in so far as was possible, to maintain a balance in their representation.[111]

But the spirit of fair play and equity which Duchene belatedly tried to reimpose on the French section was not enough or came too late. The fractious *fronde* led by Jeanne Alexandre finally separated from the rest of the Ligue in September 1938, abandoning what they called 'le beau mot liberté' and creating simply a Ligue des femmes pour la paix. As Duchene wrote in a special number of *En vigie* in March 1939, this latter statement revealed better than any long commentary the irreducible differences between the two groups. As for the women remaining true to the LIFPL ideal, 'we are more certain than ever that to abandon the defence of freedom is not to serve the cause of peace, but rather to betray it. This is why, together with the International, our Ligue will continue to put *defence of Freedom* and *defence of Peace* on the same level.'[112] Schism had finally come to the bicephalous French section—schism almost inevitable under the pressure of real political events.

The trauma of the LIFPL French section underlines what Michel Bilis has called, with regard to the Socialist Party, the 'untenable dilemma' of French pacifism.[113] The French section's acute sense of political reality finally forced a divorce between the desire for peace and that for freedom and justice. The political and pacifist trajectories had separated, or at any rate were no longer formed of parallel lines. As the Nazi menace became daily more palpable, French political pacifism became increasingly conscious of the need for unity (which it never achieved), collective security, and thus the possibility of having to defend militarily one's cherished conceptions of liberty. With each succeeding crisis in the thirties, the sands of *intégralité* poured faster through the pacifist hourglass towards September 1939.

[111] See Procès-verbal, réunion des membres de la région parisienne de la LIFPL du mercredi 4 novembre 1936, in BDIC/DD/FΔRés. 208/17. See also Circulaire no. 22 (Apr. 1937) in BDIC/DD/FΔRés. 208/18. See also 'Avis important' in *En vigie*, 4–5 (Apr. 1937), 9. See also 'Activités de la section française: Assemblée générale annuelle, 15 et 16 mai 1937' in *En vigie*, 6–7 (Oct.–Nov. 1937), 4–5.

[112] 'Avis important', *En vigie*, 10–11–12 (Mar. 1939), 1.

[113] The phrase is from the title of Michel Bilis's book *Socialistes et pacifistes 1933–1939: Ou l'intenable dilemme des socialistes français* (Paris: Syros, 1979).

11. France meets the International

Whatever the actual size of the French section, there is no doubting its importance at the international level of the Ligue, and also as an influential part of the larger peace movement in France. As has been noted above, at various times in the twenties and thirties the leading women of the French section served in different capacities on the international executive of the Ligue. Thus, despite its relatively small numbers and lack of financial power, the French played a disproportionately important role within the international councils of the LIFPL. Primarily through Duchene, the French section developed a specific approach to the problems of peace and the answers which it hoped pacifism would provide. In this endeavour they were often joined by the members of the German section. The community of spirit between the French and German sections became one of the two poles around which the theoretical and practical debates within the Ligue revolved during the interwar period. The other pole was, perhaps not surprisingly, epitomized above all by the ideas of the British section, with the Scandinavian countries and the American section playing increasingly important supporting roles as the shadows lengthened over Europe in the thirties.

AIMS, POLITICAL ORIENTATION, AND PROBLEMS OF AUTHORITARIAN LEADERSHIP

It was perhaps inevitable that in such an international organization disagreements should quickly arise over goals and methods. Hardly had the euphoria of the first post-war Congress in Zurich in 1919 subsided than discussions began which gradually became an at times acrimonious debate for the heart and soul of the Ligue. This debate spanned almost the entire interwar period and saw the British and French sections locked in an almost permanent confrontation from about 1924 onwards. If, as John Cairns has put it, the British in the interwar years were 'a nation of shopkeepers in search of a suitable France',[1] it is certainly also true that the French were a nation in search of a suitable Albion. The debates centred on three significant areas: the question of aims or goals for the Ligue, the debate over the nature of the Ligue and its executive—should it be national or international, delegative or leadership-orientated—and finally, the question of policy—whether the Ligue should be politically *engaged*, or rather pursue a primarily educative role.

The debate over the aims or object of the Ligue is one which highlights the different approaches taken by the various sections to the question of war and peace. As early as 1920, the International Executive Committee was expressing its concern that new associate members should sign a statement of 'our object' in order to effect a kind of pacifist quality control.[2] By 1923 at its meeting in Dresden, the question seemed to have become more acute, with the English pacifist Catherine Marshall (1880–1961)[3] remarking that the resolutions passed at The Hague in 1915 'are not any longer a real guarantee of pacifistic convictions, especially not in Central and Eastern Europe'.[4] She urged that sections ask their members to subscribe to a statement of aims drawn up by the American Emily Greene Balch (1867–1961),[5] which

---

[1] John C. Cairns, 'A Nation of Shopkeepers in Search of a Suitable France, 1919–40', *American Historical Review*, 79/3 (June 1974), 710–43.

[2] Minutes, IEC Meeting, Geneva, 1–4 June 1920, 14. In BDIC/DD/FΔRés. 206/June 1920.

[3] Marshall was a founding member of the LIFPL, and was also active in a variety of other pacifist organizations, notably the No-Conscription Fellowship. See Jo Vellacott, 'Catherine E. Marshall', in Harold Josephson (ed.), *Biographical Dictionary of Modern Peace Leaders* (Westport, London: Greenwood Press, 1985), 606–7.

[4] Cited in Minutes, IEC Meeting, Dresden, 1–5 Sept. 1923. In BDIC/DD/FΔRés. 206/Sept. 1923.

[5] Emily Greene Balch studied at Bryn Mawr College, and then at the Sorbonne, what later became Radcliffe College, the University of Chicago, and the University of Berlin. She was active as a social worker in Boston in the early 1890s, and from 1896 to 1918 taught economics at Wellesley College. Balch was one of some forty American women who attended the first meeting of the LIFPL in Holland in 1915. Largely because of her increasing pacifist involvement, her contract at Wellesley was terminated in 1918. Balch then became the first international secretary-treasurer of the LIFPL, effectively setting up its operating headquarters in Geneva. In 1946 she shared the Nobel Peace Prize with the ecumenical clergyman John R. Mott. See Justus D. Doenecke, 'Emily Greene Balch', in Josephson, *Dictionary*, 50–3.

included the phrase that the members of the LIFPL opposed 'all war'.[6]

But it was in 1924 that the debate over the aims of the Ligue began to become acute, and it is from that year that one can date the beginnings of the Anglo-French rivalries within the Ligue which found expression in the differing conceptions of the nature of peace work and the direction the Ligue ought to be taking. For most of the rest of the decade the battle-lines were drawn over the question of the admissibility of 'defensive' wars, with the French taking the more absolutely pacifist stand that they were not to be countenanced. As Andrée Jouve underlined forcefully in a letter to Kathleen Courtney in December 1924, 'we cannot accept partisans of defensive wars in the Ligue'. The French section had been formed while the German invasion was in full swing, and it was precisely because of their opposition to both defensive and offensive wars that the women of the LIFPL found themselves in disagreement with almost all French women. Jouve wrote that 'they would all be with us today if we declared ourselves only against offensive wars or wars of conquest'. And she added sarcastically 'we all know what the distinction between these two types of wars is worth'. The Ligue certainly had no need of members who would 'resign at the first incursion of an airplane'.[7]

The following summer at the International Executive Committee meeting in Innsbruck, the British section attacked the rewording of the object which had occurred at the Ligue's Congress in Washington in 1924. The Washington object specifically laid down that the Ligue was opposed to both offensive and defensive wars. Together with the Polish, Scandinavian, and Czech sections, the British protested that the new wording of the aims made the work of the Ligue in Britain extremely difficult.[8] By February 1926 the American section had decided that it, too, wanted the Washington object altered to remove the reference to defensive wars, and a concerted move began to amend the Ligue's constitution.[9] As Duchene pointed out, it appeared a bit illogical that the American section was prepared to accept a condemnation of 'all wars', but not of 'defensive wars'.[10]

---

[6] Minutes, IEC Meeting, Dresden, 1–5 Sept. 1923. In BDIC/DD/FΔRés. 206/Sept. 1923.

[7] Andrée Jouve to Kathleen Courtney, Dec. 1924, in BDIC/DD/FΔRés. 208/5.

[8] Minutes, IEC Meeting, Innsbruck, 10–15 July 1925, in BDIC/DD/FΔRés. 206/ July 1925.

[9] See Minutes, IEC Meeting, Paris, 6–10 Feb. 1926 in BDIC/DD/FΔRés. 206/Feb. 1926.

[10] Ibid. 5–6.

Some members thought that the Ligue's role should be to educate women about war and peace, and in so doing gradually bring them into the full work of the Ligue. But as Andrée Jouve made clear, the Ligue had been founded in wartime and had taken a very unpopular stand which it would be now rather difficult to go back on. She claimed that there was no 'pacific' association in France more radical than the French section of the LIFPL which represented 'integral pacifism'. She recognized that the British and American sections had a different way of working, but argued that 'we do not fulfil our goal if we do not hold to the very firm ideal which was set at the beginning'; this was necessary if a sense of direction was to be maintained.[11]

At the Ligue's Dublin Congress in 1926 the first great revisionist debate on the Ligue's aims and its structure occurred. Duchene agreed to accept a modification of the aims, removing the reference to defensive wars and replacing it with the more anodyne phrase that the LIFPL strove to unite 'women in all countries who are opposed to every kind of war, exploitation, and oppression, and who work for universal disarmament and for the solution of conflicts by the recognition of human solidarity, by conciliation and arbitration, by world co-operation, and by the establishment of social, political, and economic justice for all, without distinction of sex, race, class, or creed'.[12] But she was adamant that the international character of the Ligue be enshrined in a second paragraph which stated that the work of all of the national sections should be based 'upon the Statements adopted and the Resolutions passed by the International Congresses of the League'.[13]

The divergences of viewpoint may have been due to differences in national temperament. Catherine Marshall seemed to think that there were fundamental differences in outlook between the English section on the one hand, and the French and German sections on the other. She wrote to Duchene in 1926

... this much I can say, perhaps: I think there is a rather fundamental difference between the way the British Committee . . . regards the task and function of our League, and the way in which the French Section, and again the German Section, regards it. English people in general, and the women who form the greater part of our membership in particular, are inclined to be very much absorbed in the political *aspect* of things, and to attach less

[11] Cited, in French version of minutes, 5, appended to ibid.
[12] Minutes, Dublin Congress, 8–15 July 1926, 7. In BDIC/DD/FΔRés. 205/5/4.
[13] Ibid.

importance to thought and feelings and more importance to *action*, than is the case with your countrymen and the Germans. We tend to be not very much interested in the processes that prepare and determine events, and to wake up only when the events are actually happening and there is something to be *done*, here and now. We tend to dislike too much theorising . . .[14]

Marshall's analysis of the French section may be applicable to the situation in the mid-twenties, but as will become clear later on, it did not apply to the thirties when the French section became avowedly political whilst struggling to maintain its veneer of impartiality *vis-à-vis* the political parties. Even with regard to the twenties, Marshall's comments underestimate the broad interests and strengths of the French section. As early as 1921, for example, Duchene had written in her yearly report to the Ligue's secretariat in Geneva that 'unfortunately, the majority of the women who have joined us through conviction are *too busy* [emphasis added] with political action to work for the pacifist cause elsewhere other than within their party political groups. Their action is no less useful for that, but that of the Section suffers from it.'[15] The French section was always politically conscious and active, but it is true to say that in the twenties it placed more emphasis on activities like the summer schools, the preparation of the *Cahiers de la paix* (an activity which was once likened to the intellectual preparation of the Revolution of 1789[16]), aid to famine-stricken areas of Europe, and so on.

The question of the nature of the Ligue had already been raised briefly in Dresden in 1923 in a discussion of the 'Competence of the Executive Committee to take action for the whole League'.[17] But it was in 1927 at the Executive's September meeting in Geneva that the issue became an important one. The British section desired a change in the method of voting at the International Executive which would see the vote given to the consultative members from each of the sections, in addition to the vote already held by the International Executive members duly elected by the congresses. Duchene, on behalf of the French section, was completely opposed to this change. In her view, it would weaken or destroy the international character

[14] C. E. Marshall to G. Duchene, 29 Jan. 1926 in BDIC/DD/FΔRés. 206/Feb. 1926.
[15] Extraits du Rapport sur l'action de la section française au cours du dernier exercice, 1920–1921, adressé au comité central de la Ligue. In BDIC/DD/FΔRés. 206/Sept. 1923.
[16] Duchene's comment in Minutes, IEC Meeting, Dresden, 1–5 Sept. 1923. BDIC/DD/FΔRés. 208/2. [17] Ibid.

of the Ligue and leave it changed into a body of national groups.[18] The problem with national representation was that it would give too much power to 'recently enfranchised' nations which had not yet evolved enough in Duchene's view to be able to work effectively. Sections such as Greece and Bulgaria were still too imbued with a 'nationalisme aigu' and needed careful nurturing up to the level of the more advanced nations. Duchene considered the debate over the method of representation in the Ligue perhaps even more important than the debate about the object:

On this change—or on the maintenance of the present rules—depends the future orientation [of the Ligue.] We have been asked to act only by unanimous decision. But if unanimity can be achieved on the *philosophical* level, it cannot be at the level of *action*. Action is life—life is the multiplicity of actions and reactions, diversity.

Unanimity ceases to be possible in action, it would lead fatally to impotence.

. . . If our Ligue wishes to continue to be what it has been until now: a sower of new ideas; if it wishes to introduce new principles into the social, economic, and political domains, it cannot pretend to unanimity. It must choose: *action*, that is to say struggle and decisions taken by the *majority* or: unanimity in nothingness.[19]

She felt the issue to be so important that she threatened the secession of the French section if it should come to pass.[20]

The problem reared its head again the following year in Geneva with another debate on the constitution, prompting Duchene to ask what the other sections' conception of the Ligue was. For her it was to be an avant-garde international organization, but she suspected that for others it might be conceived in more conservative national terms.[21] Madeleine Rolland, one of the French section's consultative members, echoed Duchene's comments, saying that 'an avant-garde society signifies an absolutely pacifist society, and we must be very clear about what we would do in case of war and if we are opposed to all wars . . . the LIF would prefer to be a small group of absolutely pacifist women . . . a small group of convinced pacifists can have a real influence.'[22]

[18] See typescript remarks of Duchene dated Sept. 1927 in BDIC/DD/FΔRés. 206/Sept. 1927.   [19] Ibid.

[20] Minutes, IEC Meeting, Geneva, 11 Sept. 1927, afternoon session, 4. In BDIC/ DD/FΔRés. 206/Sept. 1927.

[21] Procès-verbal, comité exécutif international, Geneva, 20–4 Mar. 1928, 7. In BDIC/DD/FΔRés. 206/Mar. 1928.   [22] Ibid. 8.

The differences between the French and British sections on the question of principles converged on a number of occasions in relation to specific political issues. At the time of the Geneva Disarmament Conference in 1932 this became clear. The Ligue held its bi-annual congress that year in Grenoble and one of the main points on the agenda was the international work in favour of disarmament. Lida Gustava Heymann (1868–1943)[23] and Gertrud Baer representing Germany, and Duchene speaking for France, demanded a radical manifesto, but were opposed in this by the British. Mrs Corbett-Fisher said the difficulties remained the same as in the past. The different national sections represented different points of view. In Britain, what she termed 'radical pacifist work' was the province of the No More War Movement, and although she admitted that the LIFPL was in favour of total disarmament, she thought that its principal role was 'to be an association of women well informed and ready to demand practical and immediate measures on any pressing question'.[24]

By the beginning of the 1930s the situation had thus begun to reverse itself and the French section increasingly found itself on the defensive, having to defend its attitude to the other sections. This was no mere accident but rather the result of a change in the orientation of the French section, away from an 'integral' pacifist position towards a more ideologically Marxist view of peace and pacifism, at least at the official level. This slow evolution from what Duchene herself called pacifist idealism towards pacifist realism[25] was accompanied naturally enough perhaps by a gradual softening of the French section's official position on the question of non-violence, civil war, and the methods of the revolution. This gradual process resulted in an estrangement from the rest of the Ligue, with the exception of the German section, which finally saw Duchene lose her seat as an International Executive Committee member at the last pre-war Ligue Congress in Luhacovice, Czechoslovakia in 1937.

The 1934 Ligue Congress in Zurich is the key point at which the changing views of the French section became clear. Indeed it marked

[23] For a biographical sketch of Heymann, see Amy Hackett, 'Lida Gustava Heymann', in Josephson, *Dictionary*, 405–7.

[24] Procès-verbal, comité exécutif international, Grenoble, 11–14 May 1932, 7. In BDIC/DD/FΔRés. 206/May 1932.

[25] Gabrielle Duchene, 'Les Deux Conceptions du pacifisme', typescript of report prepared for the 1936 national conference of the French section. In BDIC/DD/FΔRés. 208/17.

a watershed for the Ligue as a whole as well. The world of 1934 was no longer even that of 1932—the accession to power of the Nazi Party in Germany had seen to that. The German pacifist Gertrud Baer remarked in the opening discussion that the Ligue was undergoing an 'intellectual crisis'.[26] In a long address, Clara Ragaz, one of the international vice-presidents, spoke of non-violence as the most important question for the Ligue in the time of trouble it faced in the international sphere, but she wondered whether 'this same strong majority' existed with regard to social struggles or the social revolution. She recognized that right became very difficult to distinguish from wrong in this area, and asked where the path of true liberation lay.[27] 1934 marked the LIFPL's first hard encounter with the real world of interwar Europe on a domestic as well as international level. In many ways, the 1920s and the experience of the Great War had presented relatively clear-cut moral decisions for the pacifist women of the Ligue, but the 1930s marked the convergence of two new factors in a startlingly violent way. First, the rise of Fascism and then the Nazi seizure of power destroyed the humanitarian, rationalistic approach to peace which had been possible in the post-World War I era. And secondly, the gradual insinuation into the LIFPL of a Marxist conception of peace led inevitably to a confrontation on the social, domestic level between converts to it and the heralds of the old doctrinaire 'idealistic' pacifism.

The French section quite obviously viewed the 1934 Congress as an important event for the future course of the Ligue's work because its delegation of twenty voting members, two executive members, and two consultative members was its largest during the interwar period. In a total voting body of 135 delegates, the French section was clearly a strong force.[28] At the next Congress in 1937 it only managed to send three voting delegates,[29] so it may perhaps be inferred from this that the 1934 Congress was viewed as a pivotal event by the French section and that thereafter its commitment to the

[26] Minutes of Proceedings, Eighth International Congress, Zurich, 3–8 Sept. 1934, 4. In BDIC/DD/FΔRés. 205/8/8.

[27] Clara Ragaz, 'Changements d'ordre politique, social et économique du monde depuis 1918: Problèmes qui en résultent pour le travail et les méthodes de la LIFPL'. This was the opening address to the 1934 Zurich Congress. In BDIC/DD/FΔRés. 205/8/5.

[28] List of Delegates, 1934 Zurich Congress, in BDIC/DD/FΔRés. 205/8/7.

[29] Roll Call, IXth International Congress of the LIFPL, Luhacovice, Czechoslovakia, 1937. In BDIC/DD/FΔRés. 205/9/2.

international work of the Ligue waned. Pivotal the 1934 Congress certainly was. Once again the aims of the Ligue were debated at great length with the usual stand-off between the Franco-German and British positions. The essentially Franco-German statement of aims that was finally voted after long and acrimonious discussion was much longer than the earlier versions and for the first time contained direct references to the need to abolish 'the present system of exploitation, privilege and profit' which caused wars and to 'facilitate and hasten by non-violent methods the social transformation which would permit the inauguration of a new system under which would be realized social, economic and political equality for all'. The women at Zurich saw as their goal 'an economic order on a world-wide basis and under world regulation founded on the needs of the community and not on profit'.[30] The British counter-proposal, much more general in its political analysis and stronger in its pacifist principles, originally read that the Ligue 'is opposed to all resort to bloodshed and violence whether by States, by Classes, or by individuals, to dictatorship whether from the "right" or from the "left"'.[31] The British proposal also contained references to the need for a 'social transformation' required before the aims could be achieved, but they did not wish to go into too much detail. 'By defining we create division,' said Kathleen Innes (1883–1967); 'The British Section is not entirely opposed to the Franco-German proposal. They do not, however, believe that any new order would necessarily bring peace nor that social, economic, and political equality alone would mean peace.'[32] Instead, she thought that the acceptance of such a tendentious statement might very well drive members, and even entire sections, out of the Ligue.

The British were apparently astonished that the French proposal

[30] See the revised version of the aims and the debate that preceded it at the 1934 Zurich Congress in 'Constitution. Paragraph II. Statement of Aims' in BDIC/DD/FΔRés. 205/8/6.

[31] See 'CI. British Section Proposals for Revision of Constitution as a whole', in BDIC/DD/FΔRés. 205/8/6.

[32] Minutes of Proceedings, Eighth International Congress, Zurich, 3–8 Sept. 1934, 17. In BDIC/DD/FΔRés. 205/8/6. Kathleen Elizabeth Innes (née Royds) took her BA at the University of London in 1912. In 1921 she married George Innes. During the War she had joined the British section of the International Committee of Women for a Permanent Peace, which later became the Women's International League for Peace and Freedom (or the LIFPL in French). She and her husband were active in Quaker circles in London and also in the League of Nations Union. See Margaret Tims, 'Kathleen Elizabeth Royds Innes', in Josephson, Dictionary, 446–7.

for a statement of aims made no reference to civil conflicts. D. Christol from the Marseilles section strongly opposed 'the suggestion that civil conflicts should be settled only by international arbitration'. In her view, the Ligue 'must stand definitely with the workers even if, as a last means, they had to resort to violence'.[33] One of the other French delegates, Y. Paquet, emphasizing that she spoke for a whole group of young delegates, urged 'the necessity of a clear definition of violence under present day conditions'. In her view it was violence if healthy young people were prevented from working, or if some people enjoyed a comfortable lifestyle while others went hungry. She argued that 'if we stand for peace we must not indulge in passivity but work out practicable methods of non-violent action'.[34]

Catherine Marshall saw the essential differences between the French and British sections hinging on two points: the question of international war and class war, and secondly, the definition of violence. She did not consider a general strike to be violence, nor was she prepared to accept responsibility for the covert violence of the system. She asked the French to define what they understood by violence to which Duchene replied that in her opinion 'bloodshed is not always the worst form of violence, oppression in all its forms is violence as well'. On the question of which sorts of violence might be more acceptable, Duchene argued that the LIFPL 'must understand and sympathize with the oppressed even if they resort to arms'; she added the caveat, however, that under no circumstances should Ligue members take up arms themselves.[35]

The extent to which the demands of a domestic social policy heavily inspired by the Communist Party impinged on the French section's ability to relate to the international debate on non-violence and pacifism can be seen in the remarks of Germaine Baurez, one of the French section's consultative members, who explained to the Congress

that to accept the workers' violence in social struggles does not mean to advocate violence but only to consider it unavoidable. In France the union effected between Socialists and Communists makes a general strike possible, within a few months, and it must be clear that if, as a result of this, Government forces are used against the workers and they are thus compelled to react with violence, our sympathy must definitely be with the workers. She

---

[33] Proceedings, Eighth International Congress, 19.
[34] Ibid.   [35] Ibid. 21.

would prefer a non-violent action but thinks that there is no time left now to build up an organization for such action which it took years to do in India.[36]

It is clear from the above that for the French section support of a social struggle the parameters of which were defined by the Communist Party had become more important than the struggle for international peace. One wonders if the French section would ever have seen the light of day in 1915 if Duchene and the other women of that first hour had considered the organized violence let loose over European society 'unavoidable'. The attitude here is in sharp contrast to that of the Munich and Jena sections during the days of the German revolution in 1918–19 when women of the LIFPL several times intervened, not always successfully, with the military authorities and the revolutionaries in an attempt to ward off violence.[37]

The Congress nevertheless passed the Franco-German proposal regarding aims, albeit in slightly amended form, but the French section voted against the clause which repudiated the use of violence under any circumstances.[38] This occasioned a rather bitter discussion at the International Executive Committee following the Congress when the French section's commitment to non-violence was openly called into question. Clara Ragaz, the Swiss pacifist, noted from the chair that there was 'some uneasiness in regard to the presence on the Executive Committee of a representative of the French Section, since the French Delegation in the Congress had voted against the clause in our new Aims which repudiates the use of violence under any circumstances'.[39] Duchene replied that the French section was 'realist' and saw things as they were. She claimed that the French detested violence as much as any other section but they did 'not believe that the social transformation which seem[ed] to them indispensable to assure peace and justice in the world' could occur without any violence at all. She declared that the French section was faced with a revolutionary situation, and that unarmed French workers were 'almost daily' the victims of violence 'on the part of the Government or of reactionary factions'.[40]

The French section had accepted Madeleine Rolland's amendment

[36] Proceedings, Eighth International Congress, 27.

[37] See Gertrud Baer's comments on this ibid. 22.

[38] Minutes, IEC Meeting, Zurich, 10 Sept. 1934, 12. In BDIC/DD/FΔRés. 205/8/7. See also Minutes of Proceedings of the 1934 Congress, 35, paragraph 279 which records the details of the vote on the Ligue's aims. It is unclear from this whether some members of the French delegation abstained or voted negatively.

[39] Minutes, IEC Meeting, Zurich, 10 Sept. 1934, 12.   [40] Ibid.

to the aims which spoke of achieving the social transformation deemed necessary 'by the methods most calculated to *lessen* [emphasis added] violence', an amendment which Duchene said showed neither 'the naïveté nor the absence of sense of reality of the other amendments'.[41] In any event, the Rolland amendment was defeated three times in the voting on the new constitution. Duchene said that it was this lack of reality in the other amendments which was the cause of the French abstention, but she added that it should in no way be construed as an acceptance of violence, or as an unwillingness to continue to work within the Ligue. She quite rightly pointed out that certain sections had achieved the removal of all condemnations of defensive wars from the aims in the past without it bringing into question a section's continued membership. At the time of the Ligue's campaign for disarmament, the British section refused to accept the phrase 'total disarmament' and yet on Duchene's suggestion it had been agreed to allow two formulas to exist side by side within the Ligue.[42]

The continued participation of Duchene and the French section in the Ligue was in fact in question. Emily Greene Balch said that when Duchene 'had asked her directly whether she thought the Ligue would be better without the French Section she had replied that she had arrived, with great pain, at the conclusion that G. Duchene was hampered in her work by her connection with the WILPF, and that the WILPF found its work made difficult by G. Duchene'. Duchene, for her part, supposed 'that her activity in the Amsterdam movement where she has accepted collaboration with personalities and groups which are not non-violent, [had] not been approved'. She was, however, of the opinion 'that in working successfully to realize unity in France she [had] done more in two years for the cause of peace and liberty than in 20 years of work in the League'.[43]

The German section, represented by Dr Anita Augspurg (1857–1943),[44] Lida Gustava Heymann, and Gertrud Baer, protested vehemently against the attacks made on Duchene and the French section. Heymann thought that many of the troubles 'have arisen because there is too much "Quakerism" in our Executive'. Quakerism was simply not up to the task of dealing with political situations

[41] Ibid. 13. See also Congress Proceedings, 25–6, 29, and 34 for the discussion and voting on the Rolland amendment.
[42] IEC Minutes, 10 Sept. 1934, 13.   [43] Ibid. 13 and 15.
[44] See Amy Hackett, 'Anita Augspurg', in Josephson, *Dictionary*, 42–3.

outside the social and humanitarian sphere in which it normally operated.[45] The comment is interesting because it shows the fundamental differences between an essentially political approach to pacifism, which was primarily that of the French and German sections, and the more idealistic, perhaps religiously inspired orientation of the Anglo-American sections. The Dutch section, too, seemed prone to view pacifism in an ethical, moral light rather than as a political problem. Mme Wulfften-Palthe, a Dutch consultative member of the executive, spoke of 'pacifism as a new religion and of the need to be 100% pacifist'.[46] None of this discussion, however, really called into question Duchene's personal commitment to non-violence. Gertrud Baer recounted how in a conversation with Duchene about the February troubles in Paris, Duchene had said that 'never in her life would *she* be found on the barricades'.[47] The meeting ended with Duchene still on the executive committee and the French section still part of the Ligue, but the incident serves to highlight the extent to which by 1934 the French section had begun to isolate itself from the rest of the Ligue.

In some respects it is difficult to understand why Duchene and the French section should have been singled out for this sort of treatment since in many respects Duchene's views were no more 'radical' than those of the German section, or for that matter those of Clara Ragaz, the Swiss international vice-president. Ragaz, for example, earlier that year at an executive meeting in Geneva had said that the Ligue's struggle

for peace must be conducted on two fronts, if not three: against *militarism* pure and simple, against *Fascism* which is but a disguised militarism, and against the *present economic system*, that is to say against *capitalism*, which is a supporter of Fascism . . . We have always wanted *peace* and *freedom*. But all of these problems are becoming more concrete and in so far as they become more concrete they put us before the necessity of taking some very clear, very precise decisions, while in the past we have perhaps contented ourselves with more or less vague theories . . .[48]

At this same meeting the executive committee passed a declaration drafted by Duchene on the Ligue's position on the current political situation. The document, especially in its final form, is imbued with a

[45] IEC Minutes, 10 Sept. 1934, 14.   [46] Ibid. 15.   [47] Ibid. 14.
[48] Extraits du discours d'ouverture prononcé par Clara Ragaz au comité exécutif international. Geneva, 24–8 Mar. 1934. In BDIC/DD/FΔRés. 206/Mar. 1934.

starkly Marxist analysis of the causes of the 'present discontents'. Duchene wrote that the complexity of the problems facing the world was so great that pacifists and intellectuals were falling into increasing confusion about what course to take. In her view the women of the LIFPL must 'reject all *dogmatism*—even pacifist—to become conscious of *reality*' and they must tear themselves 'away from the greyness of *formulas* which satisfy the mind too easily, in order to enter into *positive action*'.[49] Duchene saw the civilized world sliding into a barbarism without equal in human history and proclaimed that the 'passive cult of peace no longer suffices'; what was needed in this dangerous hour was an 'active, positive, incessant struggle' against war and Fascism. And if real peace was desired, one had also to desire the conditions for it.[50] Without the support of any doctrine, she claimed that the mere objective examination of the facts obliged one to recognize first that 'the capitalist regime is incompatible with real peace, with lasting peace'; and secondly, that 'Fascism is nothing but a manifestation of the self-defence mechanism of a capitalism under threat'.[51] She 'knew' that capitalism would disappear—as the regimes which preceded it in turn had disappeared—but she knew, too, that it would not merely abdicate, but would fight until the bitter end. She proclaimed that the hour had come to take sides, to affirm the Ligue's position and to work for a 'social transformation' (a euphemism for revolution) which was to be achieved with a 'minimum of suffering'.[52] She warned in the rough draft that for the Ligue, which considered true peace as its ultimate goal, the fear of a little blood spilt today would have as its consequence the future shedding of much more as the political situation worsened.[53] She urged her fellow Ligue members to accept the historical inevitability of this 'social transformation', to abandon neutrality in internal as well as external conflicts, and individually and collectively to adopt an objective, realistic attitude.[54]

It is interesting to note the differences between the declaration

---

[49] Déclaration adoptée à l'exécutif de la LIFPL (Genève—mars 1934), in BDIC/DD/FΔRés. 206/Mar. 1934. A rough draft of this declaration is in BDIC/DD/FΔRés. 208/15 and is dated Feb. 1934.

[50] Ibid. Cf. Romain Rolland's message to La Volonté de paix on much the same theme some years previously. Romain Rolland, 'La Volonté de paix', *Par la révolution, la paix* (Paris: Éditions sociales internationales, 1935), 100–4.

[51] Déclaration adoptée à l'exécutif de la LIFPL (Genève—mars 1934).

[52] Ibid.   [53] See the rough draft of this in BDIC/DD/FΔRés. 208/15.

[54] 'Déclaration adoptée'.

finally adopted at the international executive level, and the rough draft written by Duchene in February 1934. The draft version contains a much fuller analysis of the French reaction to the rise to power in Germany of the Nazi Party and the problem that posed for the Ligue. Duchene underlined the fact that the Ligue had never ceased to denounce the injustice of the 1919 peace treaties, and to demand equal treatment between victors and vanquished (but only through disarmament and not rearmament). The French section did not confound the German people with the new German government. Without underestimating the dangers posed by the new situation in Germany, Duchene did not think it impossible to arrive at some sort of *modus vivendi* with Hitler. A treaty of non-aggression would be more than possible provided it contained no military clauses and was not directed against any third countries. The French section believed 'that its position of principle *vis-à-vis* Germany should not be changed because of the fact of a change in government'. They also rejected categorically 'the idea of a preventive war' or a 'crusade of the democracies against the Fascist countries', and came out solidly against any thought of a boycott against Germany which they considered both dangerous and impossible to effect.[55] Finally, Duchene wrote that the French section was convinced that the danger of a war with Germany was neither the principal nor the most immediate danger, and she warned her members not to become obsessed with the 'German peril', but to keep everything in perspective.[56]

The removal of the paragraphs relating specifically to the position to be taken with regard to the new Germany, and the continued insistence in the final published version on the need to support the workers in a potentially violent struggle for historically pre-determined power, suggests not merely a preoccupation on the French section's part with a Marxist analysis of contemporary society, but perhaps more important a concentration on the domestic political situation in France in 1934. It is possible, one could argue, to see in the comparison of these two 1934 documents the beginnings of a political introversion within the French section of the Ligue, an introversion which paradoxically was often in the coming years to express itself in international terms. The draft version of Duchene's

[55] See the rough draft of the declaration in BDIC/DD/FΔRés. 208/15.
[56] Ibid.

declaration is a mixture of domestic Marxist analysis and traditional Ligue internationalism, whereas the manifesto finally adopted by the international executive committee was a Marxist political broadsheet and no more.

Despite the constitutional changes effected at Zurich, sectional peace did not descend on the Ligue. In March 1935 at a meeting in London, Kathleen Innes complained that the British section disapproved of 'any party implication in the aims accepted at Zurich' and served notice that her section wanted a 'more democratic organization of the WILPF' which they would soon be trying to achieve despite the opposition they encountered.[57] The French and German sections expressed their astonishment at the British action which they believed undermined yet again the basis for concerted international work in the Ligue. At this London meeting, Duchene was appointed treasurer of the Ligue, a position she held until the Congress in 1937. The appointment came only after a protracted debate in which the British international vice-president, Edith Pye, attacked Duchene's lack of commitment to non-violence and said that her appointment as treasurer would upset the delicate political balance amongst the officers of the Ligue. Duchene was finally appointed on the understanding that she exercise no political role as treasurer.[58]

The internecine sniping went on for another two years until at the executive meeting in April 1937 Duchene proposed a 'ladies' agreement' or a 'truce' not to raise constitutional questions 'until the present political crisis is over'. Failing that, she proposed a 'friendly divorce' between the two opposing tendencies within the Ligue. Her proposal for a truce was narrowly accepted with those dissenting reserving the right to propose constitutional amendments at the upcoming IXth International Congress in Czechoslovakia anyway.[59] But at that Congress Duchene lost the seat she had held for so many years as a member of the International Executive and returned to the ranks of the nominally non-voting consultative members.

It is tempting to conclude that no one was happy with the constitutional arrangements worked out at Zurich. The British

[57] Minutes, IEC Meeting, London, 25–30 Mar. 1935, 16. In BDIC/DD/FΔRés. 206/Mar. 1935. [58] Ibid. 23–5.
[59] Minutes, IEC Meeting, Bruges, 6–10 Apr. 1937, 42. In BDIC/DD/FΔRés. 206/Apr. 1937.

certainly were not and arguably neither were the French. Undoubtedly one of the reasons Duchene lost her seat in 1937 was the complete lack of French delegates there to support her. Unlike 1934 when the French delegation had numbered 24 women, in 1937 it consisted only of Duchene and the two consultative members.[60] This is perhaps an indication of Duchene's lack of interest in the work of the LIFPL by this time, or perhaps more correctly an example of how the strife-ridden French section was no longer the international force it once had been.

REALISM AND POLITICS: THE FRENCH CONTRIBUTION
TO INTERNATIONAL ACTION

Even in the early 1920s before the debates on an active, positive pacifism took place, Gabrielle Duchene and the French women of the Ligue saw their role as feminist pacifists in very active terms. Despite the analysis cited above of Catherine Marshall regarding the alleged propensity within the French section for theorizing, there is no doubting the French commitment to political action. Indeed, by 1936, Duchene was 'astonished that in such a characteristic case as the situation in Spain there [was] so much theoretical discussion' within the rest of the Ligue.[61]

That said, it is probably true that the nature of the action changed as the twenties rolled into the thirties. The French section, and indeed, the Ligue as a whole, in the more immediate post-war years was primarily concerned with mediation, revision of the peace treaties, practical help to famine-struck areas of Europe, disarmament, and the dissemination of ideas of international brotherhood by means of summer schools and the like. In the 1930s with the rise of Fascism, the deteriorating political and economic situation, and, arguably, with the gradual politicization in a Marxist direction of the French section's views on peace and pacifism, the calls for action became concrete in a way they had not previously been. As examples in the first category, one might note in passing Duchene's participation in a group of six women delegated by the 1919 Zurich Congress of the Ligue to present a series of resolutions to the peace conference

[60] See Roll Call, IXth International Congress, Luhacovice, Czechoslovakia, in BDIC/DD/FΔRés. 205/9/2.
[61] Cited in Minutes, IEC Meeting, Geneva, 10–14 Sept. 1936, 18. In BDIC/DD/FΔRés. 206/Sept. 1936.

of the powers in Paris.[62] The LIFPL seemed to make a speciality of this sort of delegation. Another example including French participation was a delegation composed of Andrée Jouve, Catherine Marshall, Dr Aletta Jacobs (1854–1929),[63] and Gertrud Baer which visited the Dutch, German, and French governments during the Ruhr crisis in 1923. It is a measure of the esteem in which the Ligue and these women were held that the delegation was received by the German Minister of the Interior who told them 'in a long and very serious interview the opinion of the cabinet that it is the first and most important aim to bring about an agreement between France and Germany approved by the other Allies'. He complained that this idea had been urged for several years by the German Socialist Party but had not been taken up by the French government.[64]

It is above all the 1930s, however, which demonstrate Duchene's attempts to force concrete political action on the Ligue. Duchene and the French became increasingly willing to take sides and to choose what they considered to be the moral and political high ground in the political conflicts of the thirties. While other sections of the Ligue gradually settled into a sort of post-Hitlerian pacifist lethargy, the French section demanded action. Neutrality was anathema to them. Politics was the art of choosing, and choices were made within a neo-Marxist ideological construct no matter how much Duchene might talk about arriving at purely objective conclusions. Four instances, among others, deserve mention here as an indication of the French attitude to political action: first, the Ligue's reaction to the Sino-Japanese conflict in 1932; secondly the developing Spanish situation; thirdly the official Ligue reaction to the remilitarization of the Rhineland; and finally, the overriding concern of the French section in the thirties to support the policies of the Soviet Union.

At the 1932 Ligue Congress in Grenoble, Edith Pye, the English

---

[62] See 'Resolutions to be Presented to the Peace Conference of the Powers in Paris' in BDIC/DD/FΔRés. 205/1. The other members of this delegation were Jane Addams (USA), Charlotte Despard (Great Britain), Rosa Genoni (Italy), Clara Ragaz (Switzerland), and Chrystal Macmillan (Great Britain).

[63] Aletta Henriëtte Jacobs was the first woman admitted to a Dutch university, and also the first woman medical doctor in the Netherlands. She was active for over forty years in the women's suffrage movement, and worked tirelessly in favour of birth control and against the misery of much of the working population. It was on her initiative that the first Congress of the nascent Women's International League for Peace and Freedom (or LIFPL) convened in Holland in Apr. 1915. See Peter van den Dungen, 'Aletta Henriëtte Jacobs' in Josephson, *Dictionary*, 452–4.

[64] Cited in 'News Letter from Geneva' in BDIC/DD/FΔRés. 206/Sept. 1923.

pacifist, presented a report on her recent trip to the Orient which was not at all well received by the French section. Pye argued that the Ligue should adopt a position of neutrality in the nascent Sino-Japanese conflict and avoid coming out on the side of one country or the other. Thérèse Pottecher, one of the French delegates, argued on the contrary that it was no good trying, as Pye had done, to examine impartially the wrongs committed by both sides. In her view, the 'great powers control business'. She did not have Pye's faith in the League of Nations, but thought rather that the governments of the day were but façades for financial interests. Thus, the boycott of Japan by China was completely justified.[65] Camille Drevet echoed Pottecher's calls for concrete action saying that the fact that Miss Cao, the Chinese representative to the Ligue, felt it impossible to remain a pacifist in the present situation only served to underline the extent to which the women of the Ligue had failed in their mission. Something more than the mere sending of telegrams was needed. She proposed a move on the Ligue's part to stop the shipment of men and munitions to China, and to that end suggested talks with trade unions. Léo Wanner of the Lyon section must have become quite agitated during this discussion, because Duchene felt obliged to apologize for the 'vivacité' of her colleague and to term her temperament not 'violent' but 'passionate'. Duchene emphasized the feeling of impotence and inactivity felt by the members of the French section in this instance: 'If the French temperament shocks some delegates, the impassibility of the latter annoys the French. She thought that once blood began to run, one could not simply "wait" before acting.'[66] Duchene proposed the adoption of a strong motion against the attitude of the great powers and Japan, to be sent to the League of Nations. The Grenoble Congress did not satisfy the desires of the French section; Duchene complained after its close that it had been a major disappointment for young people particularly, because it had not adopted a radical manifesto.[67]

The Nazi remilitarization of the Rhineland provided another example of an occasion when political action taken by the international vice-presidents, Clara Ragaz and Gertrud Baer, was called

[65] Cited in the debate on the report of the Commission on China, in Procès-verbal, VIIe Congrès international, Grenoble, 15–19 May 1932, 12–15.

[66] Ibid. 14.

[67] Procès-verbal, comité exécutif international, Grenoble, 20–2 May 1932, 1. In BDIC/DD/FΔRés. 206/May 1932.

into question and then condemned by the British section. In a letter of 16 March 1935 to the president of the Council of the League of Nations, Ragaz and Baer demanded that action be taken against Germany if the moral standing of the L.o.N. were to be saved. This action must not be military in nature, but they did envisage the application of moral, political, and economic pressure collectively applied, and if German troops did not leave the Rhineland, the eventual use of economic and financial sanctions. The British section argued that the letter conflicted with Ligue policy by leaving the door open for a food blockade. It furthermore succumbed to the dangerous temptation of ultimatum which had never worked in the past.[68] Significantly once again Duchene had supported the sending of the letter when consulted in early March by telephone.[69]

Far more significant perhaps than the remilitarization of the Rhineland was the French section's consistent support for the policies of Soviet Russia. These date back to the mid-twenties when there was considerable support within the Ligue as a whole for the disarmament proposals of the Soviet Foreign Minister, Litvinoff. But by the early 1930s many sections of the Ligue were beginning to become more hesitant and less fulsome in their support of the Soviet Union, a tendency certainly not reflected in the policies of the French or the German sections.

This became very clear at the September 1935 meeting of the international executive committee in Geneva at which Gertrud Baer delivered a long and wide-ranging analysis of the political situation in Europe. Baer viewed the signing of the Franco-Soviet and Czecho-Soviet Pacts as treaties of 'mutual assistance' designed to meet the situation created by the formation of 'blocks of countries aggressive and hostile to one another'.[70] She furthermore believed these pacts to be in harmony with the League of Nations Covenant because they were 'open for the free and sincere collaboration of all the states interested'.[71] Her only veiled criticism was that the two pacts contained no references to disarmament, but she thought that this question might be taken up by the LIFPL with the countries

---

[68] 'British Section protests against Chairmen's Letter' in BDIC/DD/FΔRés. 206/Apr.–May 1936.

[69] See 'First Replies: Telegrams, Telephone or Short Notes received from Executive Members elected by Congress commenting on the Draft Letter to Mr. Bruce, sent to them on March 12th 1936'. In BDIC/DD/FΔRés. 206/Apr.–May 1936.

[70] Minutes, IEC, Geneva, 12–16 Sept. 1935, 5–9. In BDIC/DD/FΔRés. 206/Sept. 1935. [71] Ibid.

concerned. That rider notwithstanding Baer concluded that the two pacts could serve as 'instruments of *collective security* [emphasis added] and peace'.[72] Not all of the Ligue's executive accepted this charitable gloss put on the Franco-Soviet Pact. Cor Ramondt-Hirschmann, the Dutch executive member and sometime vice-president, believed that far from representing a success for peace, the pact was a 'war danger because it enforces the military system'. Treaties of non-aggression were one thing, but a pact of mutual assistance like that signed between France and the Soviet Union was quite another.[73] This criticism was repeated by the normally left-leaning American pacifist Dorothy Detzer (1893–1981),[74] who felt that the pacts constituted a danger because it was now in the interest of Russia to have its allies heavily armed. She thought that this would lead the Soviet Union to ask Communists in other countries to support increases of armaments for defence against Fascist attack, and that thus the united front of Communists and pacifists would be rent asunder.[75] This was in fact precisely the price that Laval had exacted from Stalin in the signing of the Pact as American State Department documents for the period show. In return for signing the Laval–Stalin Pact, Stalin was to call off the French Communist Party's opportunistically antimilitarist line.[76]

The extent to which Duchene may or may not have been briefed in the new line to take by her Communist friends in the Amsterdam-Pleyel movement is open to question. There is no doubt, though, that she argued forcefully for support of the Soviet position. In response to the criticisms of Ramondt and Detzer she

[72] Minutes, IEC, Geneva, 12–16 Sept. 1935.   [73] Ibid. 10.

[74] See Rosemary Rainbolt, 'Dorothy Detzer', in Josephson, *Dictionary*, 210–12.

[75] Minutes, IEC, Geneva, 12–16 Sept. 1935, 10–11. In BDIC/DD/FΔRés. 206/ Sept. 1935.

[76] See for example US National Archives, 751.6111/76, Ambassador Bullitt to Secretary of State, Moscow, 15 May 1935, in which Bullitt reports a conversation he had with Pierre Laval. Laval said that Stalin had agreed to tell French Communists to stop opposition to the army budget and the two-year service bill. See also US National Archives, 851.00B/160, 'Strictly Confidential Report of Conversation between Mr Marcel Cachin and Ambassador Bullitt', Moscow, 6 July 1935. Bullitt reported that 'I asked Mr Cachin what the French Communist Party would do in case France should become involved in war with Germany. Mr Cachin replied that unquestionably the French Communists would make no attempt to hinder mobilisation and would march . . . I asked Mr Cachin if Stalin's statement to Laval, approving French armaments, had not placed the French Communist Party in an extremely embarrassing position. Cachin replied that on the contrary, it had made the position of the French Communists easier as it was now possible for a Communist in France to be both a good communist and a good patriot.'

insisted very strongly upon the fact that though pacts of mutual assistance were not the ideal solution, they had been the only way to prevent an alliance between England, France and Germany which would have been a great success for fascism. Since every country is invited to join the Franco-Soviet pact, it can become a general treaty. The pacts were therefore not directed against certain countries. She expressed her surprise that pacifists should have any objection to this system.[77]

Her further comment that 'the United Front between communists and pacifists in France was stronger than ever and they had never stopped to stand [*sic*] for general disarmament and to oppose all proposals for an increase of armaments', is inaccurate as should be clear.[78] Not only was there great dissension within her own section as to the wisdom of the Franco-Soviet Pact, but within the larger French pacifist movement there were many groups which viewed the entire Laval–Stalin exercise with a great deal of suspicion.

This official pro-Soviet policy on the part of the French section was a constant, however, in its dealings with the rest of the Ligue in the 1930s. As we have had ample opportunity to observe in the preceding chapter, this was a policy hotly contested within the French section. Internationally, however, the section managed to portray a face of monolithic support for the Soviet position.

Coupled with this pro-Soviet stance was a remarkable clear-sightedness on the part of the French section with regard to the danger posed by Hitler. By March 1935 in a debate within the International Executive Committee on the political situation, Duchene was attacking the attitude of 'Great Britain which encourages the audacity of Hitler by its politic [*sic*] of resignation, about which the French population is very alarmed'. Running throughout the minutes of this meeting is a continual stream of criticism of the British government's position by both the French and German executive members. Lida Gustava Heymann and Dr Anita Augspurg both warned their colleagues of Hitler's real designs and asked people to read *Mein Kampf* if further corroboration were needed. Heymann spoke of the 'extremely dangerous' situation and said that the 'various actions we are taking to tranquillize our own conscience are of no real effect'. What was needed was a mass movement of women dedicated to fighting Fascism. Duchene expressed the hope

[77] Minutes, IEC Meeting, Geneva, 12–16 Sept. 1935, 11. In BDIC/DD/FΔRés. 206/Sept. 1935. [78] Ibid.

that the British Section will not support the attitude of their Government towards Hitler. France always was in favour of agreements but there are different kinds of agreements. England is frightened of Russia and prefers fascism to communism. But England also fears Hitler and out of this fear delivers itself to him. The French government by fear might also come to take the same weak attitude . . .[79]

She condemned the conclusions of the British White Paper with regard to the rearmament of Britain, but believed fervently however that the LIFPL could not put its head in the sand and ignore the fact of German rearmament.

Spain, and the problem of civil war, undoubtedly marked the critical juncture in the pacifist debate of the mid-thirties, not only for the LIFPL but also for most other pacifist groups as well. The gradual politicization of the Ligue, and especially of the French and German sections, blossomed into full flower in 1936 with the eruption of hostilities south of the Pyrenees. As Clara Ragaz, the international vice-chairman, said in her opening remarks at the International Executive meeting held in Geneva in September 1936, 'let us frankly admit it, very often also we find ourselves confronted with situations in which we do not yet see our way, where we seek with fumbling and where we recognize the complexity of questions which do not permit of simple, or apparently simple solutions. I allude among other examples to the civil war in Spain.' Civil war was the question of the hour and Ragaz wondered whether the women of the Ligue would be up to the challenge of finding answers to the problem it posed.[80]

Kathleen Innes in a report on the situation in England said that the 'peace societies reflect the division of the Government'. There were political societies which had their own outlooks and divisions, and there were on the other hand societies which preached peace on moral grounds and did not seek to apply their principles to political situations. Innes thought that there was a danger in this in that the government might use the latter sort of peace society as an excuse for taking no leading part in continental political affairs.[81] For once agreeing with something said by Innes, Duchene declared in her report that the 'situation of pacifist societies [in France] is identical to that of England . . . some pacifists see that some principles must be

[79] Minutes, IEC Meeting, London, 25–30 Mar. 1935, 7–10. In BDIC/DD/FΔRés. 206/Mar. 1935.

[80] Minutes, IEC Meeting, Geneva, 10–14 Sept. 1936, 1–2. In BDIC/DD/FΔRés. 206/Sept. 1936.   [81] Ibid. 4–5.

modified in order to meet the immense danger of a near world war, while others are sticking to their doctrines'.[82]

The crisis had come to the Ligue in Gertrud Baer's view. In a résumé of the political reports, she concluded that most of them indicated 'that the Liberal element from which our League members are mostly drawn is more and more won over to Fascism. The League has therefore, as stated in Zurich, a responsibility of showing these elements the real tendency of Fascism.'[83] And Spain was the critical case which seemed to have paralysed action within the LIFPL. She recounted how she and Ragaz had wanted to issue a statement to members and to the press making it clear that the Spanish Civil War had been started by Franco and not by the Bolsheviks as some press accounts would have it, but they had been opposed in this by the third of the international vice-presidents, Cor Ramondt-Hirschmann of Holland, who 'did not think it right to say that we could not remain neutral in sympathy'.[84] Another opportunity for action had been lost, said Baer. The Ligue must have a decisive policy which would permit action between executive meetings. She concluded

it cannot be a violation of principles to state our sympathy with those who are fighting to maintain the principles we are standing for. The outcome of the Spanish war may be fatal for Europe and the whole world if, at the last moment, the democratic forces in all countries are not uniting to assist those fighting for democracy. She deplores that the message of sympathy drafted at the time of the Azaña Government could not be sent and urges the Committee to agree on a statement expressing that we cannot remain neutral in this fight for Peace and Freedom, against Fascism.[85]

The ensuing debate revolved around two opposing resolutions, the first a more hardline version by Ragaz and Baer, and the second a more conciliatory resolution by Ramondt and Pye. At issue was the difference between an 'idealistic pacifism' and a more 'realistic' approach to the problem posed by Spain. Some members of the committee thought that the Ragaz–Baer resolution was too aggressive and not becoming to a Ligue which had peace as one of its goals. The issue essentially was that of peace *or* freedom. The Ragaz–Baer resolution clearly attached blame to the Franco side in the conflict, which led the American Lola Maverick Lloyd to wonder aloud whether the Ligue would ever have been formed in 1915 if questions of blame and guilt had been allowed. She recalled that the first rule then was not to discuss these things, and she urged the members in 1936 to concentrate instead on what could be done to end the Spanish Civil War. Duchene cut through this theoretical discussion by demanding action. 'If we remain neutral we become accomplices of Fascism', she declared.[86] In the end the executive passed a compromise resolution bringing the two opposing sides together. However a Message to Spanish Women drafted by Duchene was rejected on a motion by Kathleen Innes because it was felt to be too partisan, not being directed to all Spanish women, but from the context only to Spanish women fighting against Franco.[87]

In 1938 Duchene pressed the LIFPL to pass a resolution demanding that the Pyrenees frontier with France be opened to the Spanish republicans, but Ramondt and others spoke against it, arguing that 'it may be alright for political parties to ask for it, but as a peace organization we cannot advocate it, because it means opening to arms [sic]'.[88] In the event the resolution was not passed.

The above instances demonstrate the extent to which the debate over the aims and orientation of the Ligue was mirrored in the debate over the day to day political action of the LIFPL. This debate was conducted largely around an Anglo-French axis. With the deepening crisis in Europe, the French section under the leadership of Gabrielle Duchene became increasingly strident in its demand for concrete political action, a demand which became a reflection of the policies of the Amsterdam-Pleyel movement and hence of the Third International. In a bicephalous organization such as the LIFPL, such a soul-searching debate was inevitable, confronted as these women were with the unique political situation of late interwar Europe. Some sections continued to cling to their immediate post-war conception of peace as women's highest calling. The French section did not. Like the German section and some others, the French gradually placed more and more emphasis on freedom, and indeed on a Marxist conception of freedom. Only through the 'social transformation' would true freedom be attained, and what began to matter more and more was the daily struggle to maintain what little freedom they saw around them. In so doing the moral, and perhaps feminist, fight for peace became eclipsed.

[86] Minutes, IEC Meeting, Geneva, 10–14 Sept. 1936, 13–19. [87] Ibid. 54–7.
[88] Minutes, IEC Meeting, Geneva, 7–11 Sept. 1938, 69–70. In BDIC/DD/FΔRés. 206/Sept. 1938.

Conclusions

Part I attempted to show the nature of the old-style pacifism in France. The *pacifisme ancien style* of the Association de la paix par le droit represents better than that of any other competing organization the type of pacifism from which the new-style integral pacifism of the late twenties and thirties was to evolve. The APD was important because of its relative size within the French peace movement, the quality of its membership and leadership, and the consistently high level of political comment it was able to make in the period under discussion. Because it antedated by some thirty years the associations and societies which sprang up in the immediate post-World War I period to support the idea of a League of Nations, it had obvious claims to pre-eminence within French pacifism. It was also a society which embraced a surprising spectrum of dissent and variance of views on the nature of pacifism. This spectrum was not apparent in the immediate post-war era, but it began to become an issue by the late twenties with the rise of challenges to the hegemony of political thought enjoyed within French pacifism up until then by the APD.

The APD's *raison d'être* was not bound up inextricably with the fate of the League of Nations. To be sure, the League represented the highest attainment so far in the realm of international political and juridical development, but unlike the societies which were wedded intellectually to the League, the Association had existed before the League and it would exist after it. This is not to say that the APD was not terribly disheartened by the apparent failure of the League idea in the late thirties. It was. But as Bloch pointed out in the article cited above, the League was above all an instrument in the implementation of an idea, and if the instrument failed, or rather if men and events failed it, then another one could always be constructed. The important thing was the essential truth contained in the idea.[1]

At the 1938 AGM, *en pleine crise* between Anschluss and Munich, Ruyssen had meditated on the essence of the APD's work in his report to the Fiftieth Anniversary Congress. As we have seen many times, the APD considered its pacifism above all else to be positive and constructive in its prescriptions for peace. Flowing from this general philosophical position was its commitment to social, collective action as opposed to individual gestures which, while often deserving of respect, were essentially negative in their practical effect. These positive, constructive measures for peace could be divided, broadly speaking, into two areas: the political and the pedagogical. On the political level, the APD acted as a pressure group, a think tank, speaking out during times of decision and crisis and trying by means of article, propaganda, public meetings, and letters to appropriate political figures, to further the idea of internationally organized peace. The effect of this programme of action on the political level is impossible to measure accurately.[2] So, too, is the effect of the second plank in the APD's platform, the pedagogy of peace. It was only natural that in an Association comprised of so many people in the teaching profession, the teaching of peace should occupy such a major part. With its summer schools, its contributions to international symposia on history, education, textbook reform, and its propaganda efforts once again, the APD undoubtedly left its mark on French and European society. How deep a mark it is impossible to say. There is much truth, though, in Ruyssen's comment to the 1938 Congress that it was not inconsiderable:

I spoke above of the first of our tasks: the psychological preparation of peace, the education of minds. How to contest that in this respect we have realized a considerable work in collaboration with the other Peace Societies?

---

[1] A. Bloch, 'Adaptations nécessaires de la doctrine pacifiste', PD 49/1 (Jan. 1939), 6.

[2] Ruyssen, in his report 'La Paix par le droit', to the 1938 Fiftieth Anniversary Congress in Nîmes, said as much: 'Or, en face de ce fléau de violence collective qu'est la guerre, les pacifistes peuvent bien jouer le rôle de l'ingénieur, de l'hygiéniste; ils peuvent proposer les plans d'une meilleure société humaine; mais après tout, ce n'est pas d'eux que dépend directement l'élimination de la guerre: les artisans, en l'espèce, ce sont les Gouvernements. Tout notre rôle, en face de la catastrophe imminente, se borne à offrir nos plans aux Gouvernements et à les adjurer de faire leur devoir.' Cited in J. Prudhommeaux and J. Lahargue, 'L'Assemblée générale et le Congrès du cinquantenaire, Nîmes, 19–21 avril 1938', PD 48/6–7–8 (May–June–July 1938), 263.

If the French people, whose armies have ploughed through Europe over the course of centuries, is today hostile to adventures and desirous of living in peace with all its neighbours, we are convinced we have contributed to that. We have also certainly played a role in the penetration of the spirit of peace, equity, and respect for other nations into public education in which we are proud to count so many friends.[3]

1939 closed the circle for the APD, bringing it back to the unflinching affirmation of the primacy of justice and law over peace in its device, which had been its position during the Great War. The APD's thought evolved from initial suspicion of Germany in the early twenties to a gradual conviction of the need for Franco-German *rapprochement*. Along the way, the Association was forced to debate and deal with the demands of the new, 'negative' pacifism which made its appearance in France in the late twenties. While often showing tremendous sympathy for the individual cases which the new pacifism produced, or even sometimes for the ideas behind it, the Association nevertheless consistently affirmed its attachment to the positive ideal of peace through law. One senses that it came close at times to being seduced by the charms of the new-style pacifism, but always at the last minute held back. Hitler's seizure of power in 1933 changed the political map of Europe and with it the mental universe of the APD which was quicker than many pacifist groups to understand the meaning and the threat of Nazism, although even here there was dissent within the Association.

The APD represents the dashing of the reasonable hopes of reasonable men in a most unreasonable world. But the inherent optimism behind the view of moral and political progress held by the men and women of the APD precluded anything other than temporary pessimism about the final victory of their ideals. As Ruyssen, once again, said in closing his remarks to the 1938 Congress:

As to the future . . . I don't know what it will be. Will peace be saved? Will the League of Nations, after a passing crisis, regain its confidence? I do not know. Only one thing is certain: that is that peace will not be achieved if in the tempest pacifists themselves deny their ideal or despair. In order that the work of peace may be achieved little by little, the desires for peace must remain alive. For a half-century *La Paix par le droit* has affirmed this desire. It cannot—far from it—claim to have realized all its dreams; but it is proud to have portended and, in a certain sense, marked, beaten, and levelled the

---

[3] Ibid. 267–8.

track on which humanity, weary of so many horrors and acquainted with so many sufferings, can finally wend its way towards a better destiny.[4]

In examining the political and moral trajectory of the French section of the LIFPL during the interwar years, the ideological evolution of the pacifist debate cannot be overemphasized. What in 1915 had been a tremendous leap of humanitarian, feminist, pacifist courage, became increasingly in the 1920s a politicized debate, and in the 1930s an increasingly sterile, ideologically determined struggle for *one* conception of peace for which some French women became increasingly willing to contemplate the shedding of blood. Because the women of the French section were so politically astute, their radical pacifism finally collapsed like a house of cards. The trump card was called Freedom; and it was for freedom that the French section primarily struggled in the latter years of the decade. The widening gap between moral conviction and political reality made the pacifism of the LIFPL untenable until at last it was no longer really pacifism, or at least certainly not 'integral pacifism'.

It is perhaps too easy for the historian to look back at the interwar period with the benefit of historical hindsight, and to chastise and to laud *à son gré*. But until 31 January 1933 nothing seemed inevitable about the rise to power of National Socialism across the Rhine —threatening yes, but inevitable no. Before the duplicity of the Nazi–Soviet Pact of August 1939, little or no suspension of disbelief was required for many men and women of goodwill to believe in the Soviet Union's desire for peace. September 1939 was not a pre-ordained *fait accompli*, until it had actually happened. In order to understand the brave mixture of optimism and despair of the interwar pacifists, it is necesary to remind oneself constantly of these facts.

The rise of Fascism and the Nazi seizure of power transformed the world of politics. Under the pressure of political reality, the LIFPL French section's early integral pacifism gradually disintegrated as the need to support the fight for freedom became increasingly evident. The gradually increasing ideological content of their pacifist analysis only served to widen further the space between their concern for peace and their fight for liberty.

Thus, women's peace initiatives in interwar France became in-

[4] Ruyssen, 'La Paix par le droit', 268.

fected with the same dilemmas, distortions, detours, and hard political choices as did more 'masculinist' efforts for peace. In terms of radical feminist pacifism, the 1930s was a decade of disappointments as the women of the LIFPL were gradually forced into a permanent retreat behind the mental Maginot line of collective security and support for the bourgeois democracies. That which had been specifically and originally feminist in the work of the LIFPL in France during the First World War and in the twenties, became diluted and distorted—*des idées périmées*—as the thirties drew to a close.

While some feminists argue that women are inherently pacifist,[5] in practice this was not necessarily the case. Women, like men, were susceptible to the drumbeats of their age. As in the working out of Christianity or Socialism, there would appear to be no inbuilt ideological determinism which leads to peace through feminism. Human perversity and individuality usually see to that. Women in interwar France, individually and sometimes collectively, did make a major contribution to peace. However, they did this more as pacifists than as feminists; and their pacifism gradually became overlaid, diluted, and distorted as a moral creed by the political and ideological demands of their age.[6] In thus returning to the questions posed at the outset of the section on feminist pacifism, the measured words of the feminist journalist Marcelle Capy seem particularly appropriate. Grappling with the same issues dealt with here, Capy concluded:

[5] See for example Jo Vellacott, 'Women, Peace, and Internationalism, 1914–1920', in Charles Chatfield and Peter van den Dungen (eds.), *Peace Movements and Political Cultures* (Knoxville, Tenn.: University of Tennessee Press, 1988); and Pam McAllister (ed.), *Reweaving the Web of Life* (Philadelphia: New Society Publishers, 1982).

[6] Huguette Bouchardeau comes to similar conclusions about the nature of feminist pacifism in interwar France. She writes: 'Ce débat illustre bien ce qui est en train de se passer au niveau de la lutte des femmes pour la paix. D'un côté, des actions autonomes des femmes, intéressantes dans leur portée concrète, mais souvent vouées à l'inefficacité et à l'angélisme. De l'autre, des actions qui visent à des rassemblements massifs, s'insèrent dans des luttes politiques d'envergure, mais sont rarement menées à l'initiative même des femmes.' Bouchardeau's point is that the feminist pacifist movement became de-tracked and politicized, and thus less than 100 per cent feminist or even pacifist in inspiration. 'Les thèmes des droits de la maternité, de la femme pacificatrice, qui avaient été si mobilisateurs, si "productifs" à la fin de la guerre et dans les années qui ont suivi, vont devenir clichés, manipulés comme arguments au service d'un discours qui trouve ailleurs ses fondements.' Women became, in Stalin's word, merely 'la grande réserve' of the working class. See Huguette Bouchardeau, *Pas d'histoire, les femmes . . . 50 ans d'historie des femmes: 1918–1968* (Paris: Éditions Syros, 1977), 110–11.

Many writers—of all countries—have shown themselves extremely severe with regard to women. They have admirably criticized the frivolity, the unconsciousness of some, the exasperated chauvinism of others. They are neither completely wrong, nor completely right.

Is it right to demand that women be pacific heroines? For my part, I believe that men and women have nothing to envy one another, and that they need a reciprocal indulgence in order to judge one another.[7]

Wars have a nasty habit of ruining the high hopes of pacifists. This was perhaps especially true for those of the 'ideological' variety who in the case of France defined the old-style pacifism from which the new, integral type evolved. Because the ideological pacifists of the APD were collaborative in their orientation to the political society they lived in, the failure of their pacifism was acutely felt. Failure was not interpreted as the end of the struggle, however. As we have seen, if the League of Nations idea had fallen short of the mark, this did not in any way mean that the basic premises behind the APD's pacifism were wrong. Far from it. Ruyssen, looking back over fifty years of pacifist activity in 1938, could justifiably be proud of the extent to which the theses of the APD had become accepted in political society. As Part I has made clear, the disaster of 1939 did not lessen in any appreciable way the long-term optimism with which the representatives of the old-style pacifism viewed the future. Of the final victory of their ideas they were convinced.

No doubt the political world in which the interwar pacifists moved was very different when it ended from when it had begun. In the immediate post-war years, even the old-style pacifism of the APD had been somewhat suspect in the eyes of much of public opinion. We are no longer acquainted today with the species of warmonger who honoured the fact of war and glorified it as a salutary social instrument. But in the early twenties, the memory of the vilification to which the APD had been subjected in the pre-war years was still fresh. The trauma of the Great War did much to alter the political balance in favour of the theses of the old-style pacifists. By the late 1920s it was a commonplace for politicians to support the efforts towards international reconciliation of Briand, for example.

For the new-style pacifists of the thirties, the situation was rather different. 1939 represented for them both the complete failure of all

[7] Marcelle Capy, 'Les Femmes et la paix', *Le Progrès civique*, 600 (14 Feb. 1931), 213.

that they had striven for, and at the same time a sort of perverse justification of the theses they had propounded. Peace had failed, but it had done so because of the complete rottenness of society. French political society was rejected, as we have seen, because of a historical interpretation of the recent past, and an antipolitical, dissenting stance in the present. This, coupled with the fears of the next war, produced a powerful new variant of pacifism. When that war finally arrived, French integral pacifism was already completely isolated from political society. Indeed, one of its problems had nearly always been the fact that it was continuously being squeezed from left and right in a political pincer action which finally left it marooned on its own small island of despair. Only in the first few years of the LICP's existence, from roughly 1930 to 1933, was the Ligue able to make any claims at all to limited public support. But the early thirties was still a time of relative optimism. War clouds were gathering on the horizon and causing people to reflect. Pessimism was around the corner. But in the first years of the Ligue, it was possible for pacifists to make inroads on public opinion because of the prevailing political climate of relative optimism. The failure of the Geneva Disarmament Conference, together with international tensions left unresolved by a League of Nations which was increasingly seen as impotent, and above all, the arrival in power of Hitler in Germany, caused this world of public optimism to crumble. The late arriving effects of the world depression only served to exacerbate an already bad political situation. The Popular Front provided a brief respite from the slippery slope of pessimism, but it did not last. This was perhaps the cruellest of the political blows which integral pacifism had to suffer in the thirties. So many high hopes had been vested in the Popular Front which, despite the presence of Communists within it, was initially considered a tremendous guarantor of peace. Because of the *idées maîtresses* which underpinned it, the new pacifism quickly and easily slipped into an antipolitical withdrawal from society. This was an indication of its sectarianism or of the utopianism of its ideas —either model will do. What is interesting, though, is the manner in which this antipolitical movement which was the focus for so much vitriolic dissent from the rest of French political society continued nevertheless to express itself in purely political terms.

It is important to see the links between all three types of French pacifism discussed in this book. Not only can they be classified according to either the Chickering or Ceadel typologies, but they should also be seen as part of a time continuum. Their political evolution is important because so many of the major figures of both new-style pacifism and also feminist pacifism began their political trajectories as allies, if not members, of the APD, moving slowly over time away from the original French pacifist 'faith'. Historical dissent begat political alienation, which in turn combined with the growing fears of another war, to produce a new type of pacifism which posited a radical departure from the methods of the past. The new pacifism incarnated the negation of politics, the negation of the recent past, and the affirmation of new political values drawn from, amongst other things, the ethical lessons of the Great War and a vision of French history which owed something to Robespierre.

The LICP ceased to exist with the coming of war in September 1939. Many of its leading lights signed the tract 'Paix immédiate', which was written and distributed by Louis Lecoin when war was declared, but then recanted under pressure from the authorities.[8] A fruitful area for further research would be to analyse the extent to which French integral pacifists succumbed to the temptations of collaborationism with the Nazis under the guise of working to create a new Europe. It is not the purpose of this book to examine this question—which constitutes quite another study in itself. Suffice it here to say that René Gerin, Félicien Challaye and Léon Emery, to name but three, were all tried for collaboration after the war. Gerin died in 1957 still protesting his innocence.[9]

In the case of Challaye, it seems clear that the man's visceral hatred of war had clouded his moral judgement by the time Vichy was a political fact. In a preface dated December 1941 to a book by Raoul-Albert Bodinier of the Ligue scolaire internationale de la paix, Challaye called for 'grateful recognition' to Pétain who had 'saved the country in imposing the armistice', and who had had 'the courage to go to Montoire'. Furthermore, he wrote that the politicians and journalists responsible for 'pushing' France into war ought to be sentenced to prison terms or have their civic rights removed 'for at

---

[8] A copy of this tract can be found in BDIC/O Pièce 342 Rés. It is also reprinted in Nicolas Faucier, *Pacifisme et antimilitarisme dans l'entre-deux-guerres* (Paris: Spartacus, 1983), 193. See Faucier, *Pacifisme*, 191–5 for his account of the 'Paix immédiate' affair.

[9] See René Gerin, *Un procès de la libération: ... La 'Justice' enferrée* (Paris: Éditions de 'Contre-courant', 1954). There are a number of letters from Michel Alexandre in BDIC/Dossiers Alexandre/FΔRés. 348 attesting to the character and probity of both Emery and Challaye.

least ten years'. In a terrible misapprehension of the nature of Nazism, Challaye proclaimed the 'duty to COLLABORATE with Germany, to hasten the return of our dear prisoners, to save our people, first from extreme misery, but also from political annihilation, and finally, to hasten the advent of a reconciled Europe and world'.[10]

As for the APD, in a very real sense it went underground. The Association stopped publication of the review in May 1940 at the time of the German invasion. Ruyssen wrote in October 1947 that the APD had not even attempted to continue its work so long as the German invader remained on French soil because 'success would have been more unbearable to us than failure'.[11] Ruyssen rejected the 'hypocrisy' of collaboration, and any 'conciliation' or 'international *rapprochement*' under the aegis of the 'defeatists of Vichy'.[12] The APD continued to publish its review until late 1948, but then, rather understandably, given the age of most of its leadership, seems to have disappeared.

The only one of the three main organizations examined in this book which still exists, both nationally and internationally, is the LIFPL.

For the ideological pacifists of the APD, and indeed for the feminists of the LIFPL as well, the coming of war did not mean the ultimate defeat of their ideas. It is one of the traits of the old-style pacifism and of the feminist pacifism under discussion here, that pessimism and optimism were mixed. Thus, the words of the APD's 1920 'Appel-programme' seem to sum up its approach to the temporary failure of its pacifist hopes in 1939:

We are rolling, it seems, the eternal rock of Sisyphus. A bitter observation and one which will discourage some. But we are of those who never despair. Instead, we find even in the avowal of our own disappointment, positive reasons to envisage the future with a reflective confidence.[13]

Romain Rolland astutely realized that the problem of peace had become very complicated by the early thirties. As he said, it was no longer enough to desire peace, one also had to desire the means to achieve it. Rolland represents the ideologizing of the question of

---

[10] See Félicien Challaye, 'Préface', in Raoul-Albert Bodinier, *Vérités d'avant-paix* (Paris: Éditions de 'Mon pays', n.d. [1942]), 18–19. The emphasis is Challaye's.

[11] Théodore Ruyssen, 'La Paix par le droit rentre en scène', *PD* 51/1 (Oct. 1947), 1.

[12] Ibid.

[13] La Paix par le droit, 'Appel-programme', *PD* 30/1–2 (Jan.–Feb. 1920), 3.

peace which was so rejected both by the old-style pacifists who preferred to think in terms of structures, and less in terms of the larger ideas behind them; and also by the new pacifists for whom peace was an overriding concern that relegated all else to a secondary position. It was this view of peace as the ultimate goal defining all other political considerations which caused so much friction with the representatives of a Moscow-orientated Communism which sought to define *its* peace in terms of the social revolution and defence of Soviet Russia. The integral pacifists would have none of it, and in their rejection of the Communist view, they affirmed peace as an example of Weber's 'ethic of ultimate ends', an idea which underpins much of Ceadel's analysis of pacifism.

The extent to which a political society can accommodate dissent like that of pacifism is perhaps a comment on its liberality. It is one of the paradoxes of France that a nation so individualistic in its soul should be so intolerant of political and ethical non-conformity. If nothing else, the debates occasioned by pacifism in the thirties represent a struggle for the French historical soul, an attempt to redefine the nature of French politics and the orientation it had towards the nation's revolutionary past. Pacifism struck too near the vitals of the modern French experience to be brooked gladly. The garrison mentality of the interwar years with its 'collective insecurity' was incapable of accommodating the pacifist thesis. In its ideological manifestation, pacifism was tolerated, but the political non-conformity inherent in the individualistic, dissenting new pacifism could not be accepted. Perhaps there is some grain of truth in H. N. Brailsford's rather antipathetic comment that France's 'partial eclipse during the last fifty years that followed Sedan has obliterated our recollection of the persistent military tradition of this most nationalist of peoples. . . . A nation of small peasant owners and small investors will never be Liberal in the British sense of the word.'[14]

Whatever the case, it is important to place the French pacifist experience firmly in the context of Western European political history. Pacifism was a phenomenon experienced as much by the French in the interwar years as by any of the other Western, liberal

---

[14] From H. N. Brailsford's *After the Peace*, cited in A. J. P. Taylor, *The Trouble-makers: Dissent over Foreign Policy, 1792–1939* (London: Hamish Hamilton, 1957), 177.

democracies, albeit in somewhat different forms. If this study has succeeded at all in rescuing the interwar French pacifists—men and women with different visions of the pathway to a better world, but of goodwill all of them—from the dustbin of history, then it will have partially attained its goal.

Bibliography

UNPUBLISHED PRIMARY SOURCES

Bibliothèque de documentation internationale contemporaine (Nanterre):
Fonds Duchene

1. *Ligue internationale des femmes pour la paix et la liberté:*
Section française

FΔRés. 208/1, Textes et correspondance, 1919–20.
FΔRés. 208/2, Textes et correspondance, 1921.
FΔRés. 208/3, Textes et correspondance, 1922.
FΔRés. 208/4, Textes et correspondance, 1923.
FΔRés. 208/5, Textes et correspondance, 1924.
FΔRés. 208/6, Textes et correspondance, 1925.
FΔRés. 208/7, Textes et correspondance, 1926.
FΔRés. 208/8, Textes et correspondance, 1927.
FΔRés. 208/9, Textes et correspondance, 1928.
FΔRés. 208/10, Textes et correspondance, 1929.
FΔRés. 208/11, Textes et correspondance, 1930.
FΔRés. 208/12, Textes et correspondance, 1931.
FΔRés. 208/13, Textes et correspondance, 1932.
FΔRés. 208/14, Textes et correspondance, 1933.
FΔRés. 208/15, Textes et correspondance, 1934.
FΔRés. 208/16, Textes et correspondance, 1935.
FΔRés. 208/17, Textes et correspondance, 1936.
FΔRés. 208/18, Textes et correspondance, 1937.
FΔRés. 208/19, Textes et correspondance, 1938.
FΔRés. 208/20, Textes et correspondance, 1939.
FΔRés. 208/21, Groupes de: l'Ain, Abbéville, Aix en Othe, Antibes, Autun,
    Auxerre, Bar-sur-Seine, Bordeaux, Digne, Dijon, Région parisienne,
    Seine-et-Marne, 1930–9.
FΔRés. 208/22, Groupe de Caen, 1931–8.

FΔRés. 208/23, Groupes de: Cannes, Châlons-sur-Marne, Chambéry, Chartres, Clermont-Ferrand, 1926–38.

FΔRés. 208/24, Groupes de: Marseille, Lille, Grenoble, Ile de Ré, Le Havre, 1926–37.

FΔRés. 208/25, Factures, 1920–40.

2. *LIFPL Vie internationale*

FΔRés. 207/21, Discussion sur la constitution de la LIFPL, 1934.

3. *LIFPL comités exécutifs internationaux: FΔRés. 206*

1920: Geneva, 1–4 June.

1922: Fribourg, 6–12 September.

1923: Dresden, 1–5 September.

1924: London, 4–5 February.

1925: Innsbruck, 10–15 July.

1926: Paris, 6–10 February.

1926: Geneva, 7 September, 27 and 28 September.

1927: Liège, 12–17 March.

1927: Geneva, September.

1928: Geneva, 20–4 March.

1928: Lyon, 26–30 September.

1929: Geneva, 16–19 April.

1930: Geneva, 23–6 April.

1930: Amsterdam, 11–15 October.

1931: Lille, 7–13 April.

1931: Geneva, 4–8 September.

1932: Grenoble, 11–14 May, 20–2 May.

1933: Geneva, 19–25 April.

1934: Geneva, 24–8 March.

1934: Zurich, April, May, August.

1935: London, 25–30 March.

1935: Geneva, 12–16 September.

1936: Prague, 29 April–3 May.

1936: Geneva, 9–14 September.

1937: Bruges, 6–10 April.

1937: Prague, August.

1938: Basle, 5–9 January.

1938: Geneva, 6–11 September.

4. *LIFPL Congrès internationaux*

FΔRés. 205/1, 1er Congrès international, Zurich, 12–17 mai 1919: Résolutions.

FΔRés. 205/2, Vienne, 10–16 juillet 1921: Ordre du jour.

FΔRés. 205/4, Washington, 1–8 mai 1924: Procès-verbaux, manifestes.

FΔRés. 205/5, Dublin, 8–15 juillet 1926: Rapports, résolutions.

FΔRés. 205/6, Prague, 1929: Amendement de la section allemande.

FΔRés. 205/7, Grenoble, 14–19 mai 1932: Rapports, procès-verbaux.

FΔRés. 205/8, Zurich, 3–8 septembre 1934: Rapports, résolutions, procès-verbaux.

FΔRés. 205/9, Luhacovice, 25–31 juillet 1937: Rapports, résolutions, procès-verbaux.

5. *Pacifism, general dossiers*

FΔRés. 235/1–6, Pacifisme, 1918–1939: Rapports, textes divers, résolutions, correspondance.

FΔRés. 273/1–22, Pacifisme, 1919–1939: Textes divers, comptes-rendus, résolutions, correspondance.

FΔRés. 298, Enseignement de l'histoire/New History: Congrès internationaux pour l'enseignement de l'histoire: La Haye, 1932; Bâle, 1934.

FΔRés. 312/1–4, Pacifisme, organisations diverses: 1920–1940.

FΔRés. 313, Pacifisme, 1923–1930: Congrès national de la paix: Xème (1923); XIème (1927); XIIème (1930).

FΔRés. 317, Comité mondial des femmes contre la guerre et le fascisme, section française: Paris (1932–8).

FΔRés. 348, Dossiers Jeanne et Michel Alexandre.

FΔRés. 530/I, Comité international des femmes pour la paix permanente.

Bibliothèque nationale, Paris

Fonds Romain Rolland.

Archives nationales, Paris

F7/13352, Objection de conscience.
F7/13948.

War Resisters' International

Archives in the private hands of the late Myrtle Solomon, now transferred to the International Institute for Social History, Amsterdam.

Archives of the United States of America, Washington

1. *German Foreign Ministry Archives*

Microfilm, T-120, Roll 2697, 'Viktor Margueritte'.

2. *US Department of State*

Series 851.00, Political Affairs, France (reports from Paris Embassy).
Series 851.00B, Bolshevik Activities in France.
Series 851.20, Military Affairs, France.

Swarthmore College Peace Collection, Swarthmore, Pennsylvania

CDG-B, France.
DG 107/1,4,5, André Trocmé Papers.
'Autobiographie d'André Trocmé'.

Service historique de l'armée de terre, Château de Vincennes

5N581(2), Objection de conscience.
6N468(4), Objection de conscience.
5N601(4), Propagande révolutionnaire.
5N602(2), Propagande révolutionnaire.
6N323(4), Propagande révolutionnaire.
7N2606(2), Pacifisme.
5N577(2), Organisation de la défense nationale et du haut commandement (études et projets de notes).

Interviews

Monsieur le Pasteur et Madame Philippe Vernier.
Monsieur le Pasteur et Madame Jacques Martin.
Lord (Fenner) Brockway.

Newspapers and Journals

1. *Systematically examined*

La Paix par le droit (1918–40).
En vigie (1934–9).
SOS (1930–4).
La Patrie humaine (1931–9).
Le Combat pour la paix (1933–4).
Le Barrage (1934–9).
La Volonté de paix (1928–36).

2. *Unsystematically examined*

Les Cahiers de la réconciliation.
Les Cahiers des droits de l'homme.
Évolution.
Le Semeur.
Mercure de France.

PUBLISHED PRIMARY SOURCES

'Activités de la section française, Assemblée général annuelle, 15 et 16 mai 1937', in *En vigie*, 6–7 (Oct.–Nov. 1937), 4–5.
'Addis-Abéba est prise: A bas Mussolini!', *Le Barrage*, 96 (7 May 1936), 1.

ALLÉGRET, PAUL, 'Le Devoir militaire, et le scrupule de conscience: Avant et après la Grande Guerre: Une solution: Rapport présenté à l'Assemblée générale de la "Paix par le droit"', *PD* 36/4 (Apr. 1926), 145–6.

'A M. Georges Clemenceau (lettre adressée à M. Clemenceau au lendemain de la demande d'armistice formulée par les Empires centraux par le Comité directeur de "l'Association de la paix par le droit", Bordeaux, 8 octobre 1918)', *PD* 28/21–2 (Nov. 1918), 332–3.

ANDRÉ, BERNARD, 'Désarmement', *PH* 10 (30 Jan.–14 Feb. 1932), 7.

Annuaire de la paix (Paris: Centre international de documentation anti-guerrière, 1936).

'Appel', *PH* 20 (16–23 Apr. 1932), 6.

'Appel-programme', *PD* 30/1–2 (Jan.–Feb. 1920), 1–5.

'A propos du Front populaire', *Le Barrage*, 67 (17 Oct. 1935), 4.

ARCHDEACON, ERNEST, 'Pour l'unification des sociétés pacifistes', *PD* 41/7 (July 1931), 313–4.

'Association de la paix par le droit', in *Nous voulons la paix* (Paris: SRIP, 1932), 28–31.

'Au cercle de la Russie neuve', *Le Barrage*, 56 (13 June 1935), 2.

'Autour du Congrès de Zurich', *En vigie*, 1 (Oct. 1935), 4–5.

'Avis important' in *En vigie*, 4–5 (Apr. 1937), 9.

'Avis important', *En vigie*, 10–11–12 (Mar. 1939), 1.

BABUT, HENRY, 'Les Origines de la Paix par le droit', *PD* 38/4–5 (Apr.–May 1928), 169–75.

—— 'Notes brèves sur nos origines', *PD* 48/6–7–8 (May–June–July 1938), 254–6.

BARBÉ, A., 'A ceux qui doivent bientôt "partir"', *PH* 83 (15 Sept. 1933), 4.

BAUCHET, ÉMILE, 'Rapport financier', *Le Combat pour la paix*, 10 (Mar. 1934), 5–6.

—— 'Rapport financier', *Le Barrage*, 87 (5 Mar. 1936), 4.

—— 'Rapport moral', *Le Barrage*, 43 (7 Mar. 1935), 4.

—— 'Rapport moral', *Le Barrage*, 87 (5 Mar. 1936), 4.

—— 'Rapport sur l'organisation pratique', *Le Barrage*, 44 (14 Mar. 1935), 2.

BELOT, GUSTAVE, 'Encore le mot "pacifisme"', *PD* 28/7–8 (Apr. 1918), 109.

BLOCH, A., 'Adaptations nécessaires de la doctrine pacifiste', *PD* 49/1 (Jan. 1939), 4–7.

—— 'Le Pacifisme a-t-il fait faillite?', *PD* 44/3 (Mar. 1934), 131–4.

BOIS, JACQUES, 'Enquête sur la crise du pacifisme: Réponse de M. Jacques Bois', *PD* 44/2 (Feb. 1934), 74–7.

BOSSE, LOUIS, 'Quelques réflexions sur un projet du paradis mécanique', *PD* 31/1 (Jan. 1921), 3–6.

BOUSSINOT, CHARLES, 'Le Salut n'est qu'en nous-mêmes', *Le Barrage*, 86 (27 Feb. 1936), 1.

BROUSSAUDIER, SYLVAIN, 'Brève réponse à R Messac', *Le Barrage*, 111 (27 May 1937), 3.

—— 'Comment lutter à la fois contre la guerre et contre le fascisme? Rapport sur l'aspect politique de la question', *Le Barrage*, 124 (24 Feb. 1938), 3.

—— 'Le Repli impérial', *Le Barrage*, 142 (2 Feb. 1939), 1.

—— 'Les Pacifistes dans le Parti socialiste', *Le Barrage*, 110 (13 May 1937), 2.

—— 'Nous demandons à comprendre', *Le Barrage*, 72 (21 Nov. 1935), 3.

'Bulletin officiel de la LICP: Autour du Congrès de Pâques', *PH* 61 (25 Mar. 1933), 5.

CAPY, MARCELLE, *A bas les armes! Discours prononcé à l'occasion de la "Croisade de la paix" de la Ligue internationale des combattants de la paix* (Paris: 'La Patrie humaine', 1932).

—— 'Les Femmes et la paix', *Le Progrès civique*, 600 (14 Feb. 1931), 213.

—— 'Retour d'Allemagne', *PH* 13 (27 Feb.–4 Mar. 1932), 1.

CARRÈRE, JEAN, 'L'Autriche depuis l'Anschluss', *Le Barrage*, 135 (20 Oct. 1938), 3.

'Ce que disent les autres', *PH* 12 (20–6 Feb. 1932), 3.

'Ce que disent les autres', *PH* 28 (11–18 June 1932), 3.

CHALLAYE, FÉLICIEN, 'A bas les deux ans! Lettre ouverte à Léon Blum', *Le Barrage*, 101 (25 June 1936), 1.

—— 'A propos de "l'indivisible paix": Réponse à Romain Rolland', *Le Barrage*, 83 (6 Feb. 1936), 1.

—— 'A propos du conflit italo-éthiopien: Guerre et colonisation', *Le Barrage*, 60 (18 July 1935), 1.

—— 'Antifascisme et pacifisme intégral: Réponse à Bernard Lecache', *Le Barrage*, 81 (23 Jan. 1936), 1.

—— *Georges Demartial: Sa vie, son œuvre* (Paris: A. Lahure, n.d. [1950]).

—— *La Paix sans aucune réserve: Thèse de Félicien Challaye: Suivie d'une discussion entre Th. Ruyssen, F. Challaye, G. Ganguilhem, Jean le Masaf, et de textes de Bertrand Russell et d'Alain sur: La Vraie et la folle résistance* (Nîmes: Imprimerie 'la laborieuse', 1932).

—— 'La Préparation de la guerre et l'action de certains réfugiés allemands', *Le Barrage*, 78 (2 Jan. 1936), 1.

—— *La Signification morale de la guerre actuelle (conférence faite au cours d'instruction complémentaire pour les sous-officiers du 109e régiment territorial d'infanterie le 29 mars 1916 par le Sergent Félicien Challaye)* (Paris: Comité de propagande socialiste pour la défense nationale, 1916).

—— 'Le Conflit italo-éthiopien et les principes de notre Ligue', *Le Barrage*, 64 (12 Sept. 1935), 1.

—— 'Lettre à Léon Blum', *Le Barrage*, 102 (9 July 1936), 1.

—— 'Pacifisme et antifascisme', *Le Barrage*, 140 (5 Jan. 1939), 2.

CHALLAYE, FÉLICIEN, 'Pacifistes, tolstoiens ou révolutionnaires', *Le Barrage*, 105 (20 Aug. 1936), 1.

—— 'Pas de guerre pour l'Autriche!', *Le Barrage*, 126 (31 Mar. 1938), 2.

—— *Pour la paix désarmée, même en face de Hitler* (Le Vésinet: chez l'auteur, n.d. [1933]).

—— 'Pour la paix sans aucune réserve', *PD* 41/11 (Nov. 1931), 489–97.

—— 'Pour la paix sans aucune réserve (réponse à l'article de M Ruyssen)', *PD* 42/4 (Apr. 1932), 149–52.

—— 'Pour l'union des adversaires de toute guerre', *Le Barrage*, 58 (27 June 1935), 1.

—— 'Préface', in Raoul-Albert Bodinier, *Vérités d'avant-paix* (Paris: Éditions de 'Mon pays', n.d. [1942]).

—— 'Raymond Poincaré, René Gerin, et les responsabilités de la guerre', *Le Barrage*, 26 (8 Nov. 1934), 1–2.

—— 'Robespierre et l'actualité', *Le Barrage*, 116 (30 Sept. 1937), 1.

—— 'Seconde réponse à Romain Rolland', *Le Barrage*, 90 (19 Mar. 1936), 2.

—— 'Un manifeste d'intellectuels', *Le Barrage*, 66 (10 Oct. 1935), 2.

—— 'Un terrible lapsus', *Le Barrage*, 109 (29 Apr. 1937), 1.

CHARPENTIER, ARMAND, 'Ce que coûtent les alliances franco-russes', *Le Barrage*, 107 (1 Oct. 1936), 1.

—— 'Heureuses victoires et joyeux échecs', *Le Barrage*, 96 (7 May 1936), 1.

—— 'Similitudes: 1914: Iswolsky—1938: Bénes', *Le Barrage*, 133 (22 Sept. 1938), 1.

—— 'Un héros de la paix: Gérard Leretour', *PH* 53 (28 Jan.–4 Feb. 1933), 1.

'Chez les Combattants de la paix: Le Congrès de Pâques', *PH* 66 (29 Apr. 1933), 4.

'Chronique: La Révision du traité de Versailles: La Paix par le droit et la guerre: La Paix avec la Russie' (letters from A. H. Fried, A. A. Warden, and Louis Guétant, with comments by Ruyssen), *PD* 30/3–4 (Mar.–Apr. 1920), 89–100.

'Cinquième conférence nationale de la paix par l'éducation', *PD* 45/3 (Mar. 1935), 116–34, and *PD* 45/4 (Apr. 1935), 172–92.

'Comité central de la Ligue', *PH* 10 (30 Jan.–14 Feb. 1932), 8.

'Compte-rendu du Congrès de Montargis', *Le Combat pour la paix*, 11 (Apr. 1934), 4.

'Congrès national de la LICP, 16–17 avril 1933', *Le Combat pour la paix*, 1 (May 1933), 4–10.

COT, PIERRE, 'La Conception française de la lutte contre la guerre', *PD* 39/4–5 (Apr.–May 1929), 164–70.

CUENAT, PIERRE, 'Depuis qu'Hitler est là . . . qu'y a-t-il de changé?', *PH* 88 (27 Oct. 1933), 1.

—— 'Du pacifisme à la paix', *PH* 46 (10–17 Dec. 1932), 2.

—— '1914, deuxième édition?', *PH* 71 (2 June 1933), 3.

DANDIEU, Y., 'Compte-rendu financier', *Le Barrage*, 126 (31 Mar. 1938), 4.

DÉAT, MARCEL, 'Réponse à l'Enquête sur la crise du pacifisme', *PD* 44/2 (Feb. 1934), 77–80.

DELAISI, FRANCIS, 'Le Problème des populations en surnombre', in J. Lahargue, 'Le Congrès de Marseille de la Paix par le droit (suite et fin), 28–29 décembre 1935', *PD* 46/4 (Apr. 1936), 173–5.

—— 'Les Garanties intérieures de la paix, conséquence du Pacte Kellogg', in J. Prudhommeaux, 'L'Assemblée générale de la Paix par le droit, Bordeaux, 2 et 3 novembre 1929', *PD* 39/12 (Dec. 1929), 458.

DEMARTIAL, GEORGES, *La Légende des démocraties pacifiques* (Paris: Rieder/Presses universitaires de France, 1939).

—— 'Le Problème tchèque et la paix', *Le Barrage*, 148 (4 May 1939), 1.

—— 'Les Responsabilités de la guerre: Une réponse de G. Demartial à M. Camille Bloch', *PH* 105 (2 Mar. 1934), 2.

—— 'L'Hitlérisme et la France', *Le Barrage*, 34 (3 Jan. 1935), 1.

—— *1939: La Guerre de l'imposture* (Paris: Éditions Jean Flory, 1941).

'200 délégués participent aux débats', *PH*, 31 (2–9 July 1932) 1.

'Deuxième Conférence nationale de la paix par l'éducation', *PD* 42/5 (May 1932), 201–36.

DEVALDÈS, MANUEL, 'Les Objecteurs de conscience anglo-saxons', *Mercure de France*, 166 (15 Sept. 1923), 642–69.

—— 'L'État mondial de la question de l'objection de conscience', *Mercure de France*, 198 (15 Aug. 1927), 100–22.

DOYEN, PIERRE, 'Deux lettres du Professeur Doyen', *Le Combat pour la paix*, 4 (Aug.–Sept. 1933), 4.

DREVET, CAMILLE, 'Rapport moral', *Le Barrage*, 125 (17 Mar. 1938), 3.

—— 'Rapport moral', *Le Barrage*, 145 (16 Mar. 1939), 4.

DUCHENE, G., 'Congrès mondial contre la guerre, Amsterdam, 27–28 août 1932', in *SOS* 12 (1932), 5–6.

DUMAS, ANDRÉ, 'Ligue, "*Patrie humaine*" et librairie', *PH* 58 (4–11 Mar. 1933), 4.

DUMAS, JACQUES, 'La Société française pour l'arbitrage entre nations', *PD* 32/2 (Feb. 1922), 59–65.

—— 'Les Origines de la Paix par le droit', *PD* 38/3 (Mar. 1928), 105–12.

DUMÉRIL, EDMOND, 'L'Allemagne et la Société des nations: Le Projet de Mathias Erzberger', *PD* 29/2–3 (Feb.–Mar. 1919), 65–71.

—— 'Pour notre Assemblée générale', *PD* 40/10 (Oct. 1930), 373–5.

—— and PRUDHOMMEAUX, JULES, 'L'Assemblée générale de la Paix par le droit' (Poitiers, 31 Oct.–1 Nov. 1921), *PD* 31/12 (Dec. 1921), 401–10.

—— —— and RUYSSEN, THÉODORE, 'L'Assemblée générale de la Paix par le droit', *PD* 30/11–12 (Nov.–Dec. 1920), 370–80.

DUPIN, GUSTAVE, 'La Revanche de la caste', *PH* 79 (28 July 1933), 1.

—— 'L'Individu et l'état', *PH* 47 (17–24 Dec. 1932), 2.

DUTHU, ADRIEN, 'Ange ou démon?'; *Le Barrage*, 110 (13 May 1937), 1–2.

—— 'Autriche–Tchécoslovaquie', *Le Barrage*, 127 (28 Apr. 1938), 2.

—— 'Tchécoslovaquie', *Le Barrage*, 129 (26 May 1938), 2.

—— 'Une leçon à tirer des événements d'Espagne', *Le Barrage*, 108 (22 Oct. 1936), 2.

'Échos', *Le Barrage*, 66 (10 Oct. 1935), 2.

'Échos: Distinguo', *Le Barrage*, 76 (19 Dec. 1935), 2.

EMERY, L., 'Encore la Tchécoslovaquie', *Le Barrage*, 130 (9 June 1938), 1.

—— 'Le Pacifisme et la doctrine révolutionnaire', *Le Barrage*, 146 (30 Mar. 1939), 1.

—— 'Le Pacte franco-russe et la paix européenne', *Le Barrage*, 95 (30 Apr. 1936), 2.

—— 'Le Problème colonial et la paix', *Le Barrage*, 125 (17 Mar. 1938), 3.

—— 'Les Équivoques du pacifisme', *PD* 43/7 (July 1933), 239–44.

'Enquête sur l'objection de conscience', *PD* 36/9–10 (Sept.–Oct. 1926), 337–41.

FAURE, S., 'Avant tout et à tout prix il faut empêcher la guerre', *PH* 20 (16–23 Apr. 1932).

—— 'La Sauvegarde de la paix', *Le Barrage*, 98 (21 May 1936), 2.

—— *Nous voulons la paix* (Paris: chez l'auteur, 1932).

—— 'Rapport sur le désarmement unilatéral', *Le Barrage*, 44 (14 Mar. 1935), 5–6.

FERNAU, HERMANN, 'De la nécessité d'un rapprochement franco-allemand', *PD* 31/2 (Feb. 1921), 54–7.

FOERSTER, FRIEDRICH WILHELM, 'Avertissements d'un pacifiste allemand: Pour un pacifisme sans illusions', *PD* 45/1 (Jan. 1935), 4–14.

FOLLIET, JOSEPH, *Pacifisme de droite? Bellicisme de gauche?* (Paris: Éditions du cerf, 1938).

FOUSKI, MARCEL, 'Rapport sur la déclaration de la Ligue', *PH* 58 (4–11 Mar. 1933), 3.

FRANÇOIS, LOUIS, 'Une entente franco-allemande est-elle donc impossible?', *PD* 45/3 (Mar. 1935), 139–43, and 'Suite', in *PD* 45/4 (Apr. 1935), 195–204.

FRIED, ALFRED H., 'Un dernier mot', *PD* 29/9–10 (Sept.–Oct. 1919), 401–2.

'Gaston Moch', *PD* 45/9 (Sept. 1935), 377–8.

GERIN, RENÉ, 'A ceux qui doivent bientôt "partir"', *Le Combat pour la paix*, 4 (Aug.–Sept. 1933), 5–6.

—— 'Alain a raison: C'est la paix qui commence', *Le Barrage*, 133 (22 Sept. 1938), 1.

—— 'Antimilitarisme d'abord!', *Le Barrage*, 99 (28 May 1936), 1.

—— 'A propos d'un incident', *Le Barrage*, 114 (22 July 1937), 1.

—— 'Au travail, pour la paix des peuples!', *Le Barrage*, 134 (6 Oct. 1938), 1.

—— 'Bientôt, des élections', *Le Barrage*, 47 (4 Apr. 1935), 1.

—— 'Bilan 1935', *Le Barrage*, 78 (2 Jan. 1936), 1.

—— 'Blum-Gribouille', *Le Barrage*, 140 (5 Jan. 1939), 1.

—— 'Ce que signifie le vote des Sarrois', *Le Barrage*, 37 (24 Jan. 1935), 1.

—— 'Décrets-lois', *Le Barrage*, 137 (17 Nov. 1938), 1.

—— 'Défense de libertés et "défense nationale"', *Le Barrage*, 111 (27 May 1937), 1.

—— 'Détente?', *Le Barrage*, 31 (13 Dec. 1934), 1.

—— 'Écueils', *Le Barrage*, 135 (20 Oct. 1938), 1.

—— 'Guernica . . .', *Le Barrage*, 110 (13 May 1937), 1.

—— 'Guerre étrangère et guerre civile', *Le Barrage*, 104 (6 Aug. 1936), 1.

—— *Honneur et patrie ou comment j'ai été exclu de la Légion d'honneur* (Paris: Éditions de la LICP, 1934).

—— 'Honte aux assassins!', *Le Barrage*, 66 (10 Oct. 1935), 1.

—— 'La Démocratie et la paix', *Le Barrage*, 113 (24 June 1937), 1.

—— 'La Formule d'André Delmas', *Le Barrage*, 132 (11 Aug. 1938), 1.

—— 'La Guerre de Dantzig n'aura pas lieu', *Le Barrage*, 151 (13 July 1939), 1.

—— 'La Joie mauvaise', *Le Barrage*, 14 (16 Aug. 1934), 1.

—— 'La Négociation aura lieu', *Le Barrage*, 148 (4 May 1939), 1.

—— 'La Nouvelle Alliance franco-russe est-elle une étape vers la paix?', *Le Barrage*, 51 (9 May 1935), 1.

—— *La Paix anxieuse et obstinée* (Paris: Rivière, 1938).

—— 'La Politique extérieure de l'URSS', *Le Barrage*, 96 (7 May 1936), 1.

—— 'La Pologne et nous', *Le Barrage*, 149 (18 May 1939), 1–2.

—— 'Le Coup de Staline', *Le Barrage*, 53 (23 May 1935), 1.

—— 'Le "Fascisme" a fait faillite', *Le Barrage*, 17 (6 Sept. 1934), 1.

—— *Les Causes psychologiques des guerres* (Paris: Ligue internationale des combattants de la paix, 1935).

—— 'Les Élections et la paix', *Le Barrage*, 95 (30 Apr. 1936), 1.

—— 'Les "Mentalités obstinées"', *Le Barrage*, 21 (4 Oct. 1934), 1.

—— 'L'Espoir, enfin, change de camp', *Le Barrage*, 52 (16 May 1935), 1.

—— *Les Responsabilités de la guerre de 1914* (Paris: Éditions de la LICP, 1933).

—— *Les Responsabilités de la guerre: Quatorze questions par René Gerin, ancien élève de l'École normale supérieure, agrégé des lettres: Quatorze réponses par Raymond Poincaré de l'Académie française* (Paris: Payot, 1930).

—— 'Lettre ouverte à M Daladier', *PH* 63 (8 Apr. 1933), 1–2.

—— 'On revise les traités . . .', *Le Barrage*, 125 (17 Mar. 1938), 1.

—— 'Pacifisme et antifascisme', *Le Barrage*, 141 (19 Jan. 1939), 2.

—— *Pacifisme 'intégral' et guerre civile* (Paris: Ligue internationale des combattants de la paix, 1937).

—— 'Pas de surenchère verbale!', *Le Barrage*, 122 (20 Jan. 1938), 1.

GERIN, RENÉ, 'Pas de surenchère verbale: (II) Réponse à Robert Tourly', *Le Barrage*, 123 (3 Feb. 1938), 1.

—— 'Pourquoi nous refusons toute union sacrée', *Le Barrage*, 126 (31 Mar. 1938), 1.

—— 'Pour un appel aux peuples', *Le Barrage*, 146 (30 Mar. 1939), 1.

—— 'Que veut l'Allemagne?', *Le Barrage*, 88 (12 Mar. 1936), 1.

—— 'Rapport moral sur l'activité de la Ligue de Pâques 1933 à Pâques 1934 qui sera présenté au Congrès de Montargis', *Le Combat pour la paix*, 10 (Mar. 1934), 4–5.

—— 'Rapport provisoire sur la déclaration de la Ligue', *PH* 58 (4–11 Mar. 1933), 3–4.

—— 'Rapport sur le "Barrage"', *Le Barrage*, 125 (17 Mar. 1938), 4.

—— 'Rapport sur le "Barrage"', *Le Barrage*, 145 (16 Mar. 1939), 4.

—— 'Rapport sur l'organisation de la propagande', *Le Barrage*, 87 (5 Mar. 1936), 4.

—— 'Sanctions', *Le Barrage*, 73 (28 Nov. 1935), 1.

—— *Si la guerre éclatait . . . Que faire?* (Paris: Ligue internationale des combattants de la paix, 1936).

—— 'Si Paris valut une messe . . .', *Le Barrage*, 30 (6 Dec. 1934), 1.

—— 'Un dictateur?', *Le Barrage*, 24 (25 Oct. 1934), 1.

—— 'Un discours et un entretien', *Le Barrage*, 28 (22 Nov. 1934), 1.

—— 'Une leçon à méditer', *Le Barrage*, 100 (11 June 1936), 1.

—— 'Une nouvelle loi scélérate', *Le Barrage*, 8 (5 July 1934), 1.

—— 'Union sacrée et lutte de classes', *Le Barrage*, 105 (20 Aug. 1936), 1.

—— 'Union sacrée?—Non, jamais!', *Le Barrage*, 143 (16 Feb. 1939), 1.

—— *Un procès de la libération: . . . La 'Justice' enferrée* (Paris: Éditions de 'Contre-courant', 1954).

GERLACH, HELLMUTH VON, 'Guerre préventive?', *PD* 43/6 (June 1933), 197.

GILBERT, HUBERT, 'Le Pacte Laval–Potemkine', *Le Barrage*, 51 (9 May 1935), 3.

GOBRON, GABRIEL, 'Les Crustacés intellectuels', *PH* 44 (26 Nov.–3 Dec. 1932), 3.

GOUTTENOIRE DE TOURY, FERNAND, 'Désarmement, ou catastrophe final', *Le Barrage*, 135 (20 Oct. 1938), 1.

GUÉTANT, LOUIS, and RUYSSEN, THÉODORE, 'Les Responsabilités de la guerre I et II', *PD* 30/10 (Oct. 1920), 328–33.

GUILBEAUX, HENRI, 'La Sarre est allemande', *Le Barrage*, 36 (17 Jan. 1935), 3.

—— 'La Sarre et les rapports franco-allemands', *Le Barrage*, 34 (3 Jan. 1935), 3.

—— 'Le Conflit italo-abyssin', *Le Barrage*, 33 (27 Dec. 1934), 3.

—— 'Rapport sur le programme, l'union France–Allemagne–URSS, et la lutte contre le fascisme', *Le Barrage*, 43 (7 Mar. 1935), 4–5.

GUITON, E., and RUYSSEN, THÉODORE, 'A propos de l'objection de conscience', *PD* 36/2 (Feb. 1926), 68–9.

GUKOWSKI, NADIA, 'Racisme et nationalisme', *Le Barrage*, 138 (1 Dec. 1938), 1.

HADAMARD, JACQUES, 'Pacifisme intégral?', *PD* 41/2 (Feb. 1931), 57–68.

—— 'Un nouveau pas à faire dans la voie de la paix: Les Manuels scolaires', *PD* 40/1 (Jan. 1930), 1–4.

HECQUET, MARCELINE, *L'Objection de conscience devant le service militaire* (Paris: Éditions du groupe de propagande par la brochure, 1924).

HENRY, R., 'Un bel exemple à suivre', *PH* 16 (19–26 Mar. 1932).

'Honte aux assassins', *Le Barrage*, 66 (10 Oct. 1935), 1.

HUMBERT, JEANNE, *Contre la guerre qui vient* (Paris: Éditions de la LICP, 1933).

—— 'La Surpopulation et la guerre', *Le Barrage*, 87 (5 Mar. 1936), 5.

JAMET, CLAUDE, 'La Paix inévitable', *Le Barrage*, 147 (20 Apr. 1939), 1–2.

JEANSON, HENRI, 'A bas l'union sacrée!', *Le Barrage*, 125 (17 Mar. 1938), 1.

JOSPIN, ROBERT, 'Au dessus de la paix', *Le Barrage*, 139 (15 Dec. 1938), 3.

—— 'Force ou collaboration', *Le Barrage*, 146 (30 Mar. 1939), 1.

—— 'Le Rassemblement populaire et la paix: A propos d'un programme', *Le Barrage*, 84 (13 Feb. 1936), 2.

—— 'Les Problèmes économiques et la paix', *Le Barrage*, 142 (2 Feb. 1939), 4.

—— 'Maintenant, bâtissons l'Europe', *Le Barrage*, 135 (20 Oct. 1938), 1.

—— 'Précisions nouvelles', *Le Combat pour la paix*, 4 (Aug.–Sept. 1933), 2.

—— 'Rapport sur la nationalisation des armements', *Le Barrage*, 44 (14 Mar. 1935), 4.

—— 'Rapport sur la question: Si la guerre éclatait?', *Le Barrage*, 44 (14 Mar. 1935), 6.

JOUVE, ANDRÉE, 'Jane Addams', *En vigie*, 1/1 (Oct. 1935), 1.

KAWERAU, SIEGFRIED, 'Les Livres d'histoire en Allemagne, notamment depuis 1923', *PD* 37/3 (Mar. 1926), 104–11.

—— 'Où en est l'Allemagne dans l'amélioration de ses livres d'histoire?', *PD* 41/10 (Oct. 1931), 449–52.

LACAZE-DUTHIERS, GÉRARD DE, 'Livres, revues, journaux' (review of Félicien Challaye, *Pour la paix désarmée, même en face de Hitler*), *Le Barrage*, 1 (17 May 1934), 3.

LACROIX, MAURICE, and MAN, HENRI DE, 'Les Lendemains de Munich: Faisons la paix!', *PD* 48/13 (Dec. 1938), 404–10.

'L'Activité de la Ligue', *Le Barrage*, 148 (4 May 1939), 4.

'L'Activité de la Ligue: Montargis', *Le Barrage*, 40 (14 Feb. 1935), 4.

'L'Affaire d'Éthiopie et nous', *Le Barrage*, 65 (26 Sept. 1935), 1.

LAGOT, EUGÈNE, 'Sous le signe de la peur', *Le Semeur*, 232 (22 July 1933), 1.

LAGUERRE, ODETTE, 'Le Congrès du Rassemblement universel pour la paix à Bruxelles', *PD* 46/10 (Oct. 1936), 397–400.

—— and PRUDHOMMEAUX, JULES, 'Le Congrès français du Rassemblement universel pour la paix, Paris, 25–27 septembre 1937', *PD* 47/11–12 (Nov.–Dec. 1937), 393–9.

LAHARGUE, J., 'Le Congrès de Marseille de la Paix par le droit, 28–29 décembre 1935', *PD* 46/3 (Mar. 1936), pp. 113–23.

—— and PRUDHOMMEAUX, JULES, 'Le Congrès de la Paix par le droit, Clermont-Ferrand (suite en fin)', *PD* 47/4–5 (Apr.–May 1937), 145–62.

'La Paix sans réserve?', *PD* 41/12 (Dec. 1931), 561.

LAPIERRE, GEORGES, 'La Conférence internationale pour l'enseignement de l'histoire', *PD* 42/7–8 (July–Aug. 1932), 346–9.

'La Politique internationale: Deux ordres du jour sur les réparations: La Paix par le droit et la Ligue de la République', *PD* 33/1 (Jan. 1923), 29–31.

LASKINE, EDMOND, 'La Victoire de Locarno', *PD* 35/11 (Nov. 1925), 429–33.

LAURET, RENÉ, 'Pourquoi le pacifisme est décrié', *PD* 32/2 (Feb. 1922), 72–3.

'La Vie de la Ligue', *PH* 12 (20–6 Feb. 1932), 4.

'La Vie de la Ligue', *PH* 13 (27 Feb.–4 Mar. 1932), 4.

'La Vie de la Ligue', *PH* 19 (9–16 Apr. 1931), 4.

'La Vie de la Ligue', *PH* 38 (1–15 Oct. 1932), 4.

'La Vie de la Ligue: Alger', *PH* 47 (17–24 Dec. 1932), 4.

'La Vie de la Ligue: 11e et 12e arrdt.', *PH* 40 (29 Oct.–5 Nov. 1932), 4.

'Le Bureau international de la paix', *PD* 29/7–8 (July–Aug. 1919), 357–9.

'Le Cinquantenaire de l'Association: A nos amis', *PD* 47/8–9 (Aug.–Sept. 1937), 297–8.

'Le Comité directeur de la Paix par le droit: Pourquoi ces armements?', *PD* 37/6 (June 1927), 185–7.

'Le Congrès de Bierville', *PD* 36/9–10 (Sept.–Oct. 1926), 369–72.

'Le Dossier Demartial (défense, témoignages et plaidoirie)', *Évolution*, 30 (June 1928), 34–50.

LE FOYER, LUCIEN, 'L'Union populaire pour la paix', in *Nous voulons la paix* (Paris: SRIP, 1932), 55–6.

LÉGER, LOUIS, 'Rapport financier', *Le Barrage*, 43 (7 Mar. 1935), 4.

'Le Journal de guerre d'Alfred H. Fried', *PD* 29/7–8 (July–Aug. 1919), 312–25.

LEMÉDIONI, ÉDOUARD, 'Rapport sur la tactique que la Ligue doit adopter afin de rendre efficace l'action qu'elle mène contre la guerre', *Le Combat pour la paix*, 9 (Feb. 1934), 1–4.

—— 'Rapport sur le référendum populaire', *Le Barrage*, 44 (14 Mar. 1935), 4.

LEONHARD, RUDOLF, *L'Allemagne et la paix* (Paris: Éditions de la LICP, 1932).

—— 'Le Problème de la Sarre du point de vue allemand', *Le Barrage*, 32 (20 Dec. 1934), 2.

—— 'Le Problème de la Sarre du point de vue allemand (suite)', *Le Barrage*, 33 (27 Dec. 1934), 2.

LÉONTIN, L., 'Après le Congrès de la paix de Berlin', *PD* 34/12 (Dec. 1924), 457–8.

LEPINE, F., 'Pacifisme ou défaitisme?', *PD* 28/3–4–5–6 (Feb.–Mar. 1918), 49–55.

LERETOUR, GÉRARD, 'Debout, les objecteurs!', *PH* 71 (2 June 1933), 2.

—— 'Pourquoi le manifeste?', *PH* 81 (18 Aug. 1933), 4.

'Le Sabotage de la défense nationale: La Presse et la circulaire de M Chautemps', *Écho de Paris*, 3 May 1933.

'Le Sabotage de la défense nationale: Une circulaire confidentielle du ministre de l'intérieur aux préfets', *Écho de Paris*, 1 May 1933.

'Les Jeux de soldats', *PD* 36/5 (May 1926), 193–213; and *PD* 36/6 (June 1926), 253–5.

'Les Manuels d'histoire allemands et français: Résolutions adoptées par la commission d'historiens allemands et français, réunis du 25 novembre au 1er décembre 1935, pour examen des rectifications qu'il y aurait lieu d'apporter aux manuels scolaires des deux pays', *PD* 47/6 (June 1937), 209–17, and 47/7 (July 1937), 257–71.

'Les Responsabilités de la guerre et le professeur Quidde', *PD* 29/1 (Jan. 1919), 56.

'Les Travaux du Congrès d'Agen', *Le Barrage*, 50 (2 May 1935), 4.

'Les Travaux du Congrès d'Arras', *Le Barrage*, 127 (28 Apr. 1938), 4.

'Les Travaux du Congrès de Bernay', *Le Barrage*, 94 (23 Apr. 1936), 3–4.

'Les Travaux du Congrès de Marseille', *Le Barrage*, 147 (20 Apr. 1939), 4.

'Lettre à M. Pierre Laval, président du Conseil, ministre des Affaires étrangères', *PD* 45/9 (Sept. 1935), 340–1.

'Lettre ouverte aux 30.000 signataires de notre manifeste', *La Volonté de paix* (Jan.–Feb. 1931), 1.

LÉVY, ROGER, 'Société des nations et coopération intellectuelle depuis dix ans', *PD* 40/6 (June 1930), 218–25.

LHOUMEAU, HÉLÈNE, 'Lettre à M. Ch. Rousseau à propos de "l'Allemagne contre le droit"', *PD* 44/1 (Jan. 1934), 18–19.

Ligue internationale des combattants de la paix, *Programme, tactiques et moyens d'action* (Paris: Éditions de la LICP, n.d.).

'Manifeste de la Volonté de paix', *La Volonté de paix* (Aug.–Sept. 1928), 4.

'Manifeste du Congrès', *Le Combat pour la paix*, 1 (May 1933), 3.

'Manifeste du Congrès d'Arras', *Le Barrage*, 127 (28 Apr. 1938), 1.

'Marcelle Capy en Allemagne et en Suisse', *PH* 10 (30 Jan.–14 Feb. 1932), 2.

MAURETTE, M., 'La Répartition des matières premières', in J. Lahargue, 'Le Congrès de Marseille de la Paix par le droit (suite en fin), 28–29 décembre 1935', *PD* 46/4 (Apr. 1936), 170–3.

MÉRIC, VICTOR, 'Celle d'hier, celle de demain', *PH* 23 (6–19 Aug. 1932), 1–2.

—— 'Du bon travail', *PH* 12 (20–6 Feb. 1932), 1.

—— *Fraîche et gazeuse! La Guerre qui revient* (Paris: Éditions 'Sirius', 1932).

—— 'La Bataille du Trocadéro', *PH* NS 3 (7–22 Dec. 1931), 2.

—— 'La Paix est en marche', *PH* 10 (30 Jan.–14 Feb. 1932), 2.

—— 'L'Aventure hitlérienne', *PH* 22 (30 Apr.–7 May 1932), 1.

—— 'Le Combat pour la paix: Réponse de Victor Méric', *PH* 33 (23 July–6 Aug. 1932), 1.

—— 'Lettre ouverte aux Juifs de France', *PH* 64 (15 Apr. 1933), 1.

—— 'Le Véritable Briand', *PH* 17 (26 Mar.–2 Apr. 1932), 1.

—— 'Le Véritable Pacifisme: Le Postulat d'Einstein', *PH* 19 (9–16 Apr. 1932), 1.

—— 'Nos moyens de lutte', *PH* 66 (29 Apr. 1933), 1.

—— 'Nos souhaits', *PH* 49 (31 Dec. 1932–7 Jan. 1933), 1.

—— 'Nous n'irons plus au bois ...', *PH* 30 (25 June–2 July 1932), 1–2.

—— 'On assassine un homme!', *PH* 52 (21–8 Jan. 1933), 1.

—— 'Pour tuer la guerre', *PH* 54 (4–11 Feb. 1933), 1.

—— 'Précisions', *PH* 32 (9–23 July 1932), 1.

—— 'Rapport moral', *PH* 59 (11–18 Mar. 1933), 5.

—— 'Vers la répression', *PH* 40 (29 Oct.–5 Nov. 1932), 1.

MESSAC, RÉGIS, 'Lettre à Sylvain Broussaudier', *Le Barrage*, 111 (27 May 1937), 3.

—— 'Pour un esprit civique européen', *Le Barrage*, 147 (20 Apr. 1939), 1.

—— 'Que chacun reconnaisse les siens!', *Le Barrage*, 106 (3 Sept. 1936), 1.

'Message adressé au Bureau international de la paix par la Sociéte allemande de la paix au sujet des décisions de la Conférence de Paris' (with response by Ruyssen), in *PD* 31/3–4 (Mar.–Apr. 1921), 118–21.

'Message à la Conférence tenue à Paris le 3 septembre 1935 pour la défense du peuple éthiopien', *PD* 45/9 (Sept. 1935), 339–40.

MICHON, GEORGES, 'Robespierre et la guerre révolutionnaire', *Le Barrage*, 80 (16 Jan. 1936), 1.

—— 'Union sacrée', *Le Barrage*, 102 (9 July 1936), 1.

MILHAUD, EDGAR, 'Sur la réorganisation économique du monde, condition de la paix future', in Jules Prudhommeaux and J. Lahargue, 'L'Assemblée générale et le Congrès du cinquantenaire, Nîmes, 19–21 avril 1938', *PD* 48/6–7–8 (May–June–July 1938), 293–7.

MOCH, GASTON, 'Un réquisitoire nécessaire: Alfred Hermann Fried', *PD* 29/4 (Apr. 1919), 155–68.

'Modifications aux statuts', *Le Barrage*, 130 (9 June 1938), 4.

MONBRISON, HUBERT DE, 'Les Colonies, terrain de lutte ou de collaboration entre les peuples', in Jules Prudhommeaux and J. Lahargue, 'L'Assemblée générale et le Congrès du cinquantenaire, Nîmes, 19–21 avril 1938', *PD* 48/6–7–8 (May–June–July 1938), 278–89.

MONCLIN, ROGER, 'Adieu', *PH* 86 (13 Oct. 1933), 1.

—— 'L'Activité de la Ligue', *PH* 59 (11–18 Mar. 1933), 5.

—— 'Violence . . . ou soumission?', *PH* 21 (23–30 Apr. 1932), 3.

MONOD, WILFRED, 'L'Antisémitisme et la notion de race', *PD* 43/6 (June 1933), 198–200.

MORHARDT, MATHIAS, 'Le Respect des traités', *Le Barrage*, 91 (26 Mar. 1936), 3.

NÉZELOF, PIERRE, 'Aux innocents les mains vides', *Le Barrage*, 135 (20 Oct. 1938), 1.

—— 'Le Front populaire ruiné par ses chefs', *Le Barrage*, 150 (8 June 1939), 2.

—— 'Une enquête', *Le Barrage*, 100 (11 June 1936), 1.

'Notre agitation', *PH* 28 (11–18 June 1932), 4.

'Notre Assemblée générale, Pau, 29 octobre–1er novembre 1932', *PD* 42/12 (Dec. 1932), 513–44.

'Notre meeting à Wagram', *PH* 12 (20–6 Feb. 1932), 1.

'Notre mot d'ordre', *Le Combat pour la paix*, 9 (Feb. 1934), 4.

'Nous ne marchons pas!', *Le Barrage*, 88 (12 Mar. 1936), 1.

Nous voulons la paix (Paris: SRIP, 1932).

'Pacifistes, tenez-vous prêts!', *PH* 21 (23–30 Apr. 1932), 1.

'Paix et liberté (manifeste adopté au Congrès de Montargis)', *Le Combat pour la paix*, 11 (Apr. 1934), 1–2.

PAUTHE, GASTON, 'Comment lutter à la fois contre la guerre et contre le fascisme? Rapport sur l'aspect économique de la question', *Le Barrage*, 124 (24 Feb. 1938), 3–4.

—— 'Non! Monsieur Daladier, nous ne sommes pas dupes!', *Le Barrage*, 150 (8 June 1939), 2.

PERCIN, General ALEXANDRE, *Guerre à la guerre* (Paris: Éditions Montaigne, 1927).

—— *Le Désarmement moral* (Paris: Delpeuch, 1925).

PÉRIÉ, R., 'Scrupules pacifistes', *PD* 31/7 (July 1921), 237–40.

PIOCH, GEORGES, 'Je joue la carte Léon Blum', *Le Barrage*, 100 (11 June 1936), 1–2.

—— 'L'Impossible Promiscuité', *Le Barrage*, 144 (2 Mar. 1939), 1.

—— 'Paix dans notre Ligue, d'abord!', *PH* 33 (23 July–6 Aug. 1932), 1–2.

—— 'Quand Brid'oison se double de Basile', *Le Barrage*, 61 (1 Aug. 1935), 2.

—— 'Questions à Romain Rolland', *Le Barrage*, 82 (30 Jan. 1936), 1.

—— 'Rougeur sur le Front populaire', *Le Barrage*, 111 (27 May 1937), 1–2.

'Pour la paix par le droit: Appel programme', *PD* 30/1–2 (Jan.–Feb. 1920), 1–5.

'Pour la réforme d'une loi inhumaine', *PD* 46/2 (Feb. 1936), 97–8.

'Pour la Société des nations', *PD* 28/17–18–19–20 (Sept.–Oct. 1918), 298.

Pour un désarmement réel: Compte-rendu de la Conférence libre du désarmement tenue à Paris les 23 et 24 avril 1932 (Levallois-Perret: Commission de la Conférence, n.d. [1932]).

'Précisions nécessaires', *Le Barrage*, 13 (9 Aug. 1934), 1.

'Première conférence nationale pour la paix par l'éducation', *PD* 41/3 (Mar. 1931), 129–61.

'Prenons garde!', *Le Barrage*, 20 (27 Sept. 1934), 1.

Procès de Camille Rombaut (Aubervilliers: 'La Réconciliation', 1932).

Procès de Jacques Martin (Aubervilliers: 'La Réconciliation', 1932).

Procès de Philippe Vernier (Aubervilliers: 'La Réconciliation', 1933).

'Projet de résolution soumis par le comité exécutif de "La Paix par le droit" à la "Fédération française des associations pour la SDN"', *PD* 45/9 (Sept. 1935), 338–9.

PRUDHOMMEAUX, JULES, 'A propos du fascisme français', *PD* 35/12 (Dec. 1925), 486–9.

—— 'Conseil directeur de l'Association de la paix par le droit', *PD* 32/10 (Oct. 1922), 426–9.

—— 'Et si l'Allemagne résiste?—Les Sanctions économiques', *PD* 43/11 (Nov. 1933), 458–60.

—— 'France et Allemagne: Le Péril', *PD* 46/3 (Mar. 1936), 143–5.

—— 'Guillot et Perrin, objecteurs de conscience', *PD* 40/4 (Apr. 1930), 137–8.

—— 'La Condamnation de "l'objecteur" Philippe Vernier', *PD* 43/10 (Oct. 1933), 402–3.

—— 'La Grande Pitié du pacifisme français: Pour l'unité et la coordination des efforts', *PD* 45/10 (Oct. 1935), 391–5.

—— 'La Guerre chimique et l'opinion: Un article de M de Kérillis', *PD* 40/11 (Nov. 1930), 451–2.

—— 'La Ligue des combattants de la paix: Le Congrès de Montargis: Les Dissidents', *PD* 44/6 (June 1934), 244–5.

—— 'La Ligue des droits de l'homme et la paix en péril', *PD* 48/11 (Oct. 1938), 359–63.

—— 'La Paix par l'éducation, l'histoire à l'école', *PD* 35/2 (Feb. 1925), 61–8, and 35/3 (Mar. 1925), 99–107.

—— 'La Politique internationale et la SDN: La Mise hors la loi de la guerre: L'Accord est fait', *PD* 38/7–8 (July–Aug. 1928), 316–18.

—— 'La Propagande: Le Monument de la réconciliation: Une manifestation émouvante au Trocadéro', *PD* 35/2 (Feb. 1925), 81–3.

—— 'L'Assemblée générale de Boulogne-sur-Mer', *PD* 41/1 (Jan. 1931), 17–26.

—— 'L'Assemblée générale de Boulogne-sur-Mer (suite)', *PD* 41/2 (Feb. 1931), 69–84.

—— 'L'Assemblée générale de la Paix par le droit (Marseille, 27 Dec. 1935)', *PD* 46/2 (Feb. 1936), 57–74.

—— 'L'Assemblée générale de la Paix par le droit, Bordeaux, 2 et 3 novembre 1929', *PD* 39/12 (Dec. 1929), 443–68.

—— 'L'Assemblée générale de Nancy', *PD* 39/1 (Jan. 1929), 3–18.

—— 'L'Association de la paix par le droit: Séance du conseil de direction', *PD* 44/6 (June 1934), 248–52.

—— 'Le Cartel lyonnais pour la paix et la SDN', *PD* 36/1 (Jan. 1926), 39–40.

—— 'Le Congrès de la Paix par le droit, Clermont-Ferrand, 26–7 décembre 1936', *PD* 47/3 (Mar. 1937), 101–11.

—— 'Le Congrès mondial contre la guerre impérialiste', *PD* 42/9 (Sept. 1932), 405–11.

—— 'Le Pacifisme oratoire d'Hitler et Cie', *PD* 43/11 (Nov. 1933), 455–8.

—— 'Le Pacte rhénan et la Conférence de Locarno', *PD* 35/10 (Oct. 1925), 385–7.

—— 'Le Problème des réparations et la pacifisme international', *PD* 33/3 (Mar. 1923), 119–25.

—— 'Le Rassemblement mondial des femmes contre la guerre et le fascisme', *PD* 44/9 (Sept. 1934), 343–7.

—— 'Le Rassemblement universel pour la paix: La Conférence de Londres', *PD* 46/4 (Apr. 1936), 206–8.

—— 'Les Lendemains du Congrès d'Amsterdam', *PD* 42/11 (Nov. 1932), 494–5.

—— 'Les Paroles et les actes', *PD* 43/6 (June 1933), 218–19.

—— 'Les Rapports du pacifisme et du mouvement ouvrier', *PD* 15/11 (Nov. 1905), 421–33.

—— 'Le Tour de France du Musée "guerre ou paix"', *PD* 41/7 (July 1931), 315–20.

—— 'L'Objection de conscience: Georges Chevé', *PD* 38/3 (Mar. 1928), 141–2.

—— 'L'Origine, le développement et le fonctionnement de l'Association de la paix par le droit', *PD* 38/12 (Dec. 1928), 513–18.

—— 'Notre Assemblée générale', *PD* 41/12 (Dec. 1931), 573–616.

—— 'Notre Assemblée générale', *PD* 47/2 (Feb. 1937), 52–67.

—— 'Notre Assemblée générale, Paris, 30 et 31 décembre 1933', *PD* 44/2 (Feb. 1934), 49–66.

—— 'Notre Assemblée générale: Suite et fin', *PD* 44/3 (Mar. 1934), 97–122.

—— 'Pacifisme d'avant-garde', *PD* 38/3 (Mar. 1928), 137–8.

—— 'Petite histoire des cartels de la paix', *PD* 42/4 (Apr. 1932), 179–82.

—— 'Pour la paix par l'école', *PD* 38/7–8 (July–Aug. 1928), 293–306; 'Suite', in *PD* 38/9 (Sept. 1928), 366–75; and *PD* 38/10 (Oct. 1928), 419–31.

PRUDHOMMEAUX, JULES, 'Rapport moral', in Jules Prudhommeaux, 'Notre Assemblée générale, Paris 30 et 31 décembre 1933', *PD* 44/2 (Feb. 1934), 53–8, also p. 49.

—— 'Rapport moral' in M. L. Puech, 'Notre Assemblée générale, Paris, 23 janvier, 1938', *PD* 48/3 (Feb. 1938), 65–9.

—— 'Un congrès de la paix qui s'annonce mal: Genève ou Moscou?', *PD* 42/7–8 (July–Aug. 1932), 350–1.

—— 'Un demi-siècle d'activité de la revue "La Paix par le droit"', *PD* 48/6–7–8 (May–June–July 1938), 269–77.

—— 'Un récidiviste de l'objection de conscience: Eugène Guillot', *PD* 41/2 (Feb. 1931), 107–9.

—— 'Vers l'union des forces pacifistes: Cartels et semaines de la paix', *PD* 39/11 (Nov. 1929), 425–30.

—— and CADIER, GEORGES, 'L'Assemblée générale de la Paix par le droit', *PD* 34/7–8 (July–Aug. 1924), 270–6.

—— and LAHARGUE, J., 'L'Assemblée générale et le Congrès du cinquantenaire, Nîmes, 19–21 avril 1938', *PD* 48/6–7–8 (May–June–July 1938), 209–99.

—— and PUECH, JULES L., 'L'Assemblée générale et les fêtes du XLème anniversaire', *PD* 37/12 (Dec. 1927), 435–78.

'PS à l'Enquête sur l'objection de conscience', *PD* 36/12 (Dec. 1926), 439–40.

PUECH, JULES L., 'A propos des articles Challaye–Ruyssen', *PD* 42/4 (Apr. 1932), 153–6.

—— 'Assemblée générale de la Paix par le droit, Nantes, 10 et 11 février 1923', *PD* 33/4 (Apr. 1923), 137–45.

—— 'Chronique: La Paix avec l'Allemagne', *PD* 30/1–2 (Jan.–Feb. 1920), 26–32.

—— 'La Paix par le droit (1887–1947)', *PD* 51/2 (Nov.–Dec. 1947), 33–41.

—— 'L'Assemblée générale de la Paix par le droit', *PD* 36/1 (Jan. 1926), 13–19.

—— 'Le 8ème Congrès allemand de la paix', *PD* 29/7–8 (July–Aug. 1919), 362–4.

—— 'Notre revue', *PD* 30/11–12 (Nov.–Dec. 1920), 363–9.

—— 'Notre "sainte cause"', *PD* 34/4–5 (Apr.–May 1924), 165–70.

PUECH, M.-L., 'De l'Allemagne', *PD* 34/9 (Sept. 1924), 332–5.

—— 'Notre Assemblée générale, Paris, 23 janvier 1938', *PD* 48/3 (Feb. 1938), 65–76.

'14 juillet 1935', *Le Barrage*, 60 (18 July 1935), 1.

'Quatrième conférence nationale pour la paix par l'éducation', *PD* 44/4–5 (Apr.–May 1934), 145–76.

RAUZE, MARIANNE, *L'Anti-guerre: Essai d'une doctrine et d'une philosophie de l'antimilitarisme en 1923*, Suivi d'une post-face de Romain

Rolland, Préfaces de W. Wellock et Dr Stoecker (Niort: Imprimerie du progrès, 1923).

RELGIS, EUGEN, *L'Internationale pacifiste* (Paris: André Delpeuch, 1929).

'Résolution sur les événements d'Espagne', *Le Barrage*, 108 (22 Oct. 1936), 1.

'Réunion du comité directeur', *Le Barrage*, 113 (24 June 1937), 3.

'Réunion du comité directeur', *Le Combat pour la paix*, 1 (May 1933), 10–11.

RICHET, CHARLES, 'La Paix sans réserve est un rêve!', *PD* 42/2–3 (Feb.–Mar. 1932), 70–1.

—— 'La Vraie Figure de la France', *PD* 42/7–8 (July–Aug. 1932), 321–3.

—— 'La Vraie Figure de la France', *PD* 43/3 (Mar. 1933), 97.

—— 'Soyons tous les enfants de la paix', *PD* 34/3 (Mar. 1924), 105–7.

—— 'Y-a-t-il des équivoques du pacifisme?', *PD* 43/8–9 (Aug.–Sept. 1933), 285–8.

—— and RUYSSEN, THÉODORE, 'Fusion de la Société française pour l'arbitrage et de l'Association de la paix par le droit', *PD* 32/2 (Feb. 1922), 57–8.

—— —— 'La Fin de la guerre', *PD* 28/21–2 (Nov. 1918), 329–31.

—— —— 'Pour "La Paix par le droit"', *PD* 28/1–2 (Jan. 1918), 2.

ROLLAND, ROMAIN, 'Appel de Romain Rolland aux Combattants de la paix', *PH* 31 (2–9 July 1932), 1–2.

—— 'Le Combat pour la paix: Romain Rolland intervient dans le débat', *PH* 33 (23 July–6 Aug. 1932), 1.

—— *Par la révolution, la paix* (Paris: Éditions sociales internationales, 1935).

—— 'Pour l'indivisible paix', *Le Barrage*, 83 (6 Feb. 1936), 2.

—— *Romain Rolland and Gandhi Correspondence* (New Delhi: Ministry of Information and Broadcasting, 1966).

ROSER, HENRI, 'L'Objection de conscience et la légalité: Lettre ouverte à M le rédacteur de "La Paix par le droit"', *PD* 44/1 (Jan. 1934), 22–3.

—— 'Réponse à l'Enquête sur la crise du pacifisme', *PD* 44/2 (Feb. 1934), 71–3.

ROTHEN, ÉDOUARD, 'Avec la peau des autres', *Le Barrage*, 92 (2 Apr. 1936), 1.

ROUSSEAU, CHARLES, 'La Dénonciation des Traités de Locarno devant le droit international', *PD* 46/4 (Apr. 1936), 188–98.

—— 'L'Agression italienne et les sanctions', *PD* 45/11–12 (Nov.–Dec. 1935), pp. 444–52.

—— 'La Politique internationale de la SDN', *PD* 48/5 (Apr. 1938), 184–91.

—— 'Les Données juridiques du conflit italo-éthiopien', *PD* 45/9 (Sept. 1935), 349–57.

—— 'Les Événements d'Espagne', *PD* 46/8–9 (Aug.–Sept. 1936), 354–8.

—— and PRUDHOMMEAUX, JULES, 'Dans le Gard: A Caveirac', *PD* 36/5 (May 1926), 234–5.

Rousseau, Charles, and Prudhommeaux, Jules, 'La IIème Conférence internationale pour l'enseignement de l'histoire', PD 44/10 (Oct. 1934), 399–400.

——— —— 'La Grande Pitié du pacifisme international: Le "Rassemblement universel pour la paix"', PD 46/1 (Jan. 1936), 43–6.

——— —— 'Le Conflit italo-éthiopien', PD 45/7–8 (July–Aug. 1935), 307–13.

——— —— 'Le Conseil général du RUP à Genève: Le Discours de Lord Robert Cecil: Les Résolutions', PD 47/4–5 (Apr.–May 1937), 184–7.

——— —— 'Lord Robert Cecil, Prix Nobel de la paix pour 1937', PD 47/11–12 (Nov.–Dec. 1937), 417.

Roussel, Ernest, 'Les Origines de la Paix par le droit', PD 38/1 (Jan. 1928), 10–15.

Ruyssen, Théodore, 'A nos amis de demain', PD 49/1 (Jan. 1939), 1–3.

—— 'A propos du 9me Congrès national de la paix', PD 31/5–6 (May–June 1921), 219–20.

—— 'Au travail', PD 30/11–12 (Nov.–Dec. 1920), 353–5.

—— 'De quelques polémiques allemandes sur les responsabilités de la guerre', PD 32/3–4 (Mar.–Apr. 1922), 110–14.

—— 'Désarmement? Ou désarmements?', PD 39/12 (Dec. 1929), 441–2.

—— 'Encore l'Article 231!', PD 35/5 (May 1925), 200–3.

—— 'Jacques Dumas', PD 51/2 (Nov.–Dec. 1947), 51–3.

—— 'La Crise du pacifisme', in Jules Prudhommeaux, 'Notre Assemblée générale, Paris 30 et 31 décembre 1933', PD 44/2 (Feb. 1934), 62–6.

—— 'La Guerre et la morale' (extrait d'un discours prononcé à l'ouverture du Congrès belge pour le progrès des idées morales), PD 33/2 (Feb. 1923), 49–52.

—— 'La Ligue française des droits de l'homme en Allemagne', PD 32/7–8 (July–Aug. 1922), 284–91.

—— 'La Nouvelle Crise du désarmement', PD 44/4–5 (Apr.–May 1934), 180–6.

—— 'La Paix hors du droit', PD 48/11 (Oct. 1938), 341–50.

—— 'La Paix par le droit: Rapport: Documents de l'Assemblée générale et du Congrès du cinquantenaire', PD 48/6–7–8 (May–June–July 1938), 256–68.

—— 'La Paix par le droit rentre en scène', PD 51/1 (Oct. 1947), 1–6.

—— 'La Paix sans réserves? Non!', PD 42/1 (Jan. 1932), 9–15.

—— 'La Sarre a voté', PD 45/1 (Jan. 1935), 1–2.

—— 'L'Assemblée générale de l'Association de la paix par le droit', PD 32/6 (June 1922), 237–46.

—— 'Le Cinquantenaire de la Paix par le droit', PD 47/2 (Feb. 1937), 49–51.

—— 'Le Discours du Fuehrer', PD 45/5–6 (May–June 1935), 244–9.

—— 'Le Double Visage de la politique allemande', *PD* 46/3 (Mar. 1936), 135–42.

—— 'Le Mouvement pacifiste: Pour et contre la reprise des relations pacifistes internationales', *PD* 29/1 (Jan. 1919), 47–9.

—— 'Le Renouveau du pacifisme et le Bureau international de la paix', *PD* 29/9–10 (Sept.–Oct. 1919), 403–16.

—— 'Les Femmes contre la guerre', *PD* 31/3–4 (Mar.–Apr. 1921), 140–1.

—— 'Les Pacifistes allemands et le Traité de Versailles', *PD* 30/1–2 (Jan.–Feb. 1920), 32–8.

—— *Les Sources doctrinales de l'internationalisme*, 3 vols. (Paris: Presses universitaires de France, 1954–61).

—— 'Les Voies de la paix: A propos du Rassemblement mondial', *PD* 46/8–9 (Aug.–Sept. 1936), 329–32.

—— 'Le XXIV Congrès international de la paix', *PD* 35/10 (Oct. 1925), 360–3.

—— 'L'Idolâtrie patriotique', *PD* 35/1 (Jan. 1925), 1–4.

—— 'L'Internationale des anciens combattants', *PD* 30/6–7 (June–July 1920), 204–7.

—— 'L'Objection de conscience', *PD* 36/9–10 (Sept.–Oct. 1926), 331–7.

—— 'Notre effort pour la paix,' *PD* 48/11 (Oct. 1938), 337–40.

—— 'Où allons-nous?' *PD* 43/6 (June 1933), 192–4.

—— 'Polémiques', *PD* 39/10 (Oct. 1929), 357–9.

—— 'Pour le rapprochement franco-allemand: La Ligue des droits de l'homme et le Bund neues Vaterland', *PD* 32/2 (Feb. 1922), 90–1.

—— 'Pressant appel aux membres de l'Association et aux lecteurs de la revue', *PD* 47/11–12 (Nov.–Dec. 1937), 385–90.

—— 'Réponse à quelques objections', *PD* 30/5 (May 1920), 130–5.

—— 'Un congrès féminin pour la paix à La Haye', *PD* 33/1 (Jan. 1923), 34–5.

—— 'Veillons!', *PD* 43/3 (Mar. 1933), 93–6.

—— 'Y-a-t-il des équivoques du pacifisme?', *PD* 43/8–9 (Aug.–Sept. 1935), 288–90.

SCELLE, GEORGES, 'La Défaite des démocraties', *PD* 48/4 (Mar. 1938), 129–34.

—— 'La Fin d'un système', *PD* 47/4–5 (Apr.–May 1937), 169–72.

—— 'La Paix . . . et le droit', *PD* 48/1 (15 Jan. 1938), 4–13.

—— 'Le Pacte Kellogg', *PD* 38/9 (Sept. 1928), 356–65.

—— 'Le Pacte Kellogg (fin)', *PD* 38/10 (Oct. 1928), 432–41.

—— 'Péril de mort', *PD* 49/3–4 (Mar.–Apr. 1939), 81–6.

—— 'Pourquoi doit-on et comment peut-on mettre la constitution française en accord avec le Pacte Briand–Kellogg et les prescriptions de la Société des nations?', in Jules Prudhommeaux, 'L'Assemblée générale de Nancy (suite)', *PD* 39/1 (Jan. 1929), 7–11.

—— 'Rétrospective', *PD* 46/1 (Jan. 1936), 23–31.

'Séverine', *PD* 39/6 (June 1929), 251.

SIMONDET, HENRI, 'L'Allemagne dans le gâchis', *PD* 43/2 (Feb. 1933), 62–7.

—— 'Les Élections allemandes', *PD* 40/10 (Oct. 1930), 376–82.

'Tableau des cotisations versées en 1926 au Bureau international de la paix', *Le Mouvement pacifiste* (Oct. 1927), 146–7.

TEISSONNIÈRE, P., 'Faut-il résister aux violents?', *PD* 49/1 (Jan. 1939), 12–14.

TEMPÊTE, JEAN, 'Propos incisifs: Législation', *PH* 15 (12–18 Mar. 1932), 3.

TOURLY, ROBERT, 'Bilan et souhaits', *PH* 97 (5 Jan. 1934), 1.

—— 'Le Programme de Hitler', *PH* 17 (26 Mar.–2 Apr. 1932), 3.

—— 'Les Obsèques de Victor Méric', *PH* 87 (20 Oct. 1933), 1.

—— 'L'Homme qui s'en va . . .', *PH* 86 (13 Oct. 1933), 1.

—— 'Sa vie, son œuvre', *PH* 86 (13 Oct. 1933), 1–2.

—— 'Sur une tombe', *PH* 106 (9 Mar. 1934), 1.

TRÉGARO, LOUIS, 'A la croisée des chemins', *Le Barrage*, 125 (17 Mar. 1938), 1.

—— 'Aragon–Autriche', *Le Barrage*, 131 (7 July 1938), 1.

—— 'Casse-cou!', *Le Barrage*, 145 (16 Mar. 1939), 1.

'Troisième Conférence nationale de la paix par l'éducation', *PD* 43/4–5 (Apr.–May 1933), 125–52.

'Un appel à l'opinion française: Que fera la France?', *PD* 45/10 (Oct. 1935), 386–90.

'Une idée . . . turque: Lénine, lauréat du Prix Nobel', *PD* 28/1–2 (Jan. 1918), 43.

'Une jeune garde pacifiste', *PH* 10 (30 Jan.–14 Feb. 1932), 2.

'Une politique maladroite', *Le Barrage*, 87 (5 Mar. 1936), 3.

'Une prédiction d'Albert Thibaudet', *Le Barrage*, 94 (23 Apr. 1936), 1.

'Un manifeste de la Société allemande de la paix', *PD* 29/1 (Jan. 1919), 54–6.

'Un manifeste pour l'abolition du service militaire obligatoire', *PD* 36/12 (Dec. 1926), 472.

VALFORT, RENÉ *L'Objection de conscience et l'esprit maçonnique*, Préface de Édouard E. Plantagenet (Paris: Collection des documents maçonniques de *La Paix*, n.d. [1930]).

VERMEIL, EDMOND, 'Le XXIIIème Congrès international de la paix de Berlin', *PD* 34/12 (Dec. 1924), 452–6.

VERNET, MADELEINE, *De l'objection de conscience au désarmement* (Levallois-Perret: Éditions de la Volonté de paix, 1930).

—— 'La Paix et la politique', *Le Barrage*, 113 (24 June 1937), 2.

—— 'Protestation', *Le Barrage*, 134 (6 Oct. 1938), 1.

'Volonté de paix et L.I.C.P.', *Le Barrage*, 99 (28 May 1936), 1.

VULLIOD, A., 'La Valeur du Pacte Kellogg–Briand', *PD* 39/6 (June 1929), 214–21.

WANNER, LÉO, 'La Femme et les dictatures', *SOS* 16 (Year 5) (1934), 1–2.

WEBER, MAURICE, 'Ce n'est pas par la guerre que l'on fera la paix', *Le Barrage*, 102 (9 July 1936), 2.

—— 'Excitations guerrières', *Le Barrage*, 106 (3 Sept. 1936), 3.

—— 'Fermeté et vigilance', *Le Barrage*, 86 (27 Feb. 1936), 1.

—— 'La Situation des pacifistes dans le Parti socialiste', *Le Barrage*, 109 (29 Apr. 1937), 2.

—— 'Les Pacifistes et le Parti socialiste', *Le Barrage*, 111 (27 May 1937), 3.

—— 'Pacifisme et socialisme', *Le Barrage*, 78 (2 Jan. 1936), 1.

—— 'Rapport-critique sur les idéologies nationalistes', *Le Barrage*, 44 (14 Mar. 1935), 4–5.

—— and JOSPIN, ROBERT, 'Rapport sur les partis politiques, le Front populaire et la paix', *Le Barrage*, 87 (5 Mar. 1936), 5–6; and *Le Barrage*, 88 (12 Mar. 1936), 4.

SECONDARY SOURCES

AUVRAY, MICHEL, *Objecteurs, insoumis, déserteurs: Histoire des réfractaires en France* (Paris: Stock/2, 1983).

BARBIER, J. B., *Le Pacifisme dans l'histoire de France (de l'an mille à nos jours)* (Paris: La Librairie française, 1966).

BEALES, A. C. F., *The History of Peace: A Short Account of the Organised Movements for International Peace* (London: G. Bell and Sons, 1931).

BECKER, JEAN-JACQUES, *Le Carnet B* (Paris: Klincksieck, 1973).

BILIS, MICHEL, *Socialistes et pacifistes 1933–1939: Ou l'intenable dilemme des socialistes français* (Paris: Syros, 1979).

BOUCHARDEAU, HUGUETTE, *Pas d'histoire, les femmes . . . 50 ans d'histoire des femmes: 1918–1968* (Paris: Éditions Syros, 1977).

BOUSSARD, ISABEL, 'Le Pacifisme paysan', in René Rémond and Janine Bourdin (eds.), *La France et les Français en 1938–1939* (Paris: Presses de la FNSP, 1978), 59–75.

BROCK, PETER, *Pacifism in Europe to 1914* (Princeton, NJ: Princeton University Press, 1972).

—— *Twentieth Century Pacifism* (New York: Van Nostrand Reinhold Company, 1970).

BUSSEY, GERTRUDE, and TIMS, MARGARET, *Women's International League for Peace and Freedom* (London: Allen & Unwin, 1965).

CAIRNS, JOHN C., 'A Nation of Shopkeepers in Search of a Suitable France, 1919–40', *American Historical Review*, 79/3 (June 1974), 710–43.

CATTELAIN, JEAN-PIERRE, *L'Objection de conscience* (Paris: Presses universitaires de France, 3rd edition, 1982).

CEADEL, MARTIN, *Pacifism in Britain, 1914–1945: The Defining of a Faith* (Oxford: Clarendon Press, 1980).

CEADEL, MARTIN, *Thinking about Peace and War* (Oxford and New York: Oxford University Press, 1987).

CHICKERING, ROGER, *Imperial Germany and a World Without War: The Peace Movement and German Society, 1892–1914* (Princeton, NJ: Princeton University Press, 1975).

DEFRASNE, JEAN, *Le Pacifisme*, Collection 'Que sais-je?' (Paris: Presses universitaires de France, 1983).

DELBREIL, JEAN-CLAUDE, *Les Catholiques français et les tentatives de rapprochement franco-allemand (1920–1933)* (Metz: Centre de recherches relations internationales, 1972).

Dictionnaire des parlementaires français, 1889–1940, 8 vols. (Paris: Presses universitaires de France, 1960–77).

DONAT, HELMUT, and HOLL, KARL (eds.), *Die Friedensbewegung: Organisierter Pazifismus in Deutschland, Österreich, und in der Schweiz* (Hermes Handlexikon) (Düsseldorf: ECON Taschenbuch Verlag, 1983).

DUROSELLE, J. B., 'Les Précédents historiques: Pacifisme des années 30 et neutralisme des années 50', in *Pacifisme et dissuasion: Travaux et recherches de l'Institut français de relations internationales sous la direction de Pierre Lelouche* (Paris: IFRI, 1983), 241–52.

EKSTEINS, MODRIS, 'All Quiet on the Western Front and the Fate of a War', *Journal of Contemporary History*, 15/2 (1980), 345–66.

FAUCIER, NICOLAS, *Pacifisme et antimilitarisme dans l'entre-deux-guerres* (Paris: Spartacus, 1983).

FITZPATRICK, BRIAN, *Catholic Royalism in the Department of the Gard, 1814–1852* (Cambridge: Cambridge University Press, 1983).

FRIGUGLIETTI, JAMES, *Albert Mathiez: historien révolutionnaire (1874–1932)*, translated from the English by Marie-Françoise Pernot (Paris: Société d'études robespierristes, 1974).

Gabrielle Duchêne, 1870–1954: In memoriam (Paris: Section française de la LIFPL, n.d. [1954]).

GIRARDET, RAOUL, *La Société militaire dans la France contemporaine (1815–1939)* (Paris: Plon, 1953).

GOMBIN, RICHARD, 'Socialisme et pacifisme', in René Rémond and Janine Bourdin (eds.), *La France et les Français en 1938–1939* (Paris: Presses de la FNSP, 1978), 245–60.

HERMON, ELLY, 'Approches conceptuelles de l'éducation en vue de la compréhension internationale dans l'entre-deux-guerres', *Canadian and International Education*, 15/2 (1986), 29–52.

—— 'The International Peace Education Movement, 1919–1939', in Charles Chatfield and Peter van den Dungen (eds.), *Peace Movements and Political Cultures* (Knoxville, Tenn.: University of Tennessee Press, 1988), 127–42.

INGRAM, NORMAN, 'Romain Rolland, Interwar Pacifism and the Problem of Peace', in Charles Chatfield and Peter van den Dungen (eds.), *Peace*

Movements and Political Cultures (Knoxville, Tenn.: University of Tennessee Press, 1988), 143–64.

JOSEPHSON, HAROLD, *Biographical Dictionary of Modern Peace Leaders* (Westport, Conn., and London: Greenwood Press, 1985).

KUEHL, WARREN F. (ed.), *Biographical Dictionary of Internationalists* (London and Westport, Conn.: Greenwood Press, 1983).

LÜTGEMEIER-DAVIN, REINHOLD, *Pazifismus zwischen Kooperation und Konfrontation: Das Deutsche Friedenskartell in der Weimarer Republik* (Cologne: Pahl-Rugenstein Verlag, 1982).

MCALLISTER, PAM (ed.), *Reweaving the Web of Life: Feminism and Nonviolence* (Philadelphia: New Society Publishers, 1982).

MCMILLAN, JAMES F., *Housewife or Harlot: The Place of Women in French Society 1870–1940* (Brighton: The Harvester Press, 1981).

MERLE, MARCEL, *Pacifisme et internationalisme XVIIe–XXe siècles* (Paris: Armand Colin, 1966).

PROST, ANTOINE, *Les Anciens Combattants et la société française*, 3 vols. (Paris: Presses de la FNSP, 1977).

RACINE-FURLAUD, NICOLE, 'Le Comité de vigilance des intellectuels antifascistes (1934–1939): Antifascisme et pacifisme', *Le Mouvement social*, 101 (Oct.–Dec. 1977), 87–113.

ROBRIEUX, PHILIPPE, *Histoire intérieure du parti communiste, 1920–1945* (Paris: Fayard, 1980).

SCHUMANN, ROSEMARIE, *Amsterdam 1932: Der Weltkongreß gegen den imperialistischen Krieg* (East Berlin: Dietz Verlag, 1985).

SÉE, YVONNE, *Réaliser l'espérance* (Paris: Section française de la LIFPL, n.d. [1984]).

SINGER, BARNETT, 'From Patriots to Pacifists: The French Primary School Teachers, 1880–1940', *Journal of Contemporary History*, 12 (1977), 413–34.

SIRINELLI, JEAN-FRANÇOIS, *Génération intellectuelle: Khâgneux et normaliens dans l'entre-deux-guerres* (Paris: Fayard, 1988).

—— 'Khâgneux et normaliens aux années vingt', thèse de doctorat d'état, Université de Paris-X, Nanterre, 1986, 5 vols.

SOULEYMAN, ELIZABETH, *The Vision of World Peace in Seventeenth and Eighteenth-Century France* (New York: G. P. Putnam's Sons, 1941).

STERNHELL, ZEEV, *Ni droite, ni gauche: L'Idéologie fasciste en France* (Paris: Éditions du seuil, 1983).

TAYLOR, A. J. P., *The Troublemakers: Dissent over Foreign Policy, 1792–1939* (London: Hamish Hamilton, 1957).

VAÏSSE, MAURICE, 'Le Pacifisme français dans les années trente', *Relations internationales*, 53 (spring 1988), 37–52.

VELLACOTT, JO, 'Women, Peace and Internationalism, 1914–1920: "Finding New Words and Creating New Methods"', in Charles Chatfield and

Peter van den Dungen (eds.), *Peace Movements and Political Cultures* (Knoxville, Tenn.: University of Tennessee Press, 1988), 106–24.

WINOCK, MICHEL, 'Le Fascisme passera ... Pourquoi?', *Le Monde aujourd'hui*, Supplement to No. 12852 of *Le Monde* (Sunday 25– Monday 26 May 1986), v.

WURGART, LEWIS D., *The Activists: Kurt Hiller and the Politics of Action on the German Left, 1917–1933* (Philadelphia: Transactions of the American Philosophical Society, 1977).

Index

Action française 238, 240, 241
Addams, Jane 255
Addis Ababa 215
Alain (Émile Chartier) 4 n. 9, 87, 199, 232
Alexandre, Jeanne 258, 278, 284, 285
Algeria 143
Allégret, Paul 58–61
Alsace–Lorraine 33, 44
American State Department 306
Ami du peuple, L' 148
Amis de la *Patrie humaine* 178
Amsterdam Congress against Imperialist War (1932) 8, 80–1, 153–5, 157, 191, 216, 268, 269, 272
  and Communists 154
  and conscientious objection 157–8
  and Soviet Russia 154
  attempts by Communists to control 81
  manifesto condemned by Romain Rolland for negative view of Gandhian pacifism and conscientious objection 269
Amsterdam-Pleyel 8–9, 160, 161, 173, 201, 221, 257, 275, 297, 306, 310
anarchism 32
  and conscientious objection 131
anarchists 64, 166
Andorra 73
Angers 140
Anschluss (with Austria) 96, 97, 104, 112, 113–14, 223, 229, 312
anticonceptional propaganda 195
antifascism
  and pacifism 184–93
  enemy 'within' 125–6
antimilitarism 32

and absolute pacifism 130
antiparliamentarianism 185
anti-Semitism 181, 233, 244
Association de la paix par le droit (APD) 15, 16, 122, 131, 153, 311, 318, 319
  address to German pacifists (1921) 43
  Bordeaux AGM (1928) 51–2
  claims to pre-eminence within French pacifism 311
  considers merger or dissolution (1937) 111
  crisis of pacifism 85–92
  debates division of primary materials in world 98–9
  debates problem of overpopulation 98–9
  and deteriorating international situation (1930–1) 83–92
  divisions within on Nazi Germany 98
  evolution of its thought 313
  Fiftieth Anniversary Congress (Nîmes, 1938) 114–17
  fiftieth anniversary celebrations(Nîmes, 1937) postponed 111
  fiftieth anniversary congress (Nîmes, 1938) 112
  and Franco-German *rapprochement* 47–8
  and Great War 30–3
  impact of its ideas on French and European society 312
  importance of teaching profession in 24–6
  integral pacifism 69–78
  and League of Nations 33–5, 311

APD – *cont*
  membership and circulation
    figures 22–4
  membership profile 24–6
  Nancy group 61
  Nantes AGM (1923) 48
  Nantes group 110
  nature of its pacifism 20–2
  and Nazi seizure of power 85
  Nîmes AGM (1927) 54
  and 1928 general election 53–4
  1929 AGM (Bordeaux) 62–3
  1930 AGM
    (Boulogne-sur-Mer) 63–4
  1932 AGM (Pau) 67
  1933 AGM (Paris) 85–92
  1935 Marseille Congress debates
    Ethiopian conflict 103
  1936 Clermont-Ferrand
    Congress 107–8
  1938 AGM 312
  origins 20–1, 27–9
  pacifist methods used 52–3
  Paris AGM (1925) debates
    conscientious objection 58–61
  and Paris Peace Conference 53
  Poitiers AGM (1921) 43
  political commentary determined by
    Fascist and Nazi
    pronouncements 98
  position within French pacifism 110
  principles of French Revolution 33
  and Protestantism 27–8
  reaction to Nazi seizure of
    power 94–100
  reaction to rise of Nazism 84
  rise of pessimism 93–109
  and RUP 110–11
  summer schools 55
  support for national defence 91
  and Versailles Treaty 33
  views on Germany 44
  views on Napoleon I 33
  war-guilt and reparations 34–5
  and working class 29
Appel aux consciences 41–3
Aragon, Louis 241
Archives nationales (Paris) 15
armistice, APD's reaction to German
  demand for (Oct. 1918) 32
Article 231: 122, 212
Association française pour la Société
  des nations 22

Augspurg, Dr Anita 297, 307
Auslandsdeutsche 224
Austria 49, 99, 103, 223–4, 230,
  236
Austro-Hungarian ultimatum of 23
  July 1914 70
Auvray, Michel 162
Axis powers 107
Azaña, Manuel 219, 309

Babeuf 189
Babut, Henri 27
Babut, Pastor Charles 28
Baer, Gertrud 280, 281, 292, 293,
  297, 298, 303, 304–5, 309
Balch, Emily Greene 287, 297
Balkans 204, 234
Barbé, Alphonse 172
Barbusse, Henri 32, 36–7, 81, 153,
  154, 162, 254, 269
Barcelona 140
Bardin, J. 177
Barnier, L.–A. 27
Barrage, Le 83, 127, 144, 179, 267
  number of subscribers 143–5
Basch, Victor 42
Bauchet, Émile 139, 141, 142, 143,
  144, 174, 176, 198
Baurez, Germaine 276–7
  on need to side with workers in case
    of civil strife 295
Belgium 44
belli-pacifistes 71
bellicistes 71
Belot, Gustave 31
Bergeron, Paul 131, 162
Berlin 47, 140
Bibliothèque de documentation
  internationale contemporaine
  (Nanterre) 15
Bibliothèque nationale 15
Bierville Congress 62
Bilis, Michel 285
Bloch, A. 100, 117–18, 311
Bloch, A.–M. 88, 90
Blum, Léon 201, 206, 207, 210, 221,
  238, 244
  compared to Poincaré and
    Tardieu 208
Bochum 47
Bodinier, Raoul-Albert 318
Bohemia 230
Bois, Jacques 89

Bolshevism 46
bombing aeroplane 127
Bonapartism 204
Bonnet, Georges 238, 241
Bordeaux 82
Borel, Émile 101
Bosse, Louis 36–7
Bossuet 75
Bouglé, Célestin 26, 60
Boulangism 208
Boulogne-sur-Mer (APD summer
    school) 55
Brailsford, H.N. 320
Brest 140
Brest-Litovsk, Treaty of 44
Briand, Aristide 2, 15, 50, 52, 185,
    316
  and LICP 2 n. 4
Brion, Hélène 31
British imperialism 213
Broussaudier, Sylvain 183, 209
  on political aspect of fight against
    Fascism and war 225–8
Brown, H. Runham 61
Buisson, Ferdinand 59
Bund neues Vaterland 48 n. 36
Bureau français de la paix 19
Bureau international de la paix
    23
  and discussion of war guilt 45
Burger, M. 272–3

Cadier, Georges 26, 89
Cahiers de la paix 290
Cahiers de la réconciliation 131
Cahiers des droits de l'homme 70
Cairns, John C. 287
Calvados 131
Camelots du roi 147, 149, 262–3
Cameroon 229
Canard enchaîné, Le 213, 223
Candide 103
Cao, Miss 304
capitalism 153
Capy, Marcelle 137, 140, 147, 164,
    180, 250, 257, 258, 315–16
  leaves LICP 195
Carnegie Endowment for International
    Peace 3
Carnet B 148
Cartel girondin de la paix 82
Cartel rouennais de la paix 82
cartels de la paix 81–3

Ceadel, Martin 7–8, 10–13, 128, 268,
    317–18, 320
Cecil, Lord Robert 110 and n. 1
Central Powers 123, 129
Centre international de documentation
    antiguerrière 1
Cercle de la Russie neuve 217
Ceresole, Pierre 60, 64–5
CGT 107, 220–1
Challaye, Félicien 31, 64, 70–5, 78,
    88, 121, 150, 182, 189, 198,
    207–8, 217, 219–20, 229, 241,
    256, 318, 319
  and debate with Romain Rolland
    over 'indivisible' peace
    (1936) 192–3
  compares refugees of 1935 to those
    of 1792 190
  questions linkage between
    antifascism and pacifism
    (1939) 238–9
  view on Ethiopian war 213–14
  views on German refugees in France
    189–90
Challaye, Jeanne 258, 275, 278
Chamberlain, Neville 114, 232, 233,
    238
Charpentier, Armand 124, 170–71,
    176, 206, 232
Chautemps Circular (26 January
    1933) 163–4, 172
  prefectoral reports 164
Chautemps, Camille 164
Chevé, Georges 62
Chickering, Roger 7–8, 13–14, 19,
    20, 317–18
China: Japanese aggression
    against 112
Choski, Professor 164
Chouffet, Armand 168–9
Christianity 315
Christol, D. 295
Churchill, Winston S., compared to
    Hitler 182
civil war 156–7, 269, 275, 292
Clarté 41
class struggle 265
class war 295
Clauzel, Comte 53
Clemenceau 32
collaboration (with Nazi Germany) 6,
    234–5, 318–19
collective non-resistance 88

collective security 84, 91, 102–3, 112, 115, 117–18, 156, 202, 231, 268, 315
and 'indivisible' peace 191
Colmar 74, 257
colonialism 213
Combat pour la paix, Le 179
Comité d'action pour la SDN 102
Comité d'entente des grandes associations de coopération intellectuelle 256
Comité de défense de l'objection de conscience 162
Comité français de coopération européenne 22
Comité mondial des femmes contre la guerre et le fascisme 257, 274
Communism 320
Communist party 261, 262
role of in Amsterdam-Pleyel movement 271
Communists 107, 118, 126, 166, 205–6, 220–1, 225, 317
general evolution on question of peace 216
Conference for the Defence of the Ethiopian People (1935) 101
Congrès belge pour le progrès des idées morales 69
Congrès national de la paix (IXe, 1921) 254
Congrès national de Nîmes (1904) 58
Congrès universel pour la paix (Paris, 1925) 58–9
conscientious objection 16, 51, 57–69, 88, 117, 131, 133, 151, 156, 158, 161–73, 205
amendments to law of 31 March 1928 on recruitment to the Army 167–9
and anarchism 131
Anglo-Saxon versus French conception of 57–8
development in France 161–2
draws inspiration from Britain 131
and French tradition of Catholicism and authoritarian centralism 58–9
government's response to problem (1933) 163–4
increases in 1932–3 161
and libertarianism 131
Ministry of Interior position papers on (1933) 166–7

and 'negative' pacifism 67
conscientious objectors 125
trials of 131
Constant, Benjamin 19
Corbett-Fisher, Mrs 292
Cot, Pierre 26, 38–9, 50, 110, 197
Coty, François 147, 148
cours Ruyssen 55
Courtney, Kathleen 288
croisade de la paix 128
Croix de feu 147
Cuenat, Pierre 150–1, 181
condemns French hegemony and idea that war inevitable 184
and inspirations for pacifism 151
tendencies within pacifism 151
Current Affairs 123
Czecho-Soviet Pact 305
Czechoslovakia 97, 115, 223, 229, 234, 236, 244

Daladier, Édouard 164, 168, 171, 238, 241, 244
Daladier-Forcinal law 205
Danan, Alexis 65
Danton 189
Danzig 223, 244
Danzig Corridor 97
Daudin, Louise 262
Déat, Marcel 1, 245
defeatism 6, 166
Delaisi, Francis 131, 152
on Kellogg-Briand Pact 51
Delbos, Yvon 108, 221
Délégation permanente des sociétés françaises de la paix 19, 79–80
links with LIFPL 254
Demartial, Georges 41, 42, 122, 123, 124, 211–12, 235–6
Denmark 73
Déroulède, Paul, statue of 68, 177
Detzer, Dorothy 306
Deutsche Friedensgesellschaft 44, 45–6
disarmament 99, 118, 152, 206, 282
and the APD 84
moral, economic and military 84
unilateral 117
Doriot, Jacques 238
Dortmund 47
Drevet, Camille 139, 143, 144, 251, 256, 257, 274, 279, 283, 284, 304

Duchene, Gabrielle 15, 37 n. 59, 251,
    252, 254, 257, 269, 272–3, 274,
    276–7, 279, 280, 281, 282, 285,
    289, 290, 292, 295, 296, 297,
    300, 302, 304, 305, 308, 310
  and Amsterdam-Pleyel
    movement 257
  appointed (1935) Treasurer of the
    LIFPL 301
  attempts to force concrete political
    action on LIFPL in 1930s 303–7
  and Comité d'entente des grandes
    associations internationales 257
  condemns integral pacifism 267
  on danger of allowing alienation of
    youth 277
  defines role of LIFPL (1921) 255
  evolution from absolute pacifism to
    pseudo-pacifism 268
  influence of neo-Marxist ideas
    on 269
  integral pacifism of 254–5
  loses seat on International Executive
    Committee (1937) 292
  Marxist analysis of the European
    crisis (1934) 299–301
  means v. ends in pacifism 267–8
  pacifism as function of social
    revolution 277
  paper on 'Les Deux Conceptions du
    pacifisme' 266–7, 283
  reaction to events of 6 Feb.
    1934: 264
  and RUP 257
  Stalinization of 284
  on Washington Object 288
Duhamel, Georges 162
Dumas, A. 177
Dumas, Jacques 25 and n. 23
Duméril, Edmond 26, 44–5
Dupin, Gustave 158
  attacks 'Jewish press' 181
Duthu, Adrien 220, 230–1

Eden, Anthony 114
Egypt 236
Einstein declaration 73, 150, 151
Einstein, Albert 65, 164
Eksteins, Modris 56
Emery, Léon 76–8, 88, 241–3,
    318
  condemns Franco-Soviet pact
    217

on the future of Europe (1938)
    231
  report on colonialism (1938 LICP
    Congress) 228–9
  stresses mystical nature of
    pacifism 242
Emery, Madame Léon 281
émigrés, German 96
En vigie 279, 285
Entente Cordiale 102
épuration 6
Erzberger, Mathias 44–5
Essen 47
Ethiopia 99, 108, 204, 218
Ethiopian War 100–3
  lead up to 98
Etten, Henry van 37 n. 59
Éveil normand, L' 261
Évolution 124

Fascism 94, 265, 293, 298–9, 314
Faure, Paul 183, 203
Faure, Sébastien 83, 151, 176, 195–6,
    206
  report on unilateral
    disarmament 197
fears of a coming war 127–9
Fédération française des associations
    pour la Société des nations 101
feminism and pacifism 251
feminist pacifism 319
  British and French examples
    compared 250
  defined by Vellacott 250
  as distinct from masculine
    pacifism 255
  in Great War 249
  situated between opposing poles of
    new- and old-style pacifism 252
Fernau, Hermann 46
Feu, Le 32
Flandin, P.-E. 233, 241
Foerster, Friedrich Wilhelm
  warns France of danger 97
Folliet, Joseph 9
Fouski, Marcel 139, 175
Fraîche et Gazeuse 127, 135
France, Fabien 82–3
France, politics:
  danger of civil war 49
  ideological confusion at time of
    Munich (1938) 117–18
Franco, General F. 241

Franco-German *rapprochement* 40,
    95–7, 313
  conditions of 203
Franco-German-Soviet union 204
Franco-Soviet Pact 202–3, 210, 222,
    281, 206, 218, 305
Freemasonry 3
French fascism 125
French pacifism:
  fears of a coming war 127–9
  interpenetration of French peace
    societies 257–8
  political nature of 127
  rhetoric of violence 264
French Revolution 46, 70, 189
Fried, Alfred Hermann 44, 45–6
Friedenswarte 45

Gandhi 73
Gandhian non-violent resistance
    214
  rejected by S. Faure 176
Gandhian pacifism 156
Gard (department of) 27
gas warfare 127
Gauche révolutionnaire 201
Geneva (APD summer school) 55
Geneva 53
Geneva Disarmament Conference 77,
    82, 84, 86, 95, 125, 128, 132–3,
    257, 292, 317
Geneva Protocol 59–60, 71
Gerbe, La 27
Gerin, René 83, 122, 123, 124, 131,
    142, 143, 144, 164, 176, 178,
    182, 185, 190, 198, 206–7,
    209–10, 212, 215, 220, 222, 234,
    235, 318
  in Algeria 141
  attacks opportunistic pacifism of
    right (1938) 237
  condemns Franco-Soviet
    Pact 216–17
  conscientious objection and the
    veterans 171
  debate with Challaye over linkage of
    antifascism and pacifism 239–41
  defines core of his pacifism
    (1939) 240
  doubts about *intégralité* of
    pacifism 229–30
  on meaning of 'democracy' 186
  on Munich crisis (1938) 232–3

  position on conscientious
    objection 169–70, 171
  position on Spanish Civil War 219
  reasons for failure of Fascism in
    France 188
  report on Ligue's propaganda
    (1933) 175
  speaking tour in spring of 1933 165
Gerlach, Hellmut von 46, 48 n. 36
  debate with R. de Vibraye 96
  warns French pacifists about
    Hitler 95–6
German *émigrés* 211
German Foreign Office
    (Wilhelmstraße) 95
German Peace Cartel 2
German Revolution 296
Germano-Czech Treaty (1926) 117
Germany 90, 93, 94, 99, 107, 115,
    126, 179–84
  Hitlerian: different conception of
    international law 104–6
  rise of Nazism 84
  Weimar Republic 47
Geronne 140
Gide, Charles 42, 123
Gilbert, Hubert 216
Gilles, Maurice 140, 147
Giraud, Émile 115
Giraudoux, Jean 244
Gobron, Gabriel 153
Godart, Justin 26
Gouttenoire de Toury, Fernand 42
*Grande Semaine de manifestations
    pacifistes internationales* 141
Great Britain 105, 107
Great War 121, 122, 124, 125, 127,
    129, 135, 316, 318
  impact of on pacifist thinking 77,
    86
Grenoble peace cartel 257, 271
Gringoire 238, 240, 241
Gruppe revolutionärer Pazifisten 179
Guernica 221
Guernut, Henri 107
Guétant, Louis 41
Guilbeaux, Henri 165, 204, 211–12,
    213
  leaves LICP 195
  report on a Franco-Soviet-German
    union (1935) 196
Guillot, Eugène 62, 67
Guizot, François 19

Hadamard, Jacques 70–1
Halévy, Élie 4 n. 9
Hallgarten, Wolfgang 96
Hamburg 140
Herriot, Édouard 3, 83, 189
Heymann, Lida Gustava 99 n. 23,
    276, 292, 297, 307
Hiller, Kurt 38, 133
historical dissent 121, 122-5
Hitler, Adolf 9, 15, 96, 116, 200, 210,
    212, 232, 233, 234, 235, 237,
    241, 265, 267, 274, 275, 300,
    307, 313, 317
    ambiguity of French Right
        towards 104
    Mein Kampf 96
    result of Versailles 88
    speech to Reichstag (17 May
        1933) 94–5; (21 May 1935) 99
Hugo, Victor 19, 50
Humanité, L' 154, 240
Humbert, Jeanne 164
    report (1936) on overpopulation as
        cause of war 198

imperialism 213
India 73
indivisible peace 156, 191, 202, 214
Innes, Kathleen 294, 301, 308, 310
integral pacifism 66–7, 69–78, 91
    compared to Anglo-Saxon absolute
        pacifism 147
    estrangement from political
        society 125–7
    juxtaposition of non-violent and
        violent elements 147
    origins and precursors of 129–33
    and Tolstoyan non-resistance to
        evil 72
    see also *pacifisme nouveau style*
integral pacifists 267
International Civilian Service 60, 64–5
International Court of Justice 49, 61
International Fellowship of
        Reconciliation 131, 162
    see also Mouvement international de
        la réconciliation
International Peace Congress (14th,
        Lucerne, 1905) 29
International Peace Congress (23rd,
        Berlin, 1924) 37–8
International Peace Congress (24th,
        Paris, 1925) 37 n. 59

international war 295
internationalism 3
Italian Fascism 213
Italo-Abyssinian friendship treaty
        (1928) 101
Italo-Abyssinian war 112, 210,
        213–16, 222, 237
Italy 93, 99, 107, 115, 126

Jacobs, Dr Aletta 303
Jamet, Claude 235
Japan 90, 213
Jaurès, Jean 164
Jeanson, Henri 140, 224–5
Jeune République 67, 82, 262
Jeunes Amis de la paix 27
Joan of Arc 208
Joly, Berthe 280–1
Jong van Beek en Donk, Benjamin
        de 43
Jospin, Robert 234–5, 243
    report on nationalization of
        armaments industries 196–7
    report on tactics in time of war
        197
Jospin, Robert and Weber, Maurice:
    criticize programme of Popular
        Front 201–4
    distinctions betwen political parties
        and LICP 199
    on parties of the right 199–200
    problem of Communist view of
        pacifism 200
    report on political parties, Popular
        Front, and pacifism
        (1936) 198–205
    SFIO divided on question of peace
        and pacifism 201
Journal, Le, 238
Jouve, Andrée 251, 256, 258, 280–1,
        288–9, 303
    analysis of 1933 political
        situation 265–6
    report on summer schools
        (1931) 256–7
Jouvenel, Bertrand de: interview with
        Hitler 104

Kawerau, Siegfried 54 n. 54
Kellogg-Briand Pact 38–9, 49–50, 59,
        67, 125, 152
    and Ethiopian conflict 101
    and French constitution 51–2

Kellogg-Briand – *cont.*
    impact on formation of La Volonté
        de paix 132
    impact on pacifist thinking in
        France 51
    and origins of new pacifism 131
Kerillis, M. de 238, 241
Krazinski, Commandant 263

Lᵃ Jeunesse et la paix du monde
    53
Lacaze-Duthiers, Gérard de 182
Lacroix, Maurice 117
Lafon, Louis 36
Lagot, Eugène:
    and conscientious objection 170
    and Gérard Leretour advocate
        collective CO movement 172
Lahargue, J, 107
    resolution on Spain (1936) 108
Lamartine, Alphonse de 19
Lambert, Jacques 114–15
Langevin, Professor Paul 127
Laune, Auguste 23
Laval government (1935) 102
Laval, Pierre 101, 112, 306
Laval-Stalin Pact 126, 199, 274
Le Foyer, Lucien 79
League of Nations 3, 49, 53, 54, 60–1,
    79, 84, 86, 87, 88, 89, 90–1, 92,
    94, 106, 110, 115, 118, 130, 152,
    194, 200, 201, 202, 204, 206,
    229, 304, 305, 311, 317
    Assembly 283
    Covenant 52, 112
    Convenant and Ethiopian
        conflict 101
    collective security 103–4
    differing conceptions of peace
        embodied in 38–9
    juridical, diplomatic, and moral
        defeat of 113–14
    sanctions 103
League of Nations Union 82, 102
Lebensraum 234
Leclerc, L. 274
Lecoin, Louis 318
Lecomte, André 67
Lehmann-Russbüldt, Otto 48 n. 36
Leibniz 217
Leleu, Lucienne 275–6
Lemédioni, Édouard 139, 187
    attacks juridical pacifism 194

calls for creation of local antifascist
    committees 187
on conscientious objection 194, 195
demands nationalization of
    armaments industry 195
leaves LICP 195
report on obligatory popular
    referendum before declaration of
    war 196
report on pacifist tactics
    (1935) 194–5
steps to a 'positive' pacifism 195
Lenormand, Jeanne 261
Leonhard, Rudolf 137, 179, 180, 258
    debates Saar issue with
        Gerin 210–11
Lepine, F. 32
Leretour, Gérard 68, 148, 176
    and conscientious objection 170
    decapitates Déroulède statue 177
    and Eugène Lagot advocate collective
        CO movement 172
Légion d'honneur 123, 124
Léontin, L. 61
Lhoumeau, Hélène 96–7
Lhoumeau, Pastor 96
libertarianism: and conscientious
    objection 131
LICP 14, 16, 41 n. 4, 80, 126, 128,
    133, 257, 262, 263, 268, 283, 318
    Algerian federation 139, 141, 149
    amended statutes 228
    anarchy within 177
    Angers Congress (1932) 137, 154
    Angers federation 139
    Arras Congress (1938) 142, 225–9
    Arras Congress manifesto 229
    attacks by Camelots du roi 138
    attempt to separate antifascism from
        pacifism 223
    Avallon section 137
    Caen section debates collective
        conscientious objection 165–6
    Calvados federation 139, 174
    challenge of external events
        (1934–8) 210
    challenges to its world view 153–60
    changes in statutes 159, 175–6
    and Christian pacifism 146
    civil vs. international wars 222
    civil war and problem of
        violence 218–20
    compared to APD 152

compared to Peace Pledge
Union 134
conception of pacifism 160–1
condemns anti-Semitism 190
condemns attacks on Jews both
within and outwith France 191
creation of Spanish section
(1932) 140
credited with expansion of
conscientious objection in France
(1933) 167
danger posed by French Fascism
187
differences with French
Communists 154–5
disenchantment with Popular
Front 206–9
division between internal and
external antifascism leads to break
with Romain Rolland 191–3
draws historical inspiration from
Robespierre 189–90
first Appeal 136–7
formation 127, 135–7
French elections 185–6
general position on Nazism and
Fascism 183–4
growth of Calvados federation 141
growth of local sections 137
growth of regional federations 139
heterogeneity of 134
impact of Munich crisis on 144
importance of anarchist and Socialist
elements within 134
importance of in spread of pacifist
ideas 128 n. 16
importance of Parisian intellectuals
in foundation of 139
initial growth 137
internal antifascism v. external
pacifism 220
internal threat of Fascism in
France 236
internal v. external
antifascism 188–90
Jeune Garde pacifiste; *see also* Young
Pacifist Guard 264
Limoges section 137
manifesto on Ethiopian crisis 214
Marseille Congress (1939) 143, 144
meetings in Germany and
Switzerland (1932) 140
membership figures (1933–9) 141–3

membership (1934) 138
Montargis Congress (1934) 142
nature of its pacifism 145–78
1933 Congress debates registering
Ligue 175
1933 Congress: police reports
on 138
1933 membership 138
1934 Montargis Congress 239
1934 Montargis Congress debates
report on pacifist tactics 193–5
1934 Montargis Congress
manifesto 188
1934 revised goal of Ligue 188
1935 Agen Congress 145, 195–7
1936 Bernay Congress 142,
198–205
1939 Marseille Congress 243
number of public meetings
held 143–5
number of sections 143–5
numerical size 134
organizational confusion 173–4
organizational weakness of Paris
sections 139
origins 134–8
pacifism v. antifascism 236–43
pacifist tactics 155
paradoxes within its pacifism
161
Paris Congress (1933) 149
peace crusades (1931–2 and
1932–3) 180
pessimism of 136–7
position on conscientious
objection 161
preoccupation with internal Fascist
threat 181
principles defined by Méric
(1932) 146
*Programme, tactique et moyens
d'action* 143
propaganda campaigns (1931–2 and
1932–3) 140
rapprochement with Nazi
Germany 184
reaction to Anschluss 223–5
reaction to Ethiopian war 213–16
rejection of Socialist conception of
peace 204
rhetoric of violence 147–9
rural sections compared to
urban 139

LICP – *cont.*
   Saint-Denis section 176
   St Jean d'Angely 137
   Saintes section 137
   schism with *Patrie humaine* 138
   second national Congress (Paris,
      1933) 173–8
   and SFIO 209
   significance of in France 134
   situation in Paris section (1933)
      177
   Socialist, anarchist, and Communist
      elements 146
   and Spanish Civil War 218–22
   spectrum of pacifist values 176
   support dwindling 235
   Toulouse group and 'hostages for
      peace' idea 176
   and unilateral disarmament 153
   view of Laval-Stalin pact 216
   view of remilitarization of
      Rhineland 212–13
   views on conscientious
      objection 169–70, 171
   views on German refugees in
      France 189–90
   views on L.o.N. 151–2
   violence and the new pacifism 149
Ligue internationale des femmes pour
      la paix et la liberté (LIFPL) 12,
      80, 93, 109, 127, 250, 319
   aims debate 286–98
   American section 286, 288, 289
   Anglo-French rivalries in Ligue from
      1924 288
   British section 286, 289, 290,
      301
   constitutional changes effected at
      1934 Zurich Congress 301
   Czech section 288
   debate on admissibility of 'defensive'
      wars 288
   definition of violence 295–6
   differences between British and
      French sections 292, 295
   differences in inspirations for
      pacifism of national sections 298
   disproportionately important role of
      French section 286
   Dutch section 298
   founded at The Hague (1915) 251
   Franco-German proposal on aims
      passed 296

German section 286, 289, 297, 298,
      301
   gradual insinuation of Marxist
      conception of peace 293
   Greek and Bulgarian sections 291
   influence of Quaker ideas
      within 297–8
   issue of non-violence 293
   Munich and Jena sections 296
   nature of Ligue 290–1
   nature of political action changes
      from 1920s to 1930s 302–3
   IXth International Congress in
      Czechoslovakia 301; size of
      French delegation 301
   1924 Washington Congress 288
   1926 Dublin Congress 289
   1932 Grenoble Congress 263, 292;
      major disappointment for young
      people 304; report on the Orient
      by Edith Pye 304–5
   1934 Zurich Congress 273, 276,
      292–3; aims debate 294;
      Franco-German v. British position
      on aims 294
   1937 Luhacovice Congress 285, 292
   on civil conflicts 295
   and Paris Peace Conference
      (1919) 302–3
   Polish section 288
   political debates conducted around
      Anglo-French axis 310
   reaction to remilitarization of
      Rhineland 303, 304–5
   reaction to Sino-Japanese conflict
      (1932) 303–4
   reaction to Spanish Civil War 303,
      308–10
   resolutions passed at The Hague
      (1915) 287
   revisionist debate on Ligue's
      aims 289
   role debated 289
   and Ruhr Crisis (1923) 303
   Scandinavian sections 286, 288
   summer schools in Salzburg, English
      Lake District, Bremen,
      Burg-Lauenstein, and Varese 256
LIFPL French section 252, 289, 301
   Abbéville group 261
   aid to infants stricken by famine and
      privation (1921–2) 256
   Ardèche group 276–7

attitude of right-wing groups
  towards 262–3
Auxerre group 260, 263
Besançon group 264
Bordeaux group 262
Caen group 260–1
campaign for disarmament 253–4,
  257
Cannes group 261
Chambéry group 261–2
Chartres group 261
clearly sees danger posed by
  Hitler 307
close identification of official level of
  French section with
  Amsterdam-Pleyel movement 268
Colmar and Mulhouse groups leave
  Ligue 278
Colmar group's problems with local
  Communists 272–3
compared to other national
  sections 253
in confrontation with British 287
on the defensive internationally by
  beginning of 1930s 268–9
defines its role (1922) 255
delegation to Zurich Congress
  compared to delegation to
  Luhacovice Congress 293
departure of Colmar group 273
dissent of Colmar group
  (1934) 271–3
En vigie 260
evolution of section away from
  absolute pacifism 268
financial importance 253
generational differences in approach
  to problem of peace 276–7
grass-roots revolt in Chambéry, Le
  Havre, Rouen, Nîmes, and Caen
  groups 271
grass-roots revolt in Grenoble
  group 271
Grenoble group 270
ideological differences 270–6
impact of Stalin-Laval pact
  on 274–5
importance at international level of
  Ligue 286
importance of ideological evolution
  of pacifist debate 314
increasing isolation 292
influence of Communist party

positions on 296
integral pacifists attacked 267
La Rochelle group 278
Le Havre group 260
links with other pacifist
  groups 257–8
links with *pacifisme ancien style* 254
Lyon group 274
Marseille group 275–6, 295
Marxist conception of war and
  peace 270
meeting of Paris region (November
  1936) 284
more left-wing than other national
  sections 266
Nîmes, Montpellier, Rouen, Le
  Havre, La Rochelle, Lyon, and
  Arles groups attempt to
  disenfranchise executive
  committee 282–3
1934 AGM 278
1935 AGM 278–9
1936 AGM a struggle for control of
  French section 282–3
1936 AGM 266, 282
1936 National Conference 253
numerical growth over interwar
  period 259–62
numerical size 253
orientation of the various
  groups 262
pacifism, definitions (1936) 266–7
Paris, Lyon, Drôme-Ardèche, Le
  Havre, Rouen, Arles, La Rochelle,
  Chalon-sur-Saône, Dijon,
  Chambéry, Nîmes, Roubaix,
  Troyes, Seine, Seine-et-Marne,
  Seine-et-Oise, Montpellier
  groups 259
peace education 254
political orientation called into
  question 272–3
predominance of teaching profession
  in provincial groups 262
print run of *SOS* 260
purge of Lyon group (1936) 279–82
reaction to Nazi
  Machtergreifung 300
reaction to right-wing
  intimidation 264
rebellion of 1936 279
resistance to joining Amsterdam
  committees 270–3

LIFPL – *cont.*
  rhetoric of violence 264
  role of feminist pacifists 302
  Saint Étienne group 274
  schism (1938) 285
  Stalinization of 284
  support for policies of Soviet
    Union 303, 305–7
  united front between Communists
    and pacifists in France 307
  use of French general elections for
    propaganda purposes 258
LIFPL: International Executive
    Committee
  Bruges meeting (April 1937) 282
  debates Franco-Soviet Pact 306
  Duchene proposes (April 1937) a
    truce in constitutional debate 301
  Geneva, 1936 308
  Innsbruck meeting (July 1925)
    discusses Washington Object 288
  1923 Dresden meeting 287
Ligue des droits de l'homme 8, 47–8,
    66, 79, 88, 91, 107, 117, 123,
    194, 263
  1937 Congress on defending
    democracy and peace 186
Ligue des femmes pour la paix 241,
    285
Ligue des mères et des éducatrices pour
    la paix 271 n. 65, 273
Ligue des objecteurs de conscience 172
Ligue internationale contre
    l'antisémitisme (LICA) 191
Ligue pour la reconnaissance de
    l'objection de conscience
    (LROC) 58–9, 131, 162
Ligue scolaire internationale de la
    paix 318
Limoges 165
Litvinoff, Maxim 305
Lloyd, Lola Maverick 309
Locarno 49, 50, 52, 84, 105, 203, 213,
    230
Locarno accords, abrogation of 103–4
London Conference 86
Loréal, Louis 140
Lorient 140
Lowery, Mr 63
Luxembourg 73
Lütgemeier-Davin, Reinhold 9–10
Lyon, University of, Chair of
    Peace 114

McMillan, James F. 249, 250
Man, Henri de 117
Manchuria 84
Manchuria
  Japanese invasion of 112
Maréchal, L. 280
Marguericitte, Victor 41, 123, 124, 176
Marseillaise 208
Marshall, Catherine 287, 295, 302,
    303
  on differences between British and
    French conceptions of LIFPL's
    work 289–90
Martin, Jacques 131, 162
Marty, André 83
Massis, Henri 215
Masson, Paul-Marie 116
Matin, Le 182, 240, 241
Maurras, Charles 193, 237, 238
Mazzini, Giuseppe 50
Mein Kampf 192, 307
Memel, 103
Messac, Régis 220, 243
Messageries Hachette 139
Meudon 140
Mélin, Jeanne 88
Méric, Victor 16, 126 and n. 12,
    134–8, 140, 141, 147, 158, 159,
    176, 190–1, 216
  anarchism as pacifist
    inspiration 157–8
  argues against registering Ligue 175
  and civil war 150
  compared to Dick Sheppard and the
    Peace Pledge Union 134
  death of 138, 178
  defines integral pacifism 135–6
  and definition of integral
    pacifism 146
  and *enquête* on aero-chemical
    warfare (1930) 127
  Hitler likened to Boulanger or
    Dreyfus affairs 180
  on Nazi election gains (1932) 180
  opposition to Amsterdam
    Congress 154–5
  ownership of *Patrie humaine* in
    question 173–5
  pacifism negative 149
  pacifist methods in peacetime 160
  personal rivalry with Pioch 177
  position on conscientious
    objection 169, 170

Méric-Rolland debate on integral
pacifism 155–9
Michelet, Jules 152
Michon, Georges 189, 208
Milhaud, Edgard 114
militarization 204
military service law (two-year) 205,
281
Ministry of Justice 167
Ministry of the Interior: reports on
LICP growth (1933) 138
Mirabeau 207
Moch, Gaston 19, 42
Monbrison, Hubert de 114
Monclin, Roger 137, 140, 143, 178
Monod, O.R. 177
Montauban 27
Montoire 318
moral disarmament 66
Morhardt, Mathias 41, 42, 122, 123
Morlaix (Finistère) 140
Morocco 143, 236
Moscow Purge Trials 209
Mouvement international de la
réconciliation 63
Mouvement pacifiste, Le 23
Mulhouse 74
Munich 140, 215, 223, 227, 230, 238,
241
Munich crisis (1938) 112, 116–18,
143, 312
and definition of pacifism 9
impact on LICP 144
and integral pacifism 175
Mussolini 96, 203, 235, 237, 241,
265

Napoleon I 189
National Socialism 314
nationalists, French: blamed for
Rhineland crisis 105–6
nationalization of armaments
industries 202
Nazi expansionism: debate on rightness
of within LICP 236–7
Nazi Germany 228, 244
Nazi seizure of power 121, 199, 293,
313, 314
impact on French pacifism 93
importance of in Franco-German
political debate 93
Nazi-Soviet Pact 314
Nazism 94, 130, 265, 285, 319

Nazism and Hitler: compared to
capitalist ruling classes in the
democracies 182
new pacifism
anarchist inspirations 125
fears of a coming war 127–9
origins of 121–33
Socialist inspirations 125
and violence 121
Nick, Pastor 67–8
Nicolai, Georg Friedrich 48 n. 36
Nîmes 27, 111–12
No More War Movement 292
Noël, M. 260
non-interventionism (in Spanish Civil
War) 221
non-resistance 117, 166
non-violence 156, 269, 272, 292, 301
influence of Communist party on
debate on within LIFPL 295
Nouvelle Revue française 237

Odéon, Pierre 174
Oran 164
Organisation pour une paix durable
43
Origines de la guerre, Les 41
Oxford Union debate (1933) 164

pacificism 7
pacifism
and antifascism 184–93
and Bolshevism 31–2
Christian 131, 268
and civil war 32
and class war 32
and defeatism 31, 35
differences between Anglo-Saxon and
French 161
and feminism 251
feminist 13, 14, 314–16
French and British experiences
compared 268
French v. Anglo-Saxon conception
of 38–9
growing divergences within 37–9
humanitarian or utilitarian
inspiration 128
moral versus juridical
approach 39 n. 64
and non-violence 11, 13, 14
origins of word 6 n. 14
and political culture 11–12

pacifism – *cont.*
  and strategic situation 12
  typologies 9–15
  Utopian 13
pacifism, French
  Balkanization of 91–2
  Communist influence on 269
  comparisons with Germany and
    Britain 2
  concern for collective action 130
  and conscientious objection 57–8
  definitions 4–9
  differences from Anglo-American
    pacifism 11
  divisions not apparent in early
    twenties 254
  divisions within 78–83, 86
  and Dreyfus Affair 20
  historiography 5 and nn. 11 and 12,
    and 6 and nn. 13 and 14
  impact on political society 16
  importance of political v. ethical
    aspect 268
  influence of Communism on, 4–5
  influence of Romain Rolland
    on 129–30
  interpenetration of French peace
    societies 21–2
  isolation from political society
    317
  nature of 3
  and Nazi seizure of power 93
  politicization of question of
    peace 269
  and Radicalism 20
  views on German revolution 46–7
pacifism, German
  divided on war guilt and
    reparations 45–6
  and German revolution 46
pacifism, ideological 13
pacifism, integral 7
  definitions 135–6
  ideas shared with French right
    (1935) 190
pacifisme ancien style 10, 14, 83, 121,
    311, 319, 320
  and APD 20–1
  definitions 36
  origins 19–21
pacifisme des munichois 9
pacifisme nouveau style 10, 14–15, 56,
    80, 122–245, 320

  alienation from official political
    world 136
  origins 37
  origins in the Kellogg-Briand Pact 51
  origins in fears of coming
    war 127–9
  and rejection of post-Versailles
    Europe 122
pacifisme oratoire (of Hitler) 99
pacifist tactics 193–8
pacifists, German
  in prison or exile 95
  warnings to French pacifists 95–8
Painlevé, Paul 26, 84
Paix immédiate 318
Paix par le droit, La 22, 52, 200, 211
  circulation figures 24
Palais Bourbon 206
Palais de la mutualité 139
Papen, Franz von 94–5
Paquet, Y. 277, 295
Paris-midi 104
Pascal 63
Passy, Frédéric 21, 28, 32
Patrie humaine, La 126, 127, 134, 140
  growth in readership 137
  1933 readership 138
  readership rises in 1934 138
Paul-Boncour, Joseph 26
Pauthe, Gaston 244
  report (1938 LICP Congress) on
    economic aspects of fight against
    Fascism and war 228
Pax internationale 273
PCF *see* Communists
Peace Pledge Union 2
peace treaties of 1919, revision of
    necessary 90
Percin, Général Alexandre 258
Perrin, Madame 264
Pertinax 238, 241
Petit, Jeanne 274
Peuples unis, Les 24, 52
Péri, Gabriel 241
Périé, R. 35
Pétain, Marshal Philippe 168, 318
  on French military preparedness and
    education 169
Philip, André 68–9
Pioch, Georges 58–9, 140, 147, 164,
    165, 176, 180, 191–2, 207, 209,
    220, 236, 241
  attacks Leninist view of war 157

Pivert, Marceau 201
Planche, Camille 169
Poincaré, Raymond 123, 124
Poitiers 138
Poland 99, 226, 244–5
Populaire, Le 183, 203
Popular Front 220–1, 225, 239, 281, 317
  LICP's position on 198–208
positivism 3
Pottecher, Thérèse 304
Pour la paix désarmée, même en face de Hitler 182
Poznan 74
Pratt, Hodgson 21
preventive war 300
Programme, tactique et moyens d'action 195
Prudhommeaux, Jules 22, 25 and n. 24, 27, 49, 50, 53, 62, 66, 67, 80, 81–3, 86, 89, 99, 101, 110, 116, 254
  on Rhineland crisis 105
Prudhommeaux, Mme J. 115–16
Prussians 74
pseudo-pacifism of French right 214–15, 237
Puech, Jules L. 26, 35, 47, 75
Puech, Marie-Louise 25, 47
Pye, Edith 309
  argues for neutrality in Sino-Japanese conflict 304–5
  attacks Duchene's lack of commitment to non-violence 301

quakerism 76
Quidde, Dr Ludwig 44, 46
Quimper 140

Radicals 200, 225
Ragaz, Clara 282, 293, 296, 298, 304–5, 308, 309
Ramondt-Hirschmann, Cor 306, 309, 310
Rancon, V 271
Rassemblement des femmes pour la paix et la liberté 279
Rassemblement international contre la guerre et le militarisme 257
Rassemblement mondial des femmes contre la guerre et le fascisme 264
Rassemblement universel pour la paix (RUP) 110, 201, 267

Rauze, Marianne 37 n. 59, 130
  attacks old-style pacifism 130–1
  condemns 'revolutionary' pacifism 131
rearmament 115, 233
Reformed Church of France 27
remilitarization of Rhineland 100, 103–6, 113, 203, 210, 222, 283, 304–5
Renaitour, Jean-Michel 260
reparations 48, 49
Revolution of 1789: 290
revolution 265
revolutionary deviation of 1792: 204
revolutionary methods 292
revolutionary pacifism 151
République des camarades 189
Réveil de l'Yonne 263
Rhineland 218
Ribeauville (Alsace) 257
Richard, Gaston 87
Richet, Charles 3, 4 n. 8, 26, 30, 33, 76–7
Robespierre 189, 229, 236, 318
Rochefoucauld-Liancourt, Duc de la 19
Rocque, Colonel-Count de la 193
Rolland, Madeleine 251, 256, 291, 296
Rolland, Romain 6, 15, 153, 154, 155, 160, 176, 254, 269, 319
  break with LICP over antifascist policies 191–3
  on civil war 156
  evolution away from absolute non-violence 129
  on Gandhi 156
  and idea of 'indivisible' peace 191–2
  influence on French pacifism 129–30
  material and moral resistance to Nazism (1936) 191
  message to LICP's 1933 Congress 158–9
  pacifism a function of revolutionary justice 158
  resigns as honorary president of LICP 157
Romania 226
Roser, Pastor Henri 63–5, 67–8
Rouen 62
Rouget de l'Isle 189
Rousseau, Charles 102–3, 114

Rousseau – *cont.*
    argues for strict non-intervention and
        neutrality in Spanish conflict 106
    on Ethiopian crisis 100–1
    on Rhineland crisis 105–6
Roussel, Ernest 27
Röttcher, Dr Fritz 45
Rue Saint Dominique, *see* War
    Ministry
Ruhr Crisis (1923) 48, 49, 96, 192
RUP
    French Congress (1937) 111
Russell, Bertrand 72, 127, 128 n. 15,
    192
Ruyssen, Théodore 4 n. 9, 22, 25, 30,
    31, 32, 33, 34, 35, 36, 37, 41, 43,
    45, 53, 55, 57–8, 61, 63–4, 66,
    68–9, 75, 76–8, 80, 84, 86, 89,
    98, 101, 104, 107, 111–12, 115,
    116–17, 121, 252, 254, 312, 316
    and Challaye debate (1931–2) 73–5
    changing views on Germany 48
    on the Crisis of Pacifism 86–8
    misled by Nazi propaganda 99
    on rise of Nazism 94
    reflections on changes in pacifism
        (1887-1937) 108–9
    resolution on Spain (1936) 108
    and Union internationale des
        associations pour la Société des
        nations, 4 n. 9
    views on *rapprochement* with
        Germany 47–8
Ryner, Han 176

Saar 218, 222, 231
Saar plebiscite 99, 210
    and war-guilt 212
Sadowa 114
Saint Étienne 140
Saint-Claude (APD summer school)
    55
Sainte-Lazaigne (Indre) 140
Salle Wagram 139, 147
sanctions 214, 215, 305
Sangnier, Marc 42, 62, 261, 262
Sarajevo 103
Scelle, Georges 26, 50–1, 102–3,
    112–14, 118
Schleswig 74
school history texts, French and
    German 53 and n. 54
Schweitzer, Dr Albert 256

Scize, Pierre 140
Second World War 125
secret diplomacy 202
Sedan 114, 320
Semeur, Le 131, 172
Serbia 70
Service historique de l'armée de terre
    (Château de Vincennes) 15
Séverine (Caroline Rémy) 254
SFIO 261, 285
    Montrouge Congress 209–10
Sheppard, Dick (Canon H.R.L.) 134
Singer, Barnett 24
Sino-Japanese War 84
Sirinelli, Jean-François 24
Six (6) February 1934 crisis 168, 187,
    188, 226, 264, 298
Socialism 315
Socialists 221, 225
Société d'études documentaires et
    critiques sur la guerre 41–3, 123
Société de morale chrétienne 19
Société française des amis de la paix
    21
Société française pour l'arbitrage entre
    nations 21
Society of Friends (Quakers), 27, 28,
    63
Soir, Le 127
SOS 269, 272, 275, 279
Soviet Union 267, 314, 320
Spain 115, 222
Spanish Civil War 100, 106–8, 210,
    217, 218–22, 229, 238, 308–10
    debated at APD's 1936
        congress 107–8
    non-intervention 107–8
    non-intervention wrong 113
    sympathy for Republicans within
        APD 106–7
Stalin, Josef 274, 306
Stalin communiqué 278
Stalin declaration 200, 281
Stalinism 267
Stöcker, Dr Helene 46
Strasburg 74, 165
Stresa Front 203
Stresemann, Gustav 52, 102
strikes (June 1936) 207
Sudeten Germans 224
Sudentenland 230
Swarthmore College Peace
    Collection 15, 23

Swiss federation 231
Switzerland 73

Taittinger, Pierre 147, 149
Tardieu, André 1, 238, 241
Taylor, A.J.P. 7
Teissonnière, P. 117
Temps, Le 83, 240
The Hague 252
Thibaudet, Albert 237
Third Reich 223, 224
Third Republic 224
    extreme polarization of political
        society 127
Thonon (APD summer school) 55
Thorez, Maurice 238
Tolstoy, Leo 95
    doctine of non-resistance to evil
        70
    Tolstoyan pacifism 100
Tourly, Robert 138, 140, 178, 180
Trades Union Congress (TUC), 214
treaties of 1919 116
treaty revision 78, 152, 193, 202
Trégaro, Louis 241
Trocmé, André 15
Trotskyists 267, 280, 284

unilateral disarmament 146, 151, 171,
    196, 202, 279
Union féminine pour la société des
    nations 22
Union internationale de 'secours aux
    enfants' 256
Union internationale des associations
    pour la Société des nations 22
Union populaire pour la paix
    universelle 79
Universal Peace Congress (1925,
    Berlin) 133
Upper Silesia 49, 231
USSR 104, 279, 281

Vaïsse, Maurice 98 n. 20
Valence 283
Valéry, Paul 210
Valfort, René 64–6, 72 n. 46, 89
Vautel, Clément 135, 238
Vellacott, Jo 249, 250, 251
Vermeil, Edmond 37–8, 133
Vernet, Madeleine 132, 250, 257,
    274–5, 278
Vernier, Philippe 131, 162

Versailles 116, 201
Versailles Treaty 46, 77, 94, 122, 152,
    200, 204, 212, 231
    Article 231 41, 50
    revision of necessary 179
    war-guilt clause 48
Vibraye, Régis de 63
    report on entente with Germany
        (APD's 1933 AGM) 95–6
Vichy 6, 96, 163, 318, 319
violence 173, 275, 297
violence, civil: acceptance of by some
    pacifists 133
violence, definition of 295
Vistula 244
Volonté de paix, La 132
Volonté de paix, La 80, 258, 275
    demands total disarmament 132
    manifesto and petition 132
    merger with LICP (1936) 132
    organization of two Conférences
        libres du désarmement (1932)
        132
    petition compared to British and
        German petitions 132
Von Rath, Counsellor: assassination of
    (1938) 191
Völkerfriede 45
Vulliod, A. 39 n. 64

Wanner, Léo 251, 257, 265, 266, 279,
    304
War Ministry: continued interest in CO
    problem (1933) 167
War Resisters' International
    (WRI) 61–2, 162
    1931 Lyon congress 257
war-guilt
    debate on 40
    and Saar plebiscite 212
Washington Object 288
Weber, Maurice 209, 220–1
    report on nationalist ideologies
        197
    see also Jospin, Robert
Weber, Max 320
Weimar Germany 40
Wilson, Woodrow 30, 203
Winock, Michel 126
Women's International Committee for
    a Permanent Peace 251, 252
Women's World Committee against
    Fascism and War 269

working class 155–6
working–class sanctions 282
World Committee against Fascism and
    War 269
Wulfften-Palthe, Madame 298

Yonne, department of the 260
Young Pacifist Guard 149
Yugoslavia 226

Zyromski, Jean 201